DRIVE!

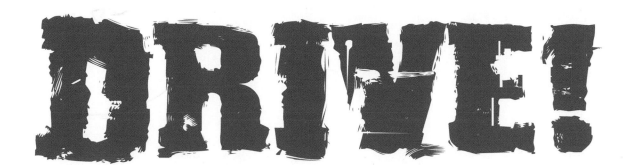

Also by Jerry Scott and Jim Borgman

Zits: Sketchbook 1
Growth Spurt: Zits Sketchbook 2
Don't Roll Your Eyes at Me, Young Man!: Zits Sketchbook 3
Are We an "Us"?: Zits Sketchbook 4
Zits Unzipped: Zits Sketchbook 5
Busted!: Zits Sketchbook 6
Road Trip: Zits Sketchbook 7
Teenage Tales: Zits Sketchbook No. 8
Thrashed: Zits Sketchbook No. 9
Pimp My Lunch: Zits Sketchbook No. 10
Are We Out of the Driveway Yet?: Zits Sketchbook No. 11
Rude, Crude, and Tattooed: Zits Sketchbook No. 12
Jeremy and Mom
Pierced
Lust and Other Uses for Spare Hormones
Jeremy & Dad
You're Making That Face Again: Zits Sketchbook No. 13

Treasuries
Humongous Zits
Big Honkin' Zits
Zits: Supersized
Random Zits
Crack of Noon
Alternative Zits
My Bad

Gift Book
A Zits Guide to Living with Your Teenager

DRIVE!

Zits® Sketchbook 14

by Jerry Scott and Jim Borgman

**Andrews McMeel
Publishing, LLC**
Kansas City • Sydney • London

Zits®is syndicated internationally by King Features Syndicate, Inc. For information, write King Features Syndicate, Inc., 300 West Fifty-Seventh Street, New York, New York 10019.

Andrews McMeel Publishing, LLC
an Andrews McMeel Universal company
1130 Walnut Street, Kansas City, Missouri 64106

www.andrewsmcmeel.com

11 12 13 14 15 SDB 10 9 8 7 6 5 4 3 2

ISBN: 978-1-4494-0107-8

Library of Congress Control Number: 2010932486

Zits® may be viewed online at
www.kingfeatures.com.

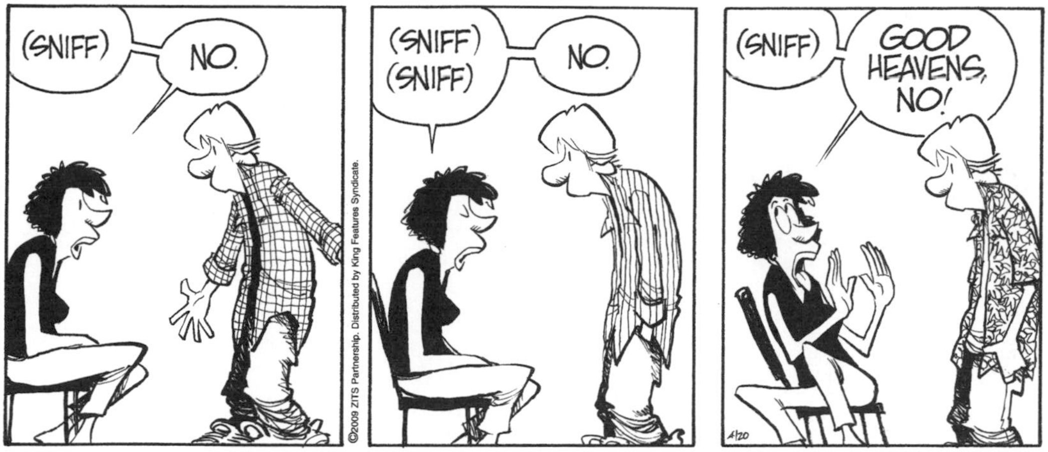
(SNIFF)
NO.
©2009 ZITS Partnership. Distributed by King Features Syndicate.
(SNIFF) (SNIFF)
NO.
(SNIFF)
GOOD HEAVENS, NO!
4/20
MOTHERS WITH DAUGHTERS PROBABLY GIVE FASHION ADVICE BASED ON HOW THINGS LOOK.
BRACE YOURSELF. THIS IS MY LAST CLEAN-ISH SHIRT.
SCOTT and BORGMAN

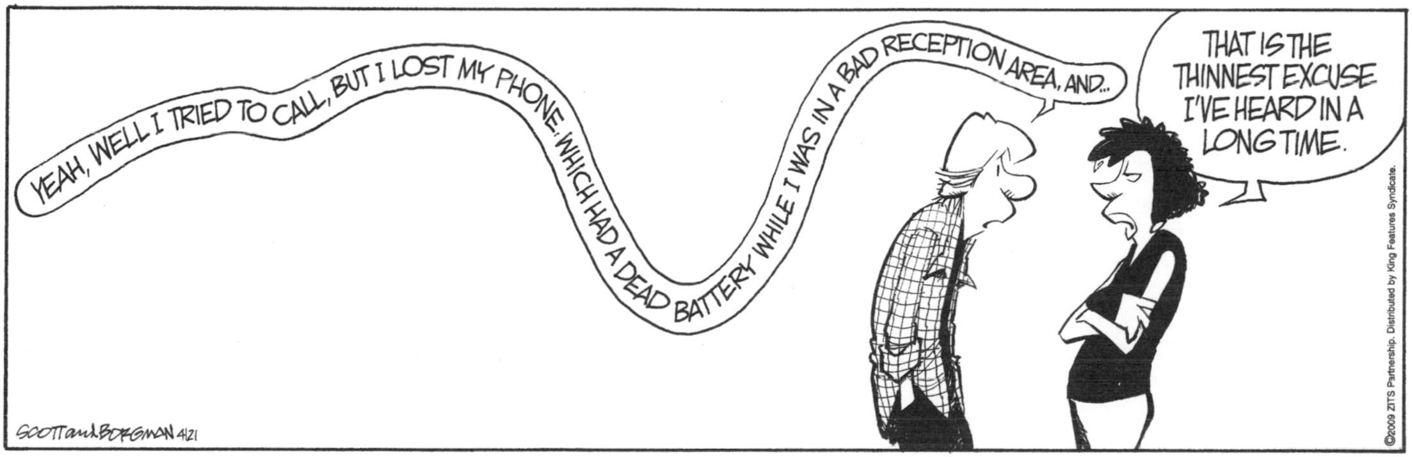
YEAH, WELL I TRIED TO CALL, BUT I LOST MY PHONE, WHICH HAD A DEAD BATTERY WHILE I WAS IN A BAD RECEPTION AREA, AND...
THAT IS THE THINNEST EXCUSE I'VE HEARD IN A LONG TIME.
SCOTT and BORGMAN 4/21
©2009 ZITS Partnership. Distributed by King Features Syndicate.

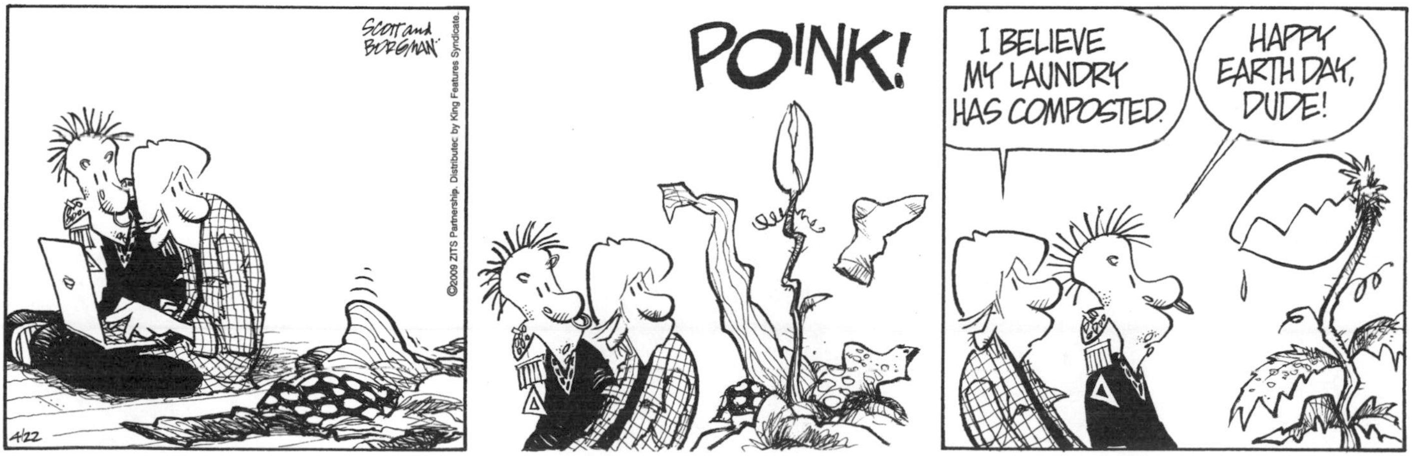
SCOTT and BORGMAN
©2009 ZITS Partnership. Distributec by King Features Syndicate.
4/22
POINK!
I BELIEVE MY LAUNDRY HAS COMPOSTED.
HAPPY EARTH DAY, DUDE!

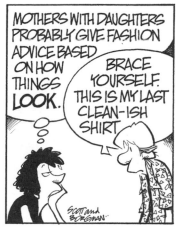

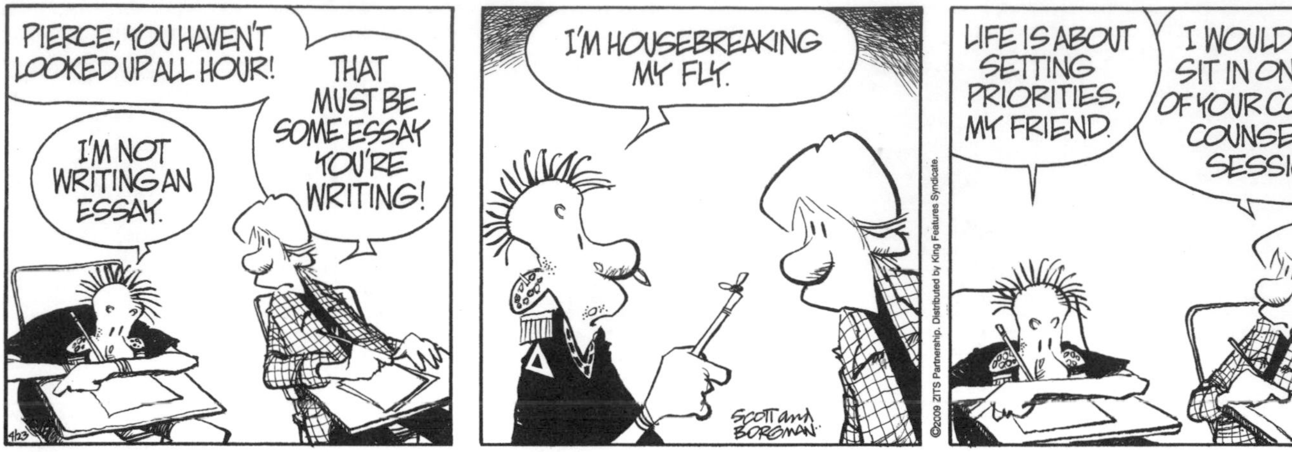
PIERCE, YOU HAVEN'T LOOKED UP ALL HOUR!
I'M NOT WRITING AN ESSAY.
THAT MUST BE SOME ESSAY YOU'RE WRITING!
I'M HOUSEBREAKING MY FLY.
LIFE IS ABOUT SETTING PRIORITIES, MY FRIEND.
I WOULD PAY TO SIT IN ON ONE OF YOUR COLLEGE COUNSELING SESSIONS.
SCOTT and BORGMAN
©2009 ZITS Partnership. Distributed by King Features Syndicate.

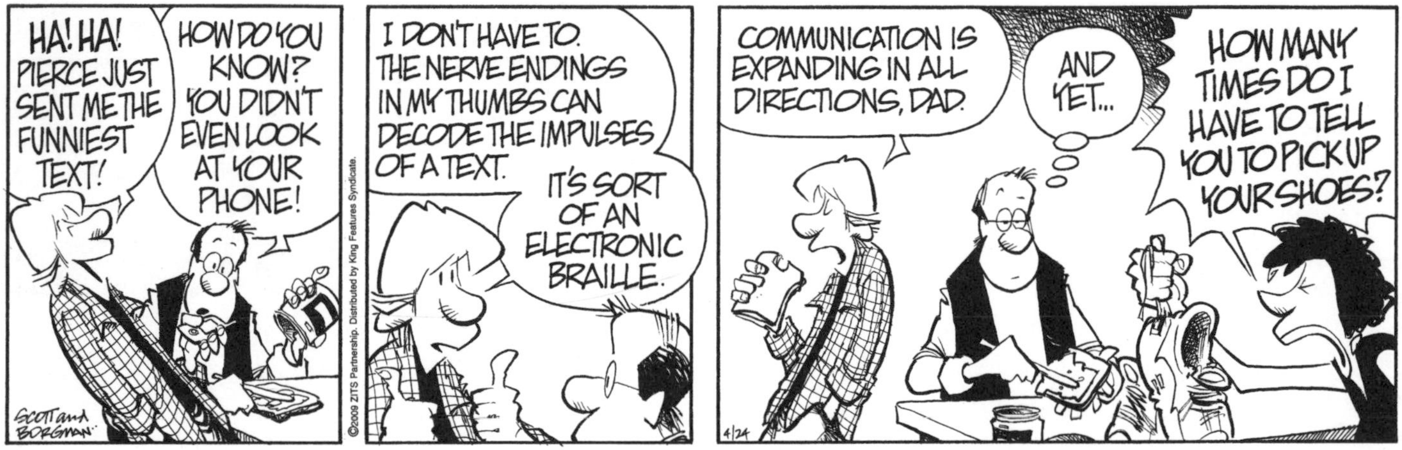
HA! HA! PIERCE JUST SENT ME THE FUNNIEST TEXT!
HOW DO YOU KNOW? YOU DIDN'T EVEN LOOK AT YOUR PHONE!
I DON'T HAVE TO. THE NERVE ENDINGS IN MY THUMBS CAN DECODE THE IMPULSES OF A TEXT.
IT'S SORT OF AN ELECTRONIC BRAILLE.
COMMUNICATION IS EXPANDING IN ALL DIRECTIONS, DAD.
AND YET...
HOW MANY TIMES DO I HAVE TO TELL YOU TO PICK UP YOUR SHOES?
SCOTT and BORGMAN
©2009 ZITS Partnership. Distributed by King Features Syndicate.

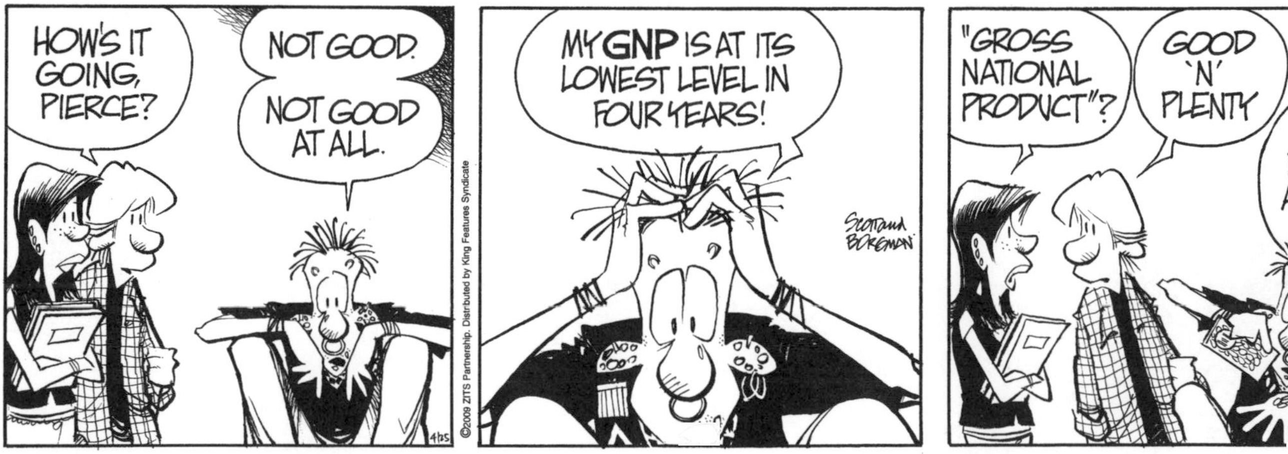
HOW'S IT GOING, PIERCE?
NOT GOOD.
NOT GOOD AT ALL.
MY GNP IS AT ITS LOWEST LEVEL IN FOUR YEARS!
"GROSS NATIONAL PRODUCT"?
GOOD 'N' PLENTY
SNACK FOODS ARE MY LIFE!
SCOTT and BORGMAN
©2009 ZITS Partnership. Distributed by King Features Syndicate

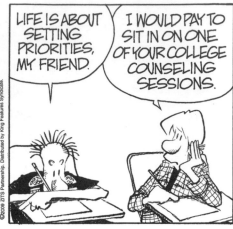

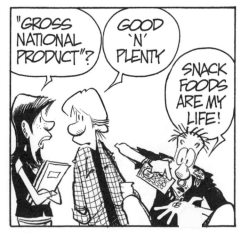

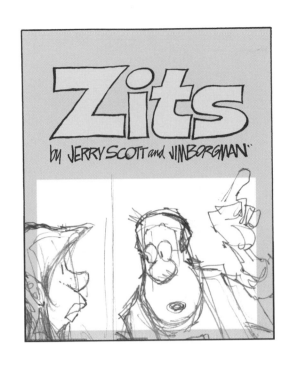

Zits
by JERRY SCOTT and JIM BORGMAN

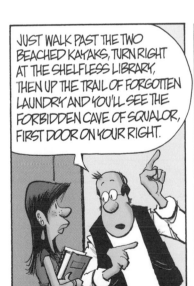

JUST WALK PAST THE TWO BEACHED KAYAKS, TURN RIGHT AT THE SHELFLESS LIBRARY, THEN UP THE TRAIL OF FORGOTTEN LAUNDRY AND YOU'LL SEE THE FORBIDDEN CAVE OF SQUALOR, FIRST DOOR ON YOUR RIGHT.
4/26
SCOTT and BORGMAN
KEEP OUT
©2009 ZITS Partnership. Distributed by King Features Syndicate.
YOUR DAD IS SO FUNNY!
THAT'S A WORD FOR IT.

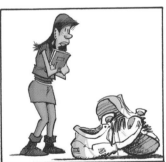

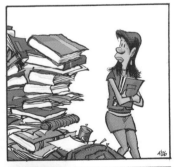

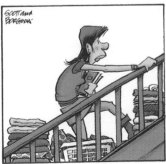

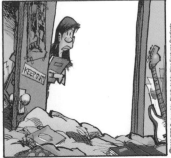

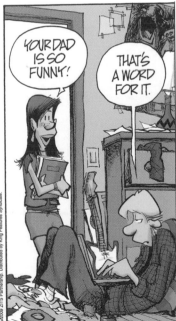

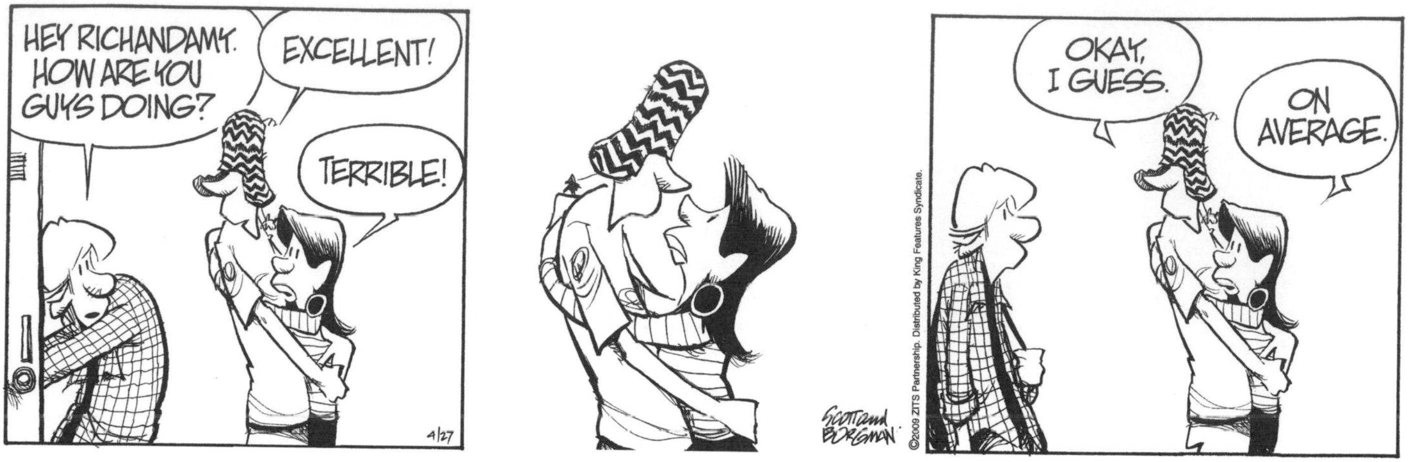
HEY RICHANDAMY. HOW ARE YOU GUYS DOING?
EXCELLENT!
TERRIBLE!
4/27
SCOTT and BORGMAN
©2009 ZITS Partnership. Distributed by King Features Syndicate.
OKAY, I GUESS.
ON AVERAGE.

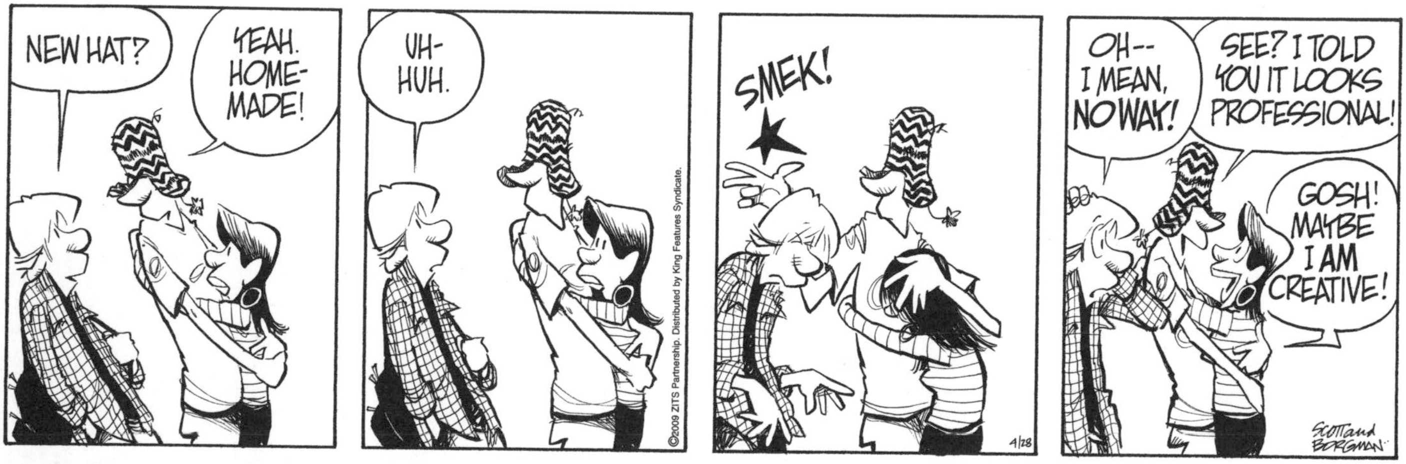
NEW HAT?
YEAH. HOME-MADE!
UH-HUH.
©2009 ZITS Partnership. Distributed by King Features Syndicate.
SMEK!
4/28
OH-- I MEAN, NO WAY!
SEE? I TOLD YOU IT LOOKS PROFESSIONAL!
GOSH! MAYBE I AM CREATIVE!
SCOTT and BORGMAN

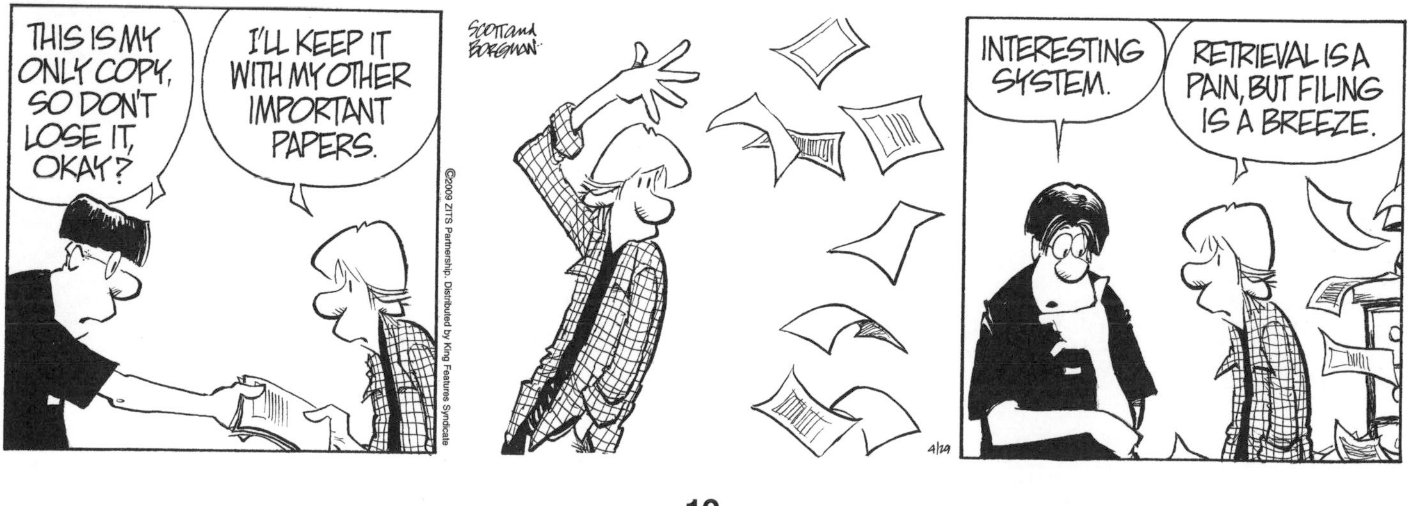
THIS IS MY ONLY COPY, SO DON'T LOSE IT, OKAY?
I'LL KEEP IT WITH MY OTHER IMPORTANT PAPERS.
©2009 ZITS Partnership. Distributed by King Features Syndicate
SCOTT and BORGMAN
4/29
INTERESTING SYSTEM.
RETRIEVAL IS A PAIN, BUT FILING IS A BREEZE.

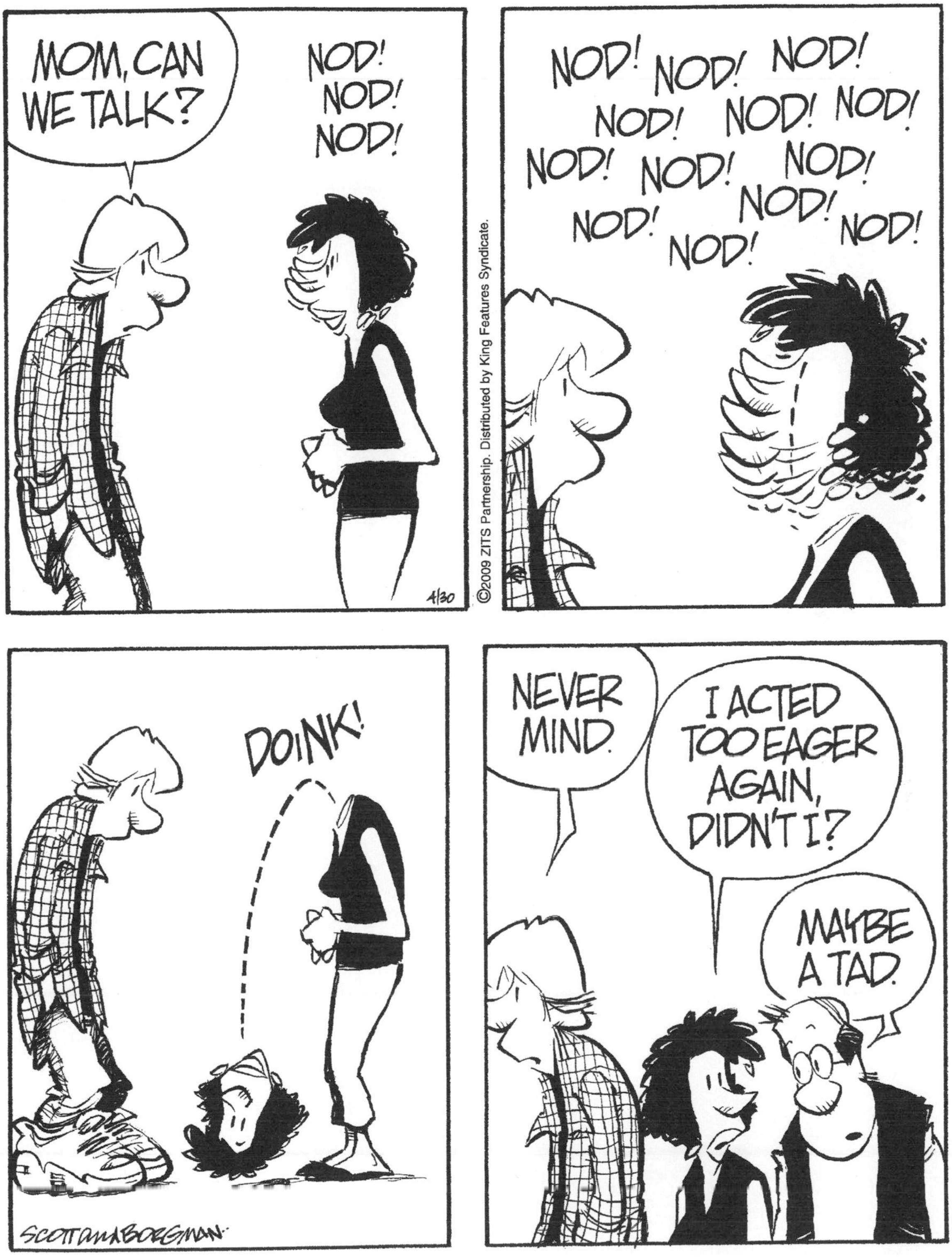
MOM, CAN WE TALK?
NOD! NOD! NOD!
4/30
©2009 ZITS Partnership. Distributed by King Features Syndicate.
NOD! NOD! NOD! NOD! NOD! NOD! NOD! NOD! NOD! NOD! NOD! NOD! NOD!
DOINK!
NEVER MIND.
I ACTED TOO EAGER AGAIN, DIDN'T I?
MAYBE A TAD.

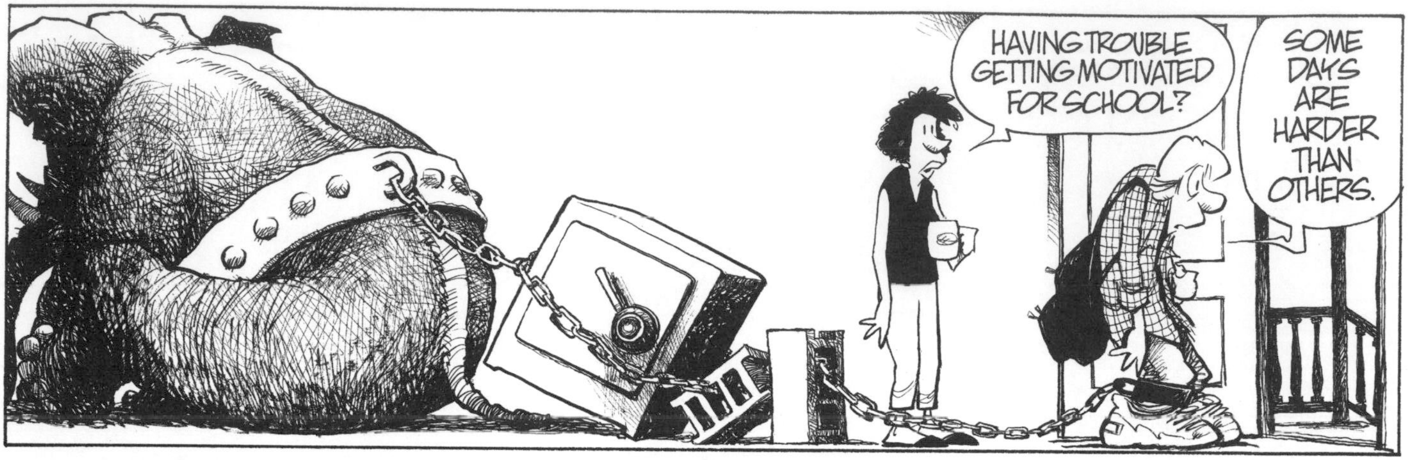
HAVING TROUBLE GETTING MOTIVATED FOR SCHOOL?
SOME DAYS ARE HARDER THAN OTHERS.

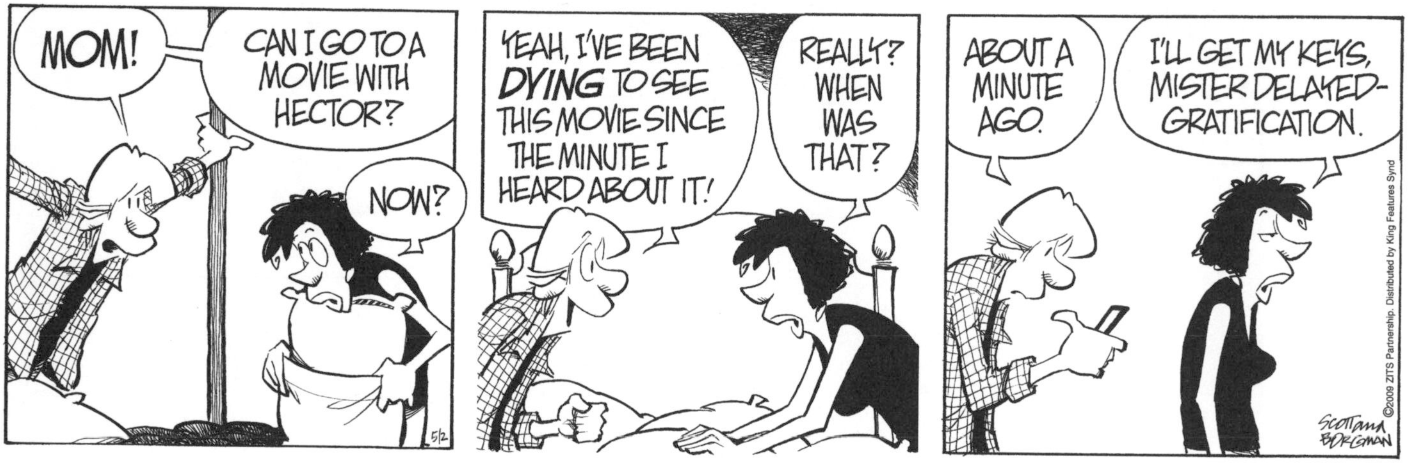
MOM!
CAN I GO TO A MOVIE WITH HECTOR?
NOW?
5/2
YEAH, I'VE BEEN DYING TO SEE THIS MOVIE SINCE THE MINUTE I HEARD ABOUT IT!
REALLY? WHEN WAS THAT?
ABOUT A MINUTE AGO.
I'LL GET MY KEYS, MISTER DELAYED-GRATIFICATION.
©2009 ZITS Partnership. Distributed by King Features Synd
SCOTT AND BORGMAN

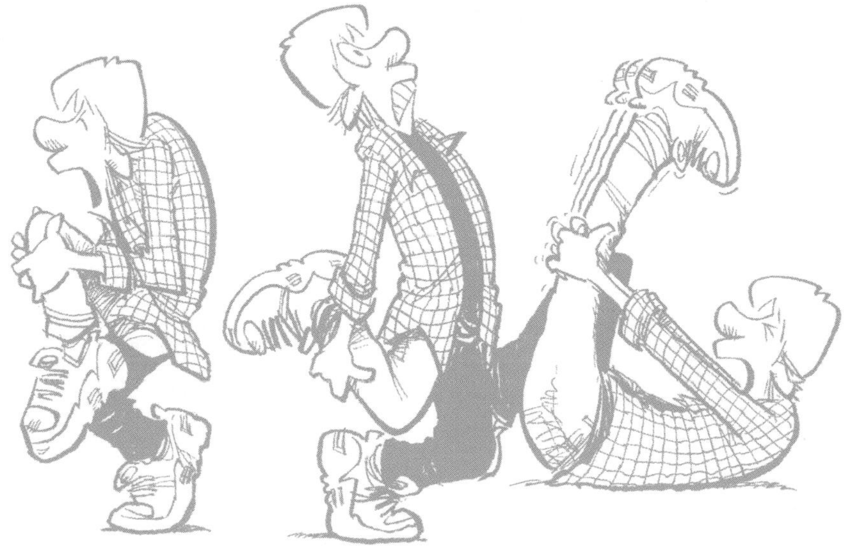

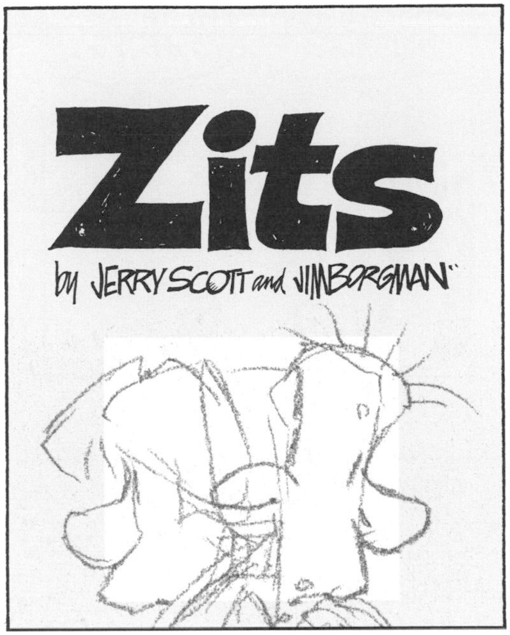
Zits
by JERRY SCOTT and JIM BORGMAN

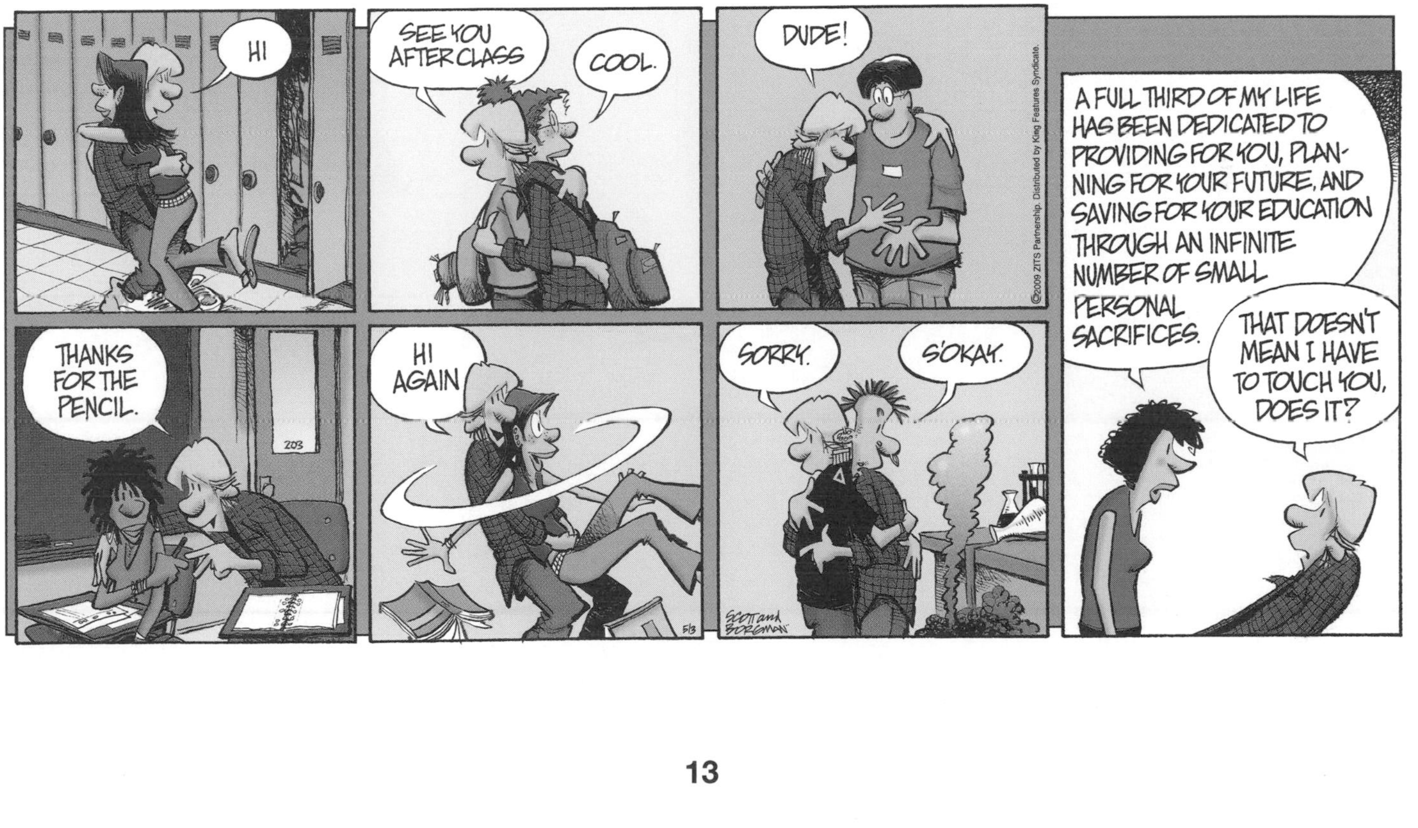
HI
SEE YOU AFTER CLASS
COOL.
DUDE!
©2009 ZITS Partnership. Distributed by King Features Syndicate.
THANKS FOR THE PENCIL.
203
HI AGAIN
SORRY.
S'OKAY.
SCOTT and BORGMAN
A FULL THIRD OF MY LIFE HAS BEEN DEDICATED TO PROVIDING FOR YOU, PLANNING FOR YOUR FUTURE, AND SAVING FOR YOUR EDUCATION THROUGH AN INFINITE NUMBER OF SMALL PERSONAL SACRIFICES.
THAT DOESN'T MEAN I HAVE TO TOUCH YOU, DOES IT?

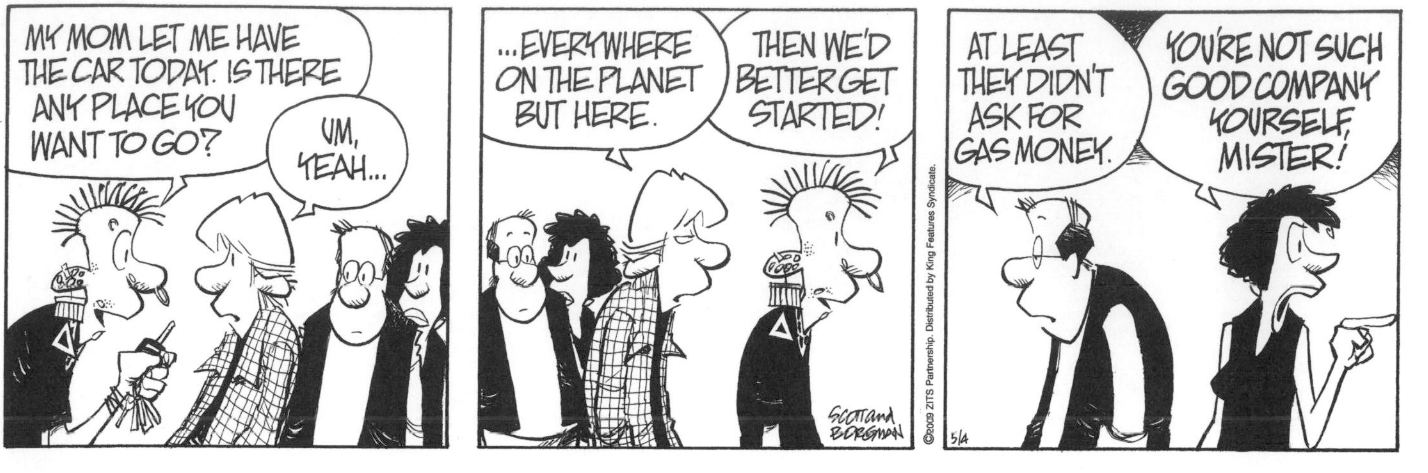
MY MOM LET ME HAVE THE CAR TODAY. IS THERE ANY PLACE YOU WANT TO GO?
UM, YEAH...
...EVERYWHERE ON THE PLANET BUT HERE.
THEN WE'D BETTER GET STARTED!
SCOTT AND BORGMAN
©2009 ZITS Partnership. Distributed by King Features Syndicate.
5/4
AT LEAST THEY DIDN'T ASK FOR GAS MONEY.
YOU'RE NOT SUCH GOOD COMPANY YOURSELF, MISTER!

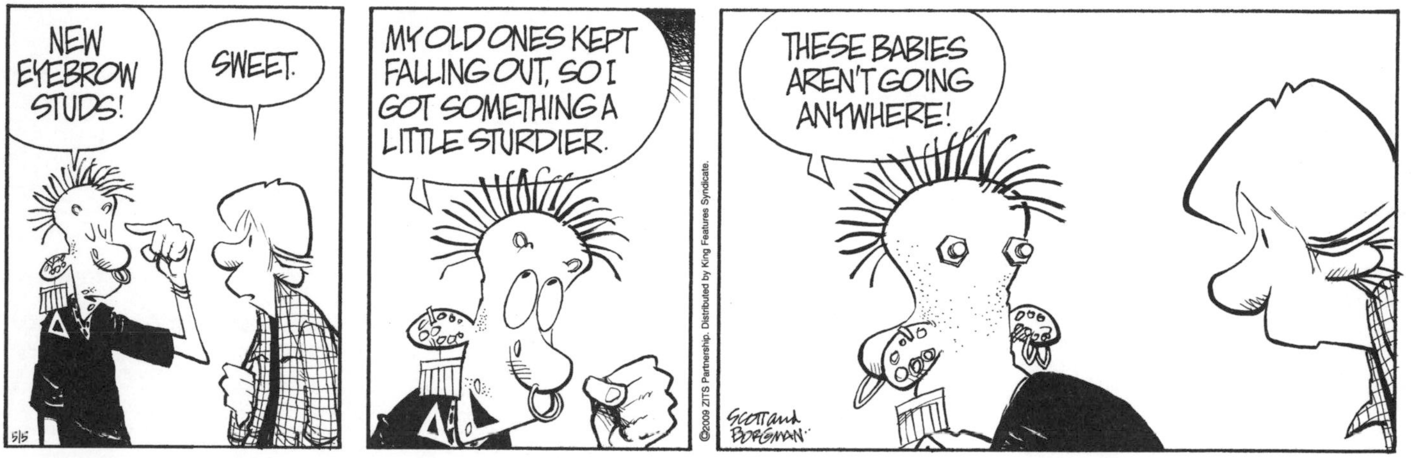
NEW EYEBROW STUDS!
SWEET.
5/5
MY OLD ONES KEPT FALLING OUT, SO I GOT SOMETHING A LITTLE STURDIER.
©2009 ZITS Partnership. Distributed by King Features Syndicate.
THESE BABIES AREN'T GOING ANYWHERE!
SCOTT AND BORGMAN

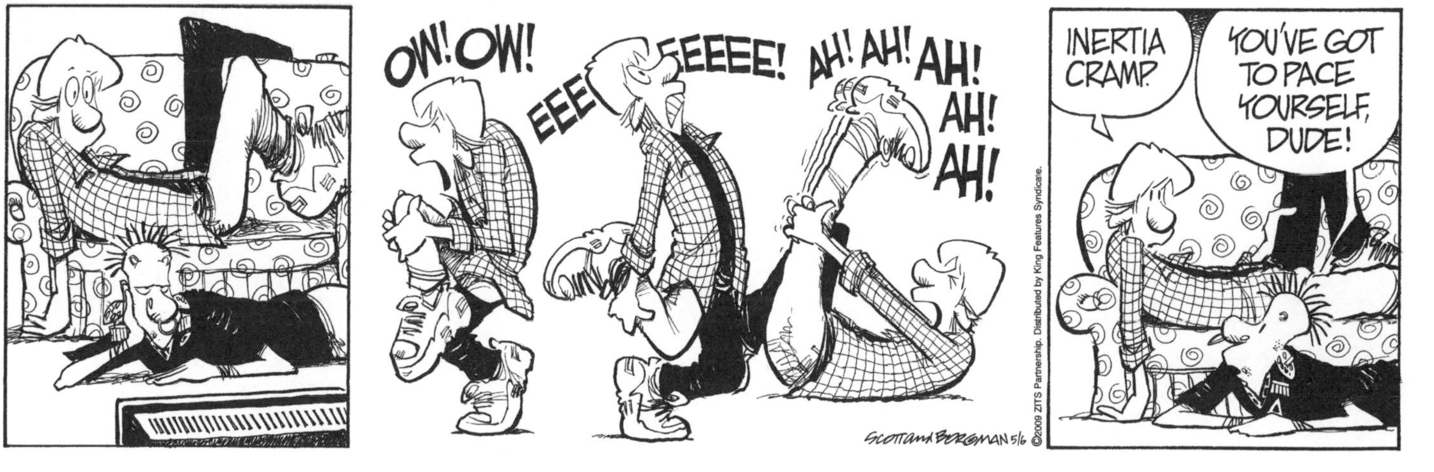
OW! OW!
EEEEEEEE!
AH! AH! AH! AH! AH!
SCOTT AND BORGMAN 5/6
©2009 ZITS Partnership. Distributed by King Features Syndicate.
INERTIA CRAMP.
YOU'VE GOT TO PACE YOURSELF, DUDE!

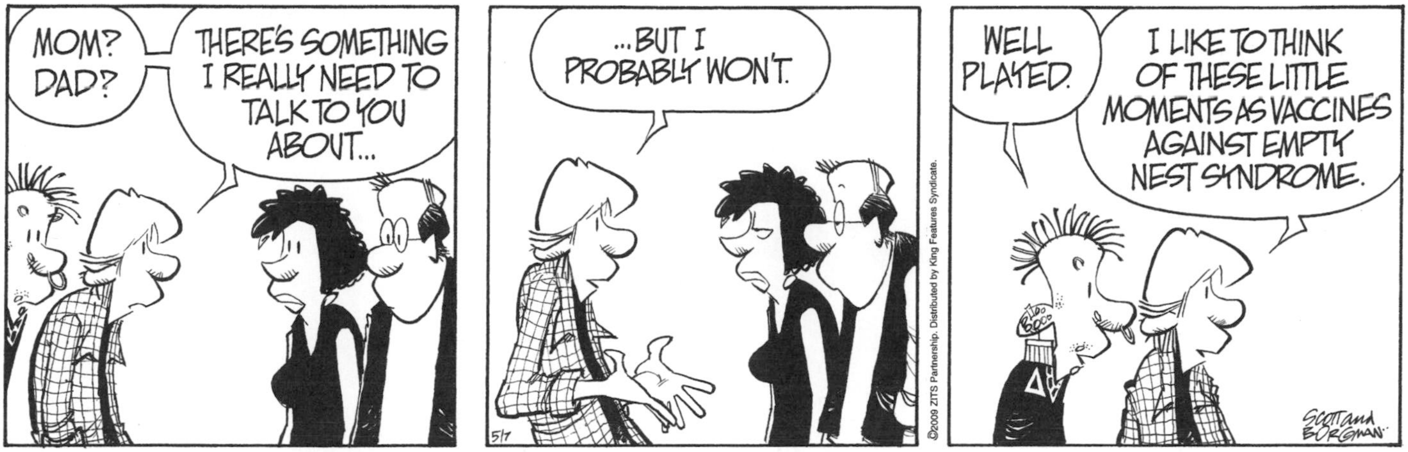
MOM? DAD?
THERE'S SOMETHING I REALLY NEED TO TALK TO YOU ABOUT...
...BUT I PROBABLY WON'T.
5/7
WELL PLAYED.
I LIKE TO THINK OF THESE LITTLE MOMENTS AS VACCINES AGAINST EMPTY NEST SYNDROME.
©2009 ZITS Partnership. Distributed by King Features Syndicate.
SCOTT AND BORGMAN

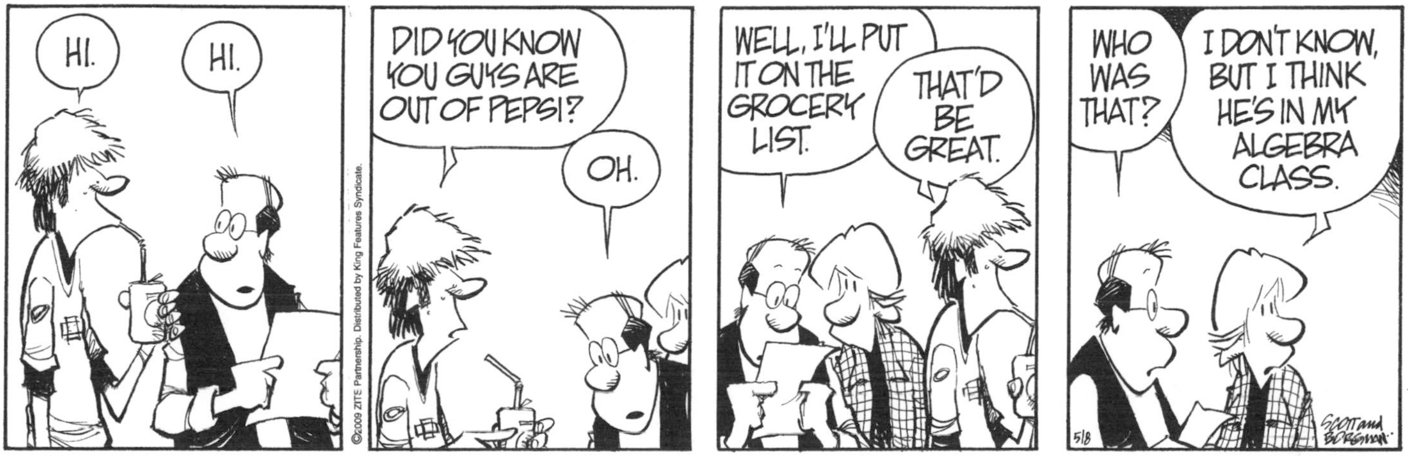
HI.
HI.
©2009 ZITS Partnership. Distributed by King Features Syndicate.
DID YOU KNOW YOU GUYS ARE OUT OF PEPSI?
OH.
WELL, I'LL PUT IT ON THE GROCERY LIST.
THAT'D BE GREAT.
WHO WAS THAT?
I DON'T KNOW, BUT I THINK HE'S IN MY ALGEBRA CLASS.
5/8
SCOTT AND BORGMAN

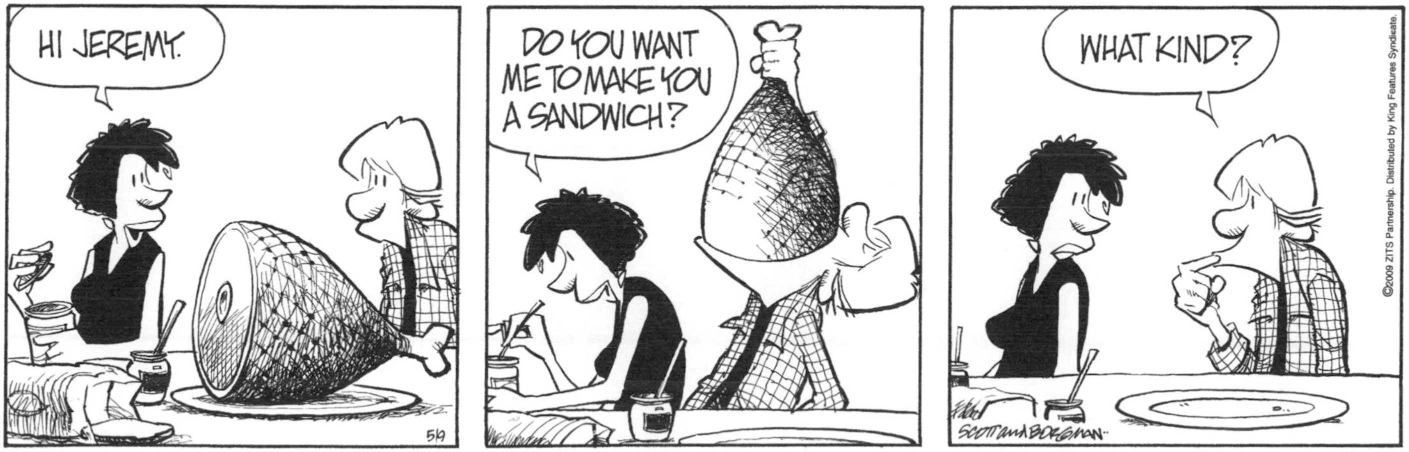
HI JEREMY.
5/9
DO YOU WANT ME TO MAKE YOU A SANDWICH?
WHAT KIND?
SCOTT AND BORGMAN
©2009 ZITS Partnership. Distributed by King Features Syndicate.

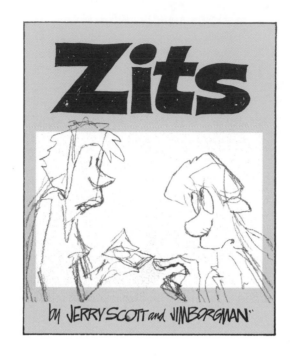

Zits
by JERRY SCOTT and JIM BORGMAN

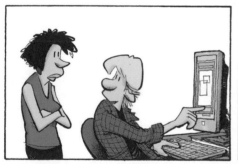

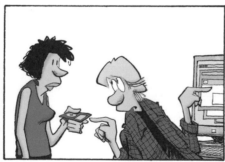

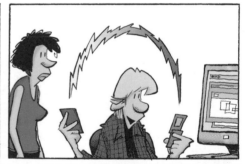

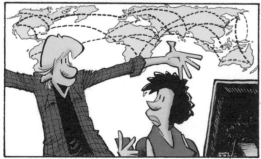

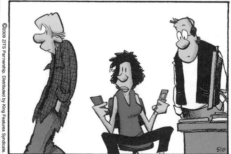

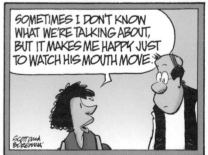

©2009 ZITS Partnership. Distributed by King Features Syndicate.
5/10
SOMETIMES I DON'T KNOW WHAT WE'RE TALKING ABOUT, BUT IT MAKES ME HAPPY JUST TO WATCH HIS MOUTH MOVE.
SCOTT and BORGMAN

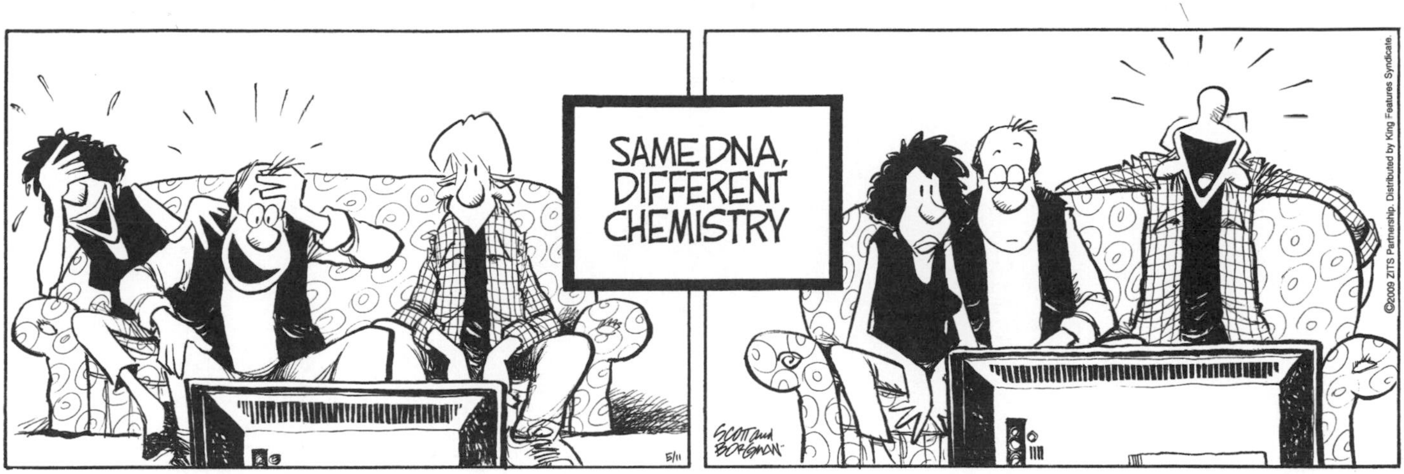
SAME DNA, DIFFERENT CHEMISTRY
SCOTT AND BORGMAN
5/11
©2009 ZITS Partnership. Distributed by King Features Syndicate.

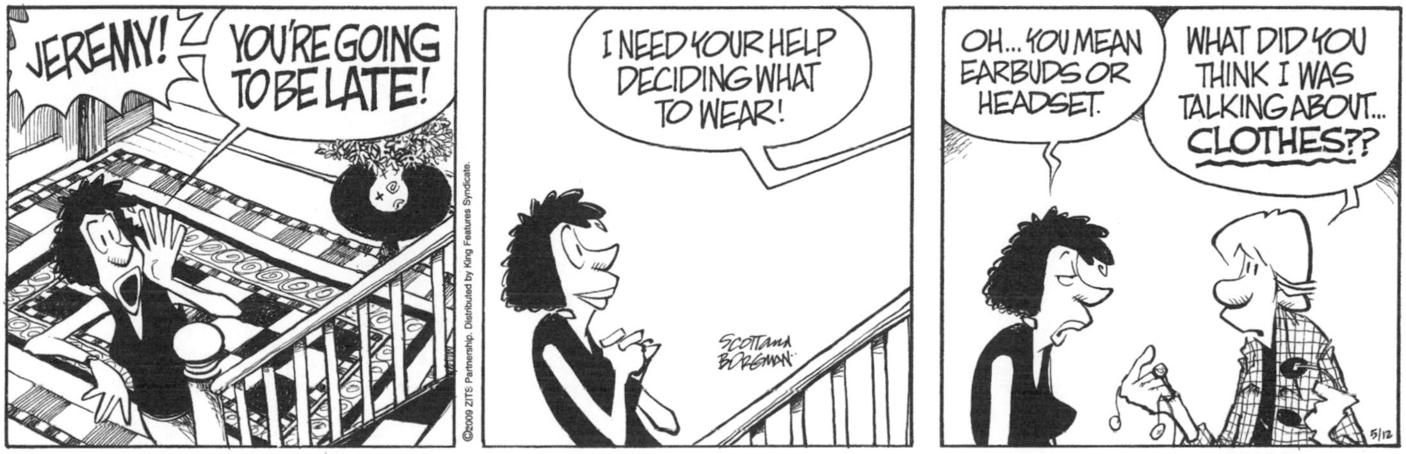
JEREMY!
YOU'RE GOING TO BE LATE!
©2009 ZITS Partnership. Distributed by King Features Syndicate.
I NEED YOUR HELP DECIDING WHAT TO WEAR!
SCOTT AND BORGMAN
OH... YOU MEAN EARBUDS OR HEADSET.
WHAT DID YOU THINK I WAS TALKING ABOUT... CLOTHES??
5/12

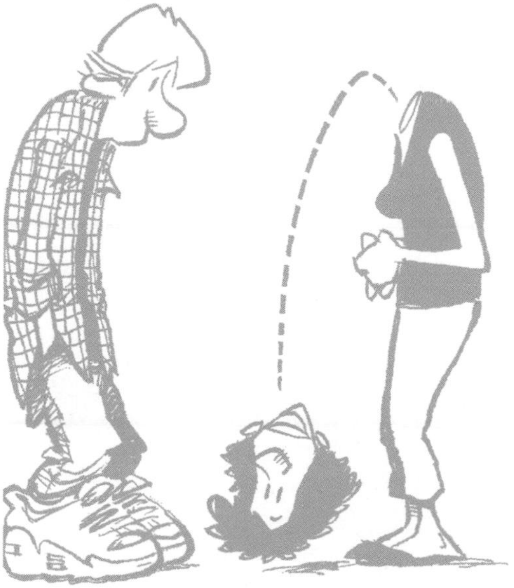

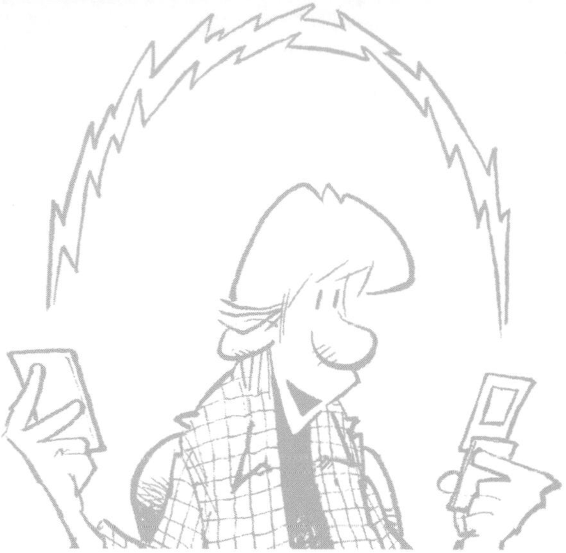

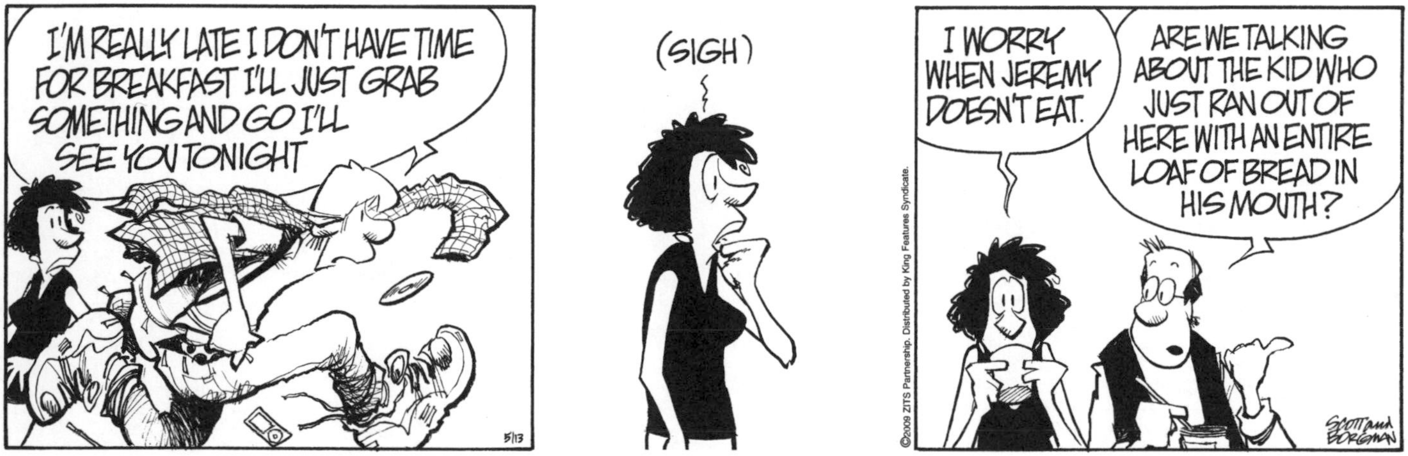

I'M REALLY LATE I DON'T HAVE TIME FOR BREAKFAST I'LL JUST GRAB SOMETHING AND GO I'LL SEE YOU TONIGHT
5/13
(SIGH)
©2009 ZITS Partnership. Distributed by King Features Syndicate.
I WORRY WHEN JEREMY DOESN'T EAT.
ARE WE TALKING ABOUT THE KID WHO JUST RAN OUT OF HERE WITH AN ENTIRE LOAF OF BREAD IN HIS MOUTH?
SCOTT and BORGMAN

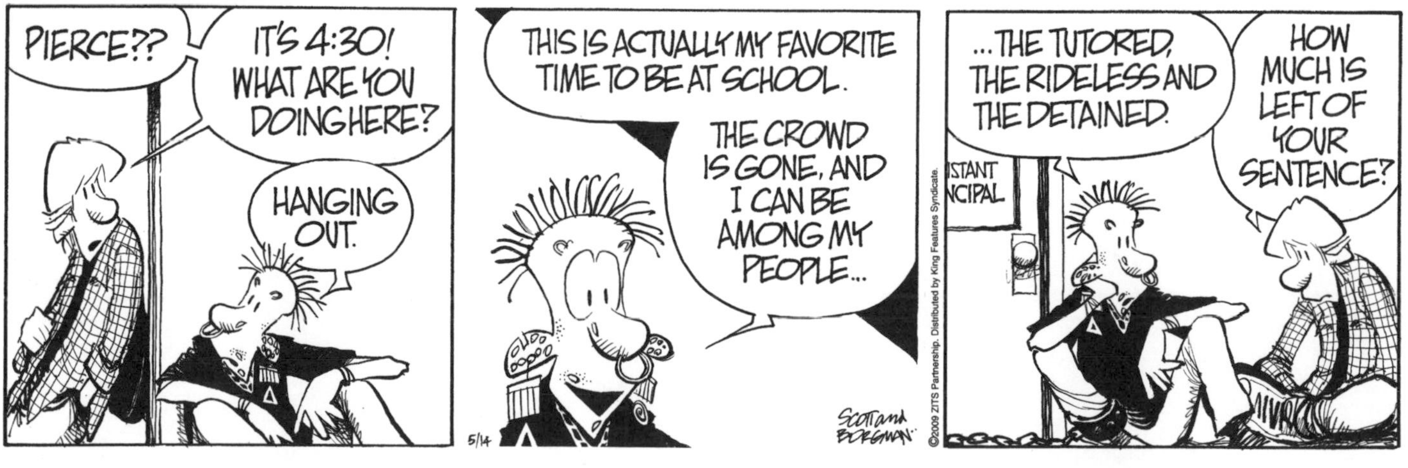

PIERCE??
IT'S 4:30! WHAT ARE YOU DOING HERE?
HANGING OUT.
THIS IS ACTUALLY MY FAVORITE TIME TO BE AT SCHOOL.
THE CROWD IS GONE, AND I CAN BE AMONG MY PEOPLE...
5/14
SCOTT and BORGMAN
©2009 ZITS Partnership. Distributed by King Features Syndicate.
...THE TUTORED, THE RIDELESS AND THE DETAINED.
HOW MUCH IS LEFT OF YOUR SENTENCE?

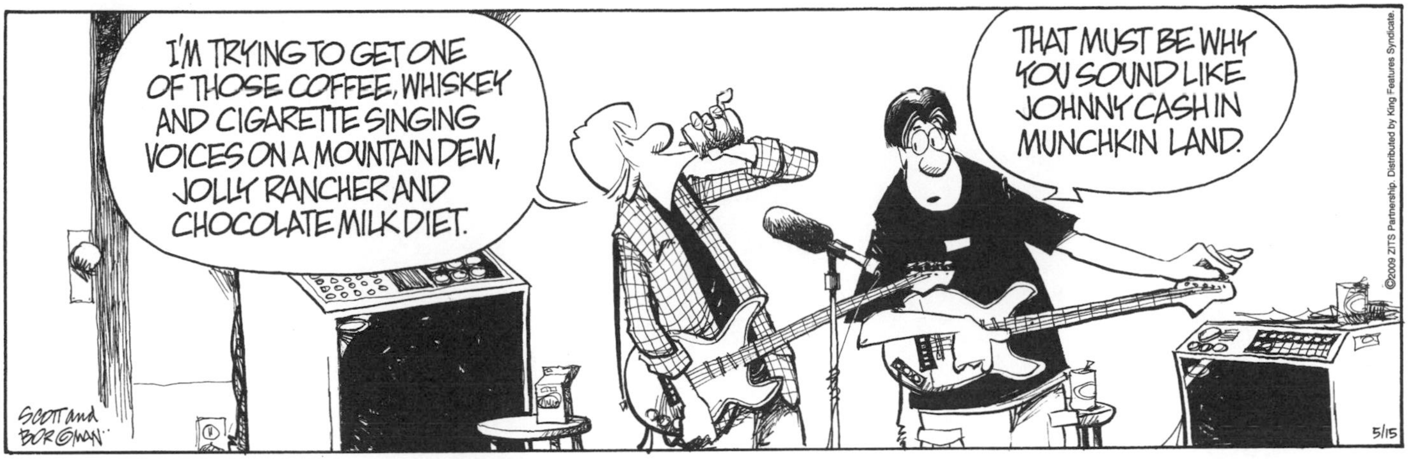
I'M TRYING TO GET ONE OF THOSE COFFEE, WHISKEY AND CIGARETTE SINGING VOICES ON A MOUNTAIN DEW, JOLLY RANCHER AND CHOCOLATE MILK DIET.
THAT MUST BE WHY YOU SOUND LIKE JOHNNY CASH IN MUNCHKIN LAND.
SCOTT and BORGMAN
5/15
©2009 ZITS Partnership. Distributed by King Features Syndicate.

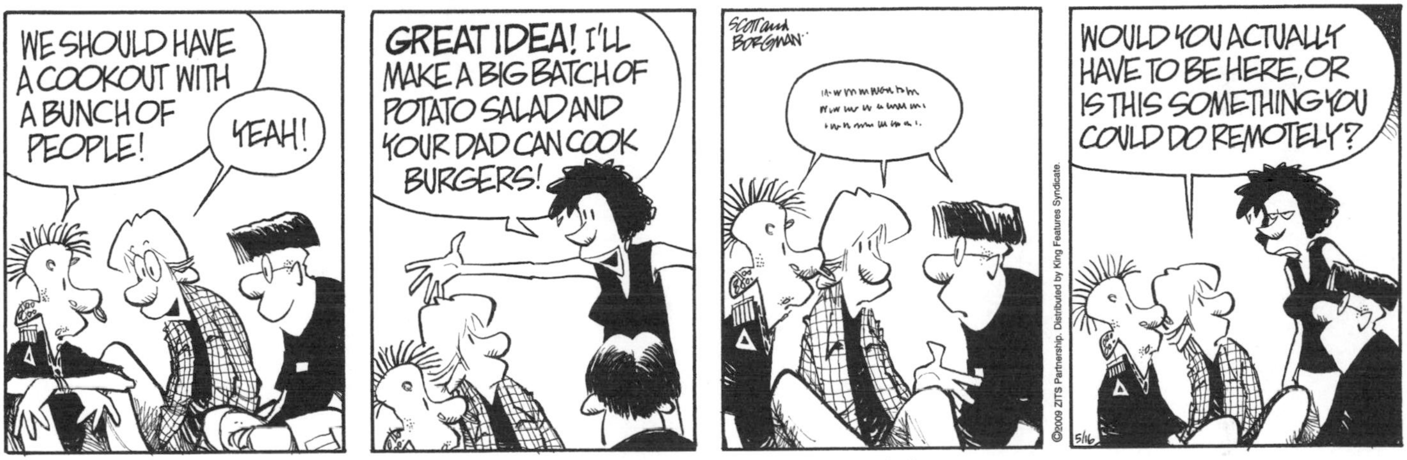
WE SHOULD HAVE A COOKOUT WITH A BUNCH OF PEOPLE!
YEAH!
GREAT IDEA! I'LL MAKE A BIG BATCH OF POTATO SALAD AND YOUR DAD CAN COOK BURGERS!
SCOTT and BORGMAN
WOULD YOU ACTUALLY HAVE TO BE HERE, OR IS THIS SOMETHING YOU COULD DO REMOTELY?
5/16
©2009 ZITS Partnership. Distributed by King Features Syndicate.

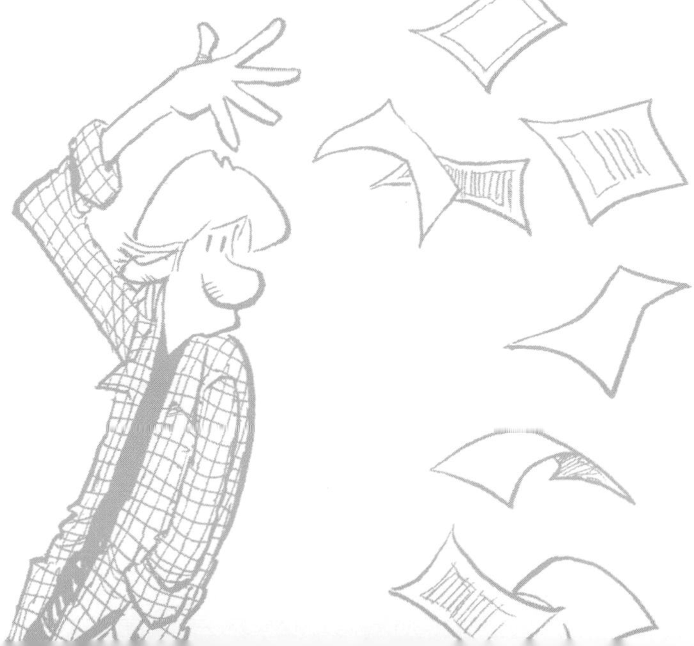

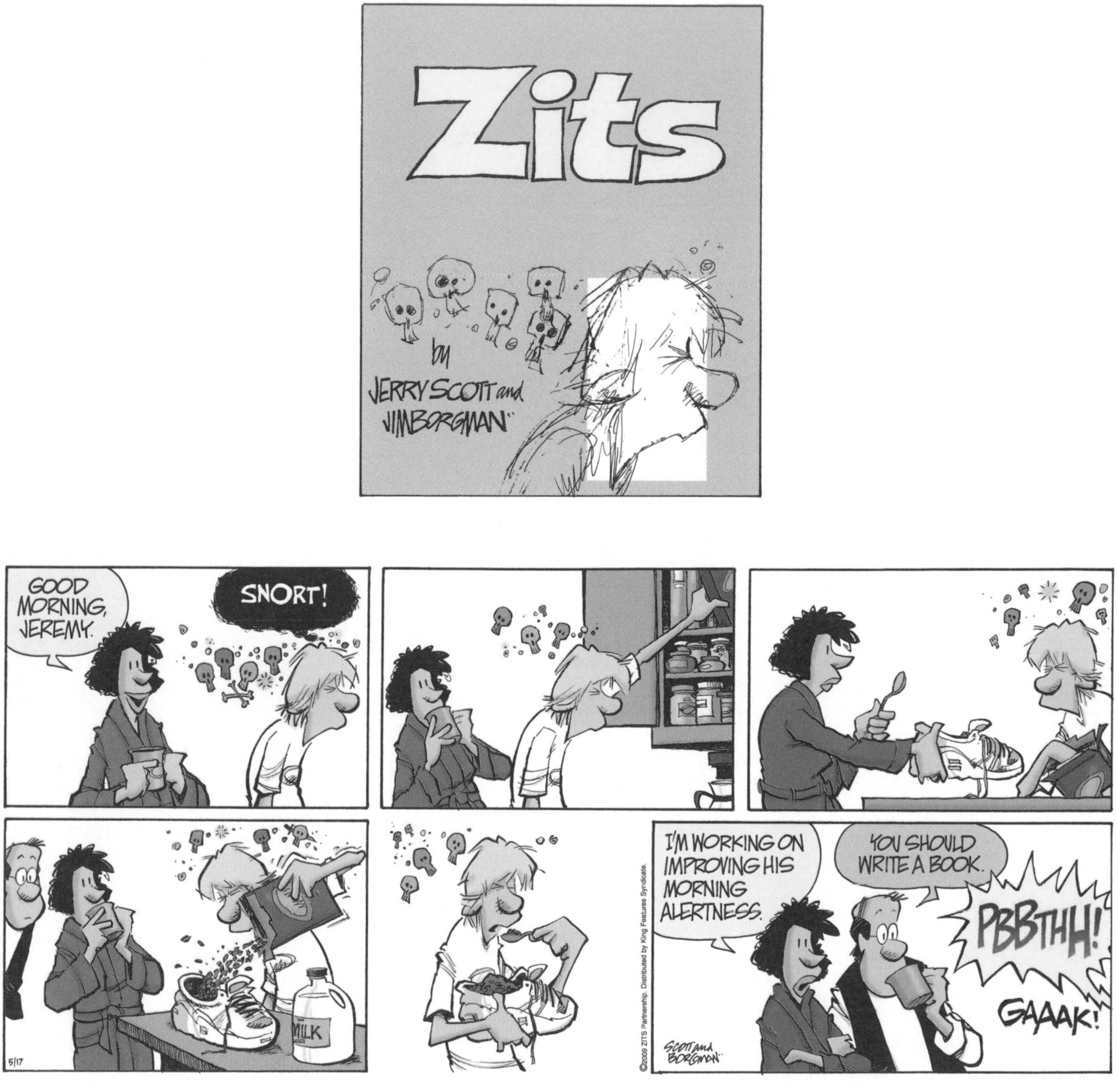
Zits
by
JERRY SCOTT and
JIM BORGMAN
GOOD MORNING, JEREMY.
SNORT!
5/17
©2009 ZITS Partnership. Distributed by King Features Syndicate.
I'M WORKING ON IMPROVING HIS MORNING ALERTNESS.
YOU SHOULD WRITE A BOOK.
PBBTHH!
GAAAK!
SCOTT and BORGMAN

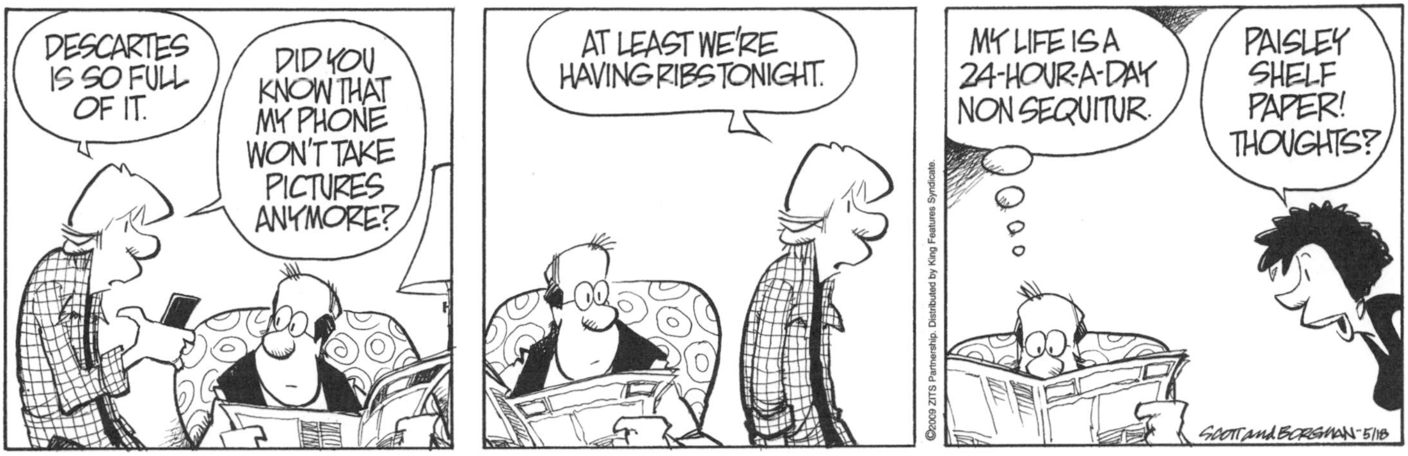
DESCARTES IS SO FULL OF IT.
DID YOU KNOW THAT MY PHONE WON'T TAKE PICTURES ANYMORE?
AT LEAST WE'RE HAVING RIBS TONIGHT.
©2009 ZITS Partnership. Distributed by King Features Syndicate.
MY LIFE IS A 24-HOUR-A-DAY NON SEQUITUR.
PAISLEY SHELF PAPER! THOUGHTS?
SCOTT and BORGMAN 5/18

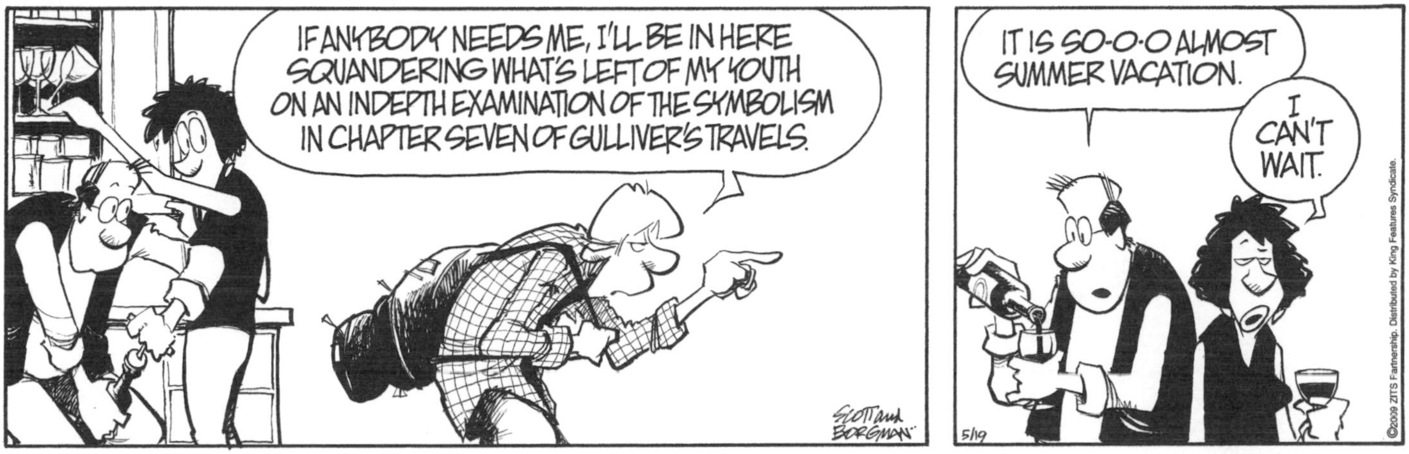
IF ANYBODY NEEDS ME, I'LL BE IN HERE SQUANDERING WHAT'S LEFT OF MY YOUTH ON AN INDEPTH EXAMINATION OF THE SYMBOLISM IN CHAPTER SEVEN OF GULLIVER'S TRAVELS.
SCOTT and BORGMAN
5/19
IT IS SO-O-O ALMOST SUMMER VACATION.
I CAN'T WAIT.
©2009 ZITS Partnership. Distributed by King Features Syndicate.

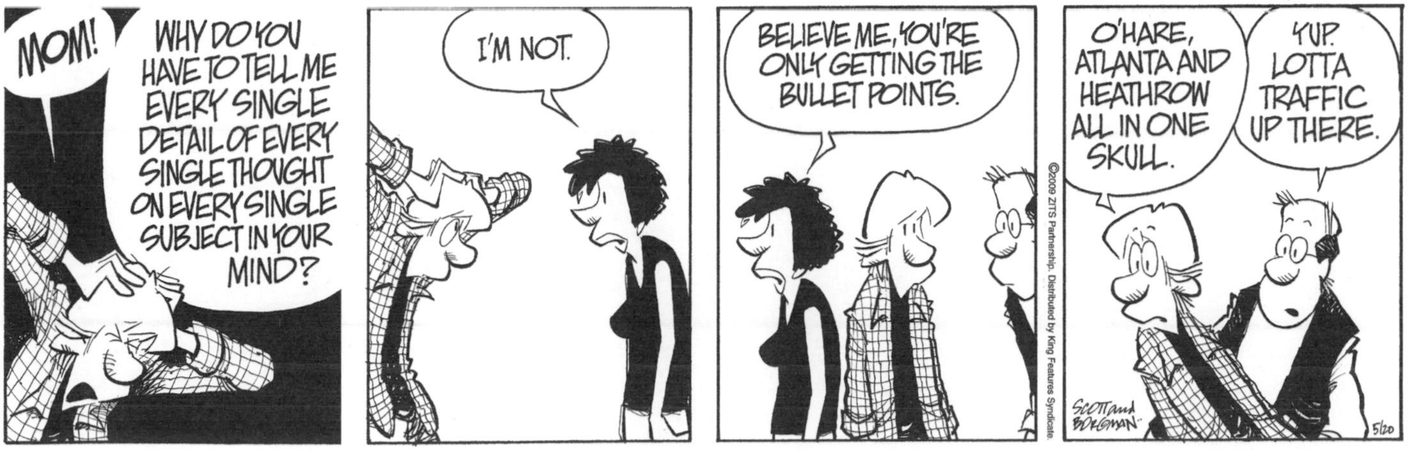
MOM!
WHY DO YOU HAVE TO TELL ME EVERY SINGLE DETAIL OF EVERY SINGLE THOUGHT ON EVERY SINGLE SUBJECT IN YOUR MIND?
I'M NOT.
BELIEVE ME, YOU'RE ONLY GETTING THE BULLET POINTS.
©2009 ZITS Partnership. Distributed by King Features Syndicate.
O'HARE, ATLANTA AND HEATHROW ALL IN ONE SKULL.
YUP. LOTTA TRAFFIC UP THERE.
SCOTT and BORGMAN
5/20

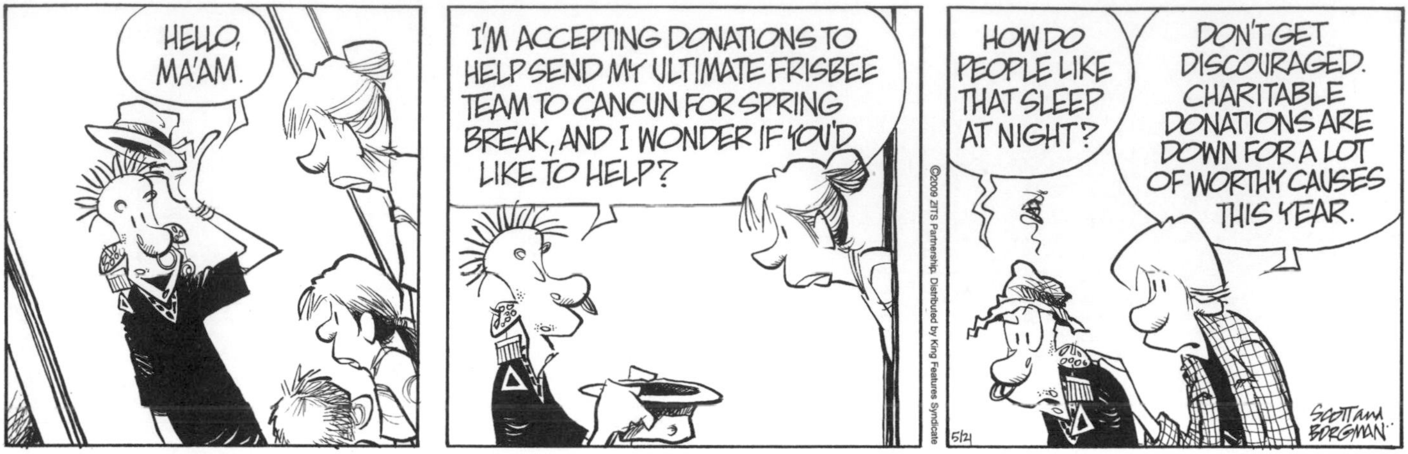
HELLO, MA'AM.
I'M ACCEPTING DONATIONS TO HELP SEND MY ULTIMATE FRISBEE TEAM TO CANCUN FOR SPRING BREAK, AND I WONDER IF YOU'D LIKE TO HELP?
HOW DO PEOPLE LIKE THAT SLEEP AT NIGHT?
DON'T GET DISCOURAGED. CHARITABLE DONATIONS ARE DOWN FOR A LOT OF WORTHY CAUSES THIS YEAR.
©2009 ZITS Partnership. Distributed by King Features Syndicate
5/24
SCOTT and BORGMAN

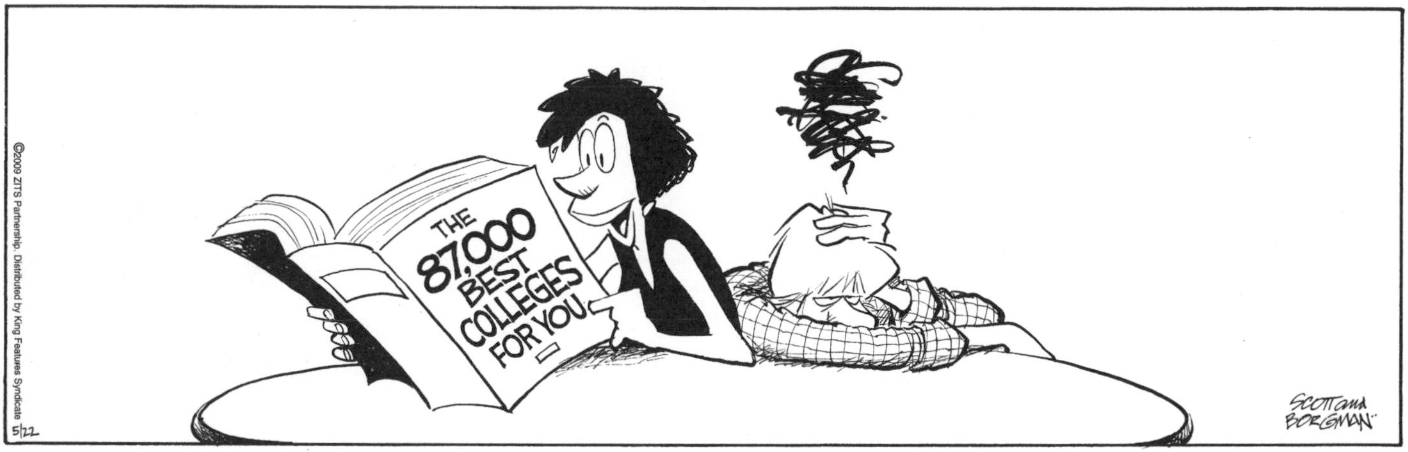
THE 87,000 BEST COLLEGES FOR YOU
©2009 ZITS Partnership. Distributed by King Features Syndicate
5/22
SCOTT and BORGMAN

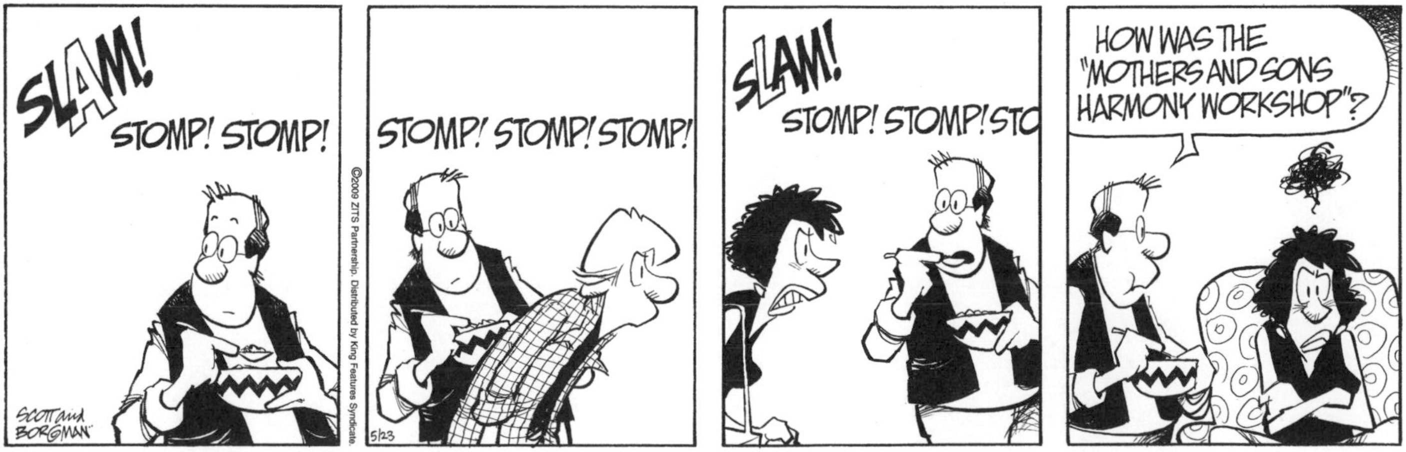
SLAM!
STOMP! STOMP!
SCOTT and BORGMAN
STOMP! STOMP! STOMP!
©2009 ZITS Partnership. Distributed by King Features Syndicate
5/23
SLAM!
STOMP! STOMP! STO
HOW WAS THE "MOTHERS AND SONS HARMONY WORKSHOP"?

Zits
TYPE O
NO ALLERGIES
by
JERRY SCOTT and
JIM BORGMAN

THE TROUBLE WITH HIGH SCHOOL IS THAT IT'S ALL JUST SO PREDICTABLE.
I KNEW YOU WERE GOING TO SAY THAT.
HEY!
PASTELS
00
SCOTT and BORGMAN
©2009 ZITS Partnership. Distributed by King Features Syndicate.

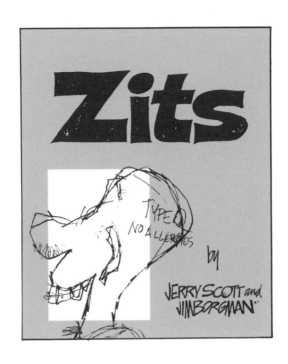

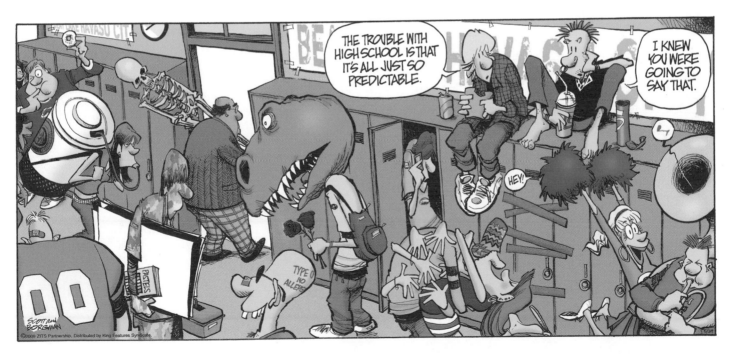

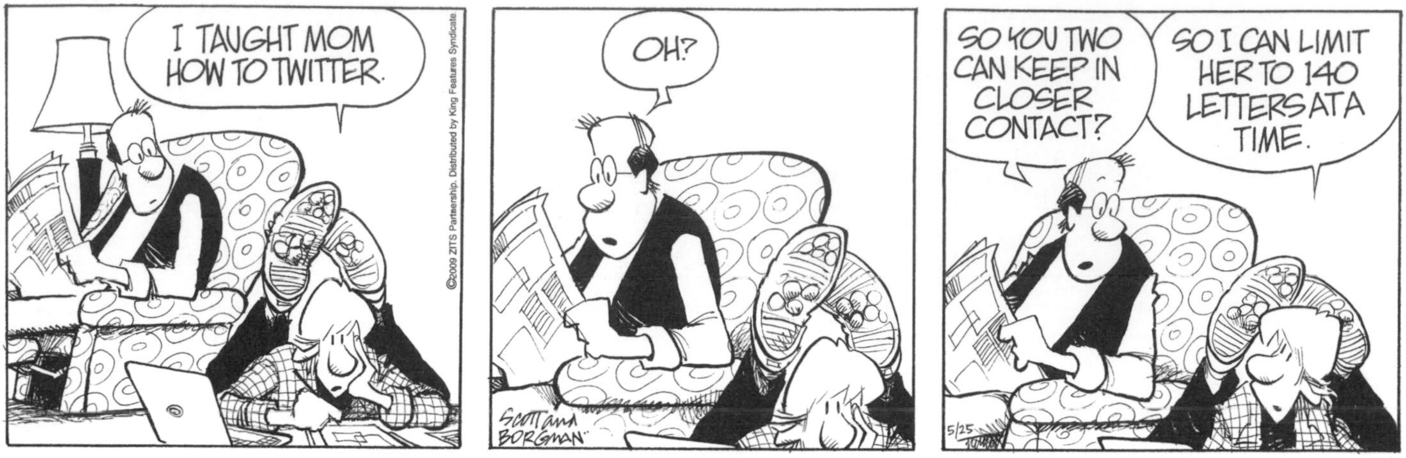
I TAUGHT MOM HOW TO TWITTER.
©2009 ZITS Partnership. Distributed by King Features Syndicate
OH?
SCOTT and BORGMAN
SO YOU TWO CAN KEEP IN CLOSER CONTACT?
SO I CAN LIMIT HER TO 140 LETTERS AT A TIME.
5/25

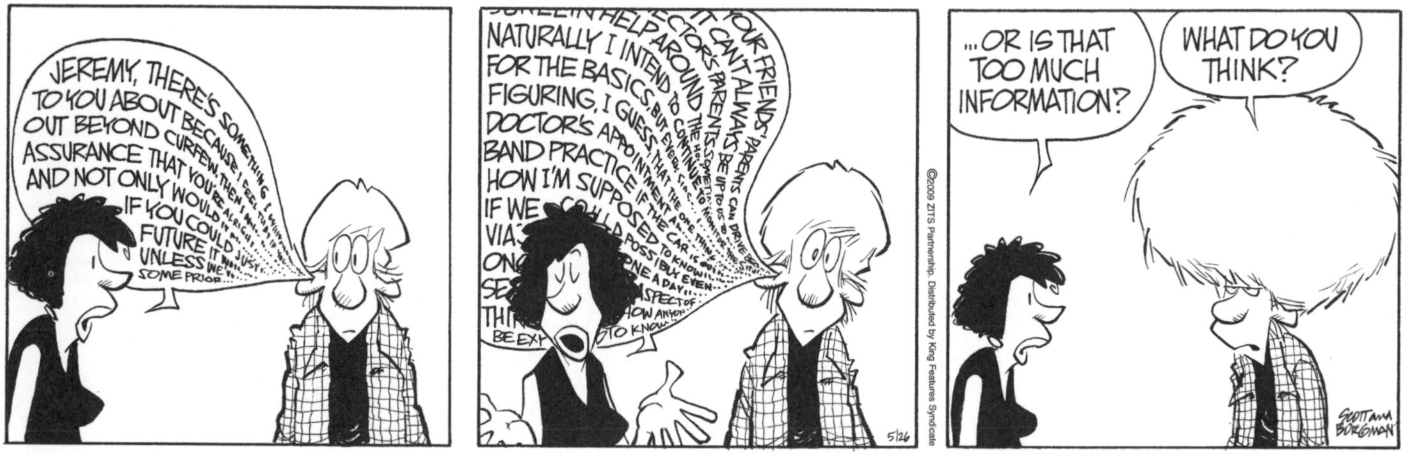
JEREMY, THERE'S SOMETHING
TO YOU ABOUT BECAUSE
OUT BEYOND CURFEW
ASSURANCE THAT YOU'RE
AND NOT ONLY WOULD
IF YOU COULD
FUTURE
UNLESS
SOME PRIOR
NATURALLY I INTEND
FOR THE BASICS
FIGURING, I GUESS
DOCTOR'S APPOINTMENT
BAND PRACTICE
HOW I'M SUPPOSED
5/26
©2009 ZITS Partnership. Distributed by King Features Syndicate
...OR IS THAT TOO MUCH INFORMATION?
WHAT DO YOU THINK?
SCOTT and BORGMAN

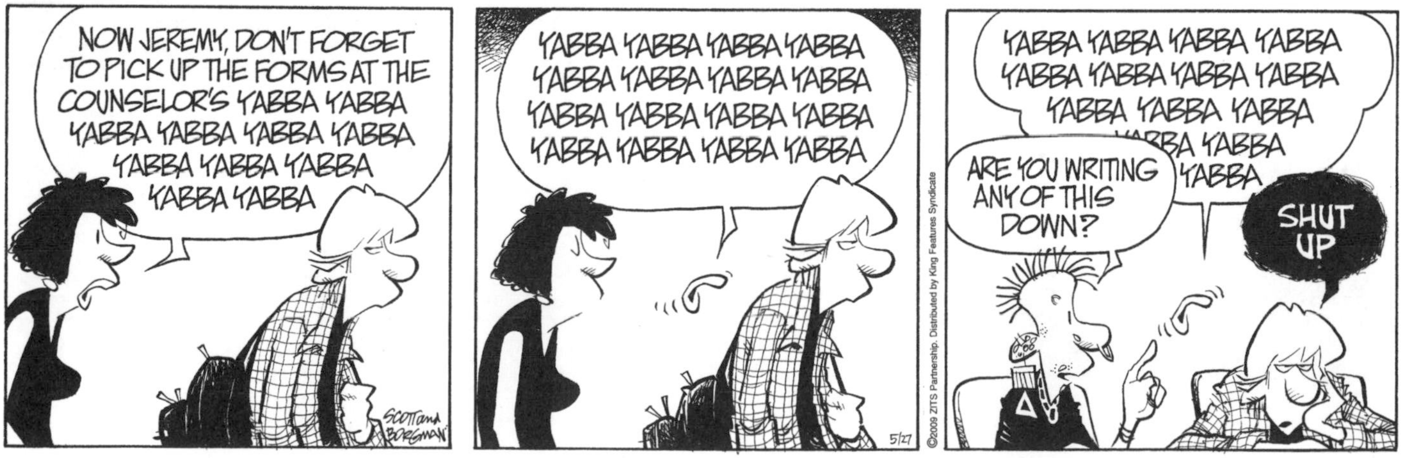
NOW JEREMY, DON'T FORGET TO PICK UP THE FORMS AT THE COUNSELOR'S YABBA YABBA YABBA YABBA YABBA YABBA YABBA YABBA YABBA YABBA YABBA
SCOTT and BORGMAN
YABBA YABBA YABBA YABBA YABBA YABBA YABBA YABBA YABBA YABBA YABBA YABBA YABBA YABBA YABBA YABBA
5/27
©2009 ZITS Partnership. Distributed by King Features Syndicate
YABBA YABBA YABBA YABBA YABBA YABBA YABBA YABBA YABBA YABBA YABBA
ARE YOU WRITING ANY OF THIS DOWN?
SHUT UP

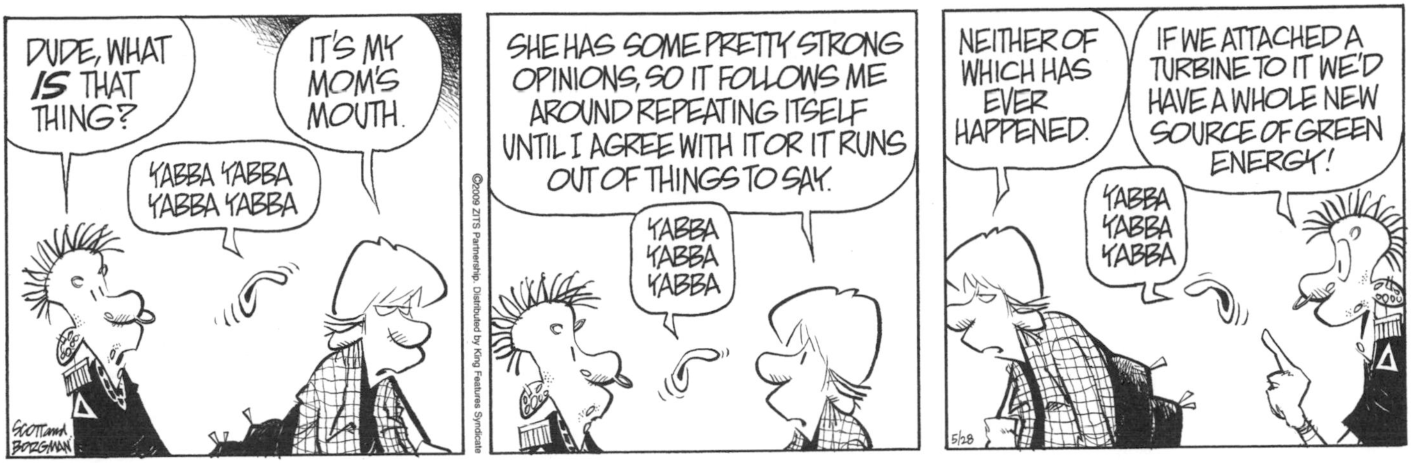
DUDE, WHAT IS THAT THING?
YABBA YABBA YABBA YABBA
IT'S MY MOM'S MOUTH.
SCOTT and BORGMAN
©2009 ZITS Partnership. Distributed by King Features Syndicate
SHE HAS SOME PRETTY STRONG OPINIONS, SO IT FOLLOWS ME AROUND REPEATING ITSELF UNTIL I AGREE WITH IT OR IT RUNS OUT OF THINGS TO SAY.
YABBA YABBA YABBA
NEITHER OF WHICH HAS EVER HAPPENED.
IF WE ATTACHED A TURBINE TO IT WE'D HAVE A WHOLE NEW SOURCE OF GREEN ENERGY!
YABBA YABBA YABBA
5/28

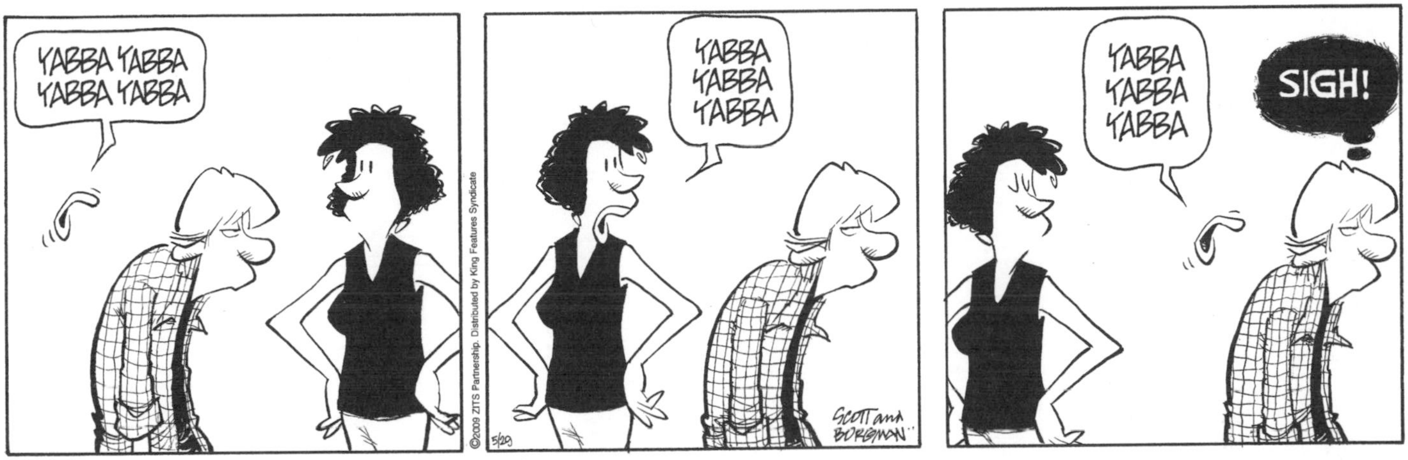
YABBA YABBA YABBA YABBA
©2009 ZITS Partnership. Distributed by King Features Syndicate
5/29
YABBA YABBA YABBA
SCOTT and BORGMAN
YABBA YABBA YABBA
SIGH!

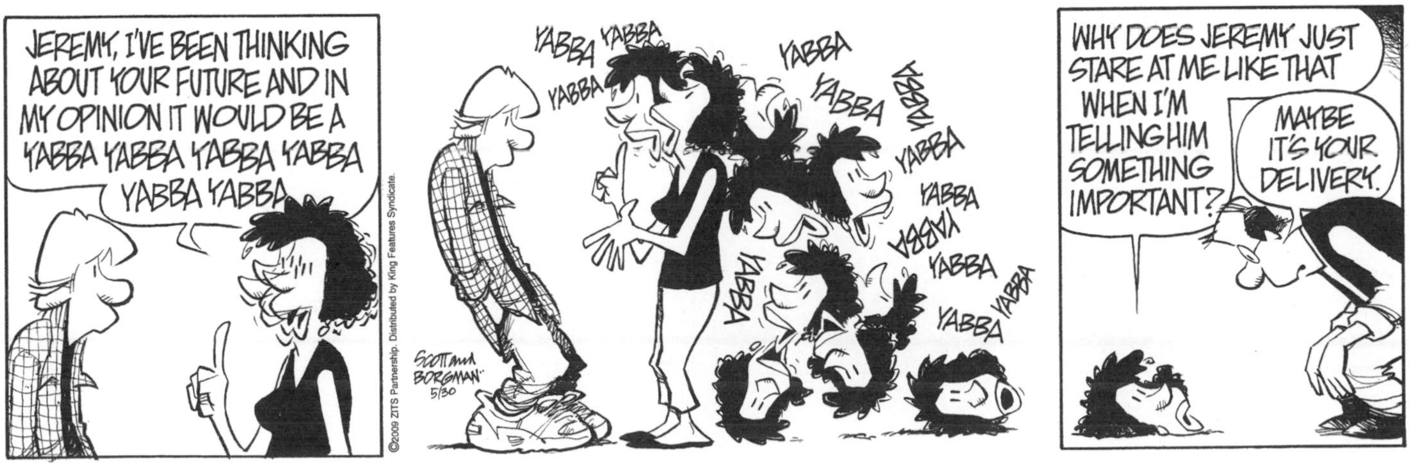
JEREMY, I'VE BEEN THINKING ABOUT YOUR FUTURE AND IN MY OPINION IT WOULD BE A YABBA YABBA YABBA YABBA YABBA YABBA
©2009 ZITS Partnership. Distributed by King Features Syndicate.
YABBA YABBA YABBA YABBA YABBA YABBA YABBA YABBA YABBA YABBA YABBA YABBA YABBA
SCOTT and BORGMAN 5/30
WHY DOES JEREMY JUST STARE AT ME LIKE THAT WHEN I'M TELLING HIM SOMETHING IMPORTANT?
MAYBE IT'S YOUR DELIVERY.

Zits
by
JERRY SCOTT and
JIM BORGMAN

JEREMY, THERE'S SOMETHING I NEED TO TALK TO YOU ABOUT.
YOU'RE HAVING A SEX CHANGE?
NO! I--
--HAVE BECOME AN EXOTIC DANCER BY DAY AND CRIME FIGHTER BY NIGHT?
NO! WE--
--ARE JOINING THE WITNESS PROTECTION PROGRAM, SO I NEED TO CHANGE MY NAME?
YOUR FATHER AND I--
ARE COUSINS?
5/31
©2009 ZITS Partnership. Distributed by King Features Syndicate.
NO!
WE'RE CHANGING SALSA BRANDS!!
SCOTT and BORGMAN
WHAT??

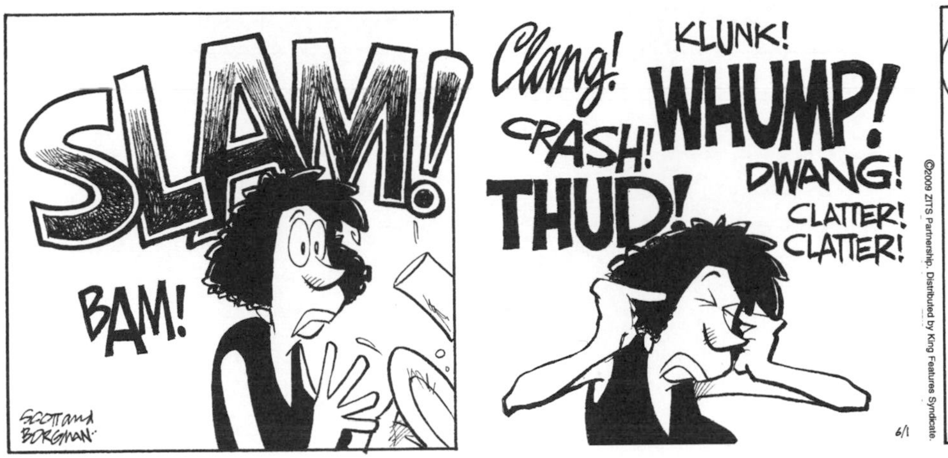
SLAM!
BAM!
SCOTT and BORGMAN
Clang!
KLUNK!
CRASH!
WHUMP!
THUD!
DWANG!
CLATTER! CLATTER!
6/1
©2009 ZITS Partnership. Distributed by King Features Syndicate.
I'M HOME.
I FIGURED IT WAS EITHER YOU OR THE APOCALYPSE.

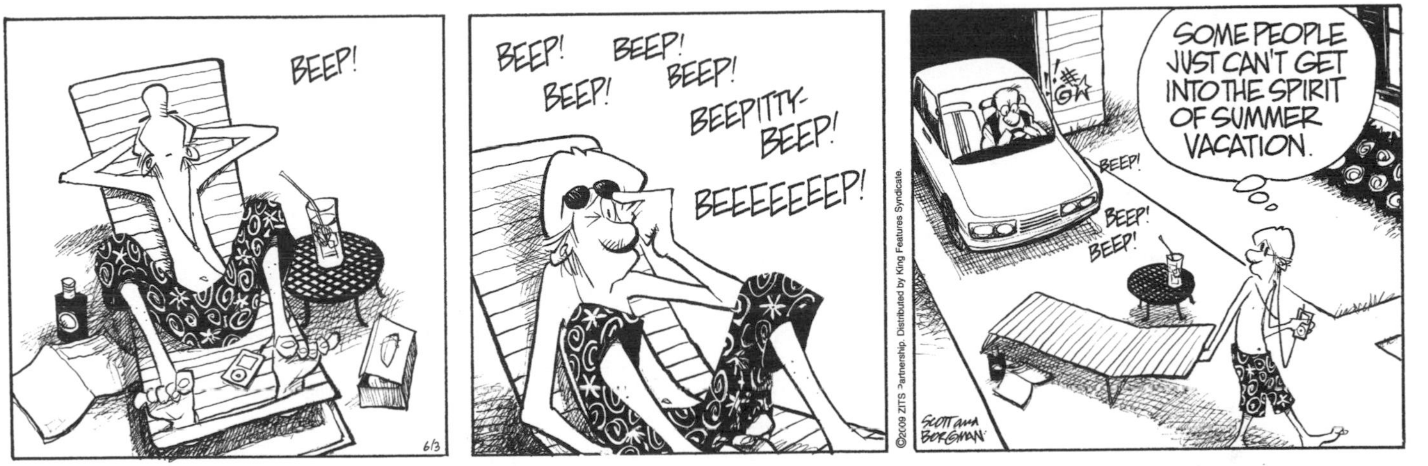
BEEP!
6/3
BEEP! BEEP!
BEEP! BEEP!
BEEPITTY-BEEP!
BEEEEEEEP!
©2009 ZITS Partnership. Distributed by King Features Syndicate.
BEEP!
BEEP! BEEP!
SOME PEOPLE JUST CAN'T GET INTO THE SPIRIT OF SUMMER VACATION.
SCOTT and BORGMAN

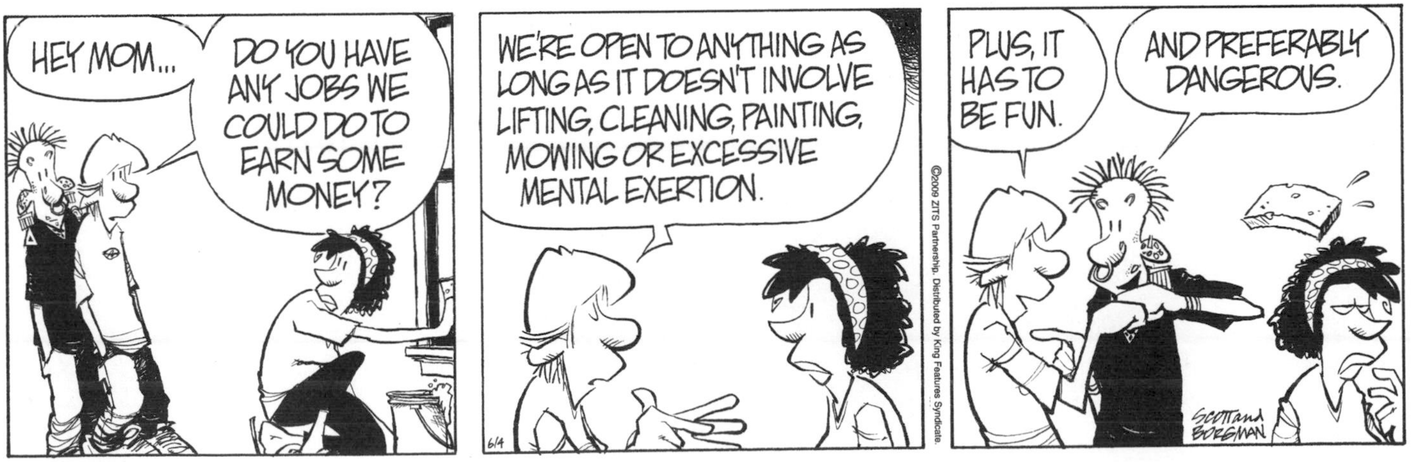
HEY MOM...
DO YOU HAVE ANY JOBS WE COULD DO TO EARN SOME MONEY?
WE'RE OPEN TO ANYTHING AS LONG AS IT DOESN'T INVOLVE LIFTING, CLEANING, PAINTING, MOWING OR EXCESSIVE MENTAL EXERTION.
6/4
©2009 ZITS Partnership. Distributed by King Features Syndicate.
PLUS, IT HAS TO BE FUN.
AND PREFERABLY DANGEROUS.
SCOTT and BORGMAN

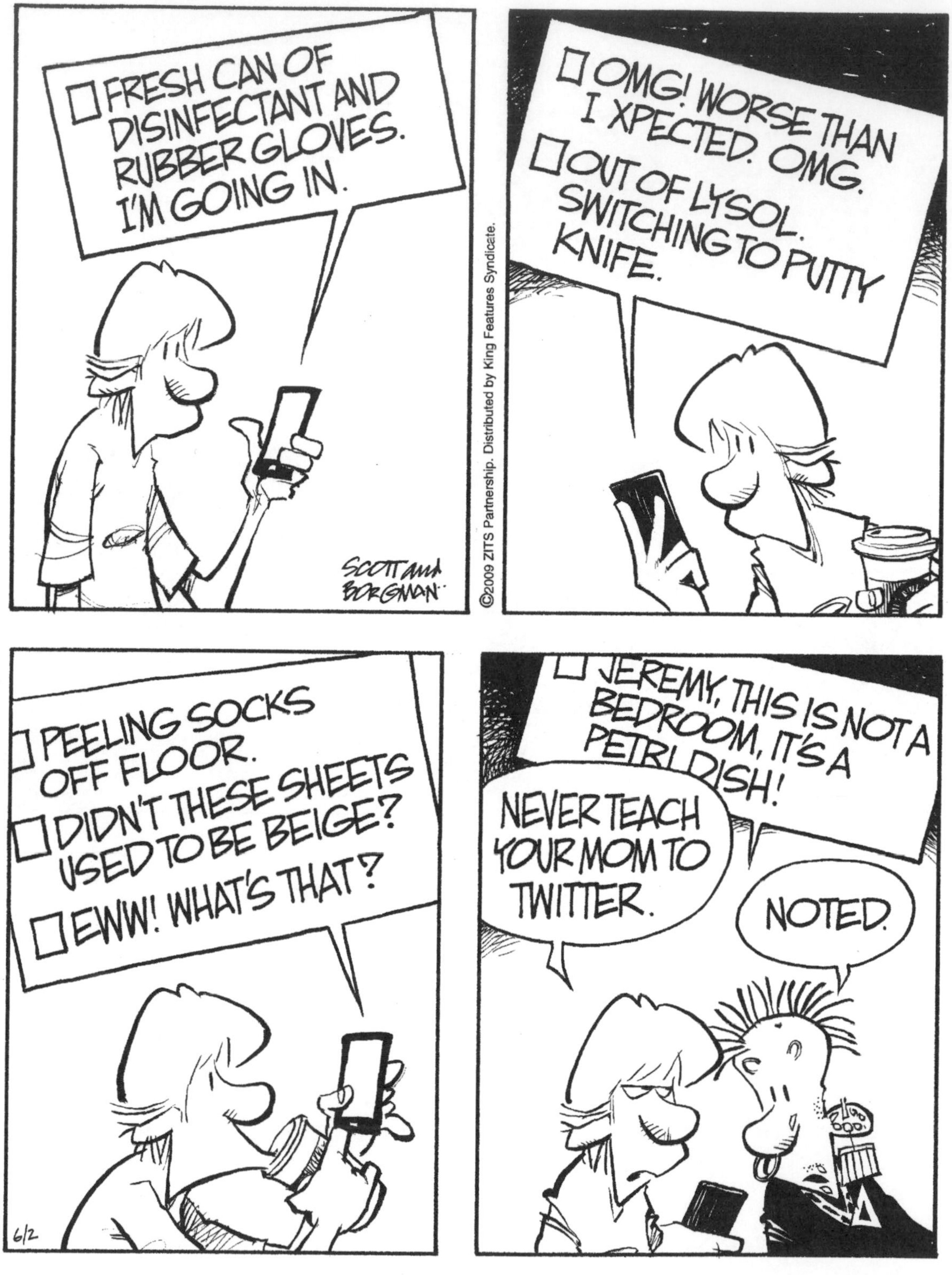
FRESH CAN OF DISINFECTANT AND RUBBER GLOVES. I'M GOING IN.
SCOTT AND BORGMAN
OMG! WORSE THAN I XPECTED. OMG.
OUT OF LYSOL. SWITCHING TO PUTTY KNIFE.
PEELING SOCKS OFF FLOOR.
DIDN'T THESE SHEETS USED TO BE BEIGE?
EWW! WHAT'S THAT?
6/2
JEREMY, THIS IS NOT A BEDROOM, IT'S A PETRI DISH!
NEVER TEACH YOUR MOM TO TWITTER.
NOTED.

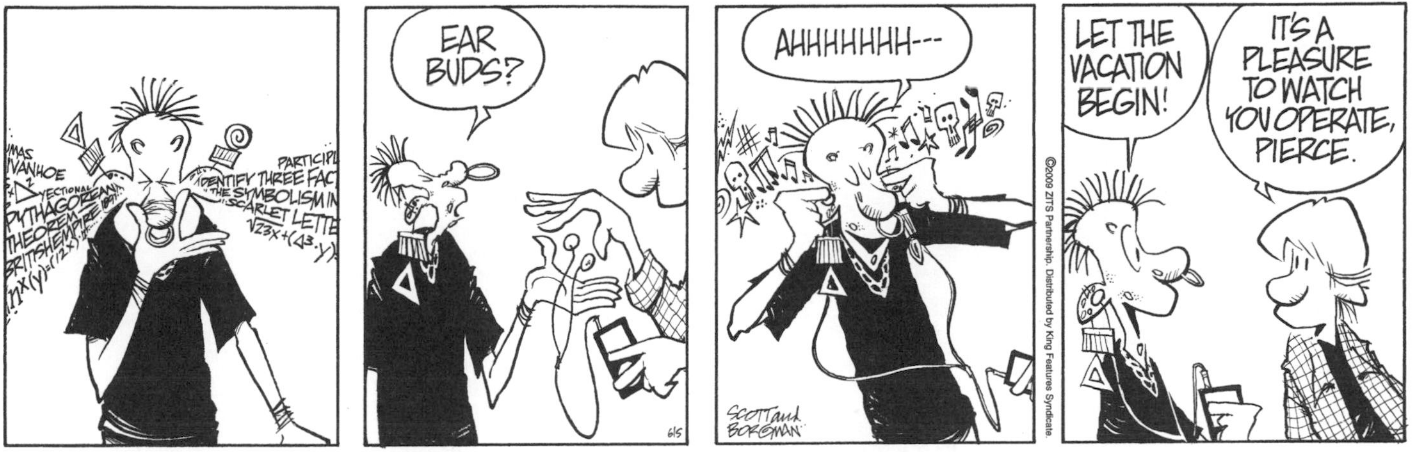
EAR BUDS?
AHHHHHHH---
LET THE VACATION BEGIN!
IT'S A PLEASURE TO WATCH YOU OPERATE, PIERCE.
©2009 ZITS Partnership. Distributed by King Features Syndicate.
SCOTT and BORGMAN
6/5

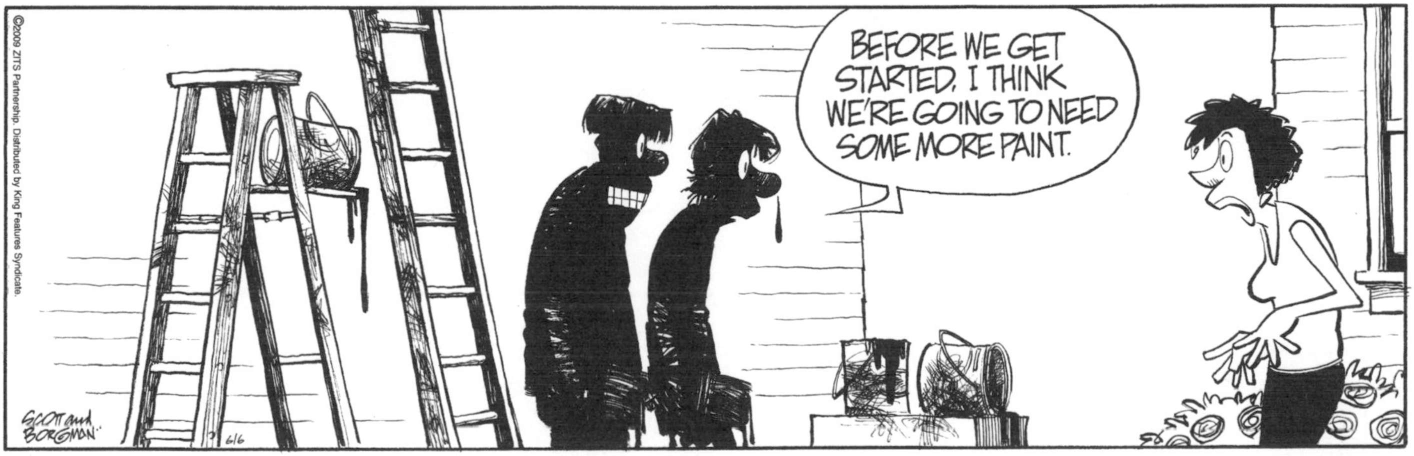
BEFORE WE GET STARTED, I THINK WE'RE GOING TO NEED SOME MORE PAINT.
©2009 ZITS Partnership. Distributed by King Features Syndicate.
SCOTT and BORGMAN
6/6

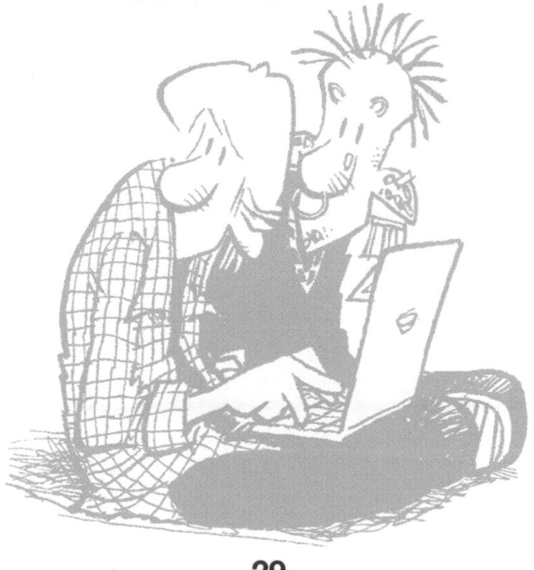

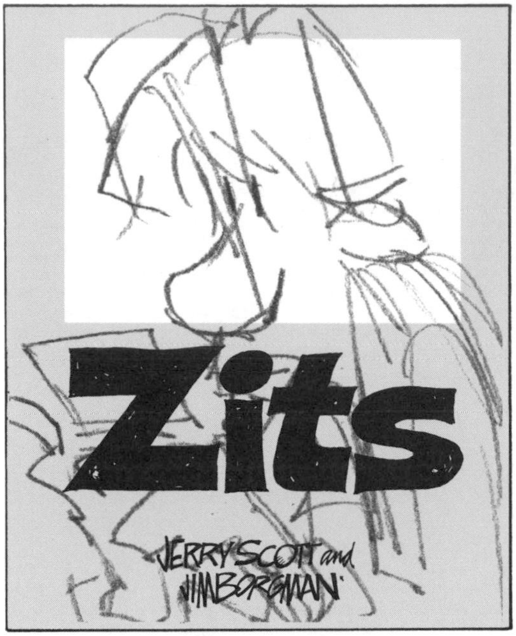
Zits
JERRY SCOTT and
JIMBORGMAN

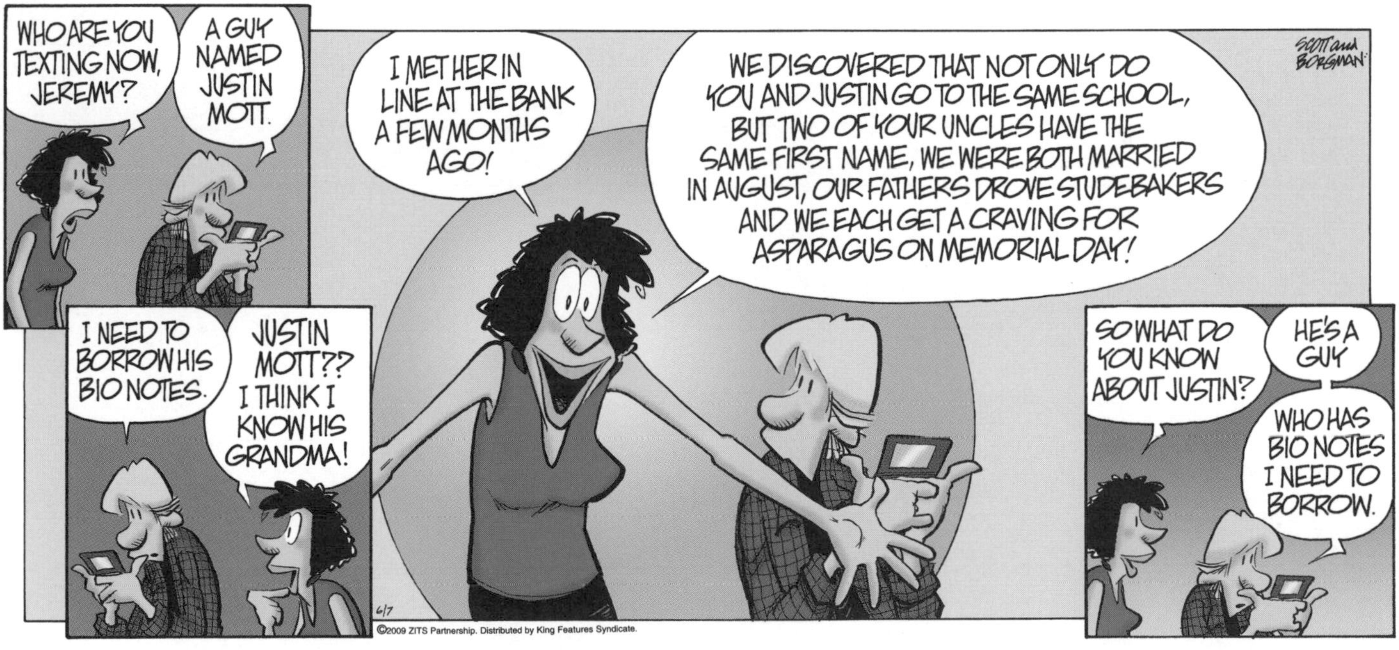
WHO ARE YOU TEXTING NOW, JEREMY?
A GUY NAMED JUSTIN MOTT.
I NEED TO BORROW HIS BIO NOTES.
JUSTIN MOTT?? I THINK I KNOW HIS GRANDMA!
SCOTT and BORGMAN
I MET HER IN LINE AT THE BANK A FEW MONTHS AGO!
WE DISCOVERED THAT NOT ONLY DO YOU AND JUSTIN GO TO THE SAME SCHOOL, BUT TWO OF YOUR UNCLES HAVE THE SAME FIRST NAME, WE WERE BOTH MARRIED IN AUGUST, OUR FATHERS DROVE STUDEBAKERS AND WE EACH GET A CRAVING FOR ASPARAGUS ON MEMORIAL DAY!
6/7
SO WHAT DO YOU KNOW ABOUT JUSTIN?
HE'S A GUY
WHO HAS BIO NOTES I NEED TO BORROW.

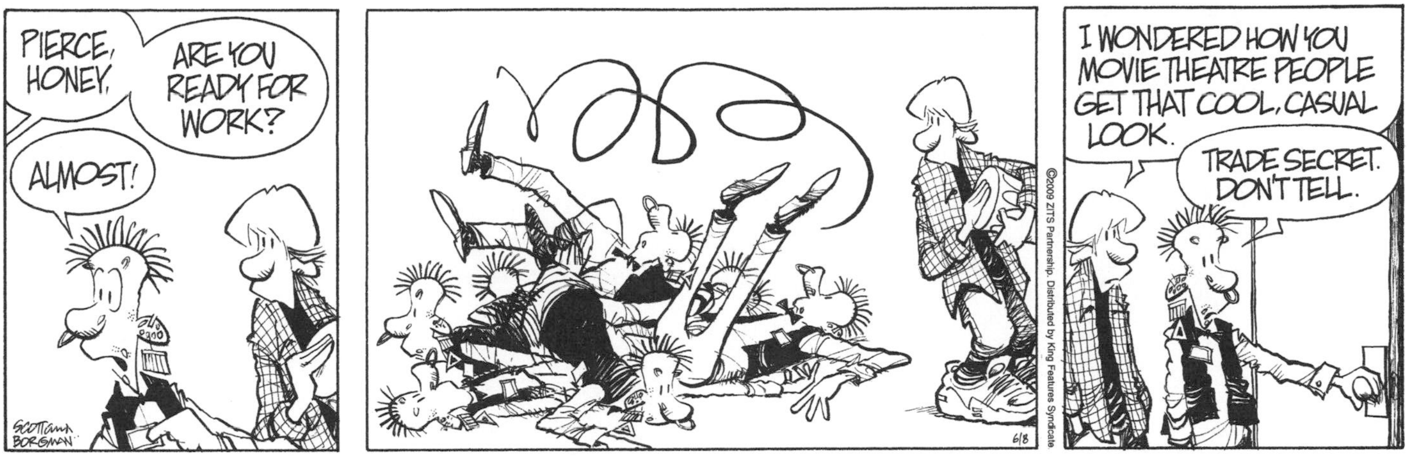
PIERCE, HONEY,
ARE YOU READY FOR WORK?
ALMOST!
SCOTT and BORGMAN
6/8
©2009 ZITS Partnership. Distributed by King Features Syndicate
I WONDERED HOW YOU MOVIE THEATRE PEOPLE GET THAT COOL, CASUAL LOOK.
TRADE SECRET. DON'T TELL.

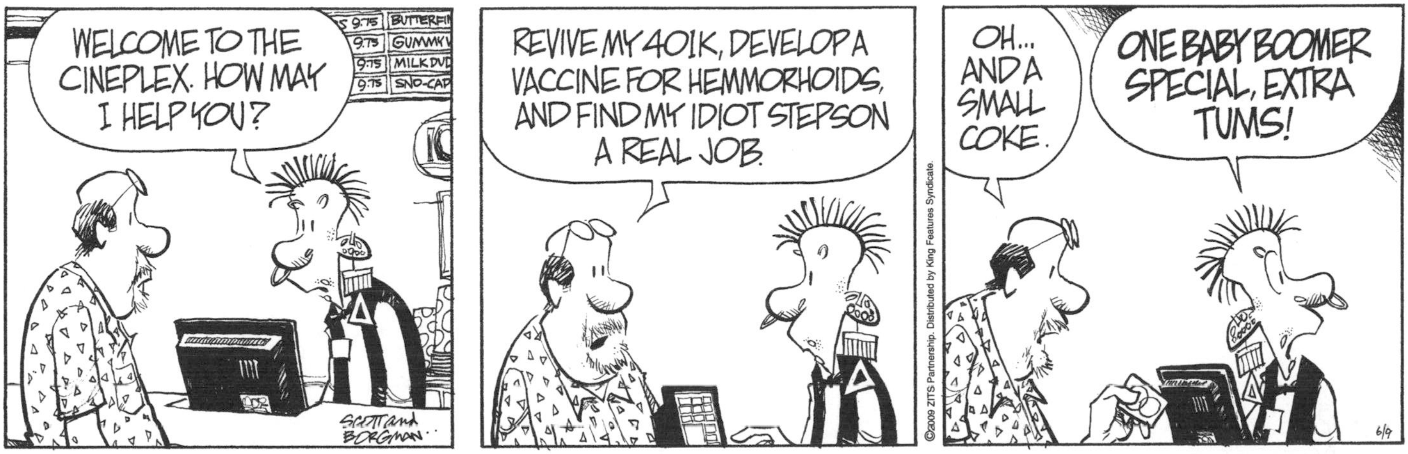
WELCOME TO THE CINEPLEX. HOW MAY I HELP YOU?
SCOTT and BORGMAN
REVIVE MY 401K, DEVELOP A VACCINE FOR HEMMORHOIDS, AND FIND MY IDIOT STEPSON A REAL JOB.
©2009 ZITS Partnership. Distributed by King Features Syndicate.
OH... AND A SMALL COKE.
ONE BABY BOOMER SPECIAL, EXTRA TUMS!
6/9

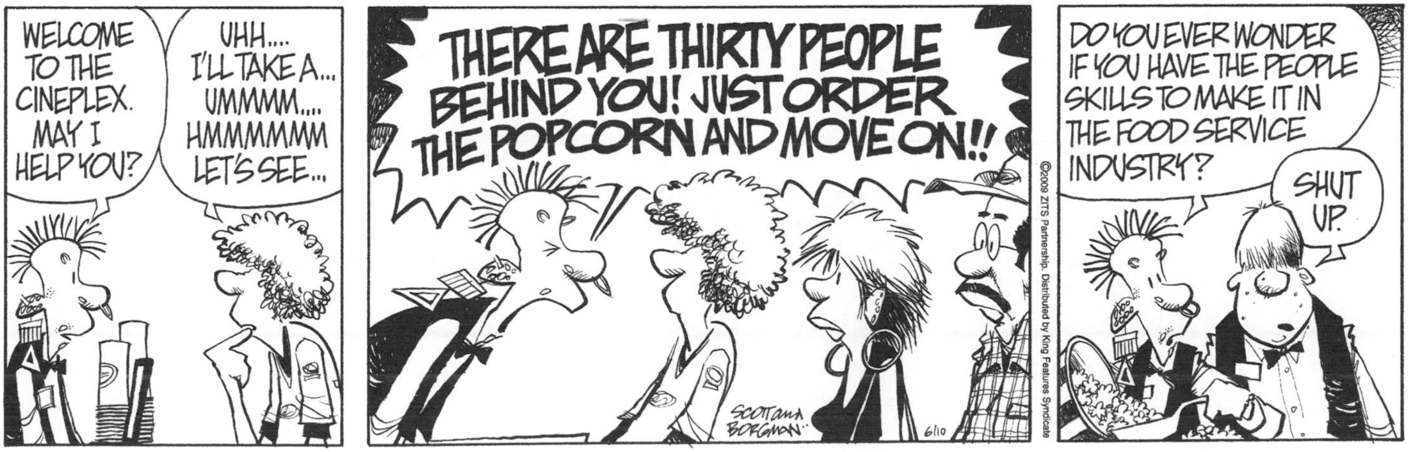
WELCOME TO THE CINEPLEX. MAY I HELP YOU?
UHH.... I'LL TAKE A... UMMMM.... HMMMMMM LET'S SEE...
THERE ARE THIRTY PEOPLE BEHIND YOU! JUST ORDER THE POPCORN AND MOVE ON!!
SCOTT and BORGMAN
6/10
©2009 ZITS Partnership. Distributed by King Features Syndicate
DO YOU EVER WONDER IF YOU HAVE THE PEOPLE SKILLS TO MAKE IT IN THE FOOD SERVICE INDUSTRY?
SHUT UP.

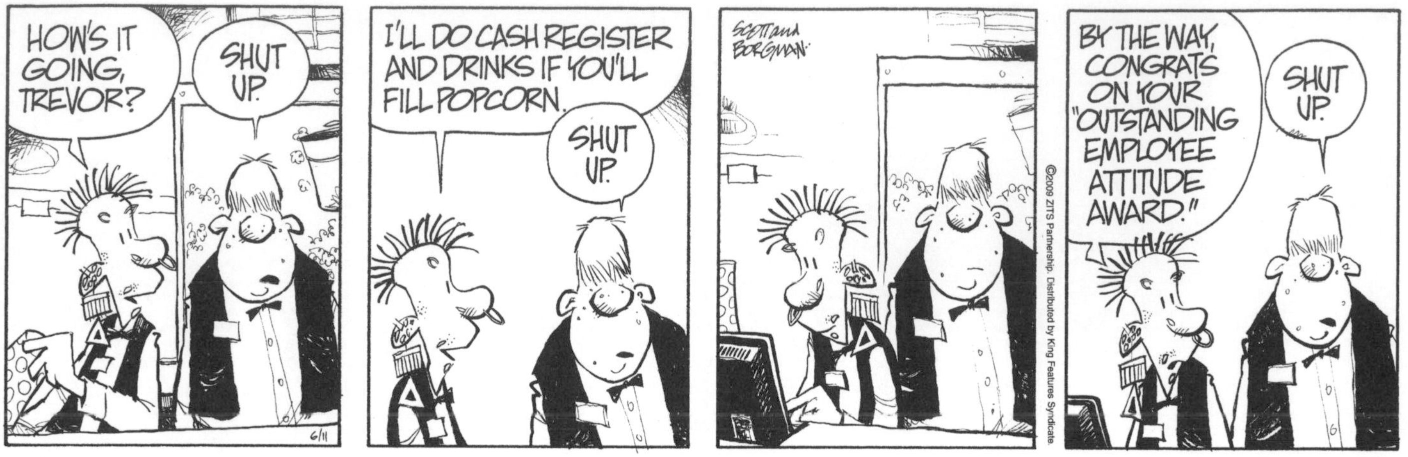
HOW'S IT GOING, TREVOR?
SHUT UP.
6/11
I'LL DO CASH REGISTER AND DRINKS IF YOU'LL FILL POPCORN.
SHUT UP.
SCOTT and BORGMAN
BY THE WAY, CONGRATS ON YOUR "OUTSTANDING EMPLOYEE ATTITUDE AWARD."
SHUT UP.
©2009 ZITS Partnership. Distributed by King Features Syndicate.

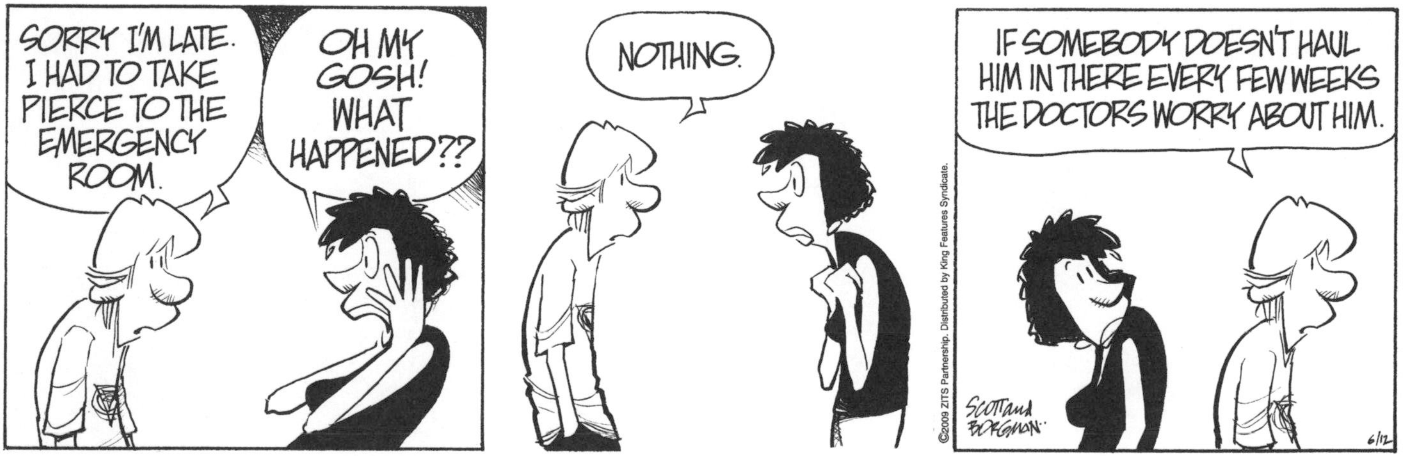
SORRY I'M LATE. I HAD TO TAKE PIERCE TO THE EMERGENCY ROOM.
OH MY GOSH! WHAT HAPPENED??
NOTHING.
©2009 ZITS Partnership. Distributed by King Features Syndicate.
IF SOMEBODY DOESN'T HAUL HIM IN THERE EVERY FEW WEEKS THE DOCTORS WORRY ABOUT HIM.
SCOTT and BORGMAN
6/12

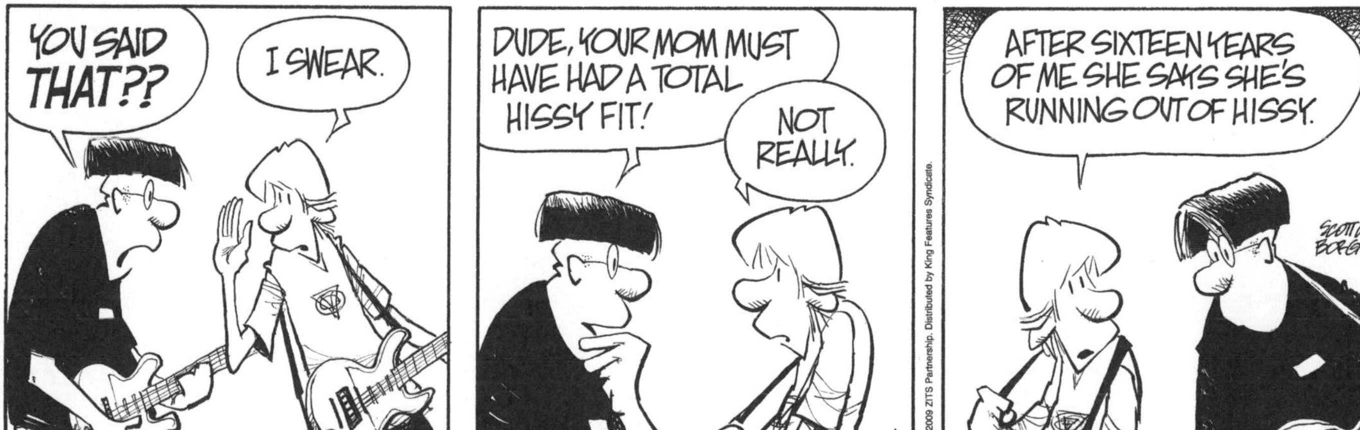
YOU SAID THAT??
I SWEAR.
DUDE, YOUR MOM MUST HAVE HAD A TOTAL HISSY FIT!
NOT REALLY.
6/13
©2009 ZITS Partnership. Distributed by King Features Syndicate.
AFTER SIXTEEN YEARS OF ME SHE SAYS SHE'S RUNNING OUT OF HISSY.
SCOTT and BORGMAN

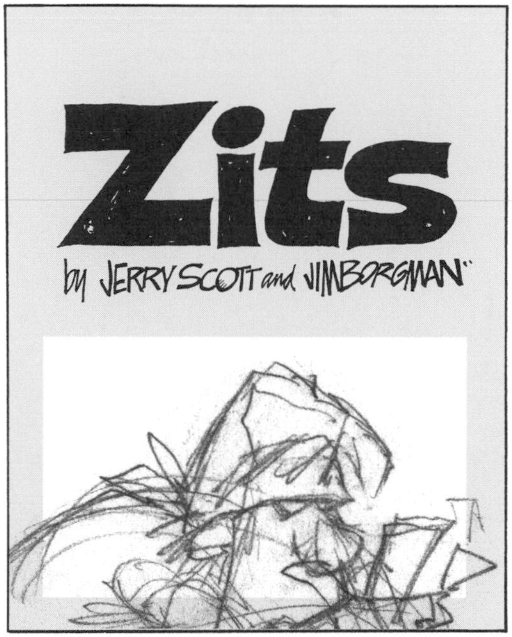
Zits
by JERRY SCOTT and JIM BORGMAN

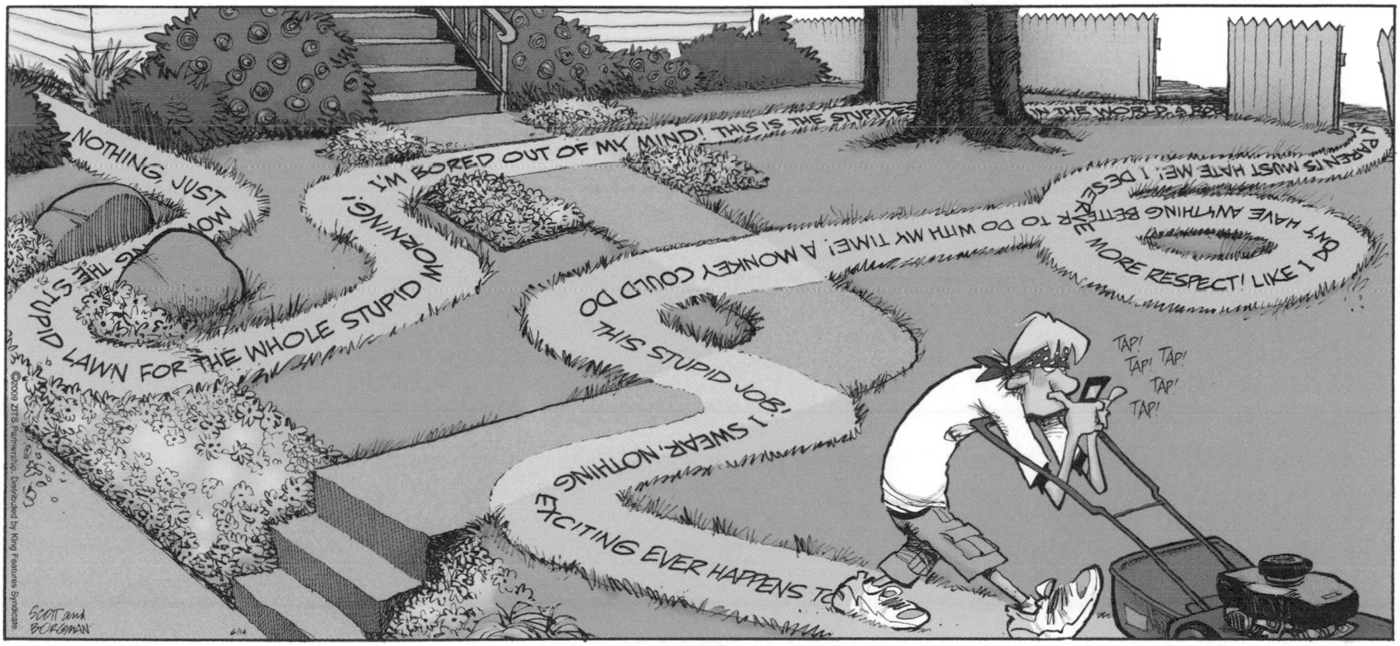
NOTHING, JUST MOW
THE STUPID LAWN FOR THE WHOLE STUPID MORNING!
I'M BORED OUT OF MY MIND! THIS IS THE STUPIDES
IN THE WORLD
PARENTS MUST HATE ME! I DESERVE MORE RESPECT! LIKE I DON'T HAVE ANYTHING BETTER TO DO WITH MY TIME! A MONKEY COULD DO THIS STUPID JOB!
I SWEAR, NOTHING EXCITING EVER HAPPENS TO
TAP! TAP! TAP! TAP! TAP!
©2009 ZITS Partnership. Distributed by King Features Syndicate
SCOTT and BORGMAN

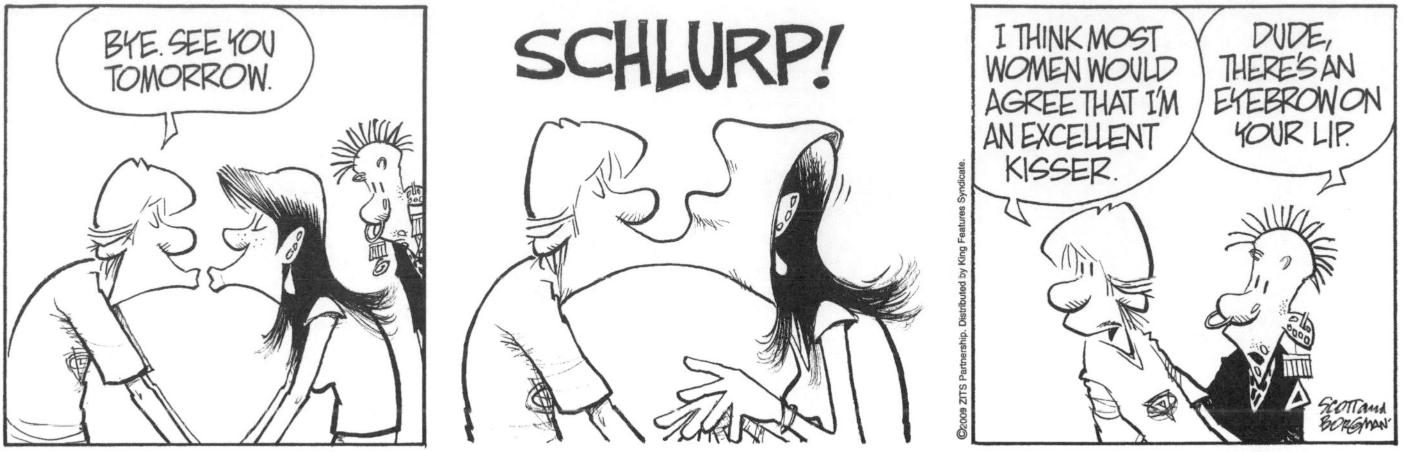
BYE. SEE YOU TOMORROW.
SCHLURP!
I THINK MOST WOMEN WOULD AGREE THAT I'M AN EXCELLENT KISSER.
DUDE, THERE'S AN EYEBROW ON YOUR LIP.
©2009 ZITS Partnership. Distributed by King Features Syndicate.
SCOTT and BORGMAN

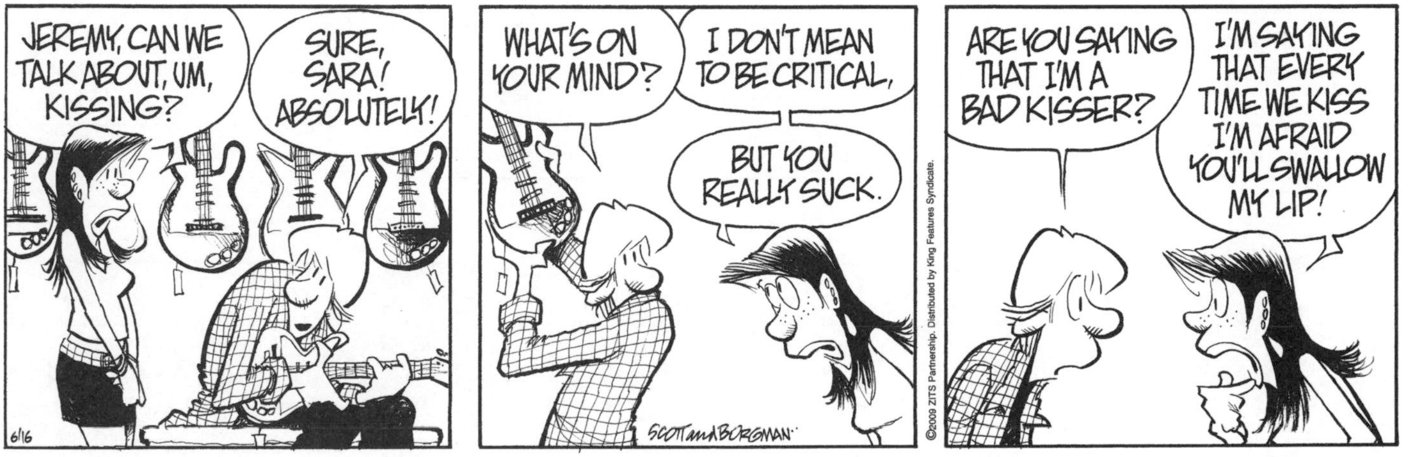
JEREMY, CAN WE TALK ABOUT, UM, KISSING?
SURE, SARA! ABSOLUTELY!
6/16
WHAT'S ON YOUR MIND?
I DON'T MEAN TO BE CRITICAL,
BUT YOU REALLY SUCK.
SCOTT and BORGMAN
©2009 ZITS Partnership. Distributed by King Features Syndicate.
ARE YOU SAYING THAT I'M A BAD KISSER?
I'M SAYING THAT EVERY TIME WE KISS I'M AFRAID YOU'LL SWALLOW MY LIP!

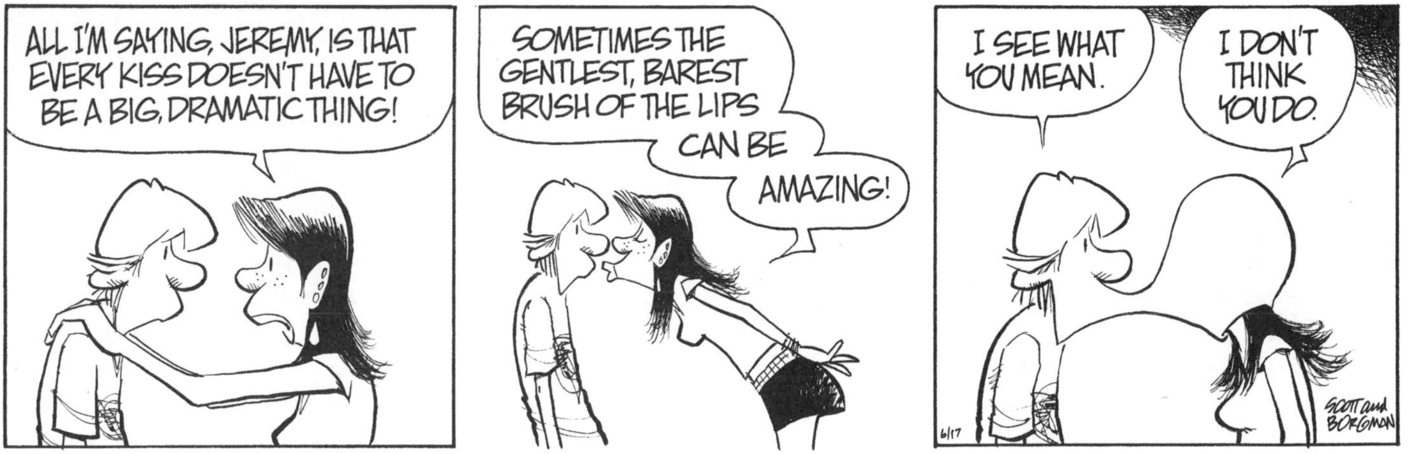
ALL I'M SAYING, JEREMY, IS THAT EVERY KISS DOESN'T HAVE TO BE A BIG, DRAMATIC THING!
SOMETIMES THE GENTLEST, BAREST BRUSH OF THE LIPS
CAN BE
AMAZING!
I SEE WHAT YOU MEAN.
I DON'T THINK YOU DO.
6/17
SCOTT and BORGMAN

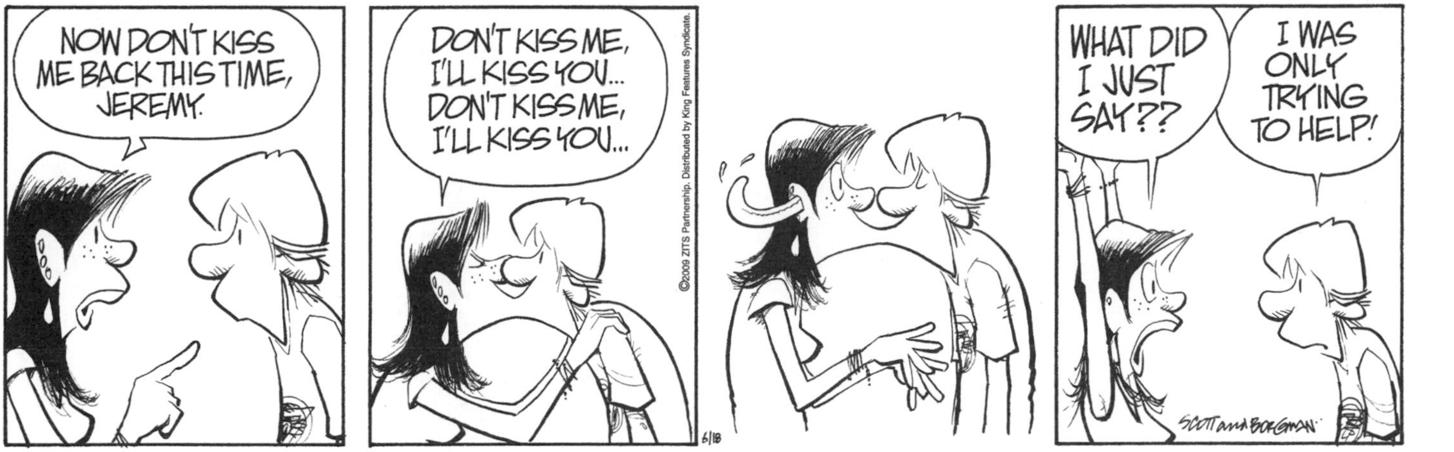
NOW DON'T KISS ME BACK THIS TIME, JEREMY.
DON'T KISS ME, I'LL KISS YOU... DON'T KISS ME, I'LL KISS YOU...
©2009 ZITS Partnership. Distributed by King Features Syndicate.
WHAT DID I JUST SAY??
I WAS ONLY TRYING TO HELP!
SCOTT and BORGMAN

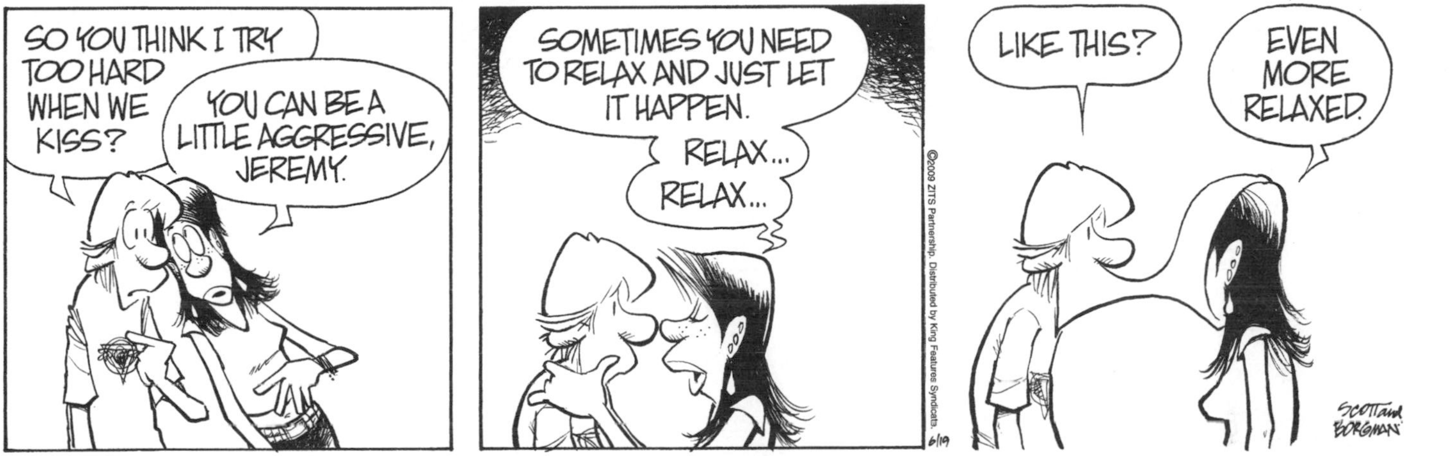
SO YOU THINK I TRY TOO HARD WHEN WE KISS?
YOU CAN BE A LITTLE AGGRESSIVE, JEREMY.
SOMETIMES YOU NEED TO RELAX AND JUST LET IT HAPPEN.
RELAX... RELAX...
©2009 ZITS Partnership. Distributed by King Features Syndicate.
LIKE THIS?
EVEN MORE RELAXED.
SCOTT and BORGMAN

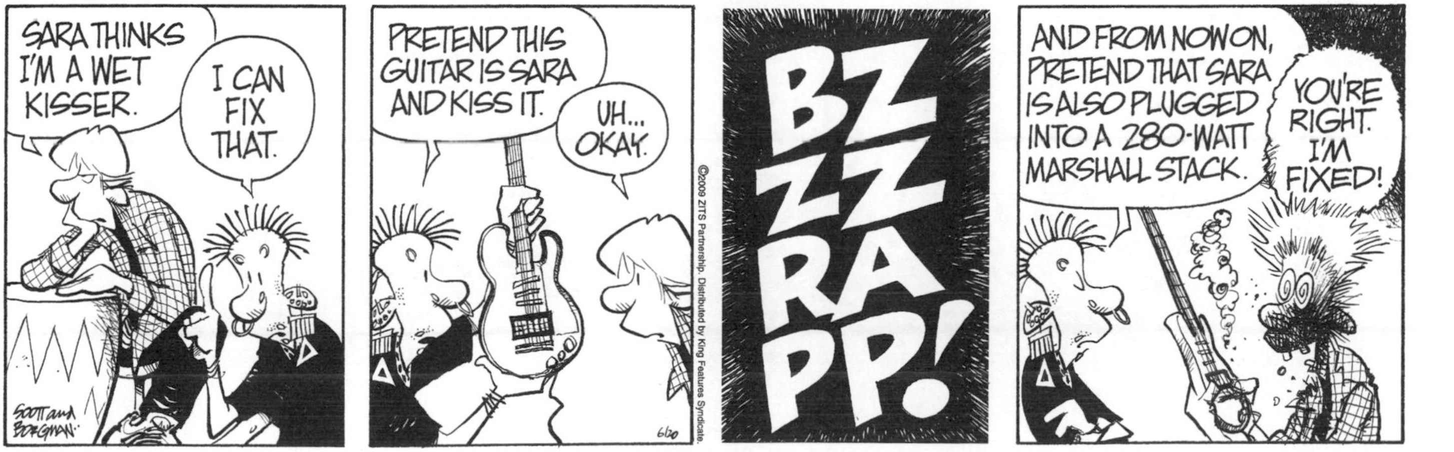
SARA THINKS I'M A WET KISSER.
I CAN FIX THAT.
SCOTT and BORGMAN
PRETEND THIS GUITAR IS SARA AND KISS IT.
UH... OKAY.
©2009 ZITS Partnership. Distributed by King Features Syndicate.
BZZZRAPP!
AND FROM NOW ON, PRETEND THAT SARA IS ALSO PLUGGED INTO A 280-WATT MARSHALL STACK.
YOU'RE RIGHT. I'M FIXED!

Zits
by JERRY SCOTT and JIM BORGMAN

SO YOU'RE JUST GOING TO SIT THERE THROUGH THE WHOLE MEAL WITHOUT SAYING A WORD, IS THAT RIGHT, JEREMY?
I THINK I CAN ANSWER THAT.
©2006 ZITS Partnership. Distributed by King Features Syndicate.
SCOTT and BORGMAN
6/21

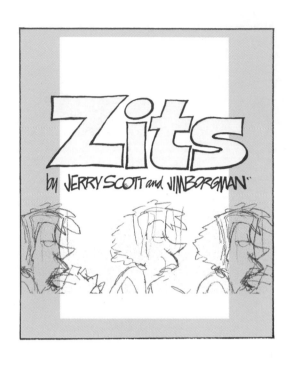

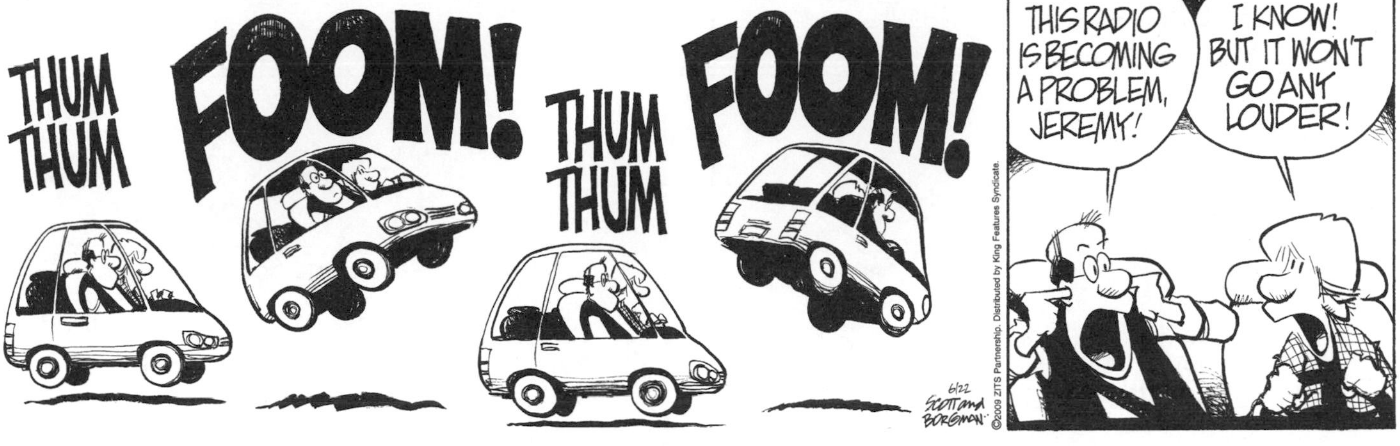
THUM THUM
FOOM!
THUM THUM
FOOM!
6/22
SCOTT and BORGMAN
©2009 ZITS Partnership. Distributed by King Features Syndicate.
THIS RADIO IS BECOMING A PROBLEM, JEREMY!
I KNOW! BUT IT WON'T GO ANY LOUDER!

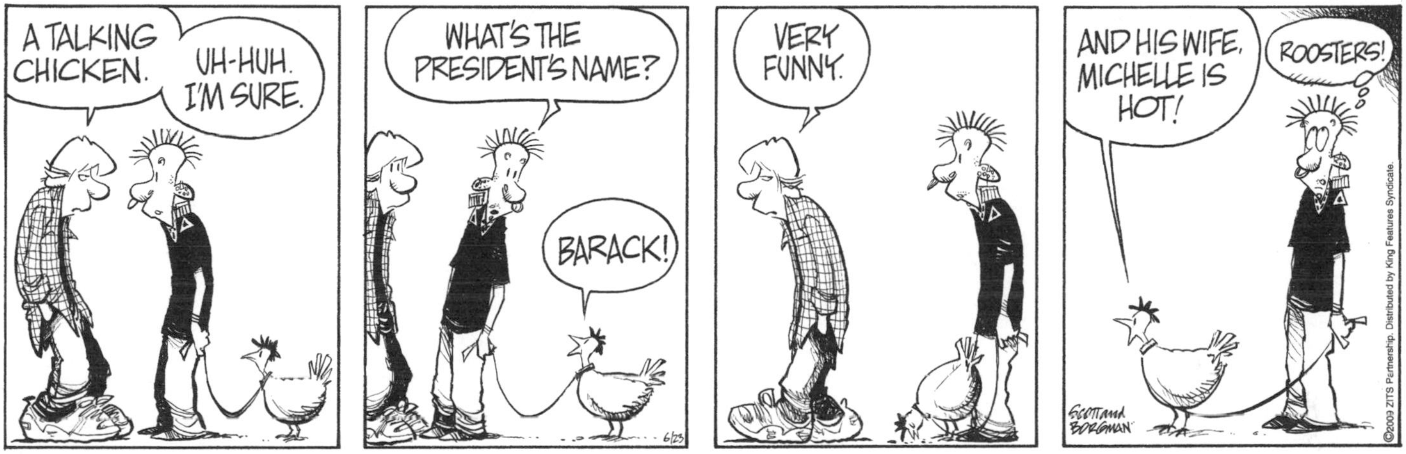
A TALKING CHICKEN.
UH-HUH. I'M SURE.
WHAT'S THE PRESIDENT'S NAME?
BARACK!
6/23
VERY FUNNY.
AND HIS WIFE, MICHELLE IS HOT!
ROOSTERS!
SCOTT and BORGMAN
©2009 ZITS Partnership. Distributed by King Features Syndicate.

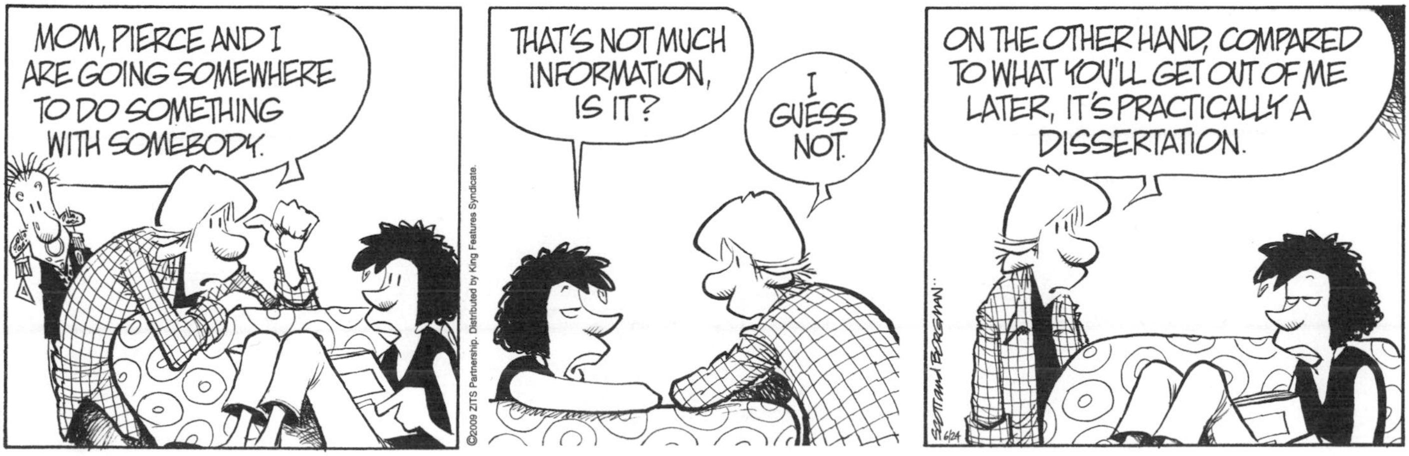
MOM, PIERCE AND I ARE GOING SOMEWHERE TO DO SOMETHING WITH SOMEBODY.
©2009 ZITS Partnership. Distributed by King Features Syndicate.
THAT'S NOT MUCH INFORMATION, IS IT?
I GUESS NOT.
SCOTT and BORGMAN
6/24
ON THE OTHER HAND, COMPARED TO WHAT YOU'LL GET OUT OF ME LATER, IT'S PRACTICALLY A DISSERTATION.

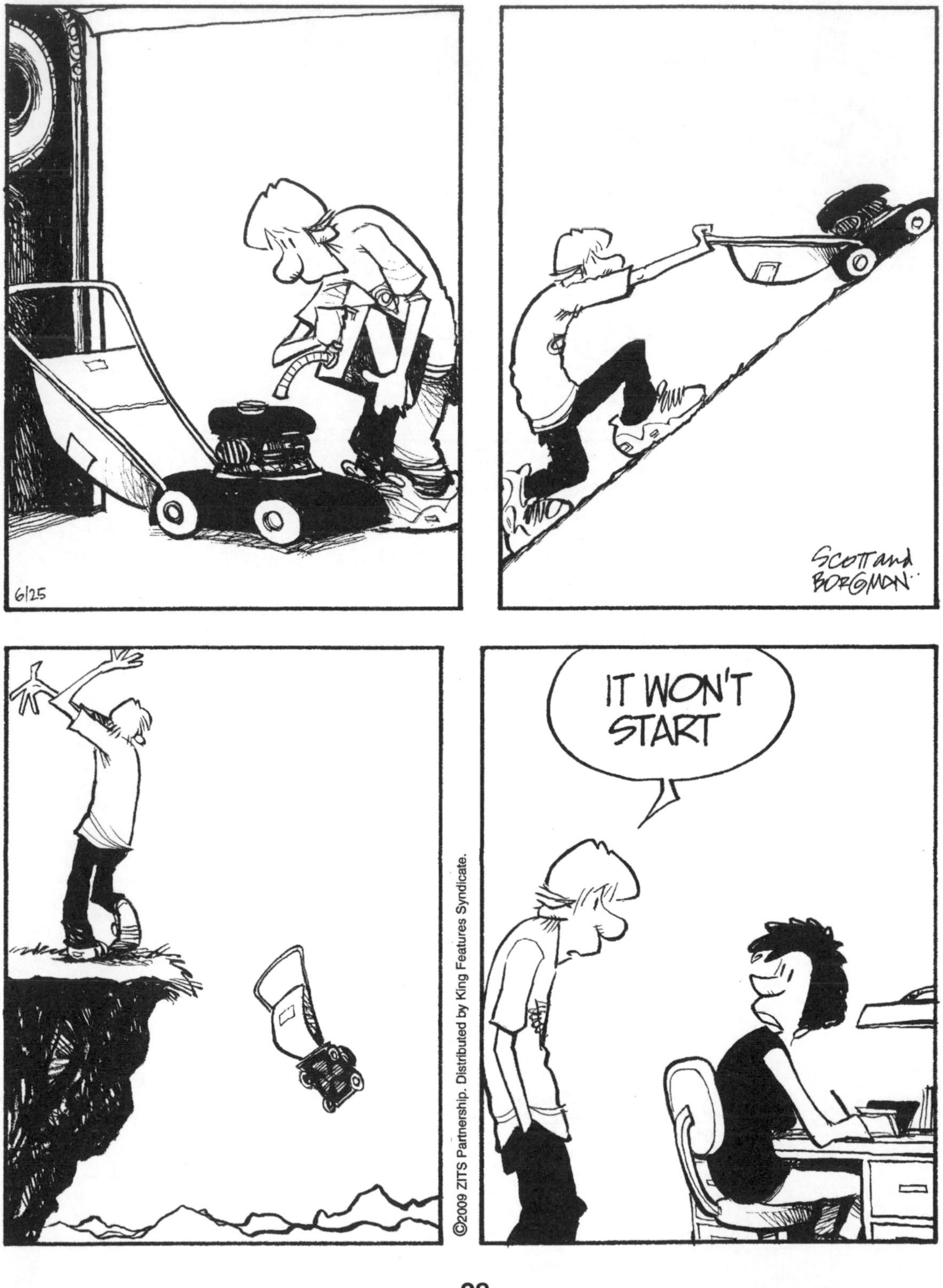
6/25
SCOTT and BORGMAN
IT WON'T START

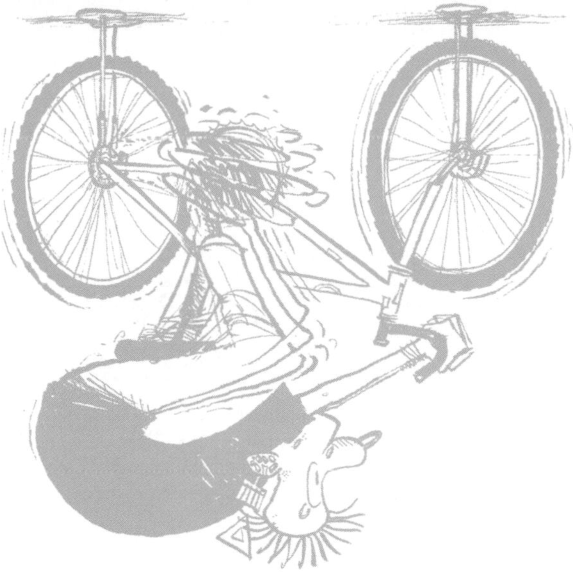

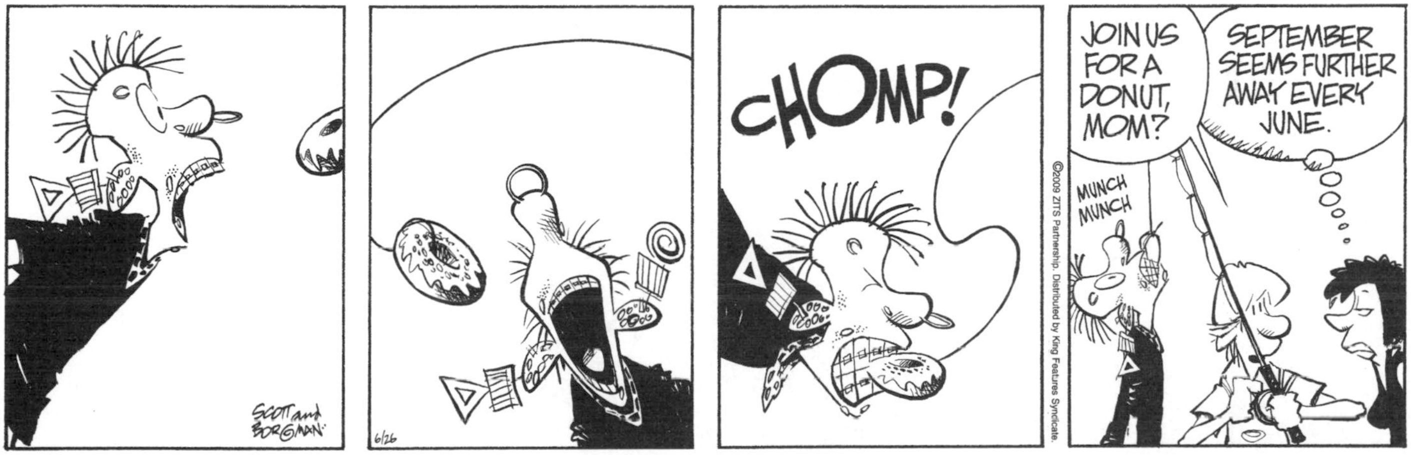

SCOTT and BORGMAN
6/26
CHOMP!
©2009 ZITS Partnership. Distributed by King Features Syndicate.
JOIN US FOR A DONUT, MOM?
SEPTEMBER SEEMS FURTHER AWAY EVERY JUNE.
MUNCH MUNCH

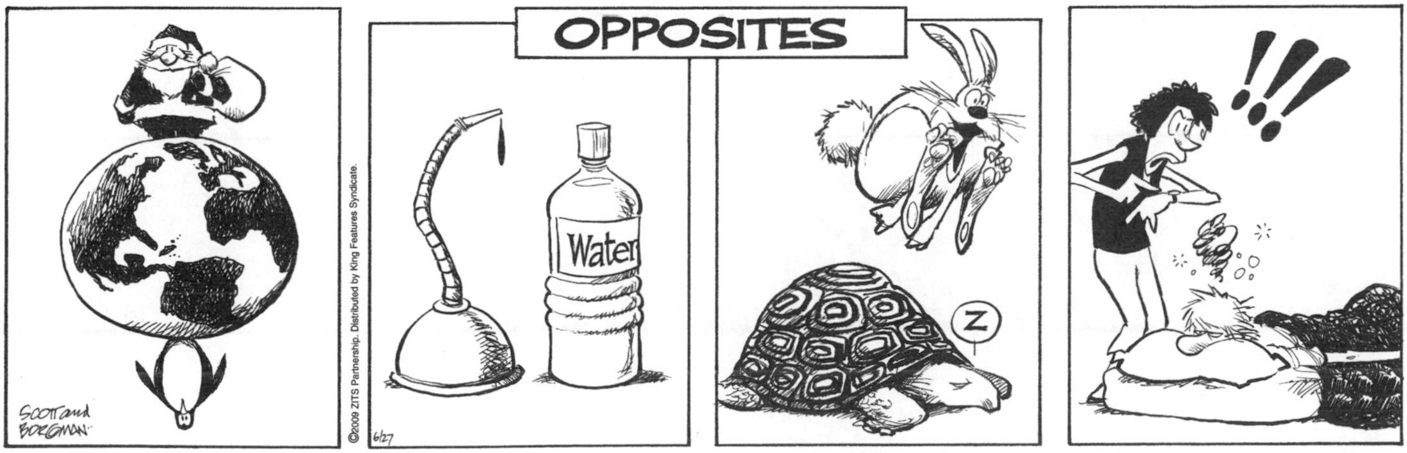

SCOTT and BORGMAN
©2009 ZITS Partnership. Distributed by King Features Syndicate.
6/27
OPPOSITES
Water
Z
!!!

Zits
by JERRY SCOTT and JIM BORGMAN

©2009 ZITS Partnership. Distributed by King Features Syndicate
SCOTT and BORGMAN 6/28
TURN IT DOWN.

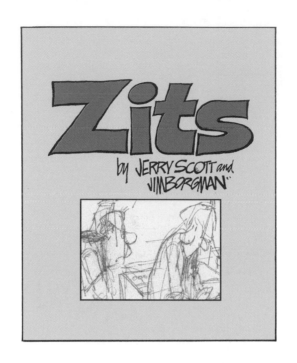

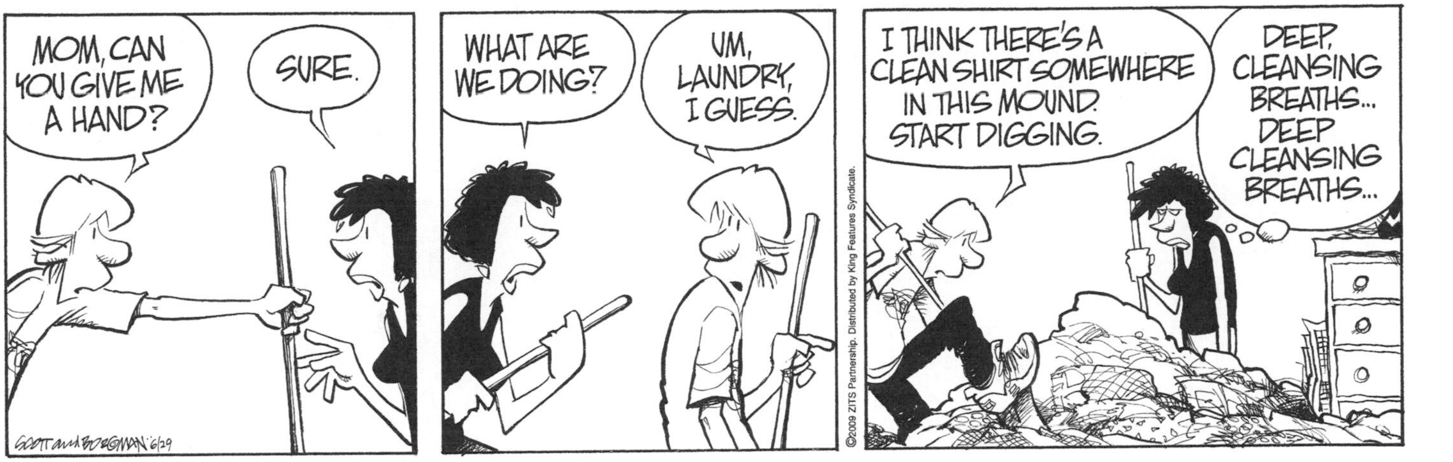
MOM, CAN YOU GIVE ME A HAND?
SURE.
WHAT ARE WE DOING?
UM, LAUNDRY, I GUESS.
I THINK THERE'S A CLEAN SHIRT SOMEWHERE IN THIS MOUND. START DIGGING.
DEEP, CLEANSING BREATHS... DEEP CLEANSING BREATHS...
SCOTT and BORGMAN 6/29
©2009 ZITS Partnership. Distributed by King Features Syndicate.

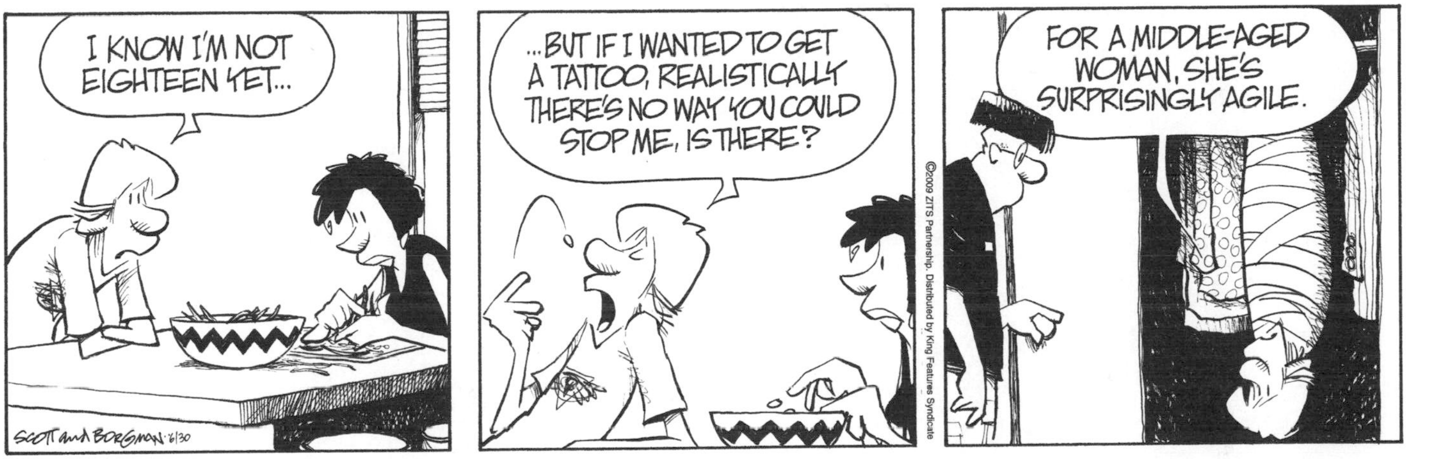
I KNOW I'M NOT EIGHTEEN YET...
...BUT IF I WANTED TO GET A TATTOO, REALISTICALLY THERE'S NO WAY YOU COULD STOP ME, IS THERE?
FOR A MIDDLE-AGED WOMAN, SHE'S SURPRISINGLY AGILE.
SCOTT and BORGMAN 6/30
©2009 ZITS Partnership. Distributed by King Features Syndicate

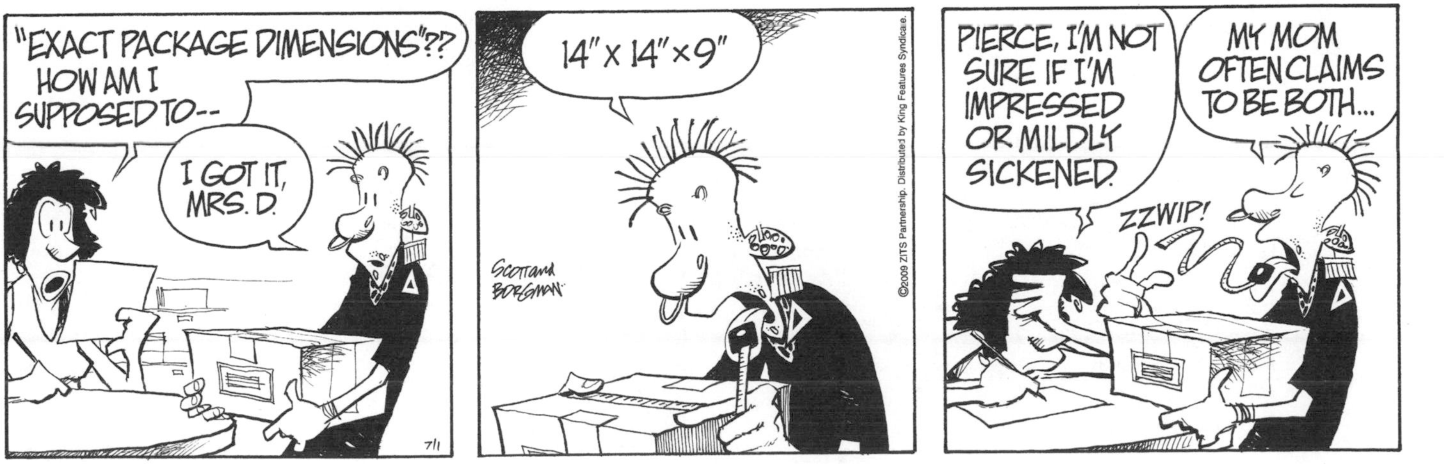
"EXACT PACKAGE DIMENSIONS"?? HOW AM I SUPPOSED TO--
I GOT IT, MRS. D.
14" x 14" x 9"
PIERCE, I'M NOT SURE IF I'M IMPRESSED OR MILDLY SICKENED.
MY MOM OFTEN CLAIMS TO BE BOTH...
ZZWIP!
SCOTT and BORGMAN
7/1
©2009 ZITS Partnership. Distributed by King Features Syndicate.

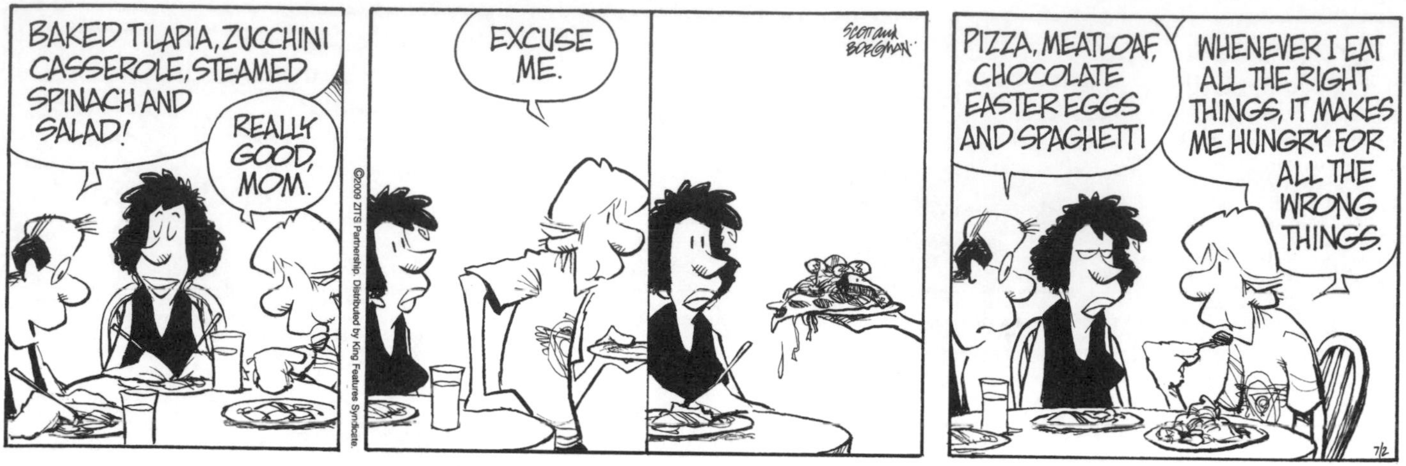
BAKED TILAPIA, ZUCCHINI CASSEROLE, STEAMED SPINACH AND SALAD!
REALLY GOOD, MOM.
EXCUSE ME.
SCOTT and BORGMAN
PIZZA, MEATLOAF, CHOCOLATE EASTER EGGS AND SPAGHETTI
WHENEVER I EAT ALL THE RIGHT THINGS, IT MAKES ME HUNGRY FOR ALL THE WRONG THINGS.
7/2
©2009 ZITS Partnership. Distributed by King Features Syndicate.

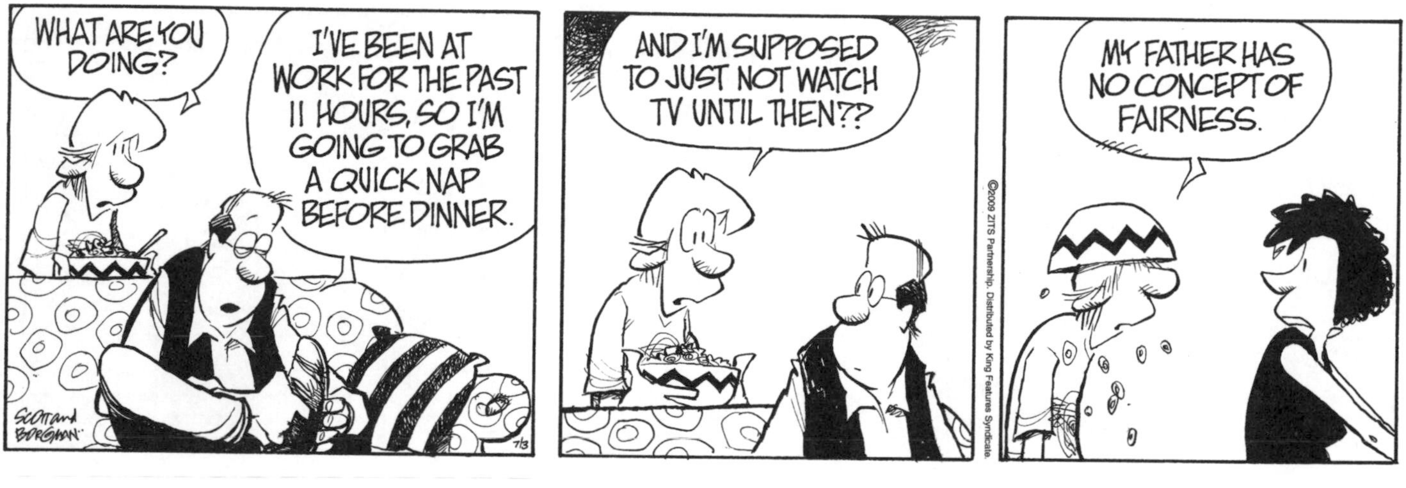
WHAT ARE YOU DOING?
I'VE BEEN AT WORK FOR THE PAST 11 HOURS, SO I'M GOING TO GRAB A QUICK NAP BEFORE DINNER.
SCOTT and BORGMAN
7/3
AND I'M SUPPOSED TO JUST NOT WATCH TV UNTIL THEN??
©2009 ZITS Partnership. Distributed by King Features Syndicate.
MY FATHER HAS NO CONCEPT OF FAIRNESS.

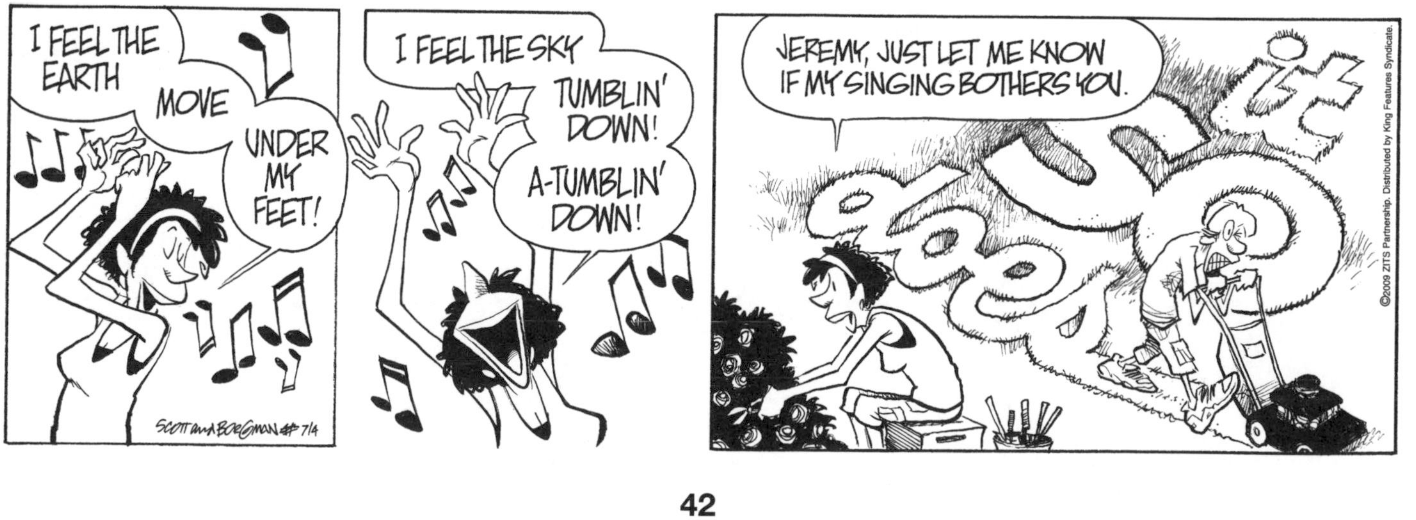
I FEEL THE EARTH
MOVE
UNDER MY FEET!
SCOTT and BORGMAN 7/4
I FEEL THE SKY
TUMBLIN' DOWN!
A-TUMBLIN' DOWN!
JEREMY, JUST LET ME KNOW IF MY SINGING BOTHERS YOU.
©2009 ZITS Partnership. Distributed by King Features Syndicate.

Zits
by
JERRY SCOTT and
JIM BORGMAN

THE REALLY COOL THING IS THAT IT USES A WHOLE DIFFERENT GROUP OF MUSCLES.
SCOTT and BORGMAN 7/5

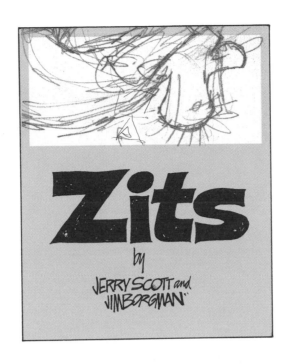

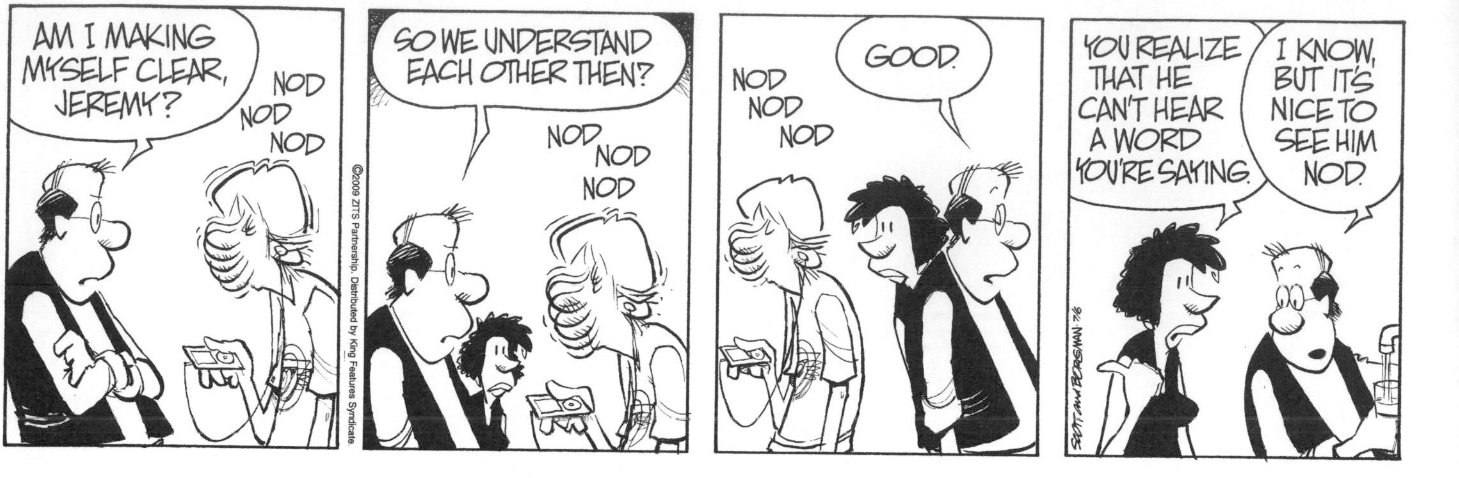

AM I MAKING MYSELF CLEAR, JEREMY?
NOD NOD NOD
SO WE UNDERSTAND EACH OTHER THEN?
NOD NOD NOD
NOD NOD NOD
GOOD.
YOU REALIZE THAT HE CAN'T HEAR A WORD YOU'RE SAYING.
I KNOW, BUT IT'S NICE TO SEE HIM NOD.
©2009 ZITS Partnership. Distributed by King Features Syndicate.
SCOTT and BORGMAN 7/6

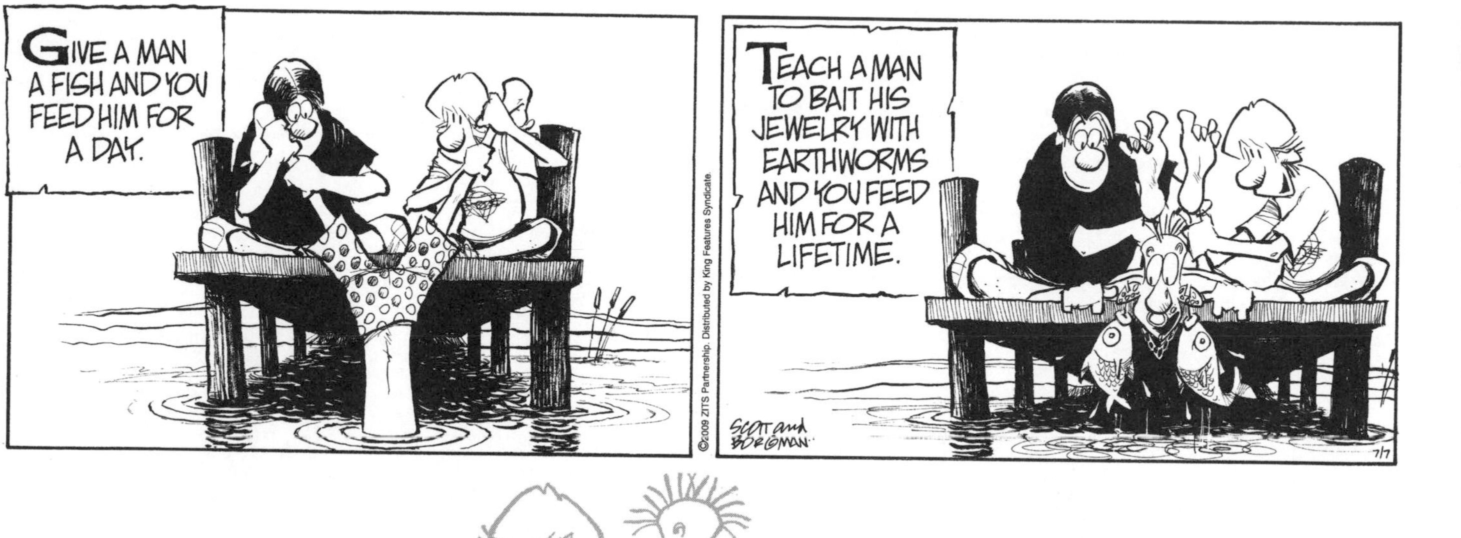

GIVE A MAN A FISH AND YOU FEED HIM FOR A DAY.
TEACH A MAN TO BAIT HIS JEWELRY WITH EARTHWORMS AND YOU FEED HIM FOR A LIFETIME.
©2009 ZITS Partnership. Distributed by King Features Syndicate.
SCOTT and BORGMAN
7/7

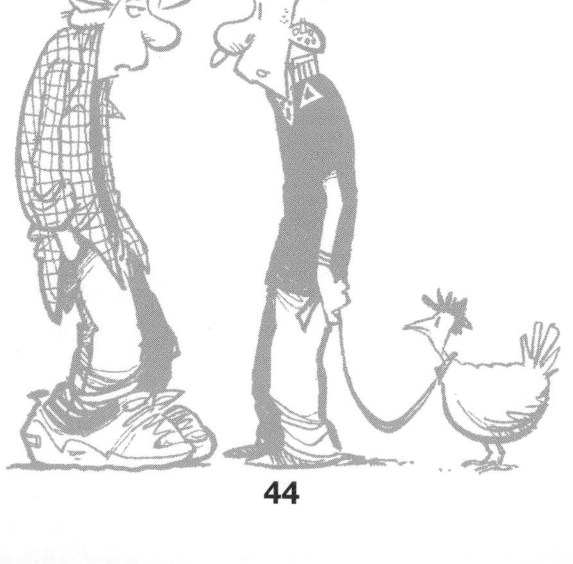

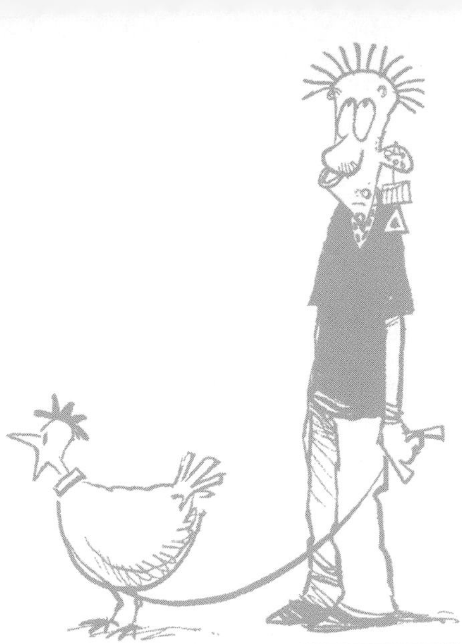

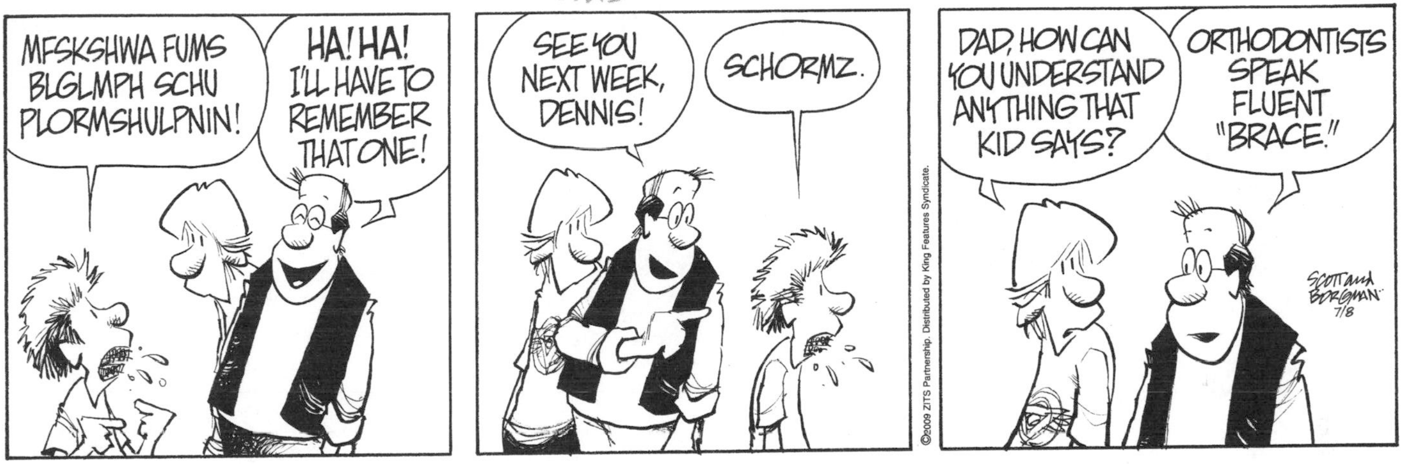
MFSKSHWA FUMS BLGLMPH SCHU PLORMSHULPNIN!
HA! HA! I'LL HAVE TO REMEMBER THAT ONE!
SEE YOU NEXT WEEK, DENNIS!
SCHORMZ.
©2009 ZITS Partnership. Distributed by King Features Syndicate.
DAD, HOW CAN YOU UNDERSTAND ANYTHING THAT KID SAYS?
ORTHODONTISTS SPEAK FLUENT "BRACE."
SCOTT and BORGMAN 7/8

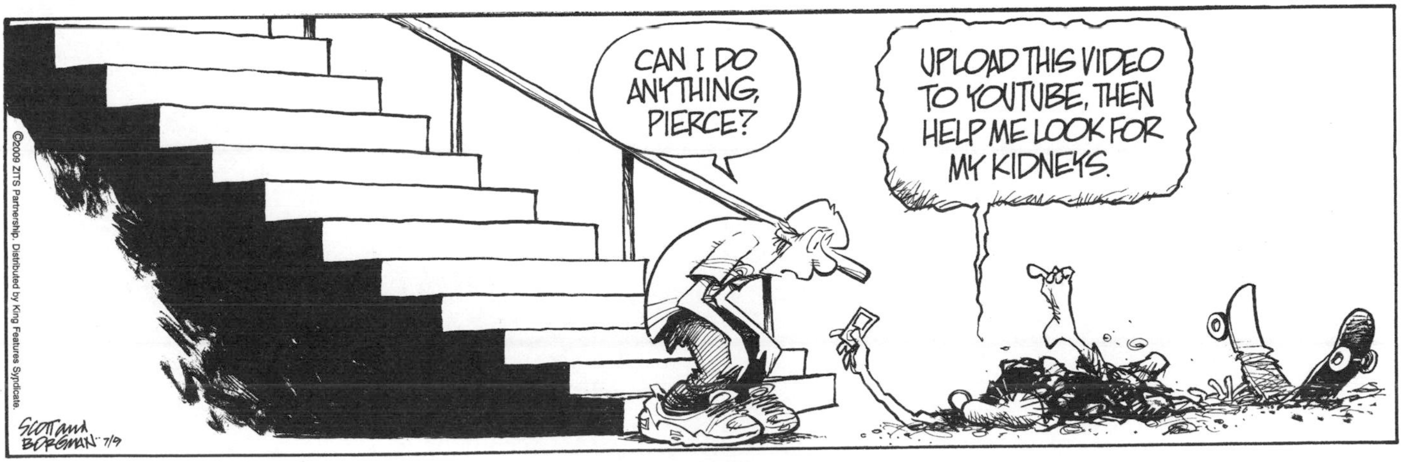
©2009 ZITS Partnership. Distributed by King Features Syndicate.
CAN I DO ANYTHING, PIERCE?
UPLOAD THIS VIDEO TO YOUTUBE, THEN HELP ME LOOK FOR MY KIDNEYS.
SCOTT and BORGMAN 7/9

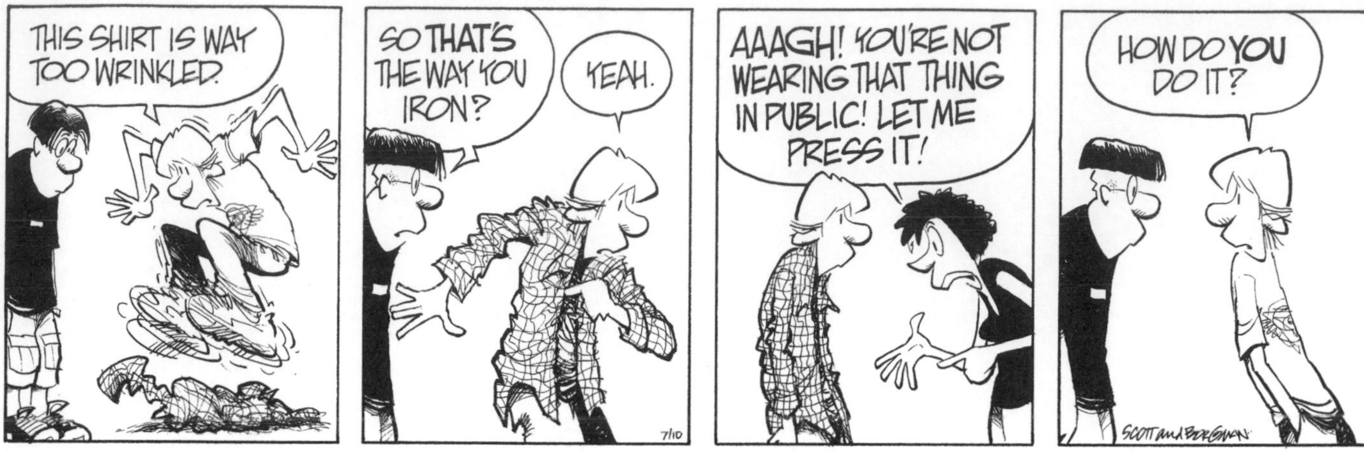
THIS SHIRT IS WAY TOO WRINKLED.
SO THAT'S THE WAY YOU IRON?
YEAH.
7/10
AAAGH! YOU'RE NOT WEARING THAT THING IN PUBLIC! LET ME PRESS IT!
HOW DO YOU DO IT?
SCOTT AND BORGMAN
©2009 ZITS Partnership. Distributed by King Features Syndicate.

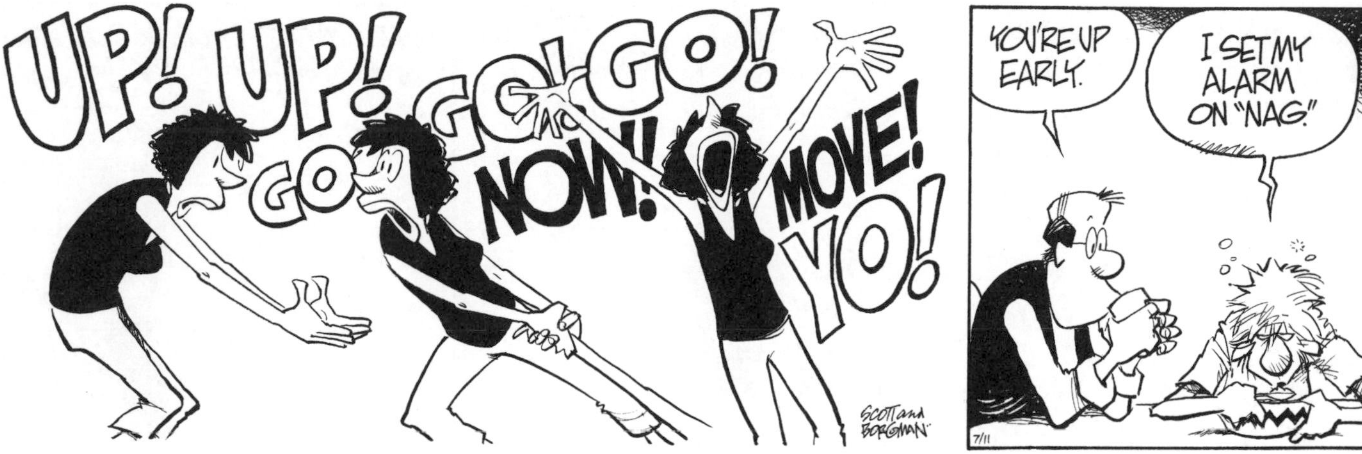
UP! UP!
GO! GO! GO!
NOW!
MOVE!
YO!
SCOTT AND BORGMAN
YOU'RE UP EARLY.
I SET MY ALARM ON "NAG."
7/11

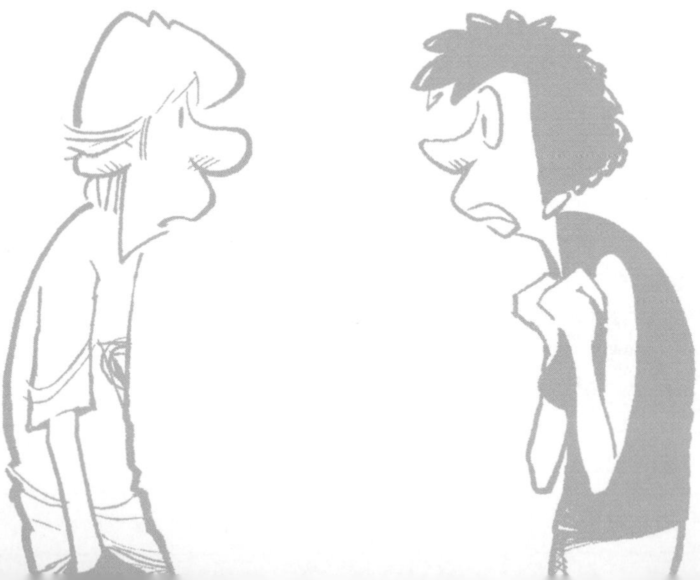

Zits
by JERRY SCOTT and
JIM BORGMAN

©2009 ZITS Partnership. Distributed by King Features Syndicate
7/12
SCOTT and
BORGMAN
WHUMP!
THUMP!
BUMP!
BUMPITTY-BUMP!
THUD!
WHIRRRRRRRR!
SCRAMBLED OR FRIED?
I'M WILLING TO BET IT'S AGAINST THE GENEVA CONVENTIONS TO WAKE SOMEONE UP BEFORE TEN DURING SUMMER VACATION.

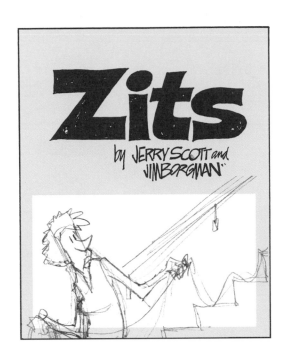

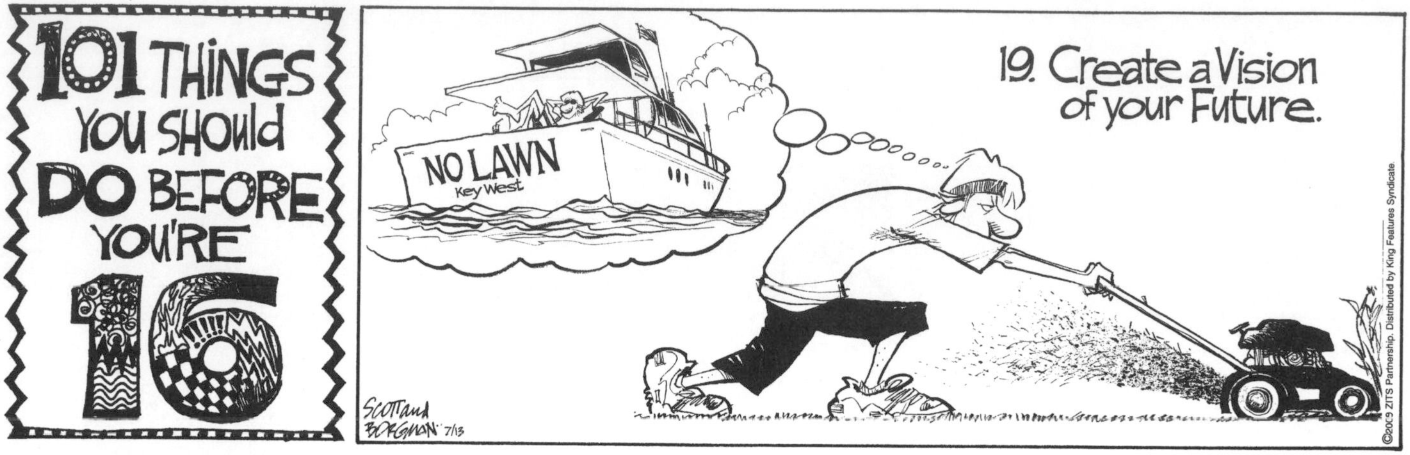
101 THINGS YOU SHOULD DO BEFORE YOU'RE 16
19. Create a Vision of your Future.
NO LAWN
Key West
SCOTT and BORGMAN 7/13
©2009 ZITS Partnership. Distributed by King Features Syndicate.

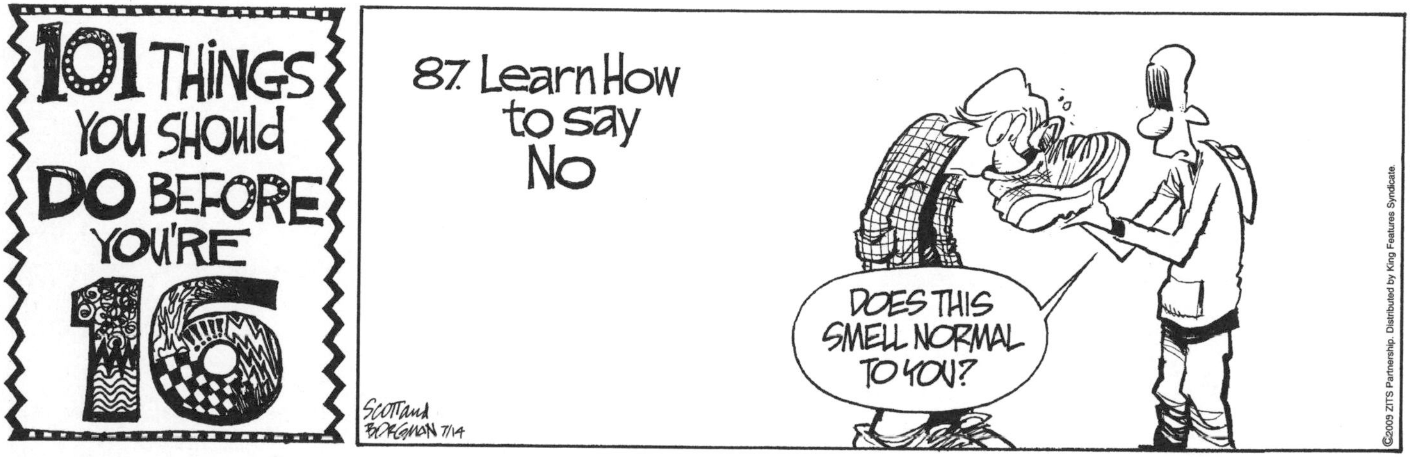
101 THINGS YOU SHOULD DO BEFORE YOU'RE 16
87. Learn How to say No
DOES THIS SMELL NORMAL TO YOU?
SCOTT and BORGMAN 7/14
©2009 ZITS Partnership. Distributed by King Features Syndicate.

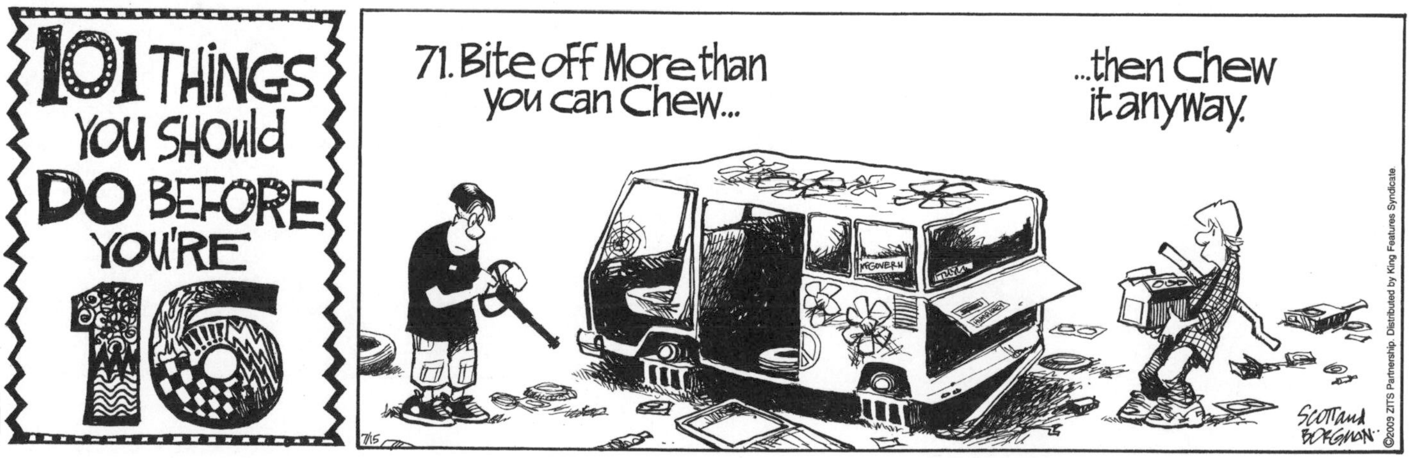
101 THINGS YOU SHOULD DO BEFORE YOU'RE 16
71. Bite off More than you can Chew...
...then Chew it anyway.
SCOTT and BORGMAN 7/15
©2009 ZITS Partnership. Distributed by King Features Syndicate.

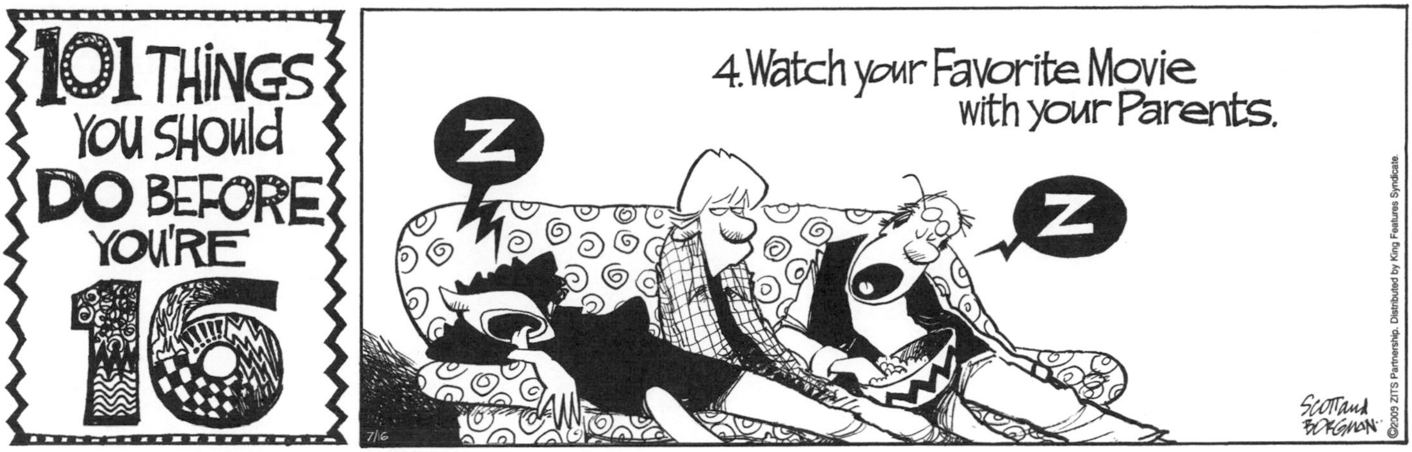
101 THINGS YOU SHOULD DO BEFORE YOU'RE 16
4. Watch your Favorite Movie with your Parents.
Z
Z
7/16
SCOTT and BORGMAN
©2009 ZITS Partnership. Distributed by King Features Syndicate.

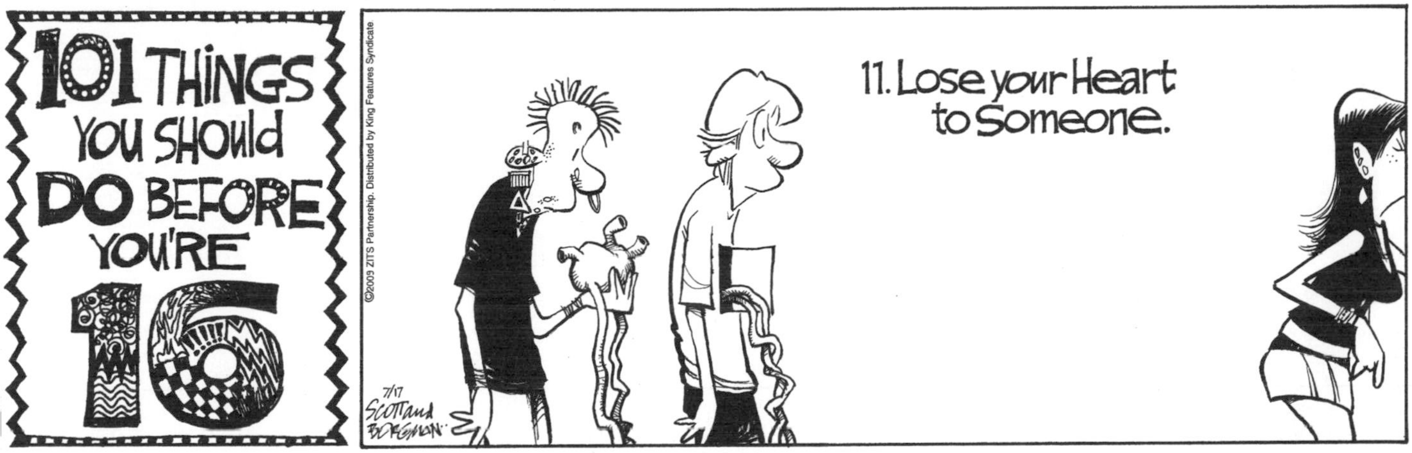
101 THINGS YOU SHOULD DO BEFORE YOU'RE 16
©2009 ZITS Partnership. Distributed by King Features Syndicate
11. Lose your Heart to Someone.
7/17
SCOTT and BORGMAN

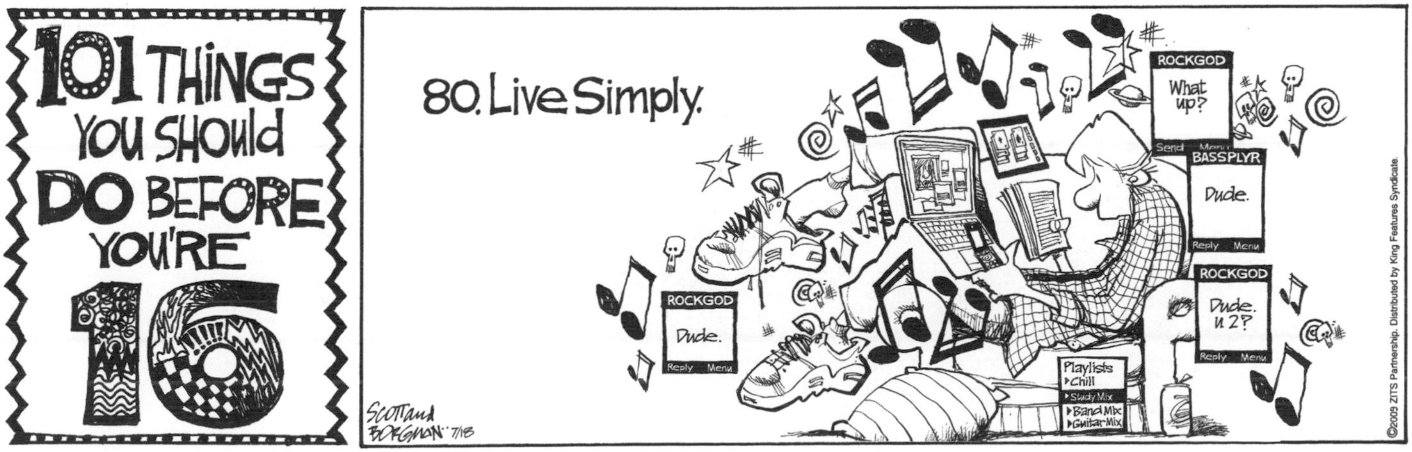
101 THINGS YOU SHOULD DO BEFORE YOU'RE 16
80. Live Simply.
ROCKGOD
What up?
BASSPLYR
Dude.
Reply Menu
ROCKGOD
Dude. u 2?
Reply Menu
ROCKGOD
Dude.
Reply Menu
Playlists
Chill
Study Mix
Band Mix
Guitar Mix
SCOTT and BORGMAN 7/18
©2009 ZITS Partnership. Distributed by King Features Syndicate.

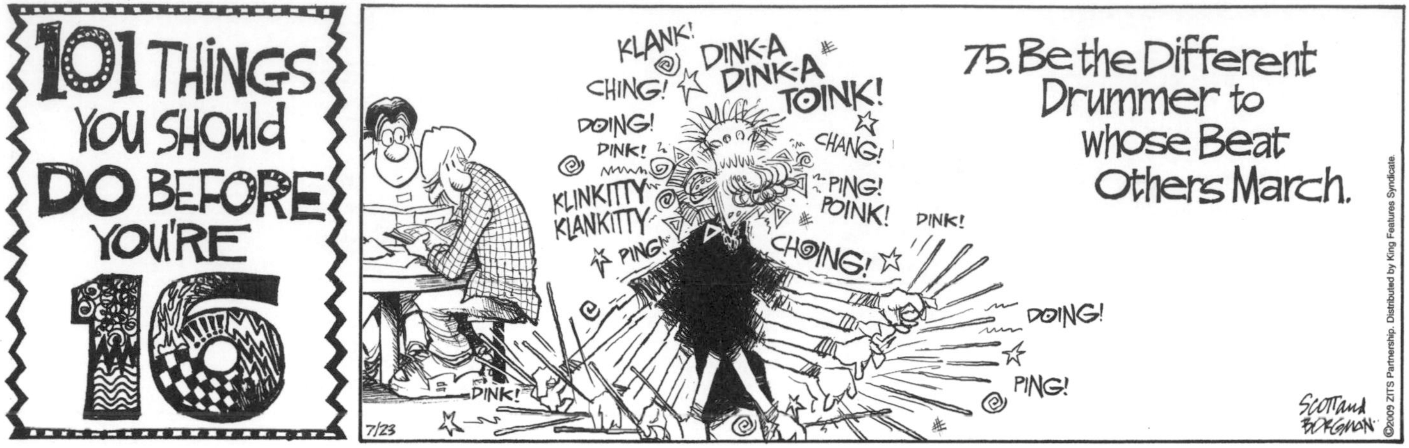
101 THINGS YOU SHOULD DO BEFORE YOU'RE 16
75. Be the Different Drummer to whose Beat Others March.
KLANK!
DINK-A DINK-A
TOINK!
CHING!
DOING!
DINK!
CHANG!
KLINKITTY KLANKITTY
PING!
POINK!
PING!
DINK!
CHOING!
DOING!
PING!
DINK!
7/23
SCOTT and BORGMAN
©2009 ZITS Partnership. Distributed by King Features Syndicate.

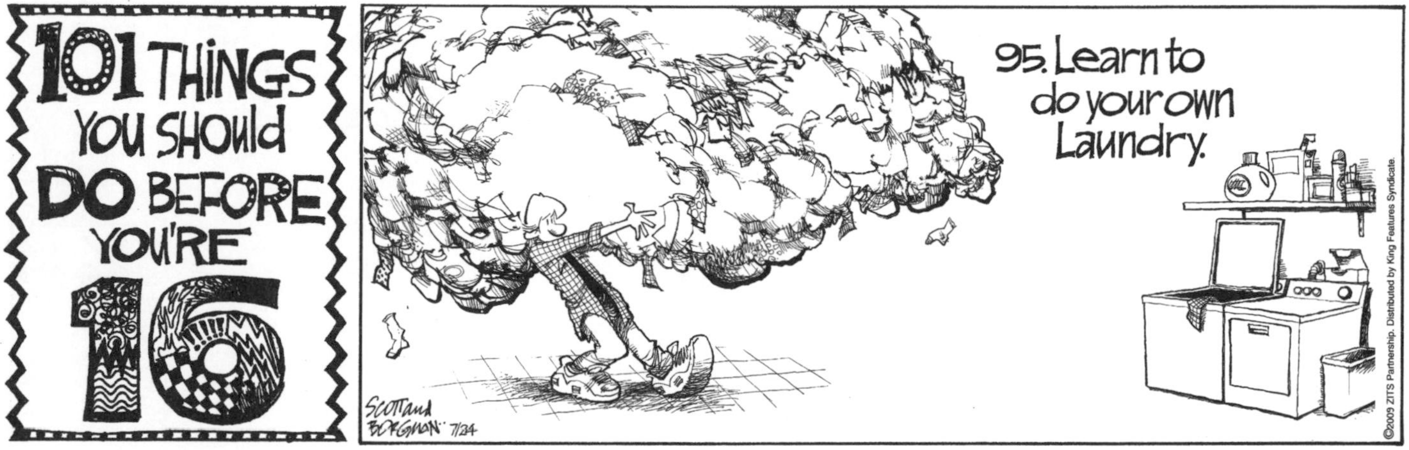
101 THINGS YOU SHOULD DO BEFORE YOU'RE 16
95. Learn to do your own Laundry.
SCOTT and BORGMAN 7/24
©2009 ZITS Partnership. Distributed by King Features Syndicate.

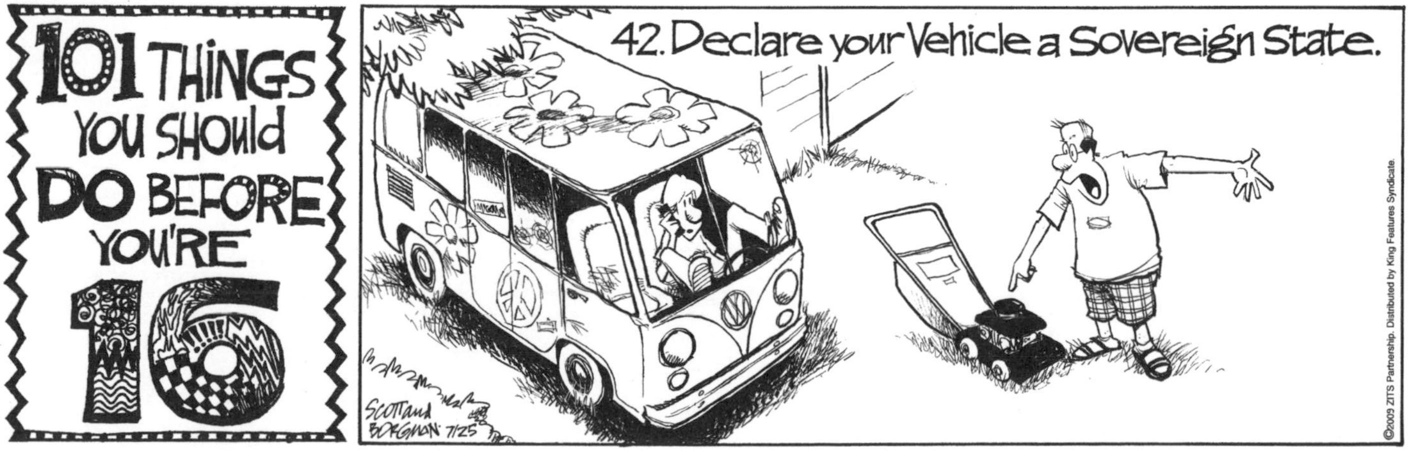
101 THINGS YOU SHOULD DO BEFORE YOU'RE 16
42. Declare your Vehicle a Sovereign State.
SCOTT and BORGMAN 7/25
©2009 ZITS Partnership. Distributed by King Features Syndicate.

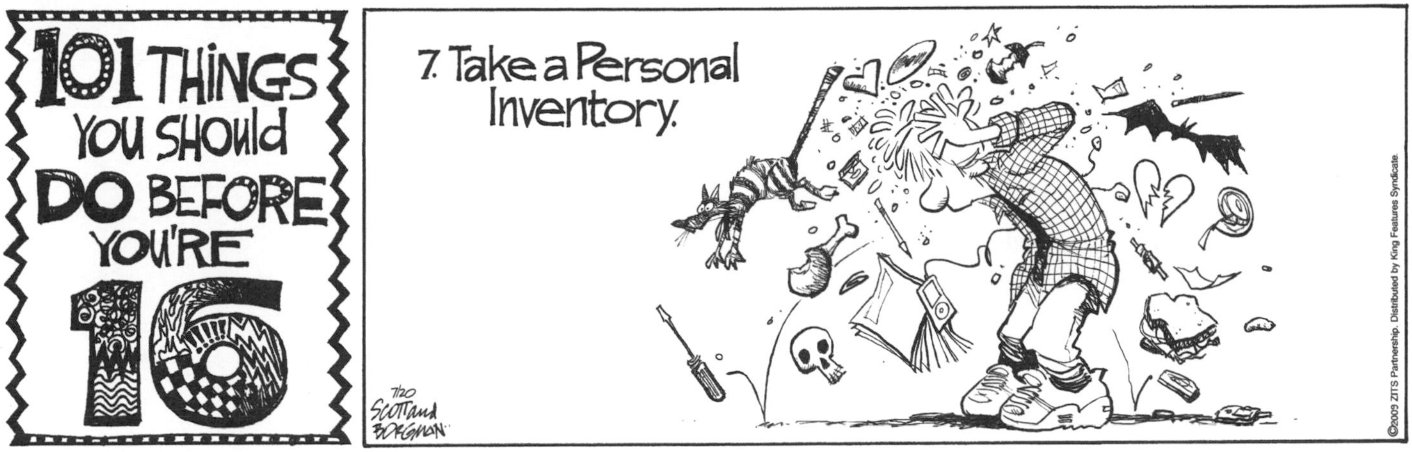
101 THINGS YOU SHOULD DO BEFORE YOU'RE 16
7. Take a Personal Inventory.
7/20 SCOTT and BORGMAN
©2009 ZITS Partnership. Distributed by King Features Syndicate.

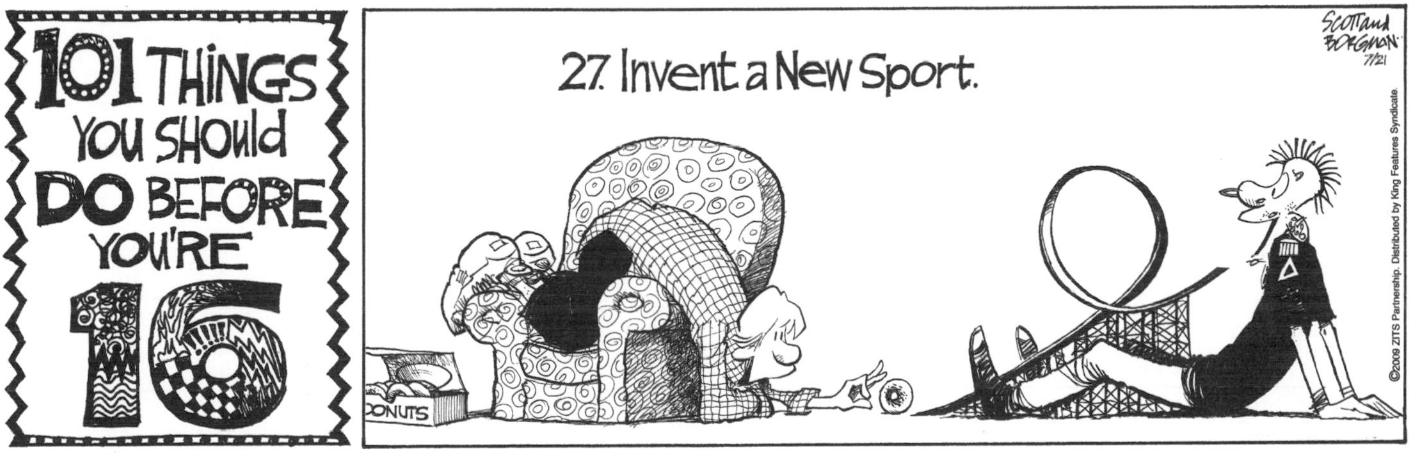
101 THINGS YOU SHOULD DO BEFORE YOU'RE 16
27. Invent a New Sport.
DONUTS
SCOTT and BORGMAN 7/21
©2009 ZITS Partnership. Distributed by King Features Syndicate.

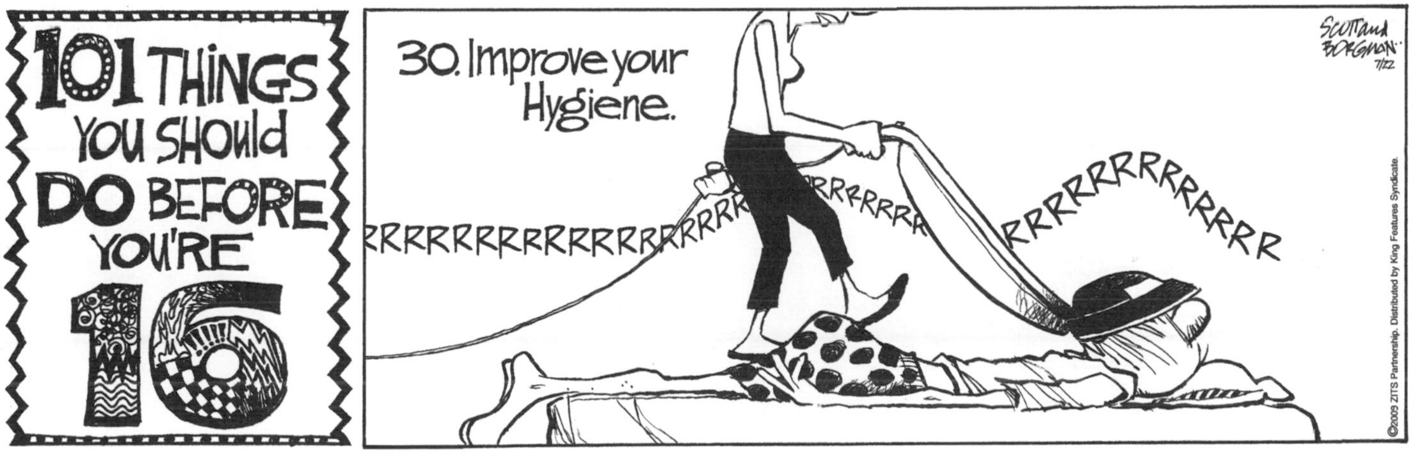
101 THINGS YOU SHOULD DO BEFORE YOU'RE 16
30. Improve your Hygiene.
SCOTT and BORGMAN 7/22
©2009 ZITS Partnership. Distributed by King Features Syndicate.

Zits
by JERRY SCOTT and JIM BORGMAN

I'D LIKE TO GO ON ONE OF THOSE WILDERNESS ADVENTURES
WHERE THEY DROP YOU OFF IN THE MIDDLE OF NOWHERE
WITH ONLY A LOINCLOTH
AND A SHARP PIECE OF FLINT
AND YOU HAVE TO SURVIVE BY YOUR WITS AND
MOM! CAN YOU NUDGE THE A.C. DOWN A DEGREE? MY POPSICLE IS SPONGY!
WOULD THAT BE COOL OR WHAT?
YEAH. AND MAYBE YOU COULD WHITTLE YOURSELF A CAPUCCINO MAKER OUT OF A LOG.
7/19
SCOTT and BORGMAN
©2009 ZITS Partnership. Distributed by King Features Syndicate.

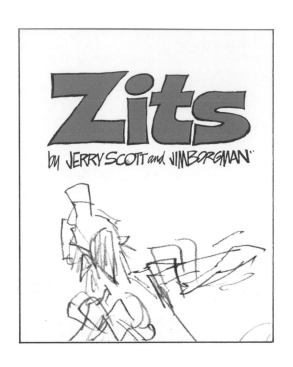

Zits
by JERRY SCOTT and JIM BORGMAN

SO...
YEAH...
UM...
A DENT.
SCOTT and BORGMAN 7/26
©2009 ZITS Partnership. Distributed by King Features Syndicate.
CREAK!
AAA AAU UGH!
RANT! RANT! RANT! RAVE! RAVE!
YOU HAVE TO PAY US BACK.
OKAY.
I THOUGHT DAD WOULD BE MORE UPSET ABOUT THIS.
HE DOES HIS FRETTING ON THE INSIDE.

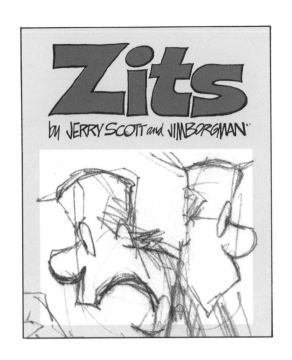

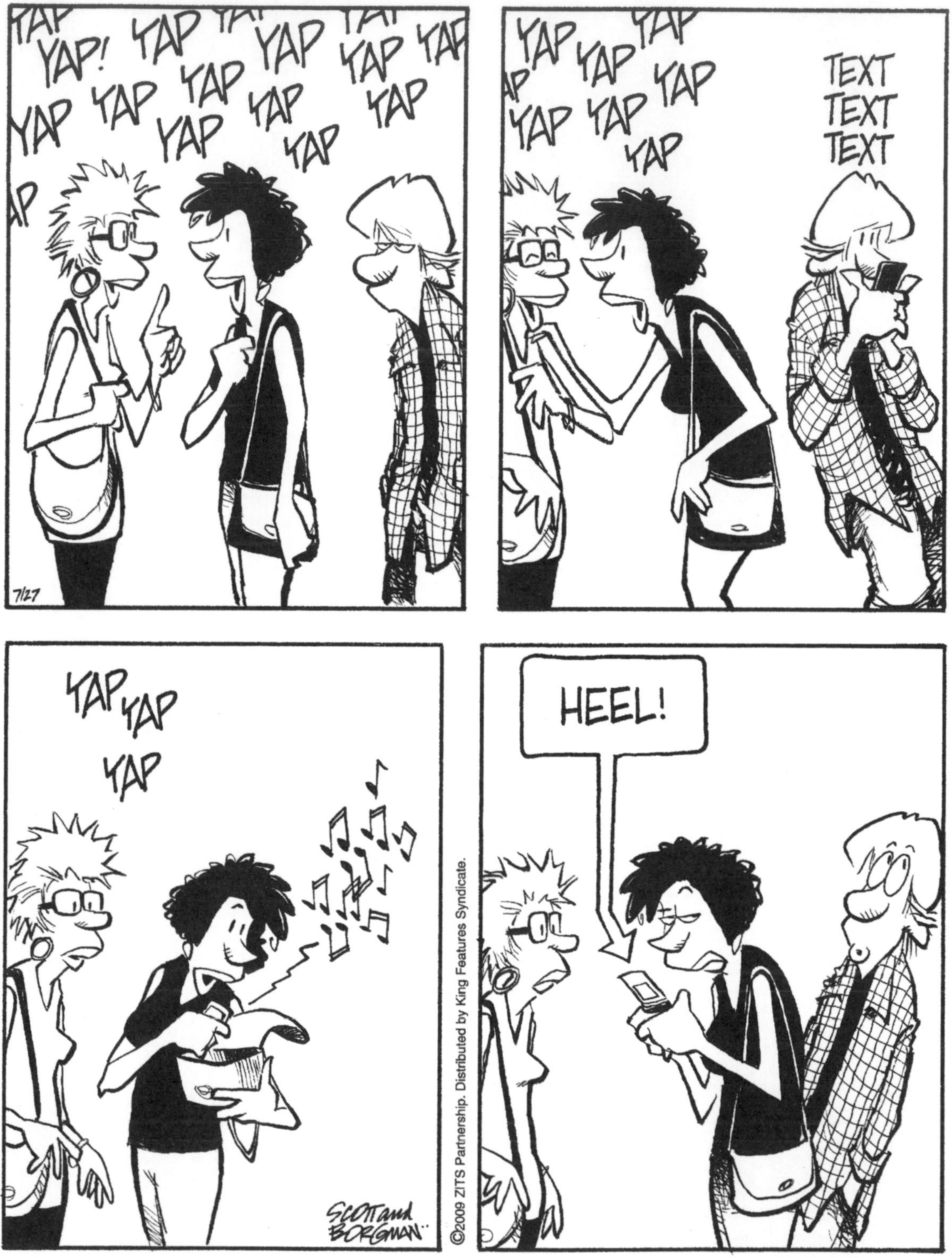
7/27
YAP!
YAP YAP YAP YAP YAP YAP YAP YAP YAP YAP YAP YAP
YAP YAP YAP YAP YAP YAP YAP
TEXT
TEXT
TEXT
YAP YAP
YAP
HEEL!
SCOTT and BORGMAN

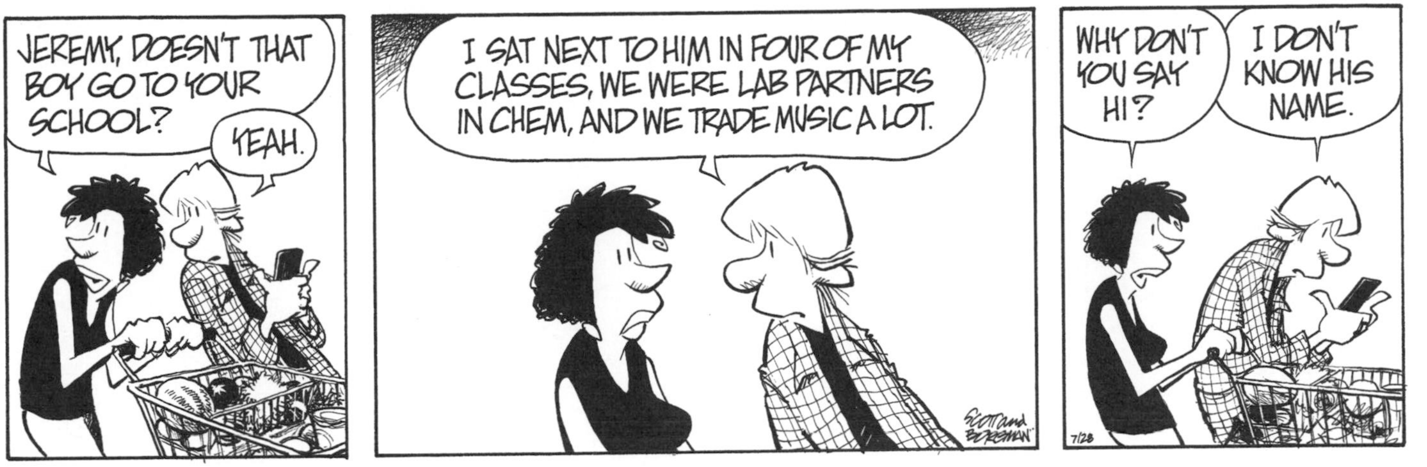
JEREMY, DOESN'T THAT BOY GO TO YOUR SCHOOL?
YEAH.
I SAT NEXT TO HIM IN FOUR OF MY CLASSES, WE WERE LAB PARTNERS IN CHEM, AND WE TRADE MUSIC A LOT.
WHY DON'T YOU SAY HI?
I DON'T KNOW HIS NAME.
SCOTT and BORGMAN
7/28

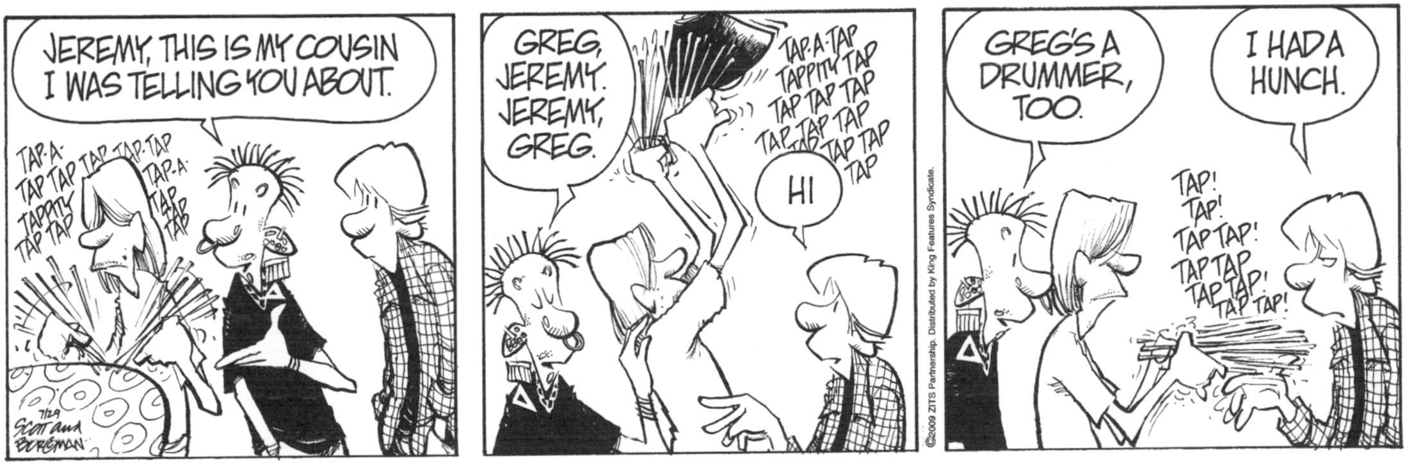
JEREMY, THIS IS MY COUSIN I WAS TELLING YOU ABOUT.
TAP-A-TAP TAP TAP TAP-TAP TAPPITY TAP TAP
TAP-A-TAP TAP TAP
7/29
SCOTT and BORGMAN
GREG, JEREMY. JEREMY, GREG.
TAP-A-TAP TAPPITY TAP TAP TAP TAP TAP-TAP TAP TAP TAP TAP TAP
HI
©2009 ZITS Partnership. Distributed by King Features Syndicate.
GREG'S A DRUMMER, TOO.
I HAD A HUNCH.
TAP! TAP! TAP TAP! TAP TAP, TAP TAP! TAP TAP!

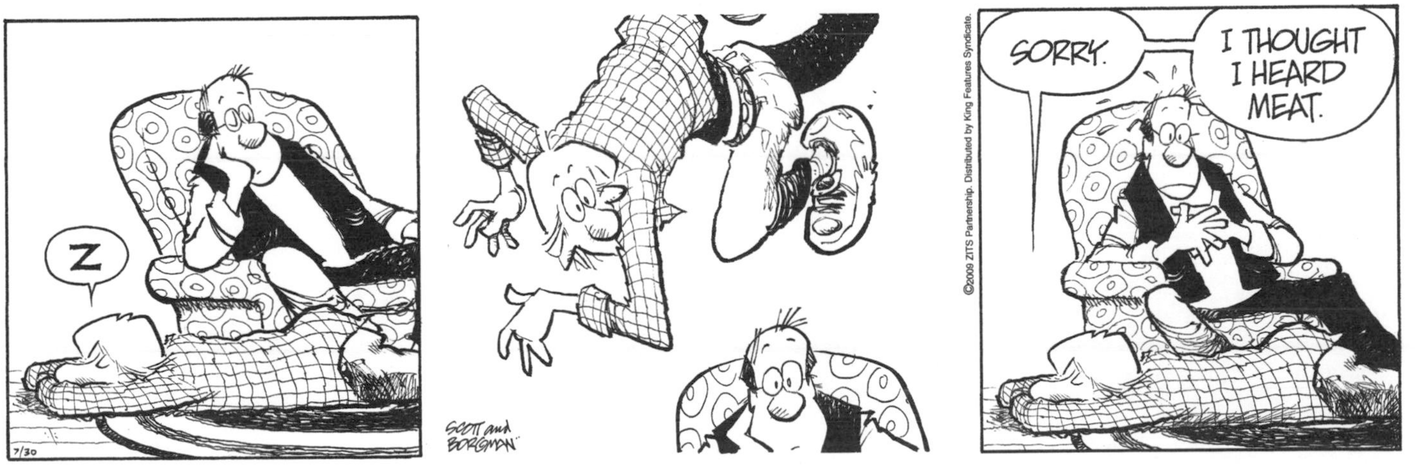
Z
7/30
SCOTT and BORGMAN
©2009 ZITS Partnership. Distributed by King Features Syndicate.
SORRY.
I THOUGHT I HEARD MEAT.

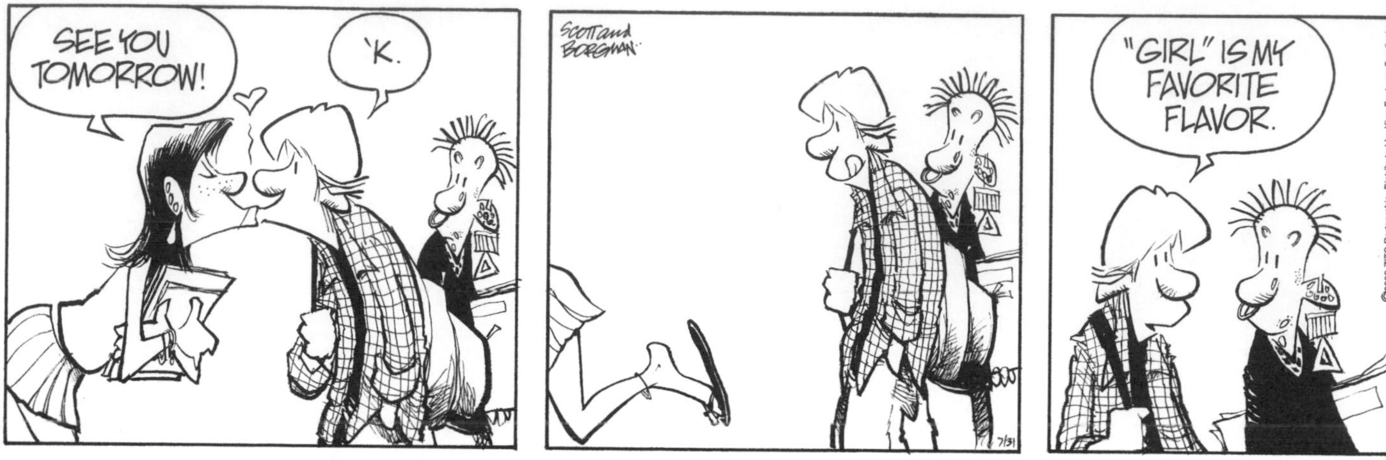
SEE YOU TOMORROW!
'K.
SCOTT and BORGMAN
7/31
"GIRL" IS MY FAVORITE FLAVOR.
©2009 ZITS Partnership. Distributed by King Features Syndicate.

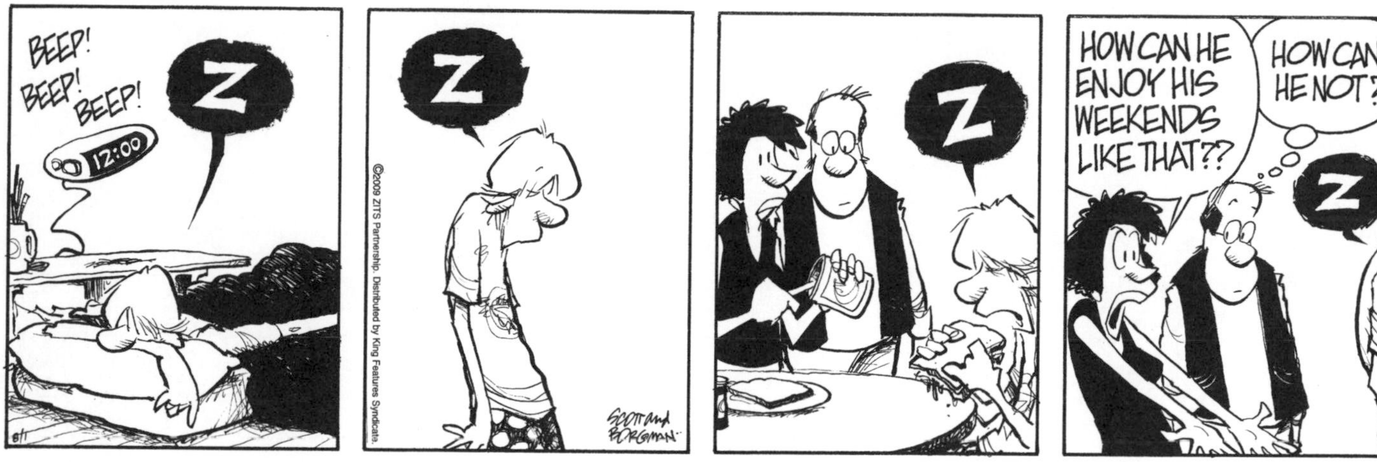
BEEP! BEEP! BEEP!
12:00
Z
8/1
©2009 ZITS Partnership. Distributed by King Features Syndicate.
Z
SCOTT and BORGMAN
Z
HOW CAN HE ENJOY HIS WEEKENDS LIKE THAT??
HOW CAN HE NOT?
Z

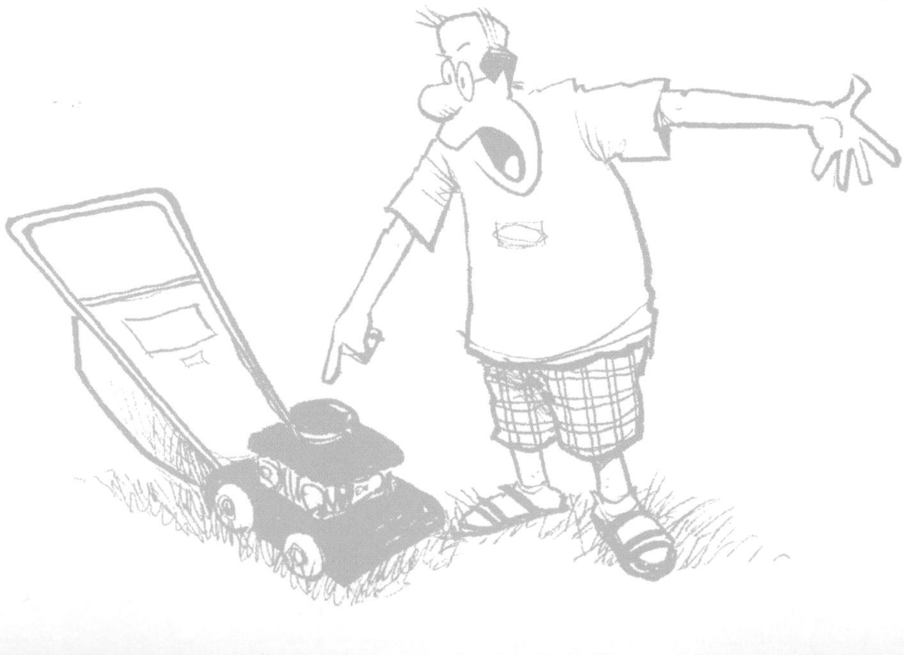

Zits
by JERRY SCOTT and JIM BORGMAN

BACKPACK AROUND EUROPE
!!!
BACKPACK AROUND EUROPE
8/2
©2009 ZITS Partnership. Distributed by King Features Syndicate.
PPTHHHHHHHHHHHHHHHHHHH
MORE HOPES AND DREAMS HAVE ENDED WITH "I'LL ASK MY MOM" THAN ANY OTHER PHRASE KNOWN TO MAN.
I AM SO OVER ADOLESCENCE.
SCOTT and BORGMAN

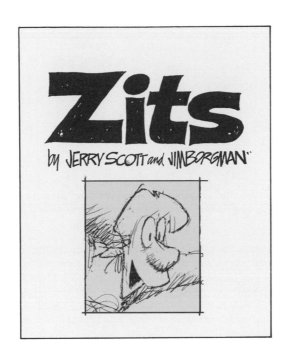

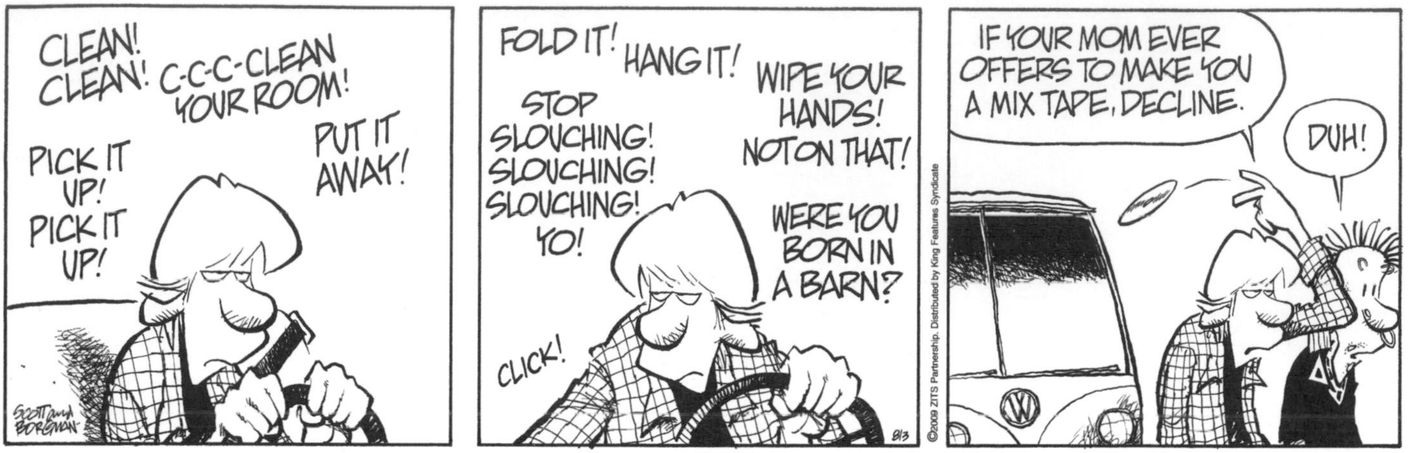
CLEAN! CLEAN! C-C-C-CLEAN YOUR ROOM!
PICK IT UP! PICK IT UP!
PUT IT AWAY!
FOLD IT! HANG IT!
WIPE YOUR HANDS! NOT ON THAT!
STOP SLOUCHING! SLOUCHING! SLOUCHING! YO!
WERE YOU BORN IN A BARN?
CLICK!
IF YOUR MOM EVER OFFERS TO MAKE YOU A MIX TAPE, DECLINE.
DUH!
©2009 ZITS Partnership. Distributed by King Features Syndicate

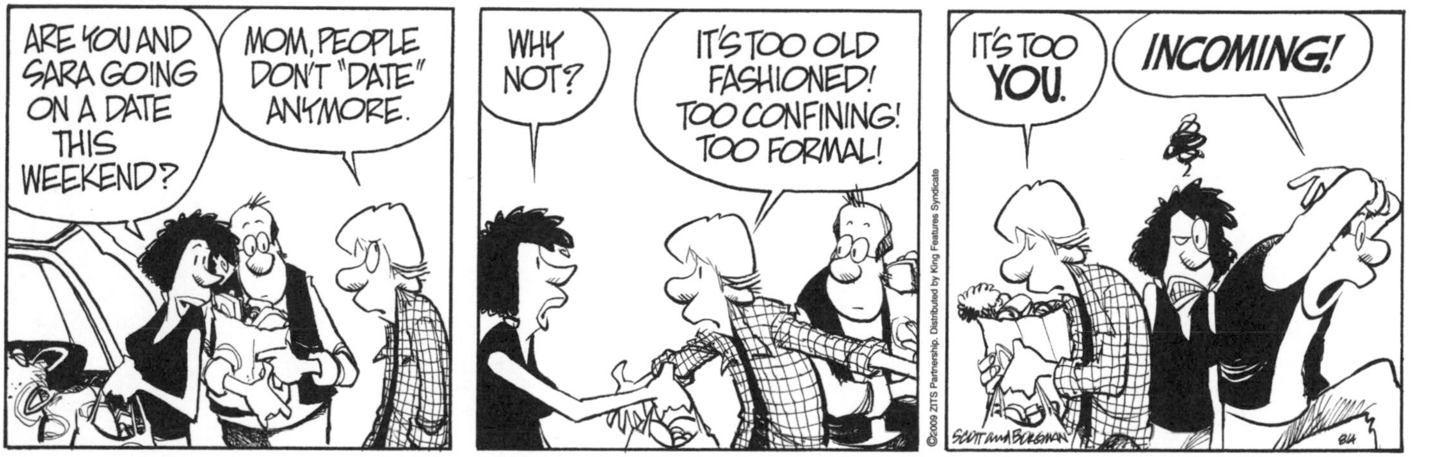
ARE YOU AND SARA GOING ON A DATE THIS WEEKEND?
MOM, PEOPLE DON'T "DATE" ANYMORE.
WHY NOT?
IT'S TOO OLD FASHIONED! TOO CONFINING! TOO FORMAL!
IT'S TOO YOU.
INCOMING!
©2009 ZITS Partnership. Distributed by King Features Syndicate

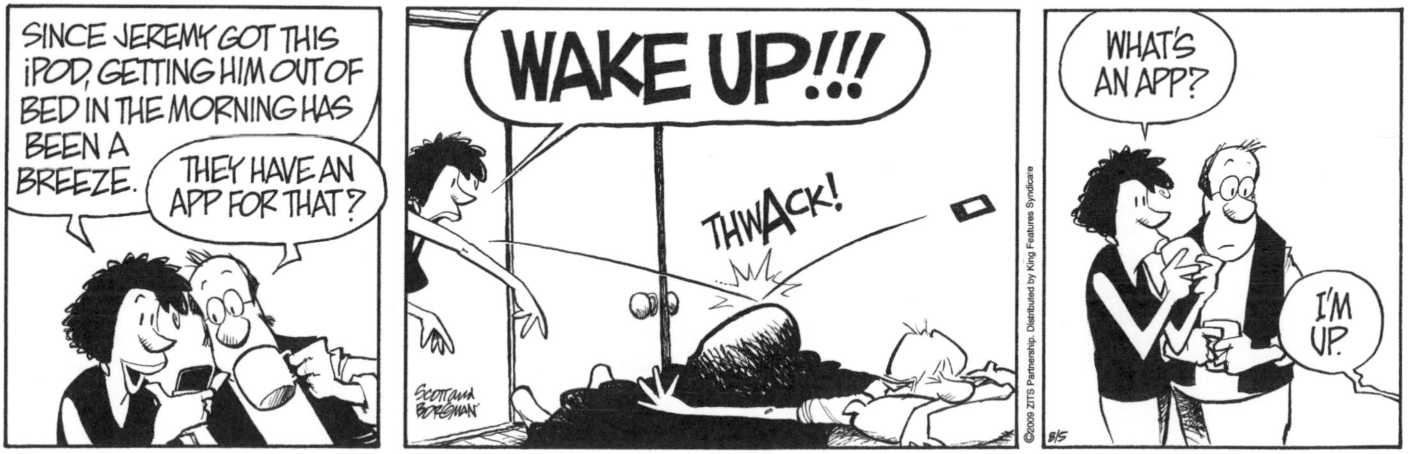
SINCE JEREMY GOT THIS iPOD, GETTING HIM OUT OF BED IN THE MORNING HAS BEEN A BREEZE.
THEY HAVE AN APP FOR THAT?
WAKE UP!!!
THWACK!
WHAT'S AN APP?
I'M UP.
©2009 ZITS Partnership. Distributed by King Features Syndicate

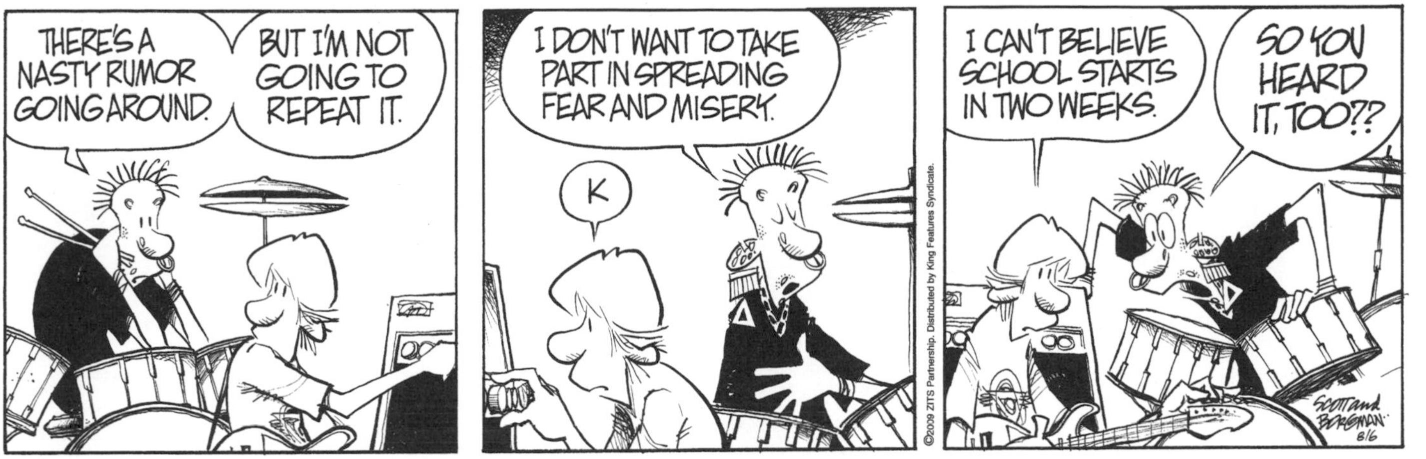
THERE'S A NASTY RUMOR GOING AROUND.
BUT I'M NOT GOING TO REPEAT IT.
I DON'T WANT TO TAKE PART IN SPREADING FEAR AND MISERY.
K
I CAN'T BELIEVE SCHOOL STARTS IN TWO WEEKS.
SO YOU HEARD IT, TOO??
©2009 ZITS Partnership. Distributed by King Features Syndicate.
SCOTT and BORGMAN
8/6

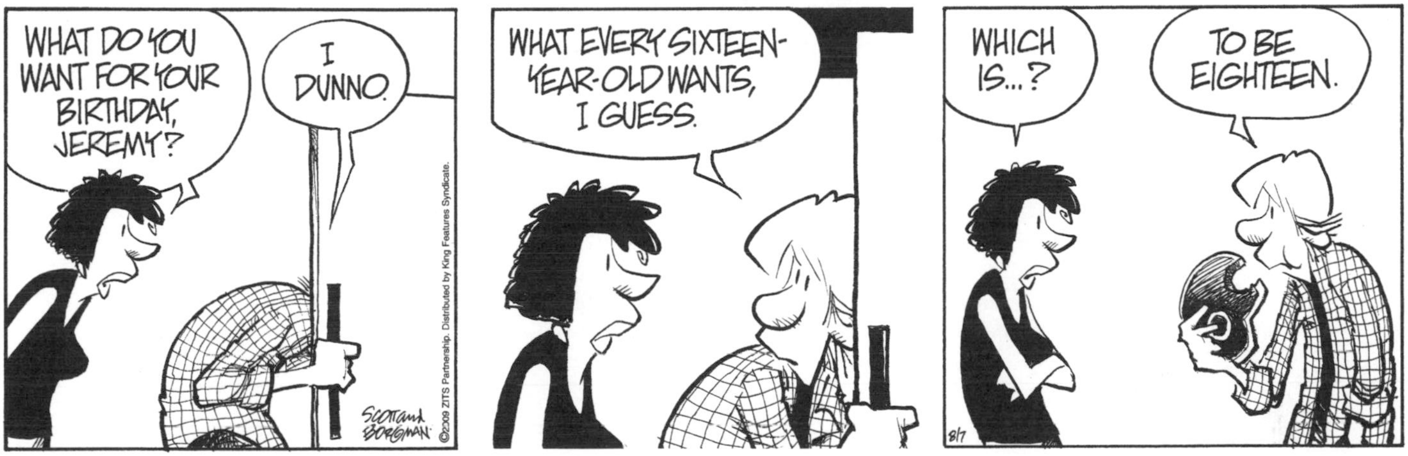
WHAT DO YOU WANT FOR YOUR BIRTHDAY, JEREMY?
I DUNNO.
©2009 ZITS Partnership. Distributed by King Features Syndicate.
SCOTT and BORGMAN
WHAT EVERY SIXTEEN-YEAR-OLD WANTS, I GUESS.
WHICH IS...?
TO BE EIGHTEEN.
8/7

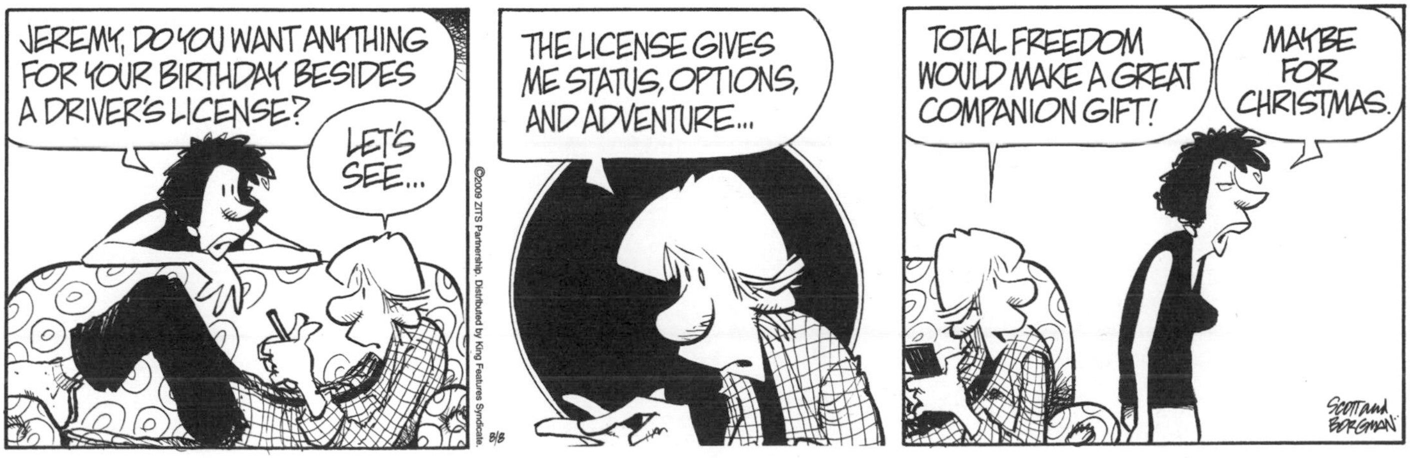
JEREMY, DO YOU WANT ANYTHING FOR YOUR BIRTHDAY BESIDES A DRIVER'S LICENSE?
LET'S SEE...
©2009 ZITS Partnership. Distributed by King Features Syndicate.
8/8
THE LICENSE GIVES ME STATUS, OPTIONS, AND ADVENTURE...
TOTAL FREEDOM WOULD MAKE A GREAT COMPANION GIFT!
MAYBE FOR CHRISTMAS.
SCOTT and BORGMAN

Zits
by JERRY SCOTT and JIM BORGMAN

SCOTT and BORGMAN
SLAM!
©2009 ZITS Partnership. Distributed by King Features Syndicate.
FOR THE RECORD, I WAS **NOT** CROWDING THE CENTER LINE WHEN THAT CEMENT TRUCK WENT BY.
YOU SURE?

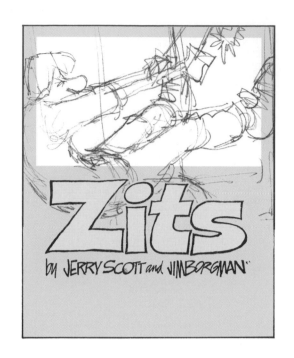

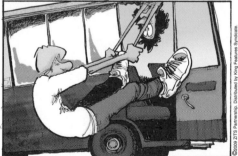

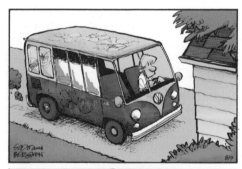

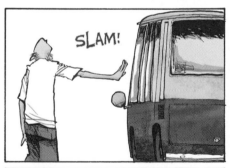

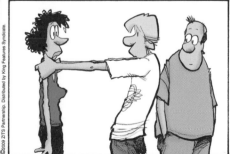

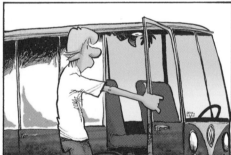

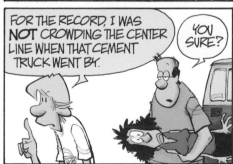

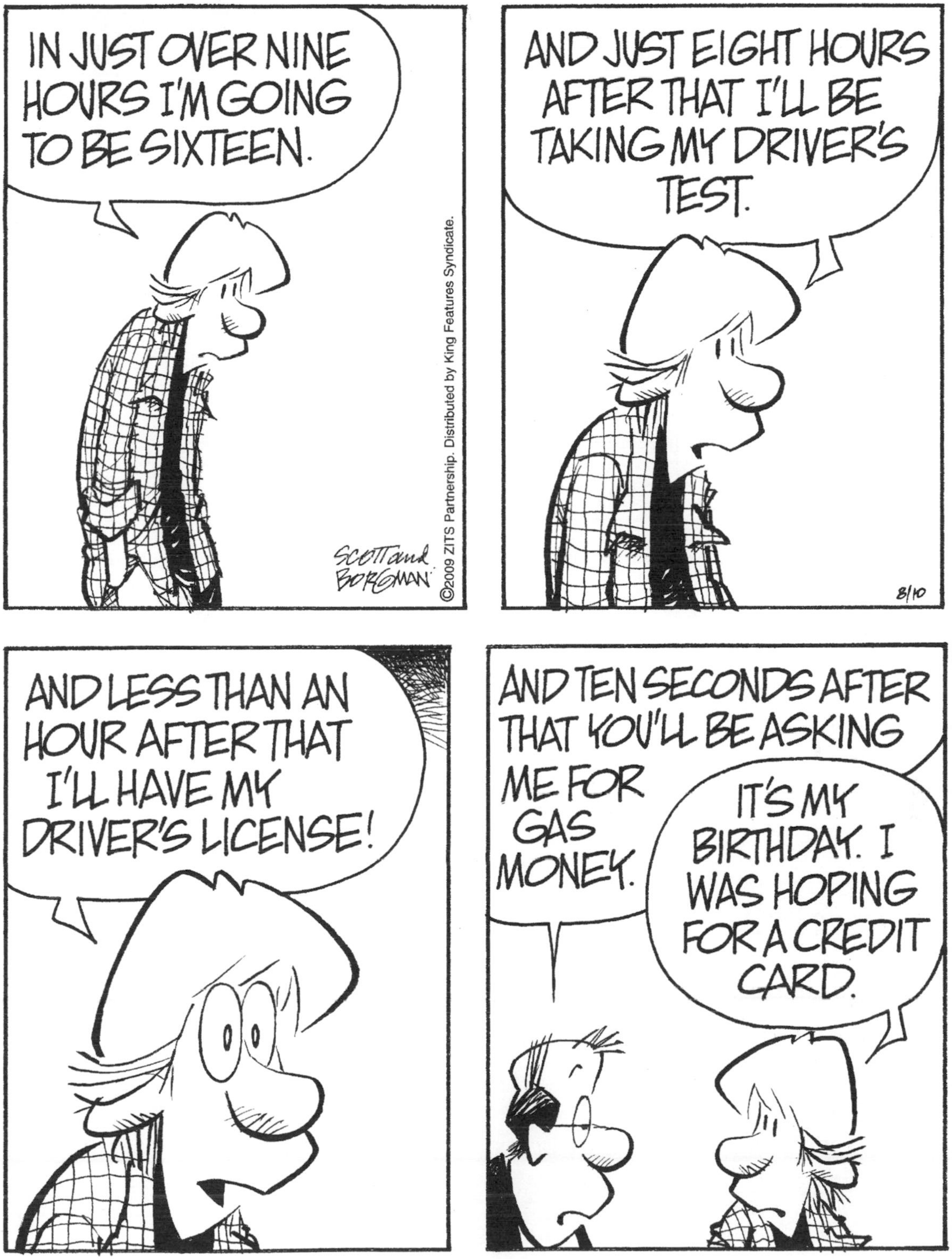
IN JUST OVER NINE HOURS I'M GOING TO BE SIXTEEN.
SCOTT and BORGMAN
©2009 ZITS Partnership. Distributed by King Features Syndicate.
AND JUST EIGHT HOURS AFTER THAT I'LL BE TAKING MY DRIVER'S TEST.
8/10
AND LESS THAN AN HOUR AFTER THAT I'LL HAVE MY DRIVER'S LICENSE!
AND TEN SECONDS AFTER THAT YOU'LL BE ASKING ME FOR GAS MONEY.
IT'S MY BIRTHDAY. I WAS HOPING FOR A CREDIT CARD.

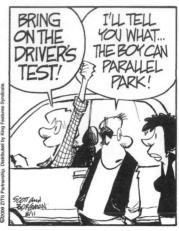

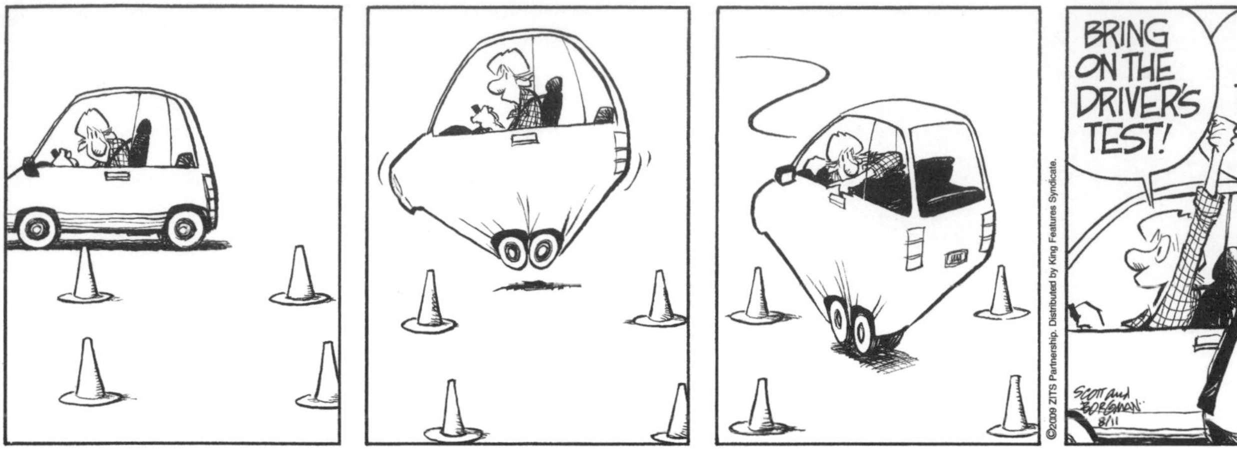
BRING ON THE DRIVER'S TEST!
I'LL TELL YOU WHAT... THE BOY CAN PARALLEL PARK!
©2009 ZITS Partnership. Distributed by King Features Syndicate.

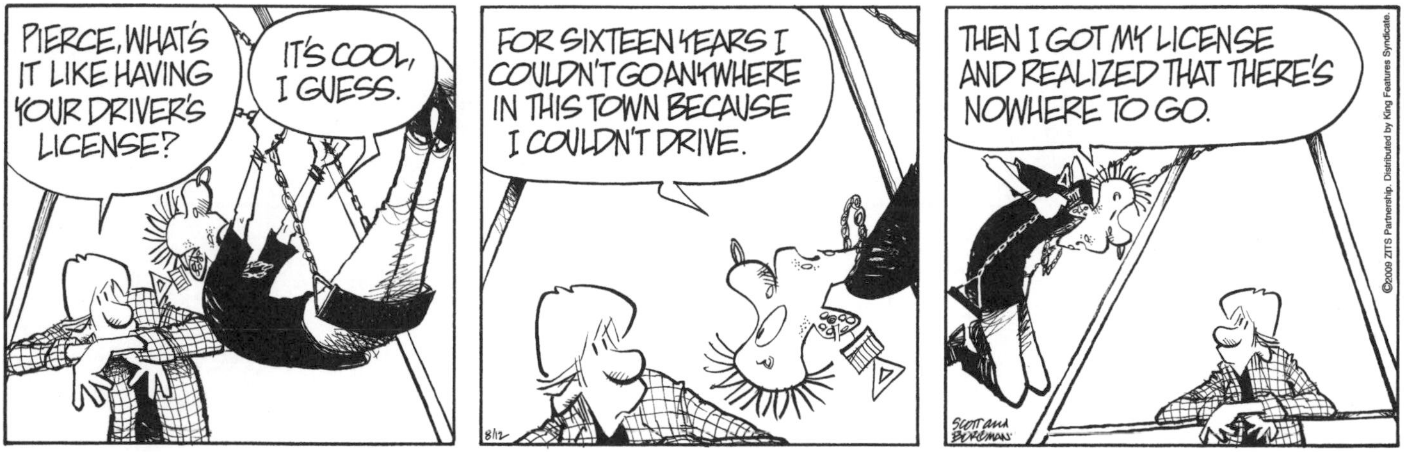
PIERCE, WHAT'S IT LIKE HAVING YOUR DRIVER'S LICENSE?
IT'S COOL, I GUESS.
FOR SIXTEEN YEARS I COULDN'T GO ANYWHERE IN THIS TOWN BECAUSE I COULDN'T DRIVE.
THEN I GOT MY LICENSE AND REALIZED THAT THERE'S NOWHERE TO GO.
©2009 ZITS Partnership. Distributed by King Features Syndicate.

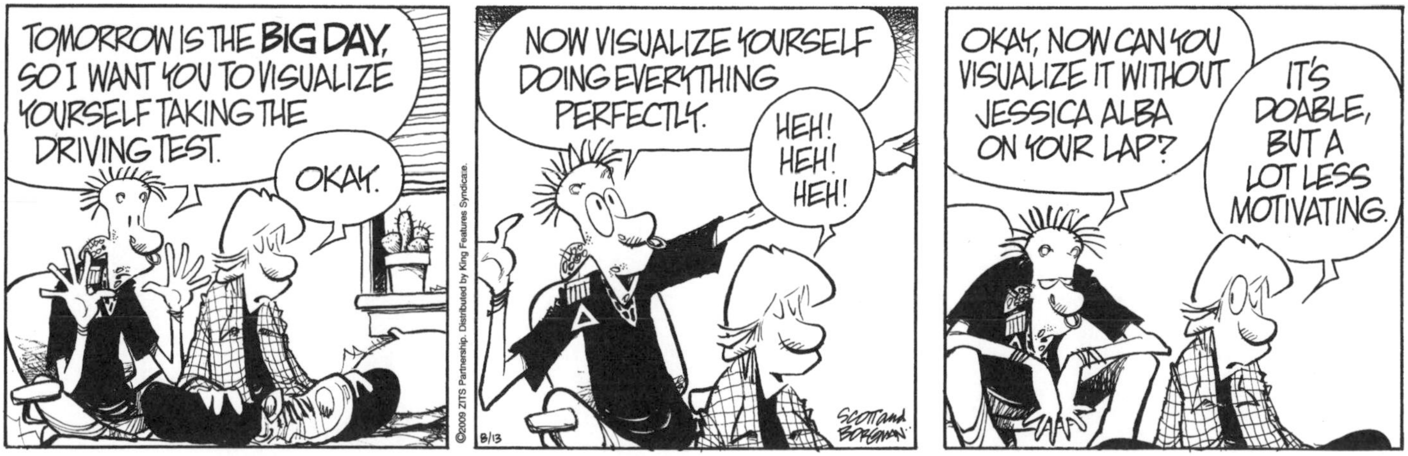
TOMORROW IS THE **BIG DAY**, SO I WANT YOU TO VISUALIZE YOURSELF TAKING THE DRIVING TEST.
OKAY.
©2009 ZITS Partnership. Distributed by King Features Syndicate.
NOW VISUALIZE YOURSELF DOING EVERYTHING PERFECTLY.
HEH! HEH! HEH!
OKAY, NOW CAN YOU VISUALIZE IT WITHOUT JESSICA ALBA ON YOUR LAP?
IT'S DOABLE, BUT A LOT LESS MOTIVATING.

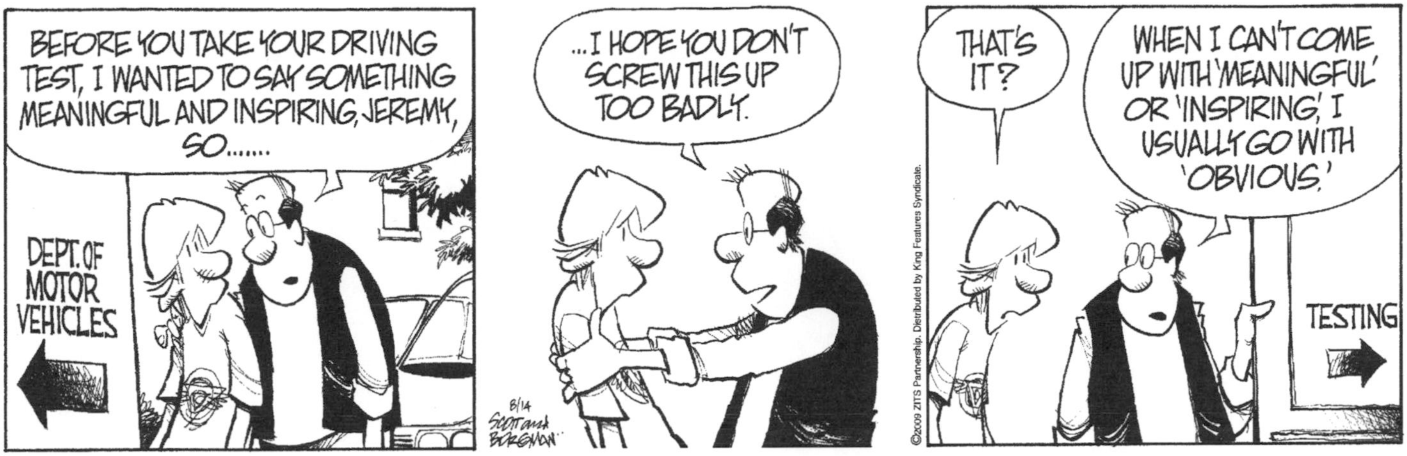
BEFORE YOU TAKE YOUR DRIVING TEST, I WANTED TO SAY SOMETHING MEANINGFUL AND INSPIRING, JEREMY, SO.......
DEPT. OF MOTOR VEHICLES
...I HOPE YOU DON'T SCREW THIS UP TOO BADLY.
8/14
SCOTT and BORGMAN
THAT'S IT?
WHEN I CAN'T COME UP WITH 'MEANINGFUL' OR 'INSPIRING,' I USUALLY GO WITH 'OBVIOUS.'
TESTING
©2009 ZITS Partnership. Distributed by King Features Syndicate.

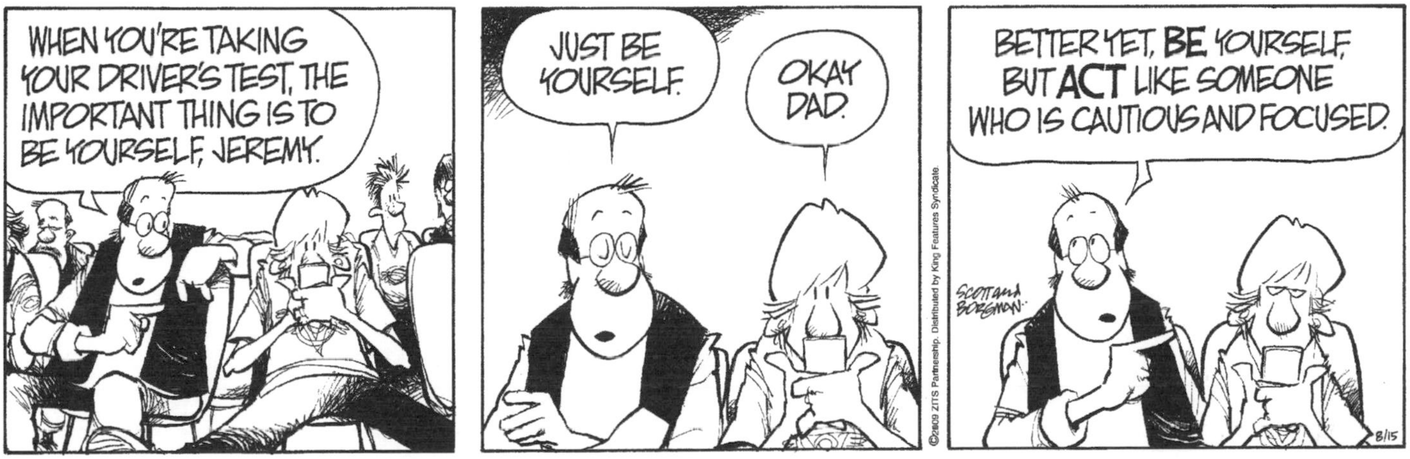
WHEN YOU'RE TAKING YOUR DRIVER'S TEST, THE IMPORTANT THING IS TO BE YOURSELF, JEREMY.
JUST BE YOURSELF.
OKAY DAD.
©2009 ZITS Partnership. Distributed by King Features Syndicate.
BETTER YET, BE YOURSELF, BUT ACT LIKE SOMEONE WHO IS CAUTIOUS AND FOCUSED.
SCOTT and BORGMAN
8/15

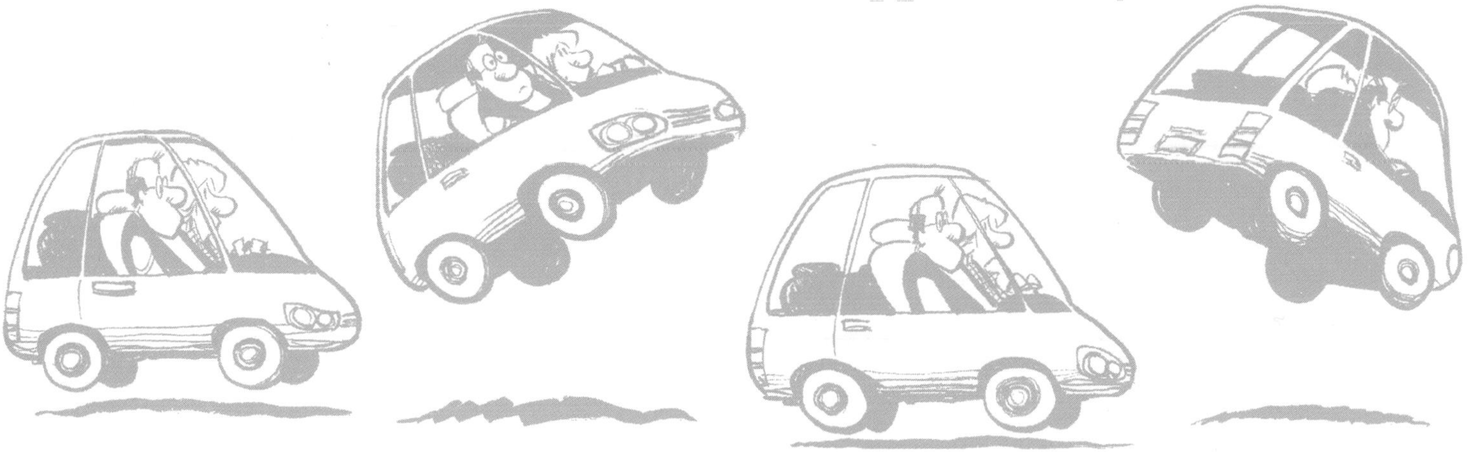

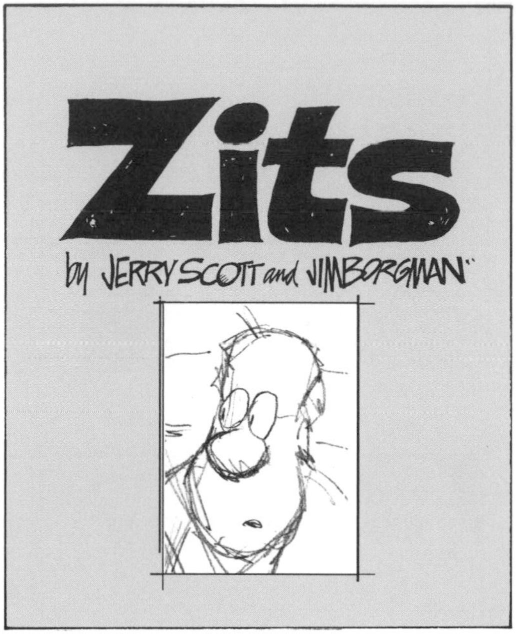
Zits
by JERRY SCOTT and JIM BORGMAN

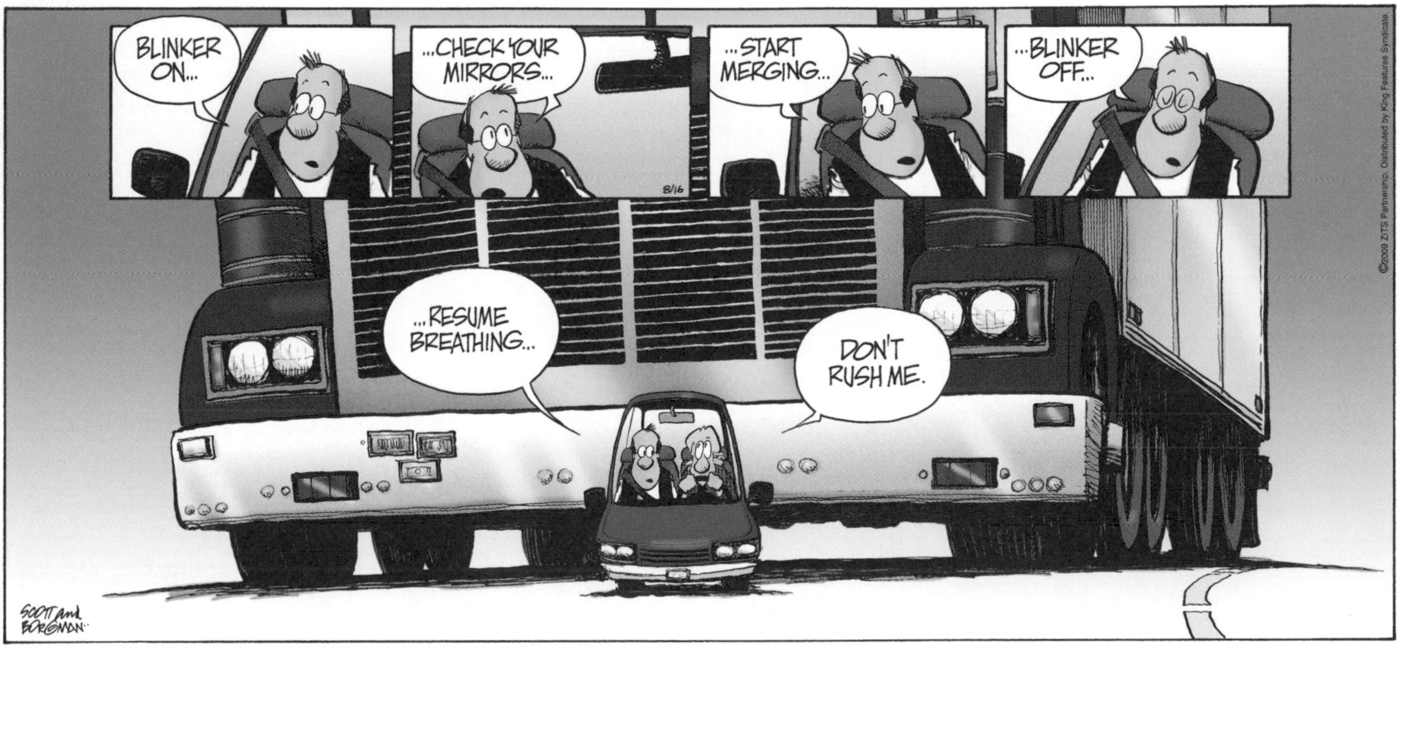
BLINKER ON...
...CHECK YOUR MIRRORS...
...START MERGING...
...BLINKER OFF...
8/16
...RESUME BREATHING...
DON'T RUSH ME.
SCOTT and BORGMAN
©2008 ZITS Partnership. Distributed by King Features Syndicate

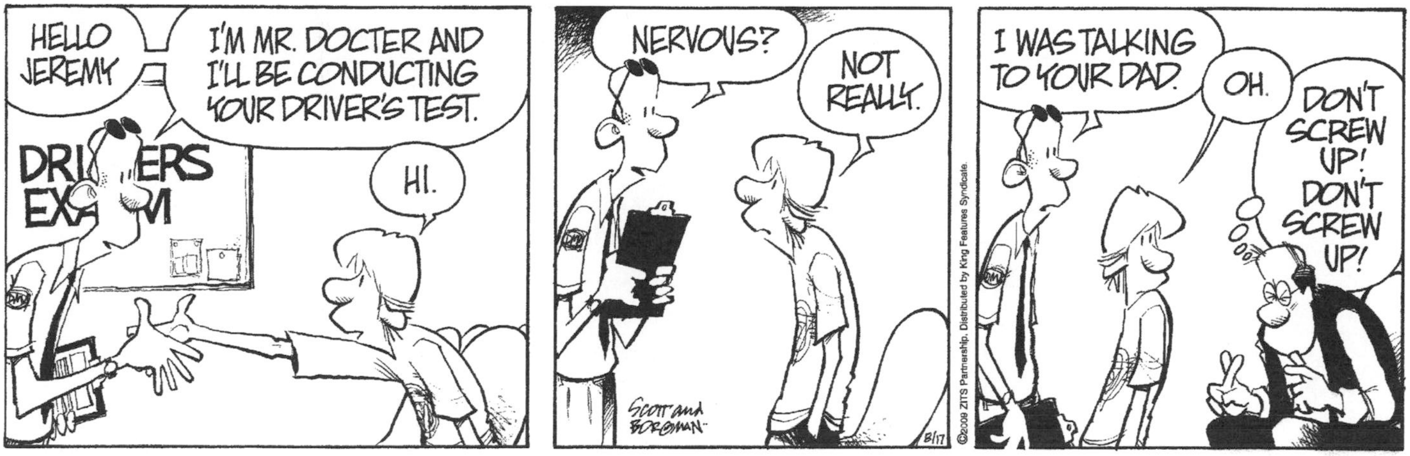
HELLO JEREMY
I'M MR. DOCTER AND I'LL BE CONDUCTING YOUR DRIVER'S TEST.
DRIVERS EXAM
HI.
NERVOUS?
NOT REALLY.
SCOTT and BORGMAN
8/17
©2009 ZITS Partnership. Distributed by King Features Syndicate.
I WAS TALKING TO YOUR DAD.
OH.
DON'T SCREW UP! DON'T SCREW UP!

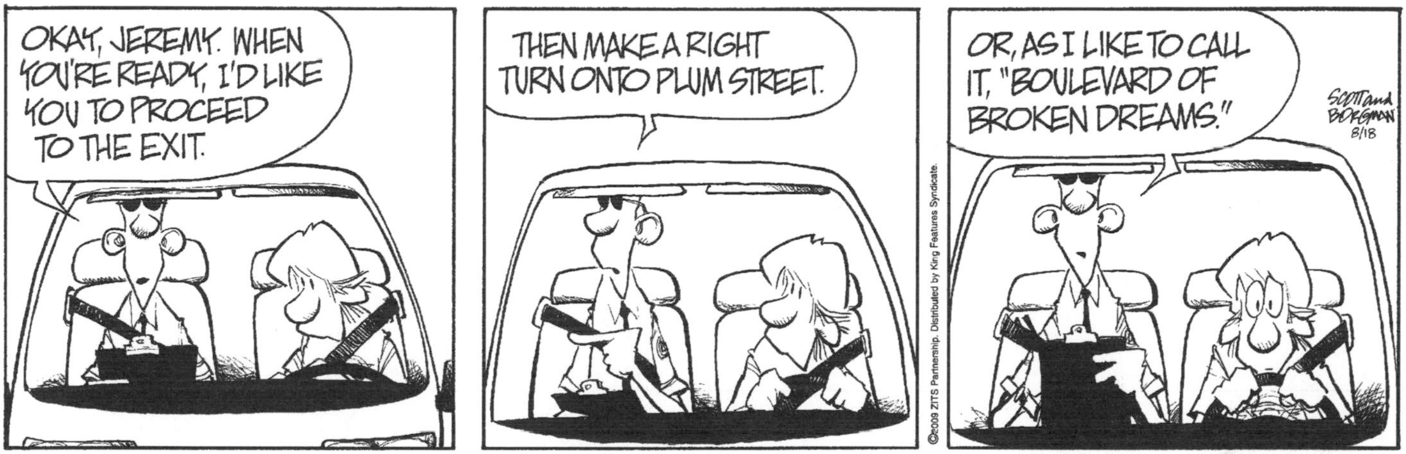
OKAY, JEREMY. WHEN YOU'RE READY, I'D LIKE YOU TO PROCEED TO THE EXIT.
THEN MAKE A RIGHT TURN ONTO PLUM STREET.
©2009 ZITS Partnership. Distributed by King Features Syndicate.
OR, AS I LIKE TO CALL IT, "BOULEVARD OF BROKEN DREAMS."
SCOTT and BORGMAN
8/18

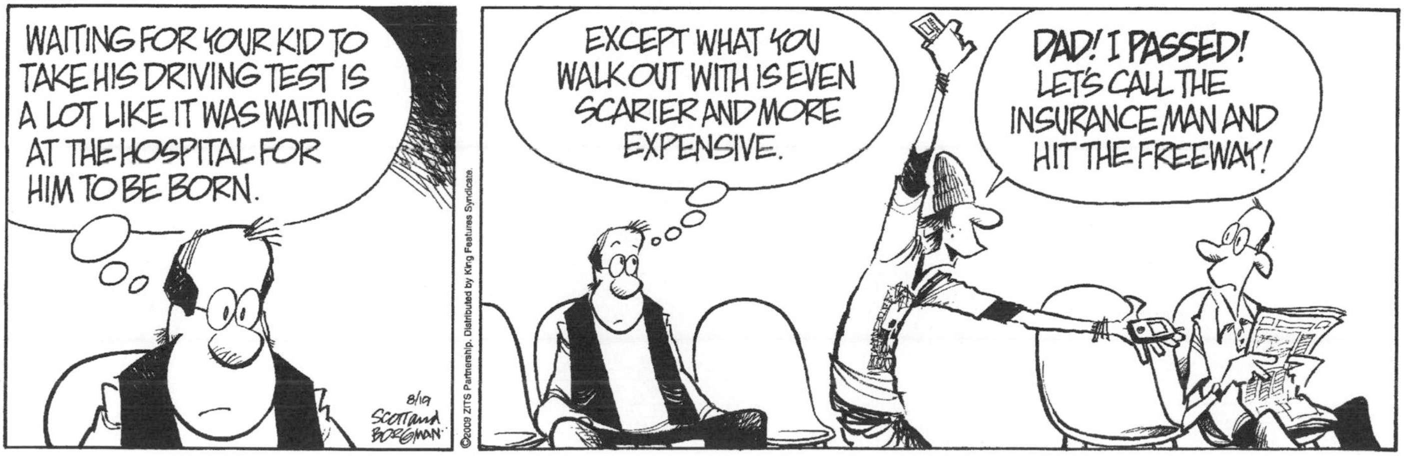
WAITING FOR YOUR KID TO TAKE HIS DRIVING TEST IS A LOT LIKE IT WAS WAITING AT THE HOSPITAL FOR HIM TO BE BORN.
8/19
SCOTT and BORGMAN
©2009 ZITS Partnership. Distributed by King Features Syndicate.
EXCEPT WHAT YOU WALK OUT WITH IS EVEN SCARIER AND MORE EXPENSIVE.
DAD! I PASSED! LET'S CALL THE INSURANCE MAN AND HIT THE FREEWAY!

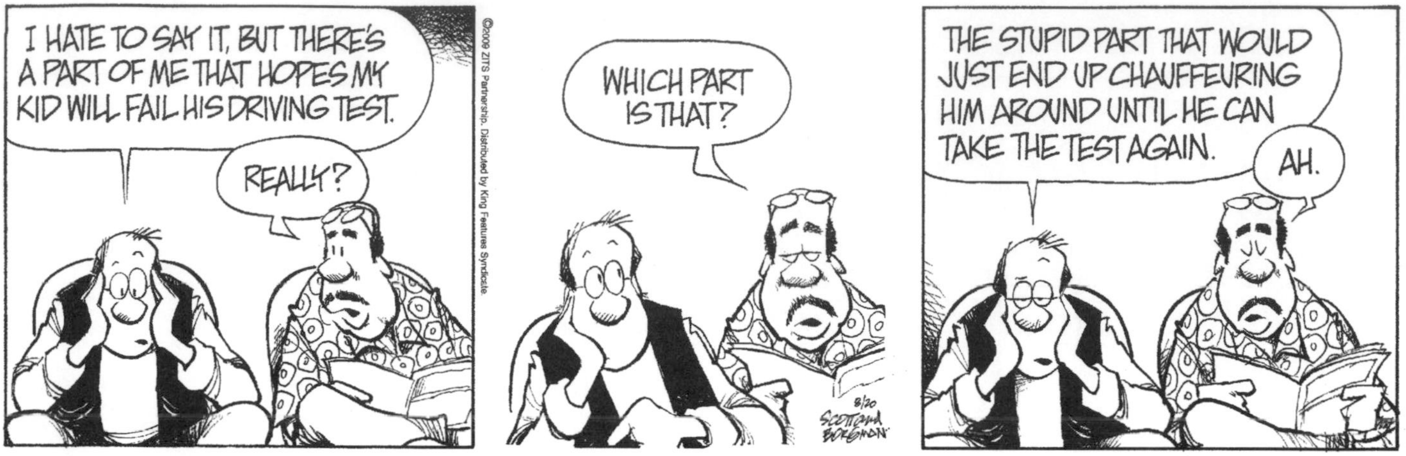
I HATE TO SAY IT, BUT THERE'S A PART OF ME THAT HOPES MY KID WILL FAIL HIS DRIVING TEST.
REALLY?
©2009 ZITS Partnership. Distributed by King Features Syndicate
WHICH PART IS THAT?
8/20
SCOTT and BORGMAN
THE STUPID PART THAT WOULD JUST END UP CHAUFFEURING HIM AROUND UNTIL HE CAN TAKE THE TEST AGAIN.
AH.

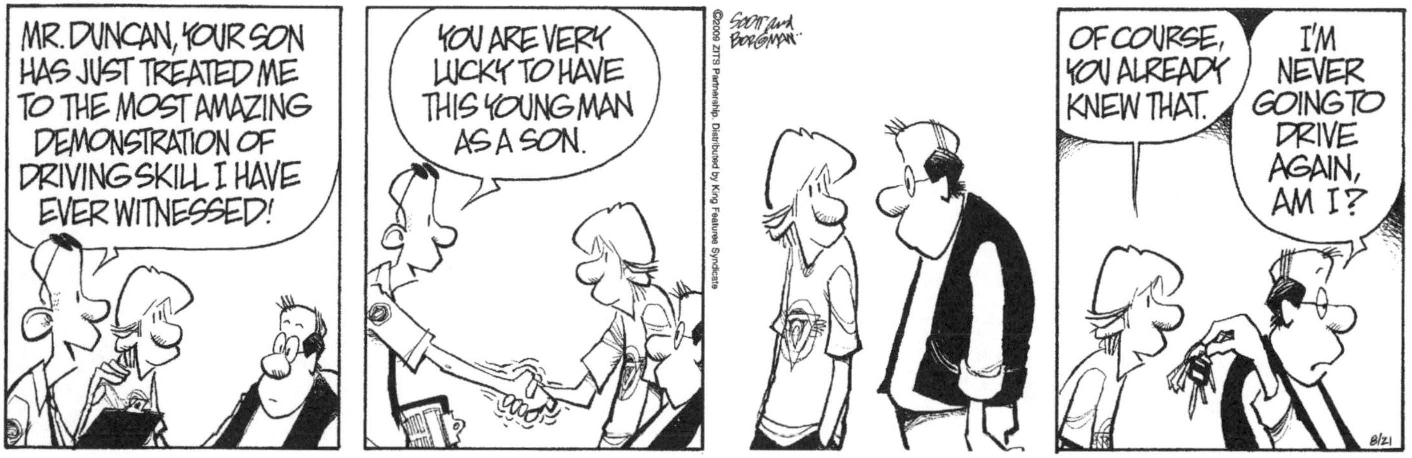
MR. DUNCAN, YOUR SON HAS JUST TREATED ME TO THE MOST AMAZING DEMONSTRATION OF DRIVING SKILL I HAVE EVER WITNESSED!
YOU ARE VERY LUCKY TO HAVE THIS YOUNG MAN AS A SON.
©2009 ZITS Partnership. Distributed by King Features Syndicate
SCOTT and BORGMAN
OF COURSE, YOU ALREADY KNEW THAT.
I'M NEVER GOING TO DRIVE AGAIN, AM I?
8/21

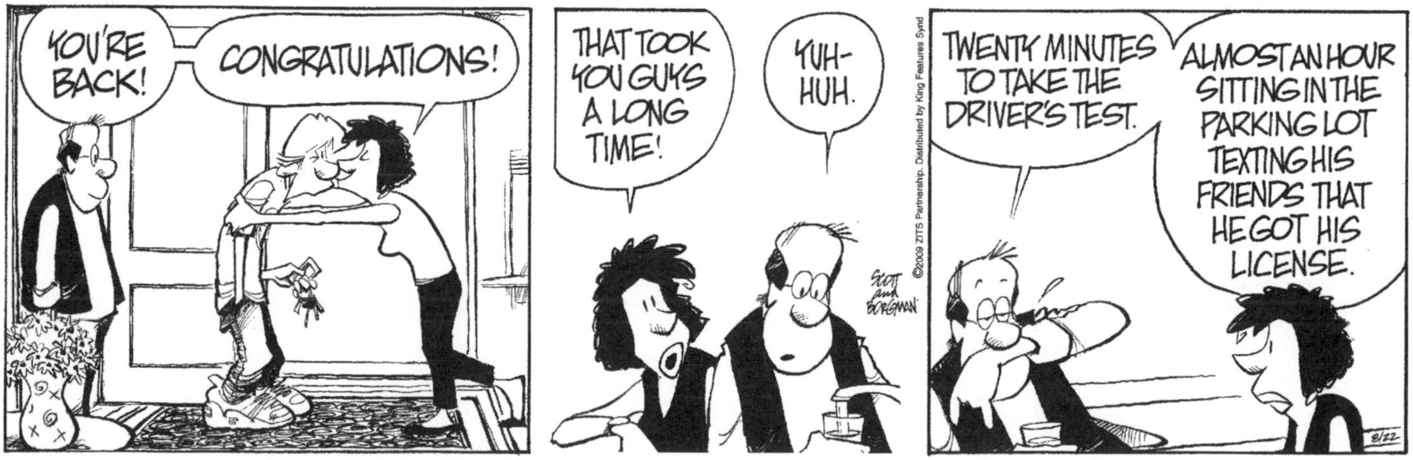
YOU'RE BACK!
CONGRATULATIONS!
THAT TOOK YOU GUYS A LONG TIME!
YUH-HUH.
SCOTT and BORGMAN
©2009 ZITS Partnership. Distributed by King Features Synd
TWENTY MINUTES TO TAKE THE DRIVER'S TEST.
ALMOST AN HOUR SITTING IN THE PARKING LOT TEXTING HIS FRIENDS THAT HE GOT HIS LICENSE.
8/22

Zits
by JERRY SCOTT and JIM BORGMAN

DRIVER'S LICENSE
YESSS!
License#RQ973J622F
Class C Issued 08/23/09
JEREMY DUNCAN
2201 HUMMINGBIRD LANE
Sex M
Height 5'11"
Weight 160
Eyes BLUE
Hair BLND
Donor♡
Jeremy Duncan
NICE PHOTO.
SCOTT and BORGMAN 8/23
©2009 ZITS Partnership. Distributed by King Features Syndicate.

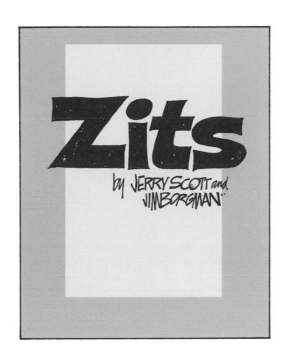

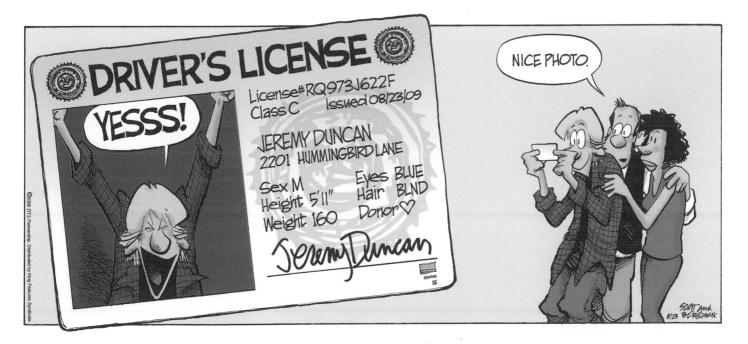

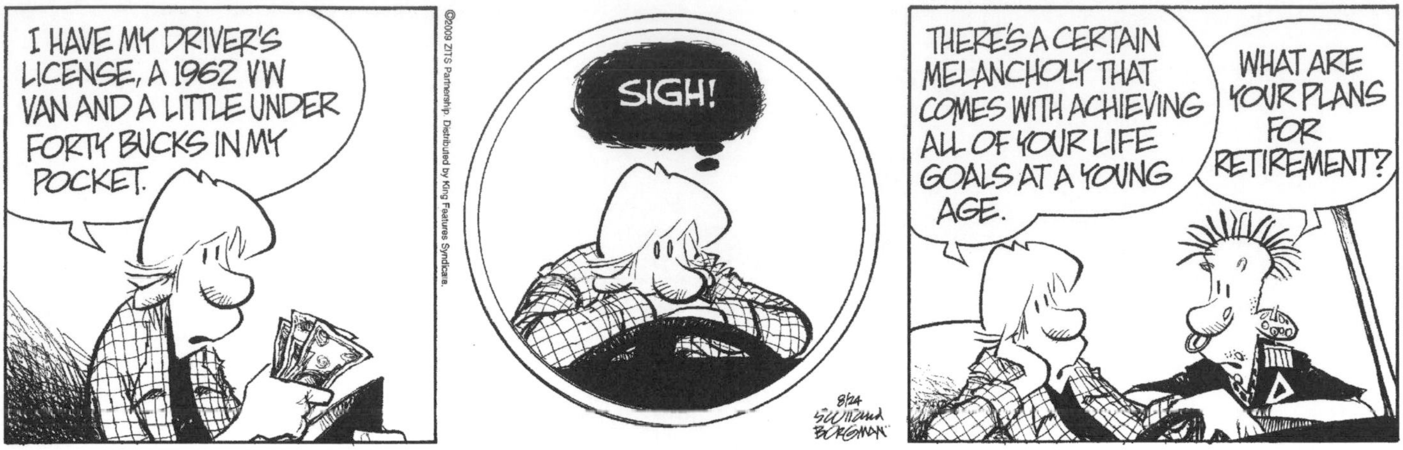
I HAVE MY DRIVER'S LICENSE, A 1962 VW VAN AND A LITTLE UNDER FORTY BUCKS IN MY POCKET.
©2009 ZITS Partnership. Distributed by King Features Syndicate.
SIGH!
THERE'S A CERTAIN MELANCHOLY THAT COMES WITH ACHIEVING ALL OF YOUR LIFE GOALS AT A YOUNG AGE.
WHAT ARE YOUR PLANS FOR RETIREMENT?
8/24
SCOTT and BORGMAN

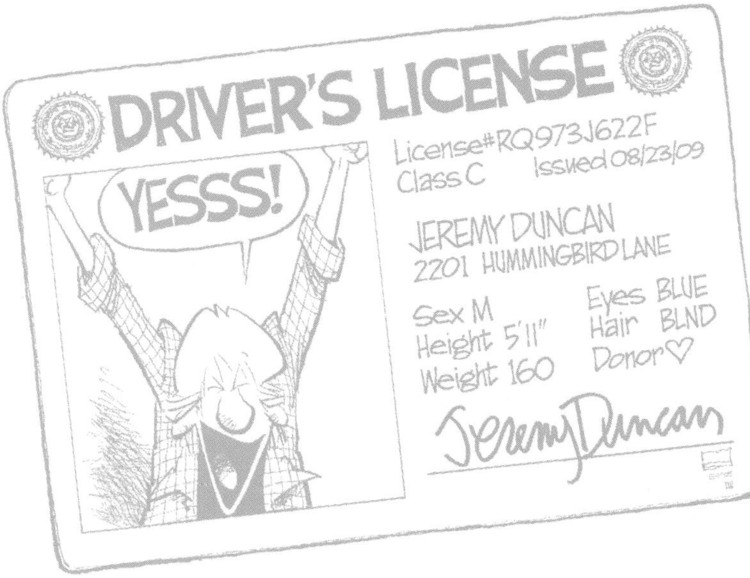
DRIVER'S LICENSE
YESSS!
License#RQ973J622F
Class C
Issued 08/23/09
JEREMY DUNCAN
2201 HUMMINGBIRD LANE
Sex M
Height 5'11"
Weight 160
Eyes BLUE
Hair BLND
Donor♡
Jeremy Duncan

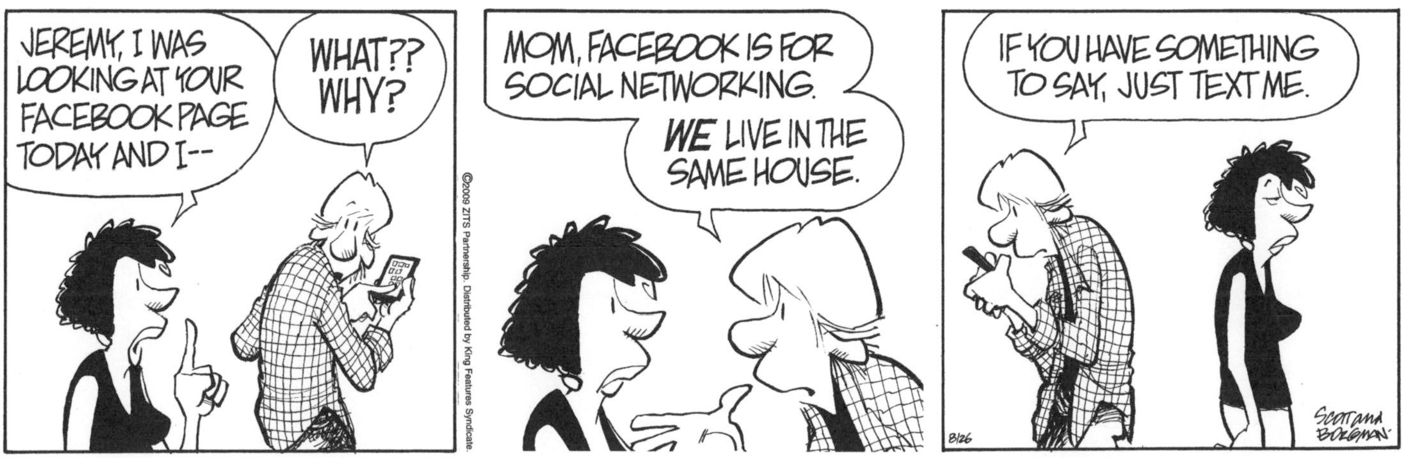
JEREMY, I WAS LOOKING AT YOUR FACEBOOK PAGE TODAY AND I--
WHAT?? WHY?
©2009 ZITS Partnership. Distributed by King Features Syndicate.
MOM, FACEBOOK IS FOR SOCIAL NETWORKING.
WE LIVE IN THE SAME HOUSE.
IF YOU HAVE SOMETHING TO SAY, JUST TEXT ME.
8/26
SCOTT and BORGMAN

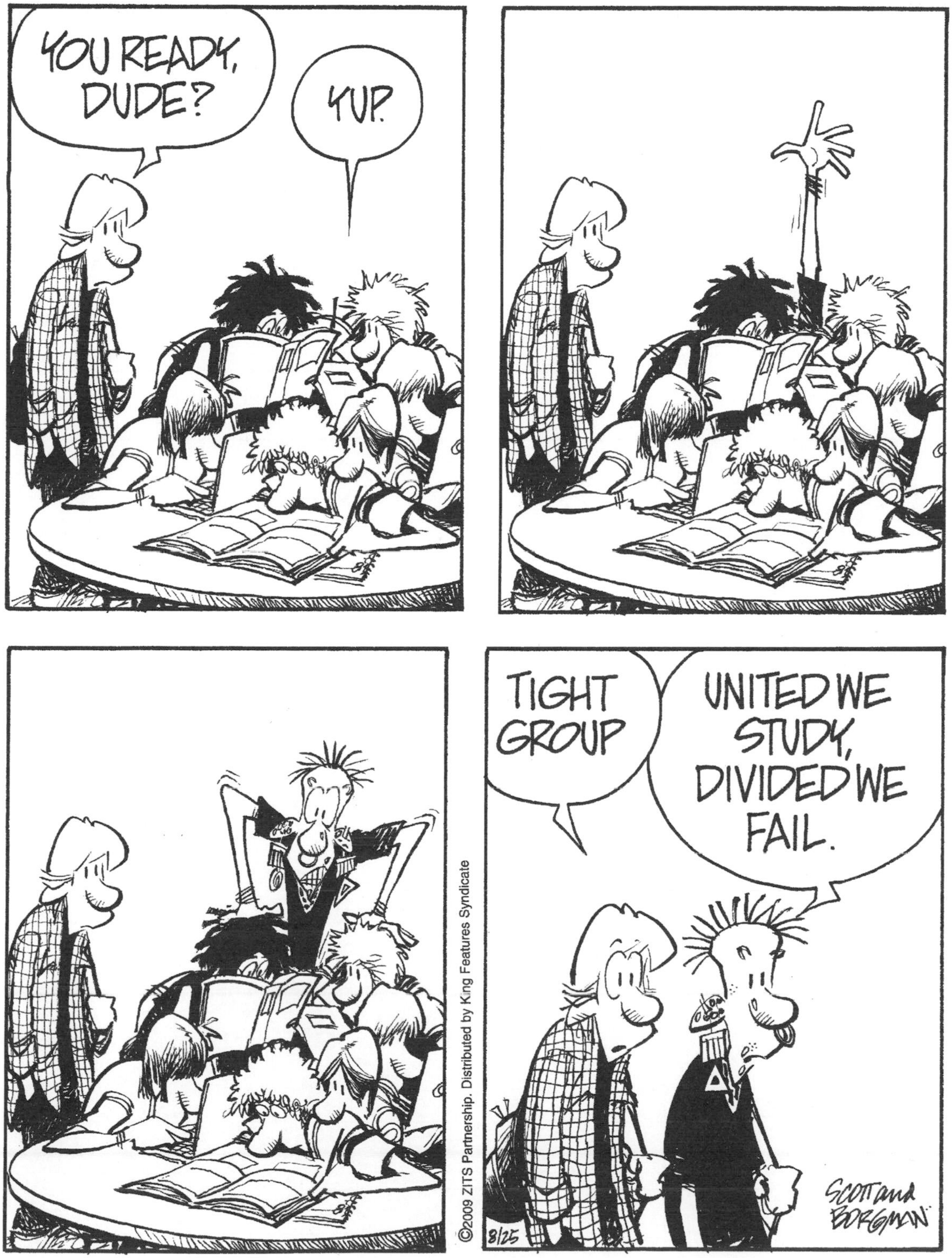
YOU READY, DUDE?
YUP.
TIGHT GROUP
UNITED WE STUDY, DIVIDED WE FAIL.
©2009 ZITS Partnership. Distributed by King Features Syndicate
8/25
SCOTT and BORGMAN

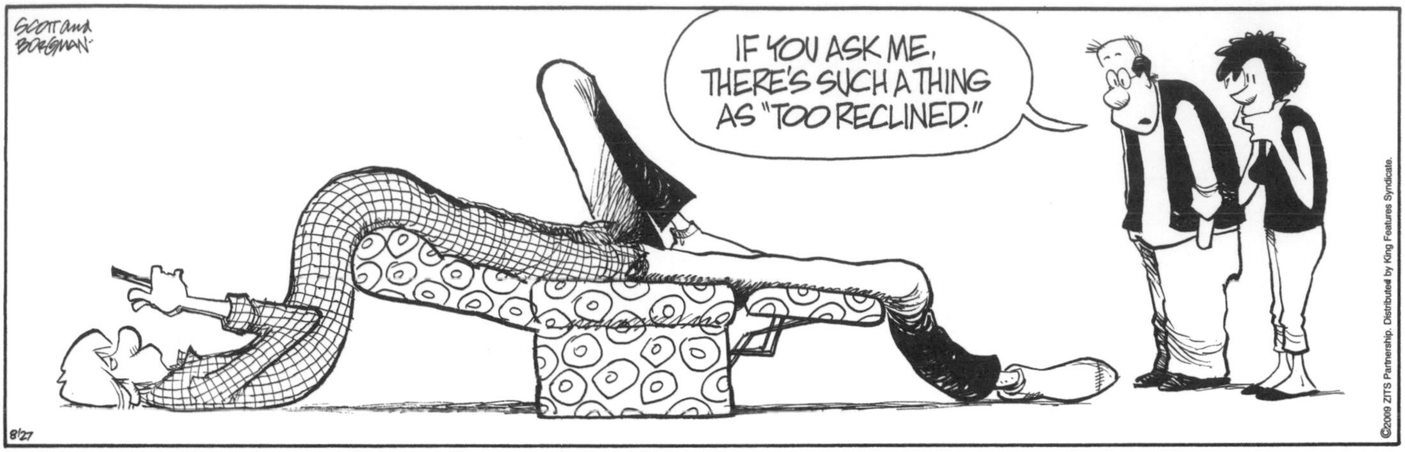
SCOTT and BORGMAN
IF YOU ASK ME, THERE'S SUCH A THING AS "TOO RECLINED."
8/27
©2009 ZITS Partnership. Distributed by King Features Syndicate.

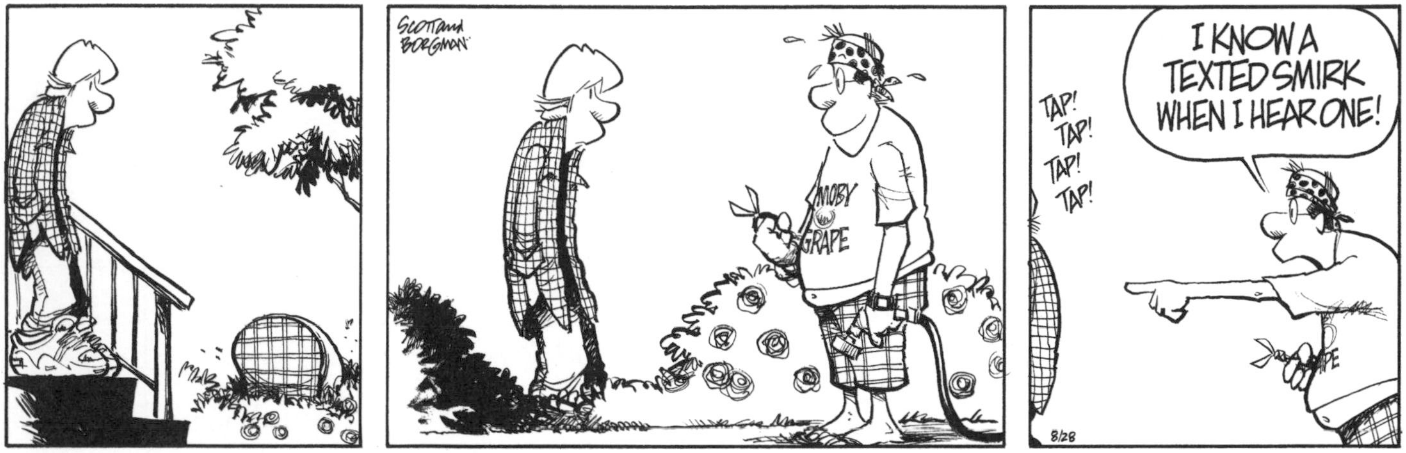
SCOTT and BORGMAN
MOBY GRAPE
TAP! TAP! TAP! TAP!
I KNOW A TEXTED SMIRK WHEN I HEAR ONE!
8/28

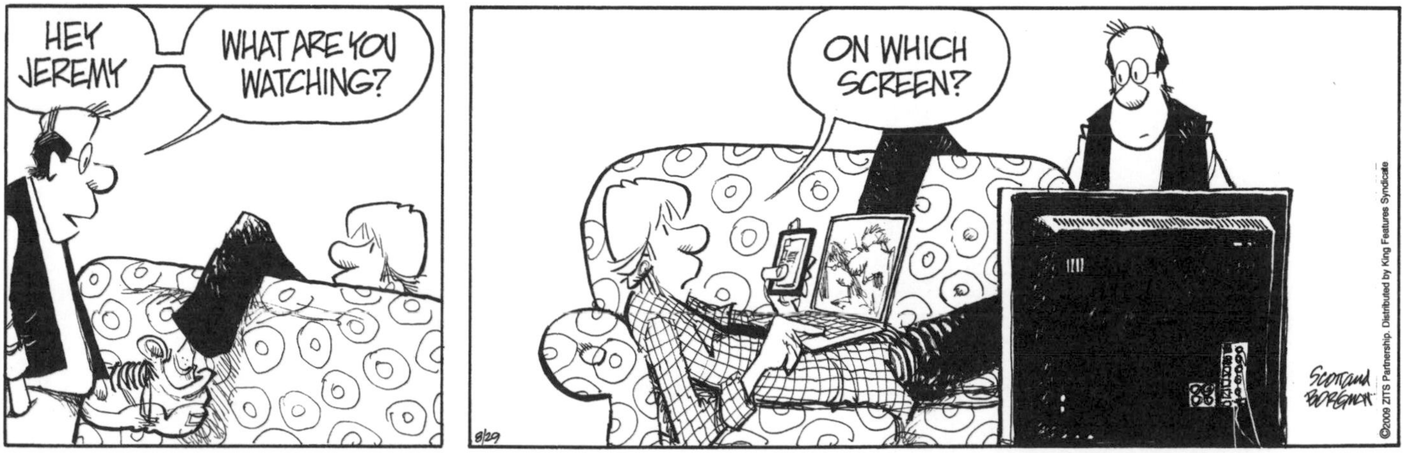
HEY JEREMY
WHAT ARE YOU WATCHING?
ON WHICH SCREEN?
8/29
SCOTT and BORGMAN
©2009 ZITS Partnership. Distributed by King Features Syndicate

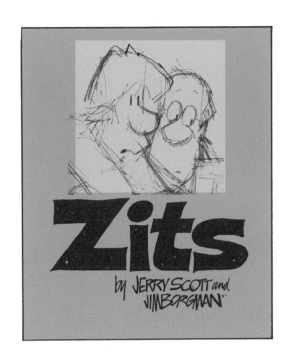

Zits
by Jerry Scott and Jim Borgman

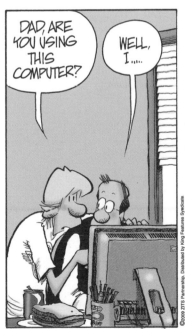

DAD, ARE YOU USING THIS COMPUTER?
WELL, I.....
'CUZ MOM IS ON HER LAPTOP AND I LEFT MINE AT HECTOR'S HOUSE.
I'M RIGHT IN THE MIDDLE OF BALANCING THE CHEC--
SCOTT and BORGMAN
©2009 ZITS Partnership. Distributed by King Features Syndicate.
I JUST NEED IT FOR A SECOND TO CHECK THE MOVIE SCHEDULES-OH!-AND I SAW THIS HILARIOUS VIDEO THAT PIERCE TOLD ME ABOUT, SO I SHOULD POST A THANKS ON HIS FACEBOOK TO, YOU KNOW... BE POLITE, AND--
--ARE YOU DRINKING THIS COKE?

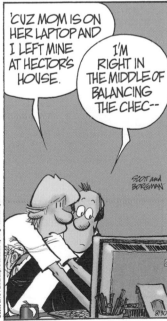

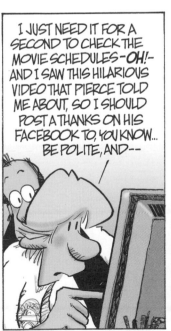

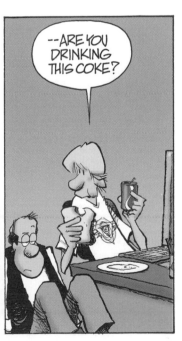

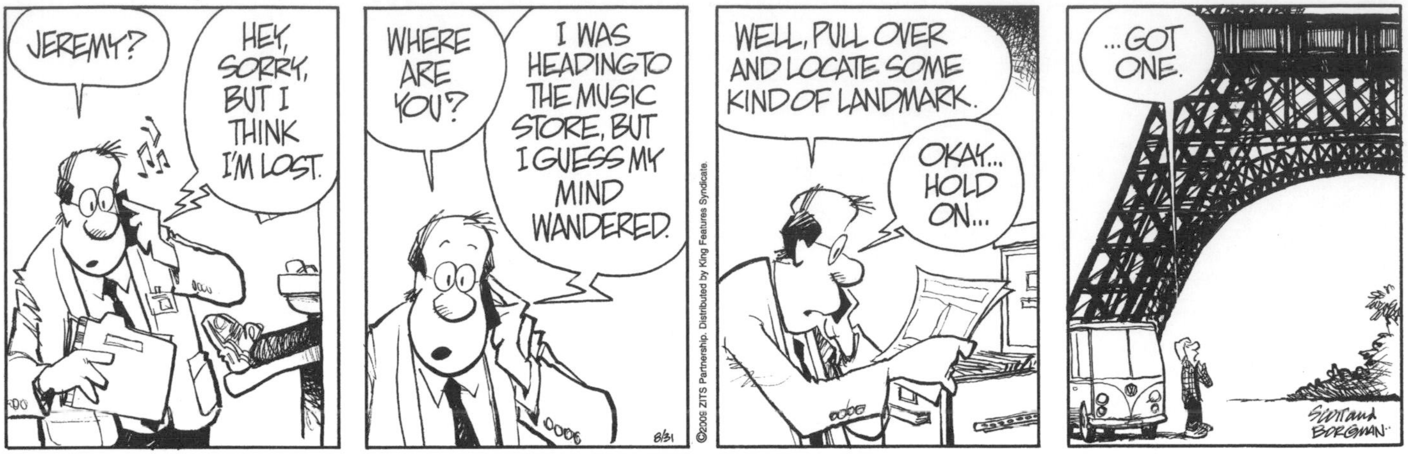
JEREMY?
HEY, SORRY, BUT I THINK I'M LOST.
WHERE ARE YOU?
I WAS HEADING TO THE MUSIC STORE, BUT I GUESS MY MIND WANDERED.
8/31
WELL, PULL OVER AND LOCATE SOME KIND OF LANDMARK.
OKAY... HOLD ON...
...GOT ONE.
SCOTT and BORGMAN

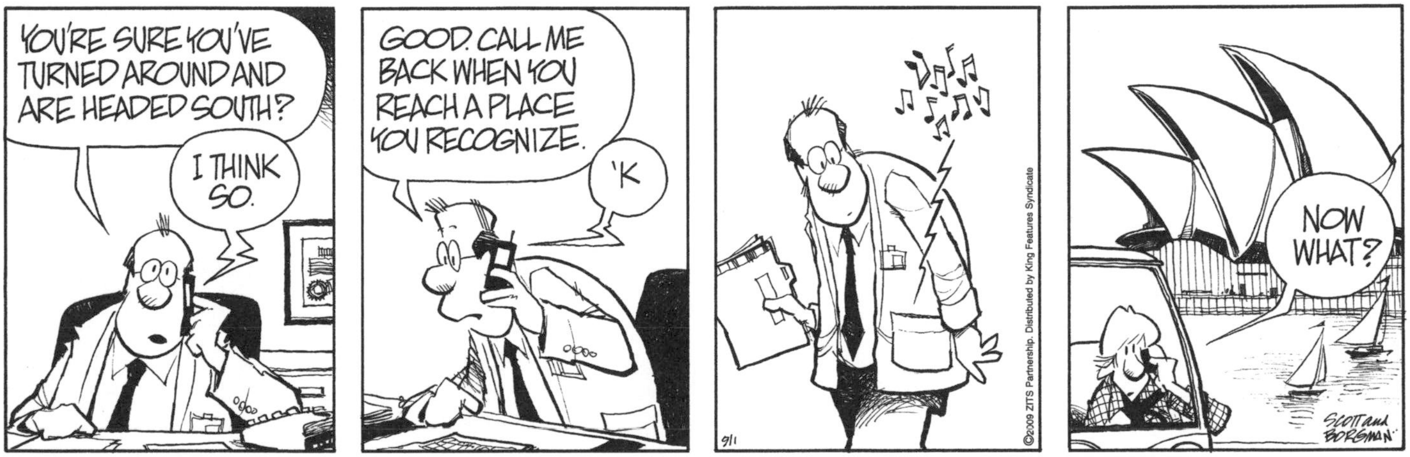
YOU'RE SURE YOU'VE TURNED AROUND AND ARE HEADED SOUTH?
I THINK SO.
GOOD. CALL ME BACK WHEN YOU REACH A PLACE YOU RECOGNIZE.
'K
9/1
NOW WHAT?
SCOTT and BORGMAN

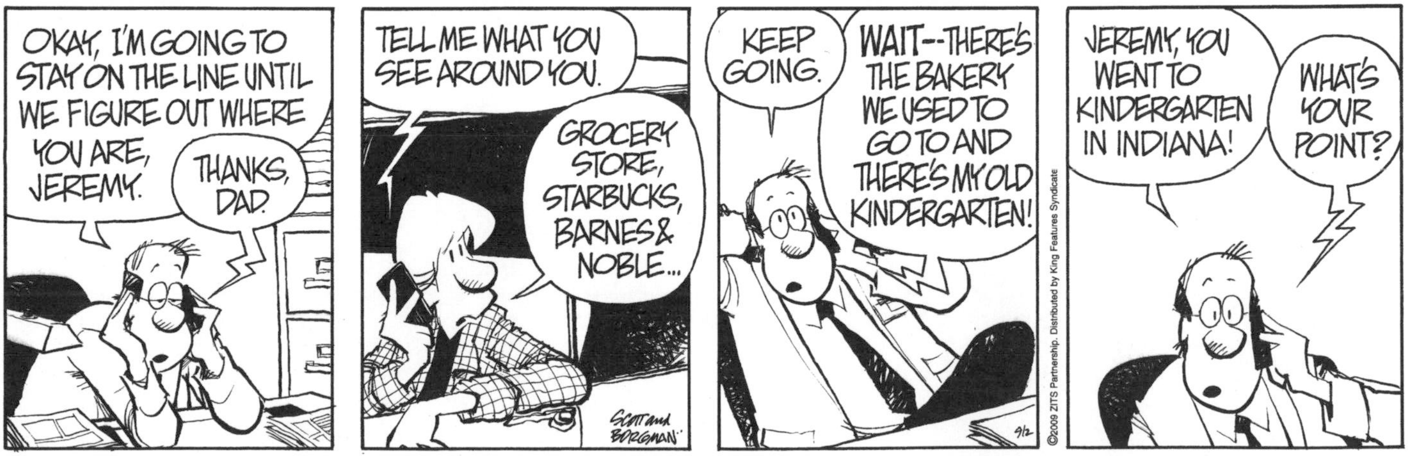
OKAY, I'M GOING TO STAY ON THE LINE UNTIL WE FIGURE OUT WHERE YOU ARE, JEREMY.
THANKS, DAD.
TELL ME WHAT YOU SEE AROUND YOU.
GROCERY STORE, STARBUCKS, BARNES & NOBLE...
SCOTT and BORGMAN
KEEP GOING.
WAIT--THERE'S THE BAKERY WE USED TO GO TO AND THERE'S MY OLD KINDERGARTEN!
9/2
JEREMY, YOU WENT TO KINDERGARTEN IN INDIANA!
WHAT'S YOUR POINT?

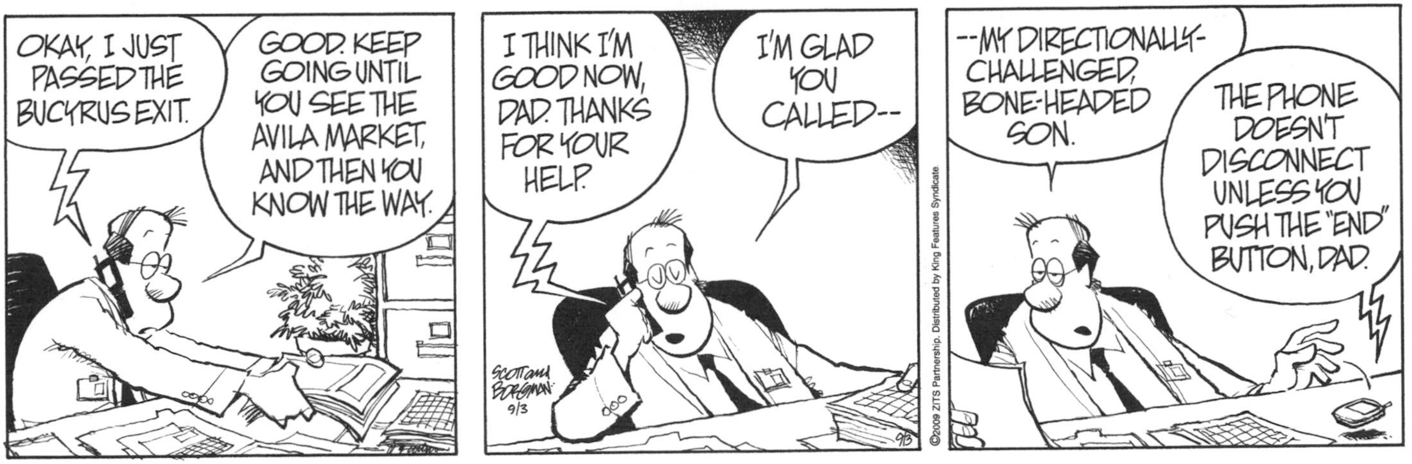
OKAY, I JUST PASSED THE BUCYRUS EXIT.
GOOD. KEEP GOING UNTIL YOU SEE THE AVILA MARKET, AND THEN YOU KNOW THE WAY.
I THINK I'M GOOD NOW, DAD. THANKS FOR YOUR HELP.
I'M GLAD YOU CALLED--
--MY DIRECTIONALLY-CHALLENGED, BONE-HEADED SON.
THE PHONE DOESN'T DISCONNECT UNLESS YOU PUSH THE "END" BUTTON, DAD.
SCOTT and BORGMAN 9/3
©2009 ZITS Partnership. Distributed by King Features Syndicate.

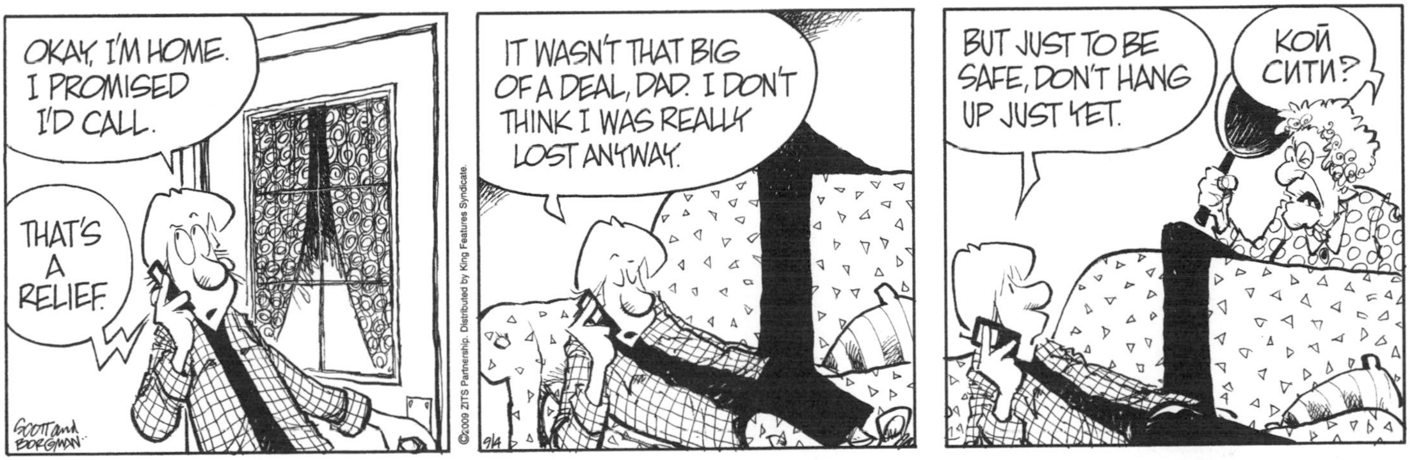
OKAY, I'M HOME. I PROMISED I'D CALL.
THAT'S A RELIEF.
SCOTT and BORGMAN
©2009 ZITS Partnership. Distributed by King Features Syndicate.
IT WASN'T THAT BIG OF A DEAL, DAD. I DON'T THINK I WAS REALLY LOST ANYWAY.
BUT JUST TO BE SAFE, DON'T HANG UP JUST YET.
КОЙ СИТИ?

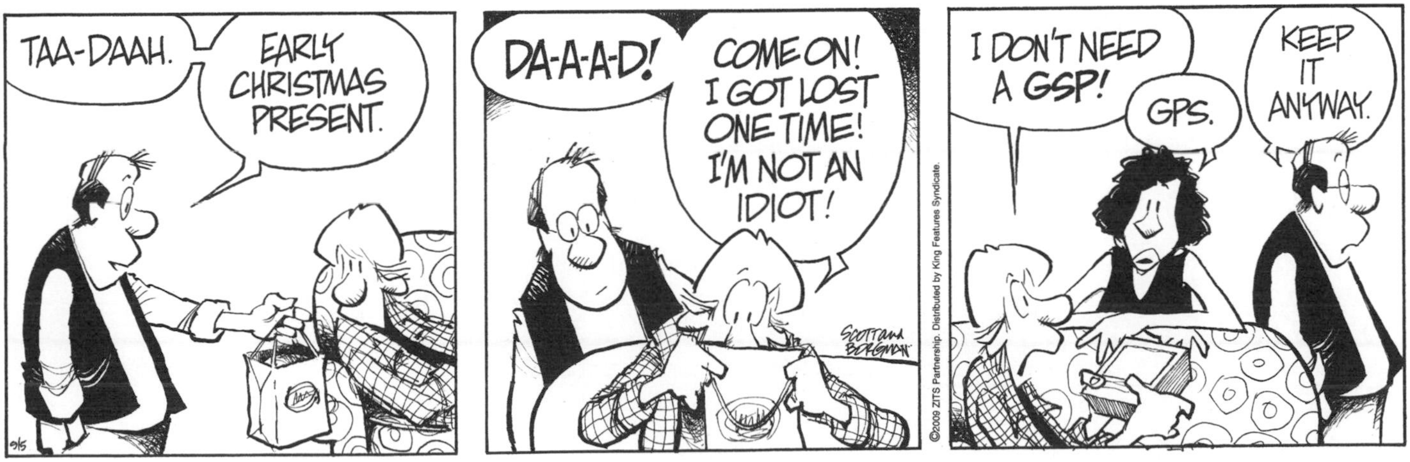
TAA-DAAH.
EARLY CHRISTMAS PRESENT.
DA-A-A-D!
COME ON! I GOT LOST ONE TIME! I'M NOT AN IDIOT!
SCOTT and BORGMAN
I DON'T NEED A GSP!
GPS.
KEEP IT ANYWAY.
©2009 ZITS Partnership. Distributed by King Features Syndicate.

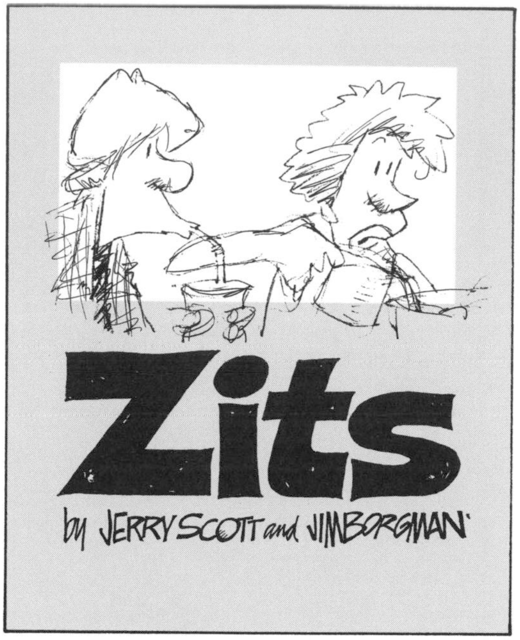
Zits
by JERRY SCOTT and JIM BORGMAN

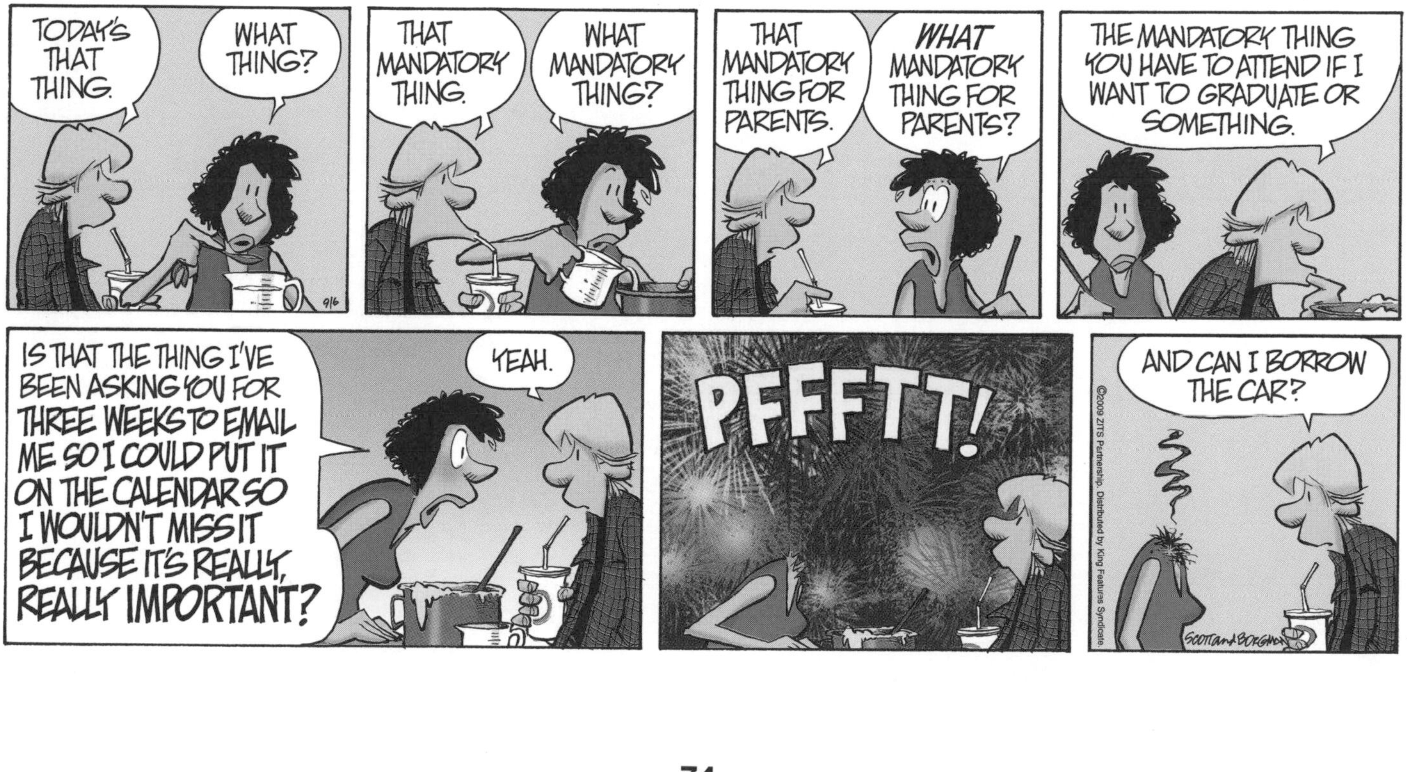
TODAY'S THAT THING.
WHAT THING?
9/6
THAT MANDATORY THING.
WHAT MANDATORY THING?
THAT MANDATORY THING FOR PARENTS.
WHAT MANDATORY THING FOR PARENTS?
THE MANDATORY THING YOU HAVE TO ATTEND IF I WANT TO GRADUATE OR SOMETHING.
IS THAT THE THING I'VE BEEN ASKING YOU FOR THREE WEEKS TO EMAIL ME SO I COULD PUT IT ON THE CALENDAR SO I WOULDN'T MISS IT BECAUSE IT'S REALLY, REALLY IMPORTANT?
YEAH.
PFFFTT!
©2008 ZITS Partnership. Distributed by King Features Syndicate.
AND CAN I BORROW THE CAR?
SCOTT and BORGMAN

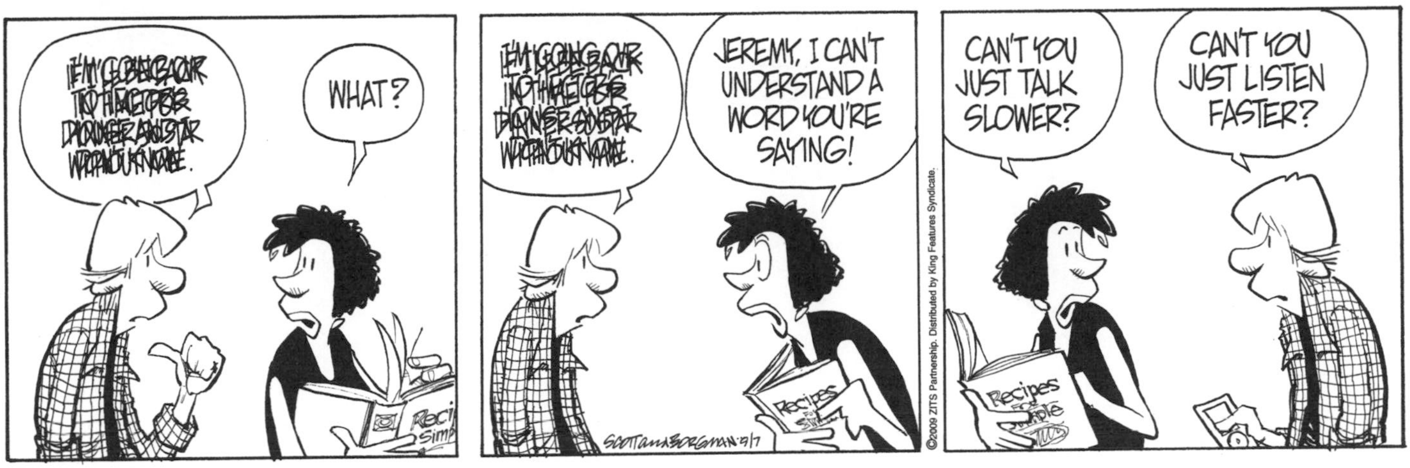
WHAT?
JEREMY, I CAN'T UNDERSTAND A WORD YOU'RE SAYING!
SCOTT and BORGMAN 9/7
©2009 ZITS Partnership. Distributed by King Features Syndicate.
CAN'T YOU JUST TALK SLOWER?
CAN'T YOU JUST LISTEN FASTER?

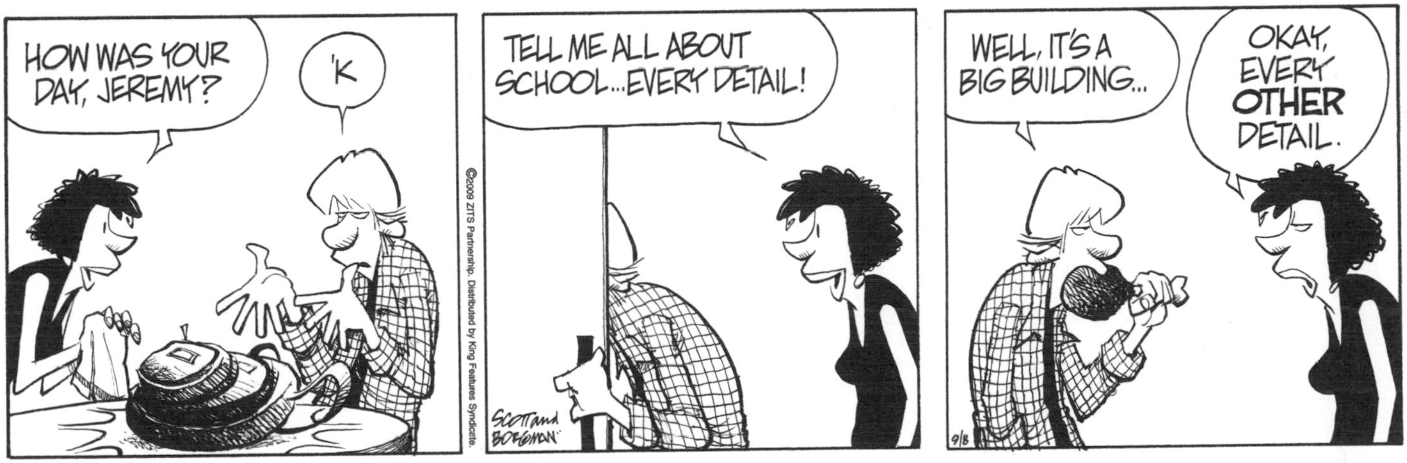
HOW WAS YOUR DAY, JEREMY?
'K
©2009 ZITS Partnership. Distributed by King Features Syndicate.
TELL ME ALL ABOUT SCHOOL...EVERY DETAIL!
SCOTT and BORGMAN
WELL, IT'S A BIG BUILDING...
OKAY, EVERY **OTHER** DETAIL.
9/8

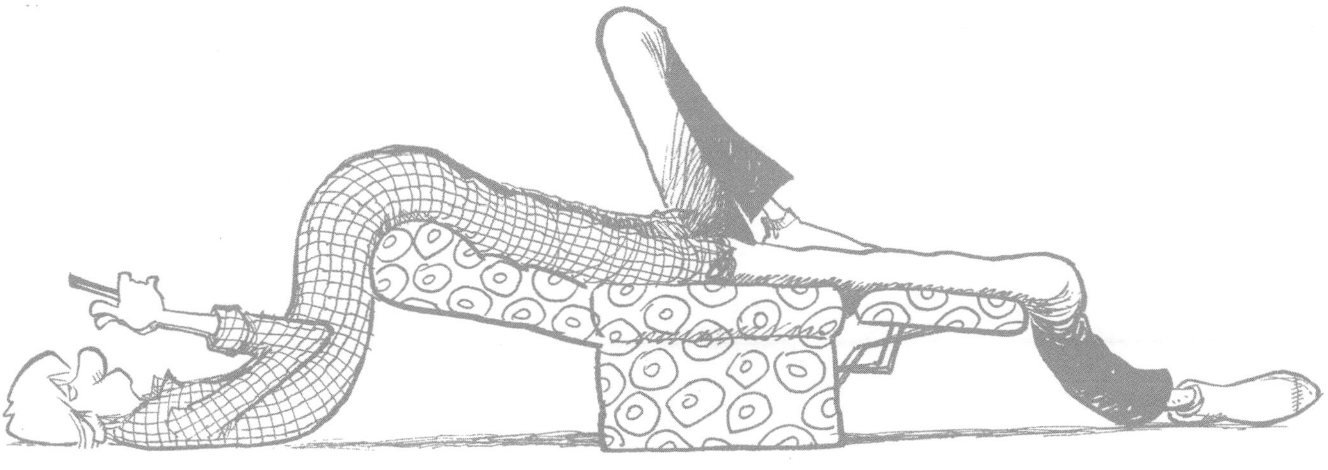

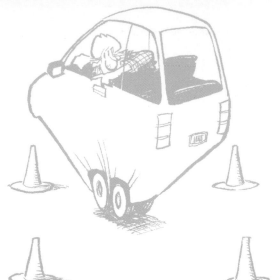

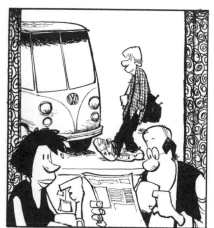

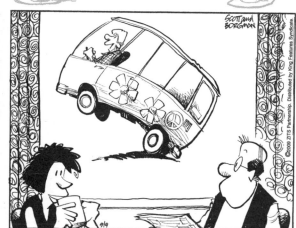

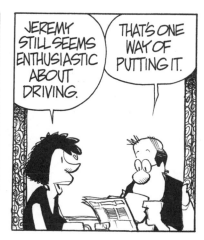

SCOTT and BORGMAN
©2009 ZITS Partnership. Distributed by King Features Syndicate.
9/9
JEREMY STILL SEEMS ENTHUSIASTIC ABOUT DRIVING.
THAT'S ONE WAY OF PUTTING IT.

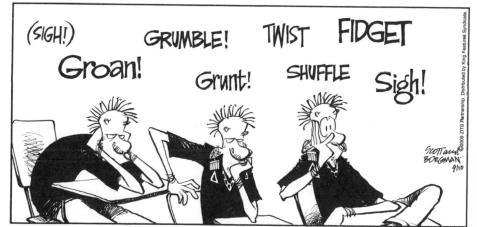

(SIGH!)
GRUMBLE!
TWIST
FIDGET
Groan!
Grunt!
SHUFFLE
Sigh!
©2009 ZITS Partnership. Distributed by King Features Syndicate.
SCOTT and BORGMAN
9/10
IS IT JUST ME, OR IS IT ACADEMIC IN HERE?
SUMMER STAYS WITH YOU LONGER THAN IT DOES MOST PEOPLE, DOESN'T IT?

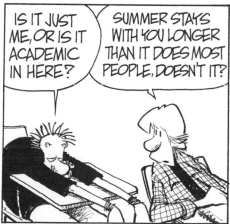

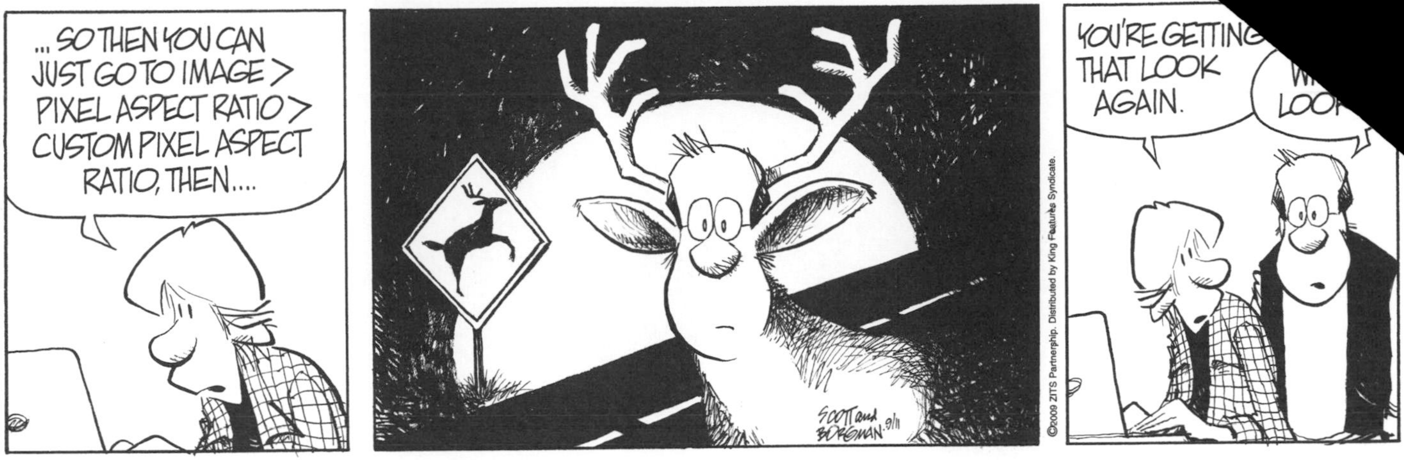

... SO THEN YOU CAN JUST GO TO IMAGE > PIXEL ASPECT RATIO > CUSTOM PIXEL ASPECT RATIO, THEN....
SCOTT and BORGMAN 9/11
©2009 ZITS Partnership. Distributed by King Features Syndicate.
YOU'RE GETTING THAT LOOK AGAIN.

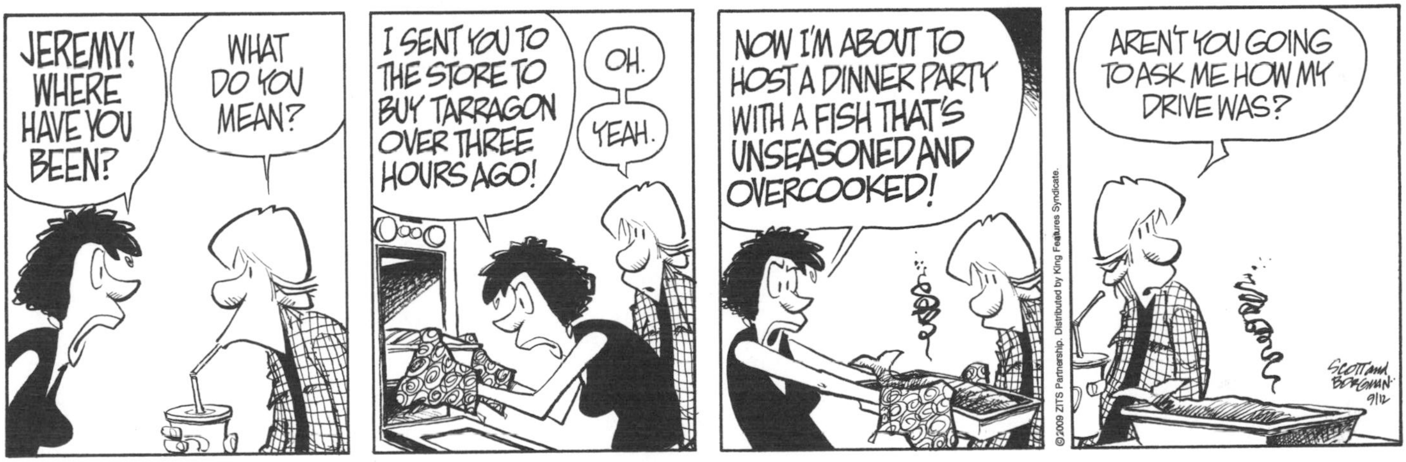

JEREMY! WHERE HAVE YOU BEEN?
WHAT DO YOU MEAN?
I SENT YOU TO THE STORE TO BUY TARRAGON OVER THREE HOURS AGO!
OH.
YEAH.
NOW I'M ABOUT TO HOST A DINNER PARTY WITH A FISH THAT'S UNSEASONED AND OVERCOOKED!
©2009 ZITS Partnership. Distributed by King Features Syndicate.
AREN'T YOU GOING TO ASK ME HOW MY DRIVE WAS?
SCOTT and BORGMAN 9/12

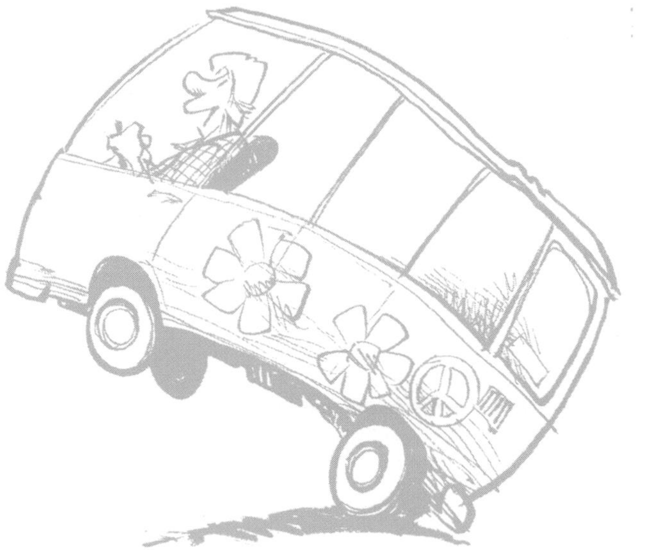

Zits
by JERRY SCOTT and JIM BORGMAN

SCOTT and BORGMAN
©2009 ZITS Partnership. Distributed by King Features Syndicate.
YOU'RE SICK?? IS SOMETHING GOING AROUND AT SCHOOL?
YOU MIGHT SAY THAT.

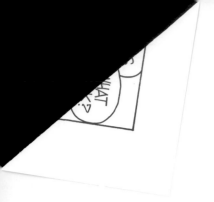

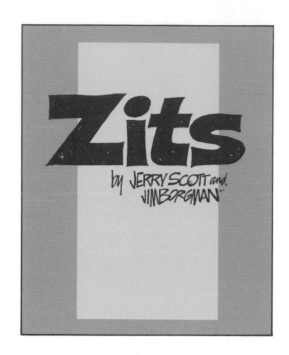

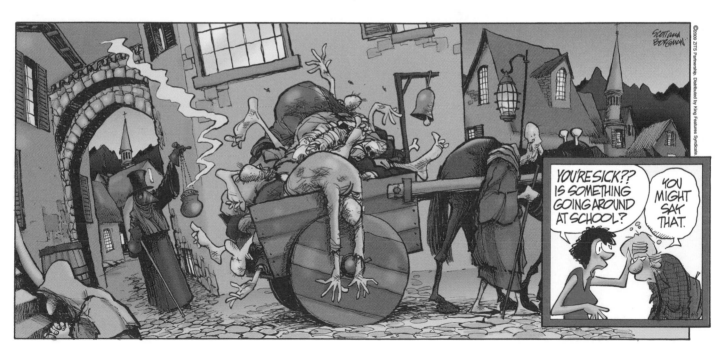

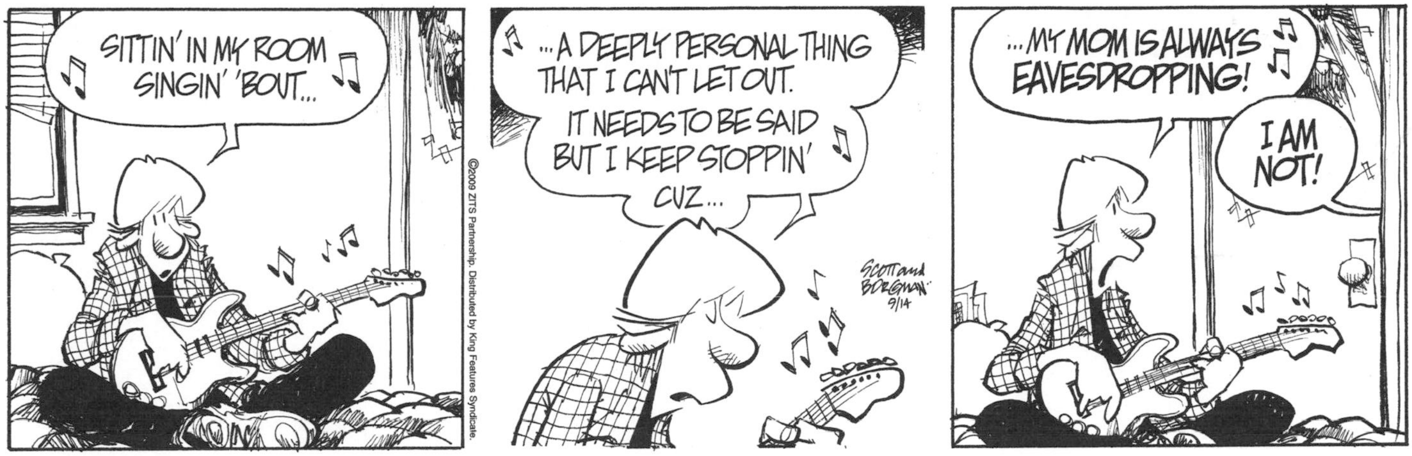
SITTIN' IN MY ROOM SINGIN' 'BOUT...
...A DEEPLY PERSONAL THING THAT I CAN'T LET OUT.
IT NEEDS TO BE SAID BUT I KEEP STOPPIN' CUZ...
©2009 ZITS Partnership. Distributed by King Features Syndicate.
SCOTT and BORGMAN 9/14
...MY MOM IS ALWAYS EAVESDROPPING!
I AM NOT!

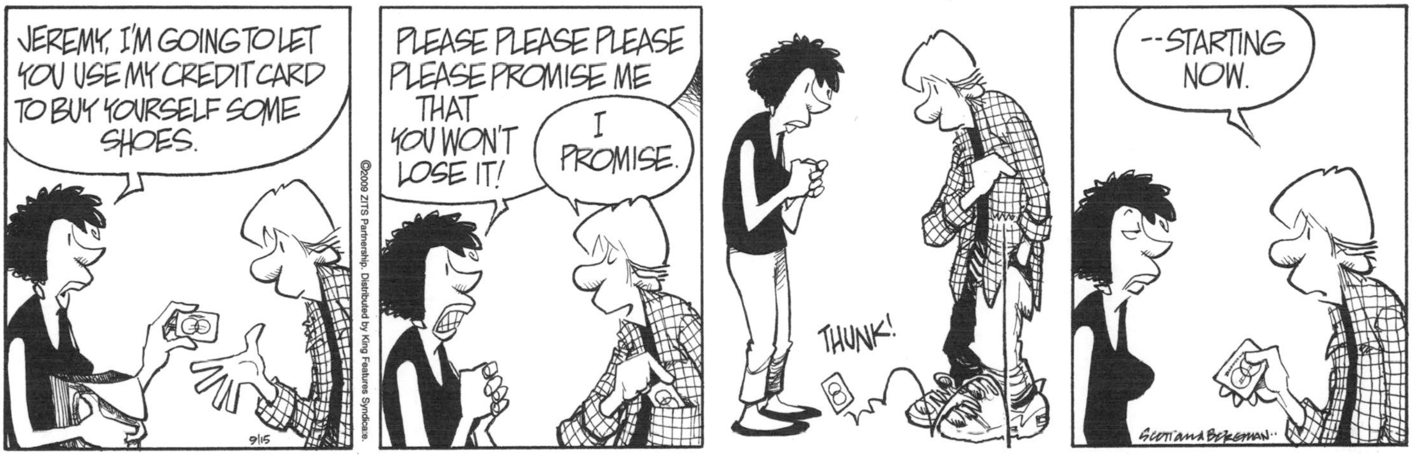
JEREMY, I'M GOING TO LET YOU USE MY CREDIT CARD TO BUY YOURSELF SOME SHOES.
9/15
©2009 ZITS Partnership. Distributed by King Features Syndicate.
PLEASE PLEASE PLEASE PLEASE PROMISE ME THAT YOU WON'T LOSE IT!
I PROMISE.
THUNK!
--STARTING NOW.
SCOTT and BORGMAN

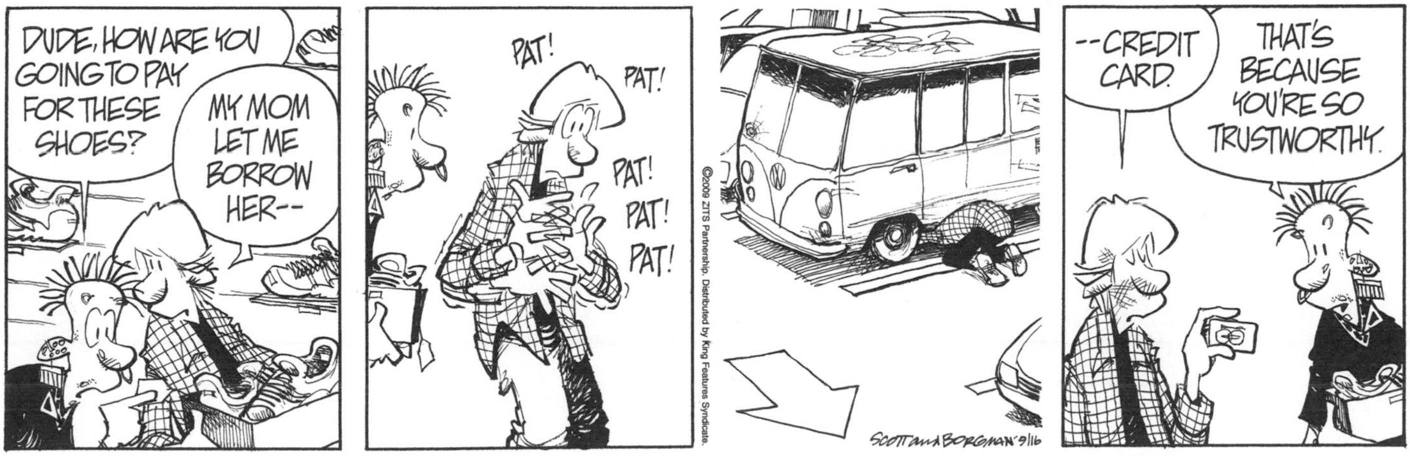
DUDE, HOW ARE YOU GOING TO PAY FOR THESE SHOES?
MY MOM LET ME BORROW HER--
PAT!
PAT!
PAT!
PAT!
PAT!
©2009 ZITS Partnership. Distributed by King Features Syndicate.
SCOTT and BORGMAN 9/16
--CREDIT CARD.
THAT'S BECAUSE YOU'RE SO TRUSTWORTHY.

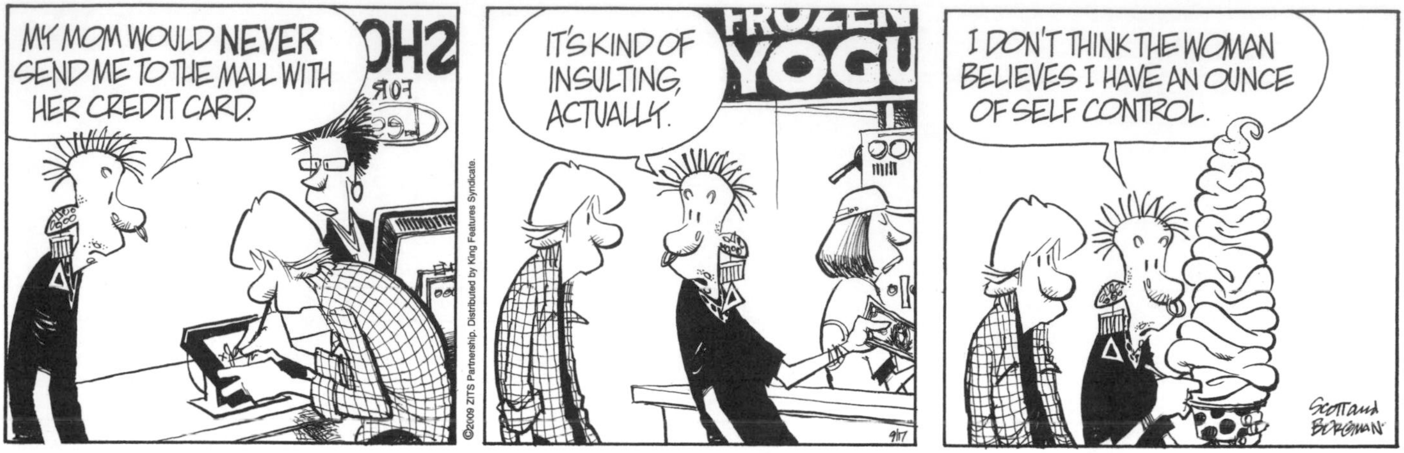
MY MOM WOULD NEVER SEND ME TO THE MALL WITH HER CREDIT CARD.
IT'S KIND OF INSULTING, ACTUALLY.
I DON'T THINK THE WOMAN BELIEVES I HAVE AN OUNCE OF SELF CONTROL.
FROZEN YOGU
©2009 ZITS Partnership. Distributed by King Features Syndicate.
SCOTT and BORGMAN

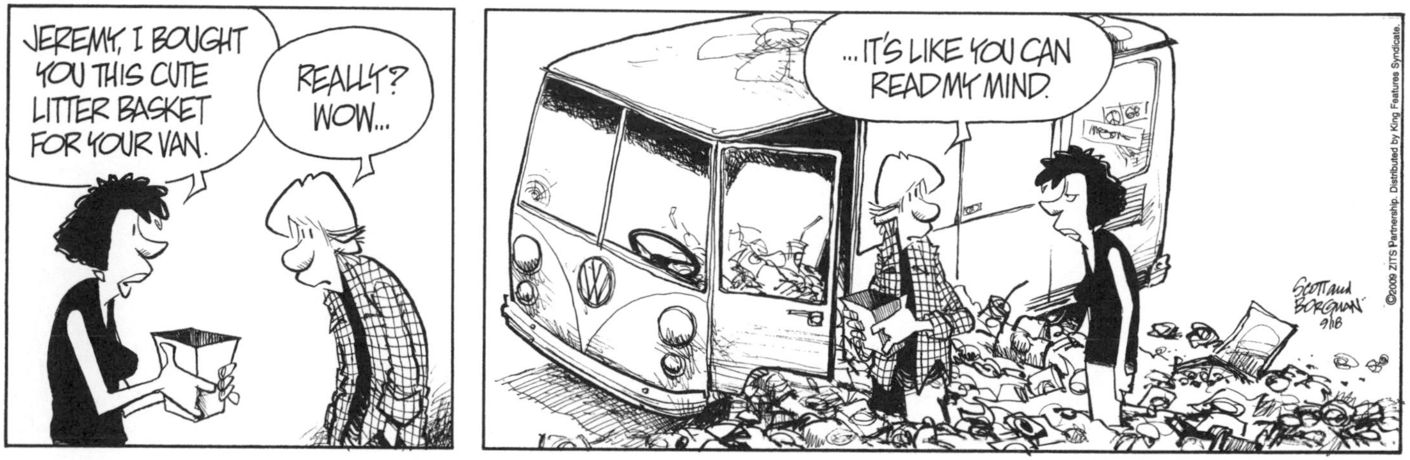
JEREMY, I BOUGHT YOU THIS CUTE LITTER BASKET FOR YOUR VAN.
REALLY? WOW...
...IT'S LIKE YOU CAN READ MY MIND.
©2009 ZITS Partnership. Distributed by King Features Syndicate.
SCOTT and BORGMAN

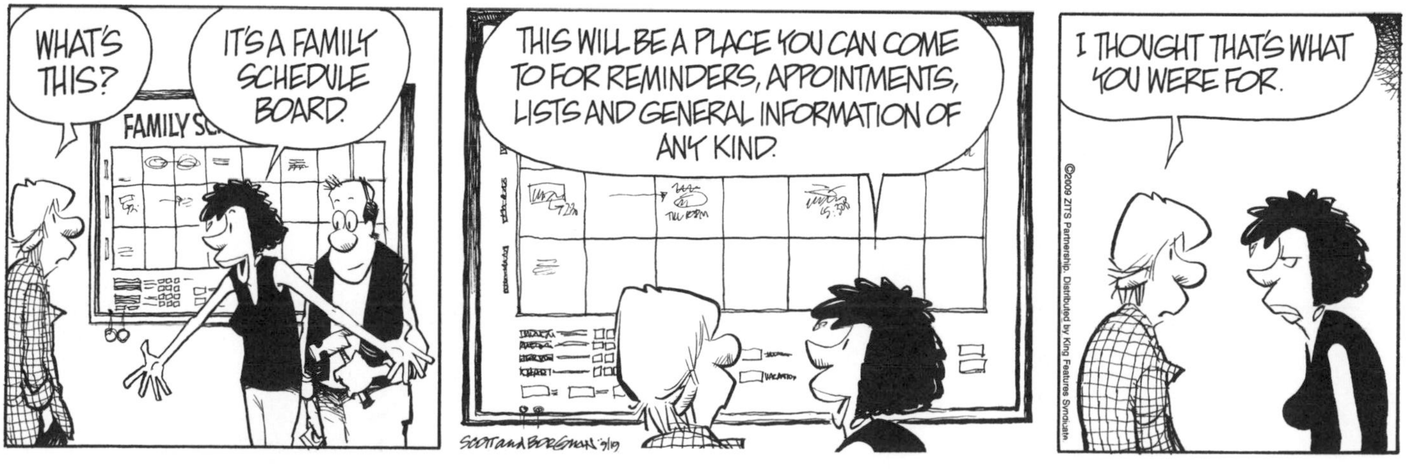
WHAT'S THIS?
IT'S A FAMILY SCHEDULE BOARD.
FAMILY SC
THIS WILL BE A PLACE YOU CAN COME TO FOR REMINDERS, APPOINTMENTS, LISTS AND GENERAL INFORMATION OF ANY KIND.
I THOUGHT THAT'S WHAT YOU WERE FOR.
©2009 ZITS Partnership. Distributed by King Features Syndicate.
SCOTT and BORGMAN

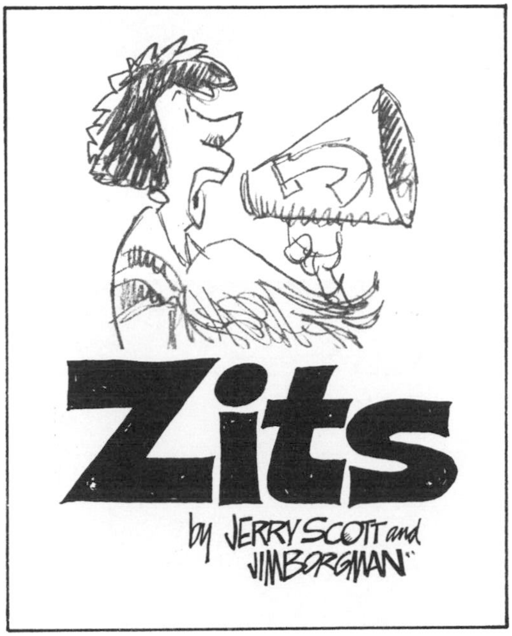
Zits
by JERRY SCOTT and JIM BORGMAN

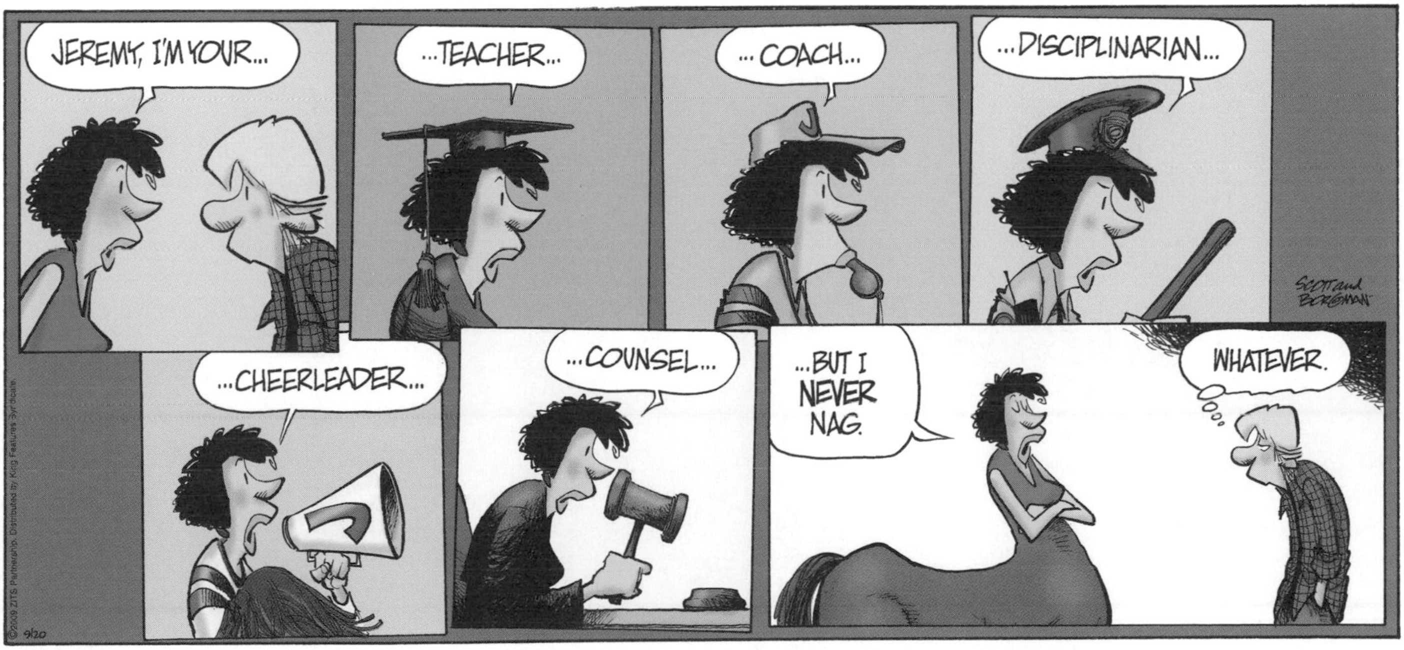
JEREMY, I'M YOUR...
...TEACHER...
... COACH...
...DISCIPLINARIAN...
SCOTT and BORGMAN
...CHEERLEADER...
...COUNSEL...
...BUT I NEVER NAG.
WHATEVER.
©2009 ZITS Partnership. Distributed by King Features Syndicate.

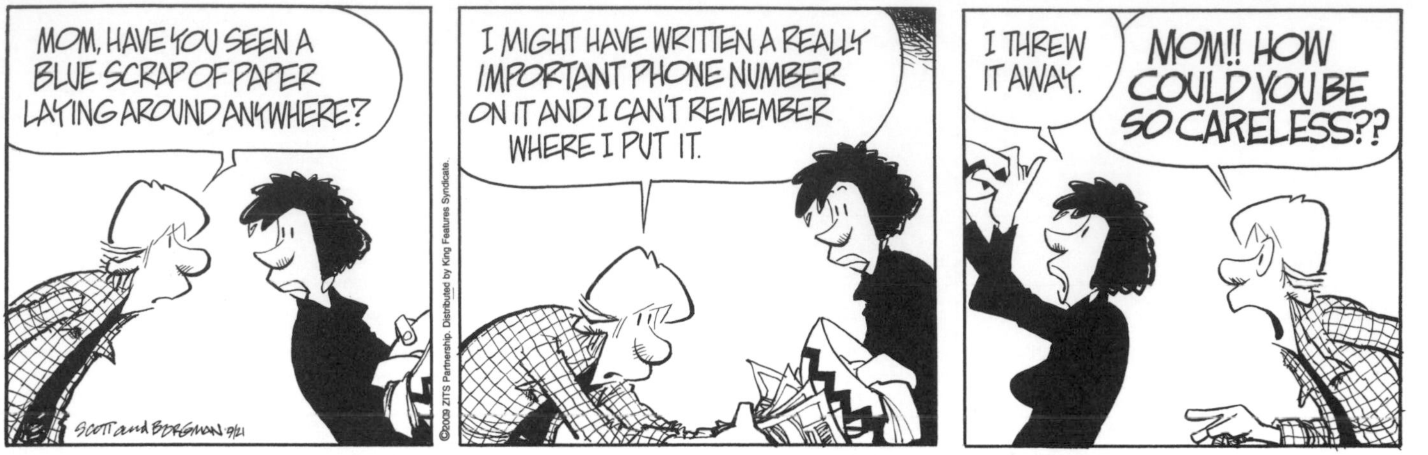
MOM, HAVE YOU SEEN A BLUE SCRAP OF PAPER LAYING AROUND ANYWHERE?
SCOTT and BORGMAN 9/21
©2009 ZITS Partnership. Distributed by King Features Syndicate.
I MIGHT HAVE WRITTEN A REALLY IMPORTANT PHONE NUMBER ON IT AND I CAN'T REMEMBER WHERE I PUT IT.
I THREW IT AWAY.
MOM!! HOW COULD YOU BE SO CARELESS??

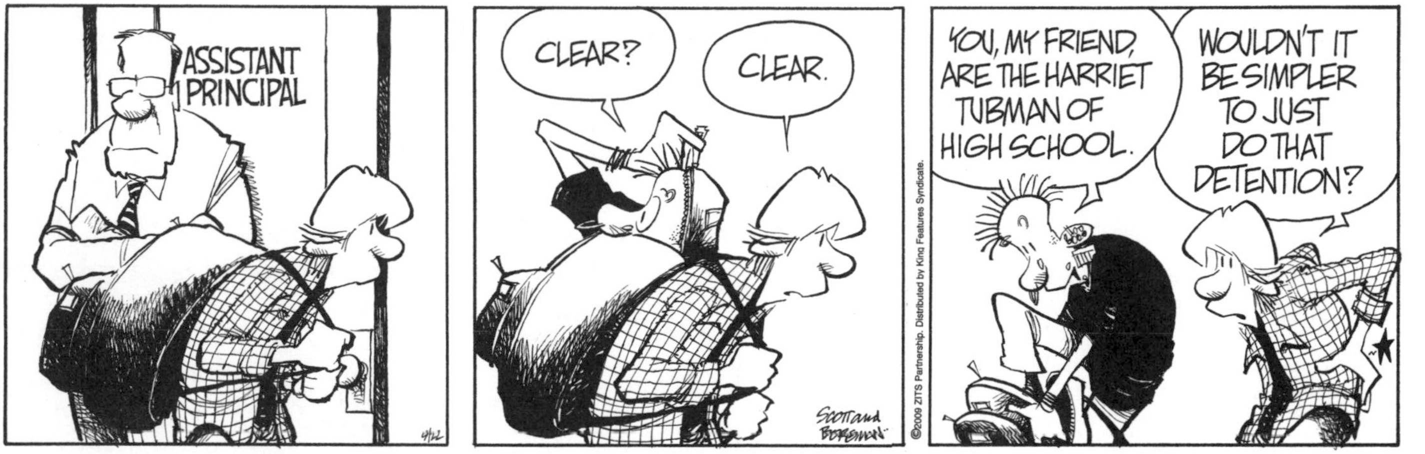
ASSISTANT PRINCIPAL
9/22
CLEAR?
CLEAR.
SCOTT and BORGMAN
©2009 ZITS Partnership. Distributed by King Features Syndicate.
YOU, MY FRIEND, ARE THE HARRIET TUBMAN OF HIGH SCHOOL.
WOULDN'T IT BE SIMPLER TO JUST DO THAT DETENTION?

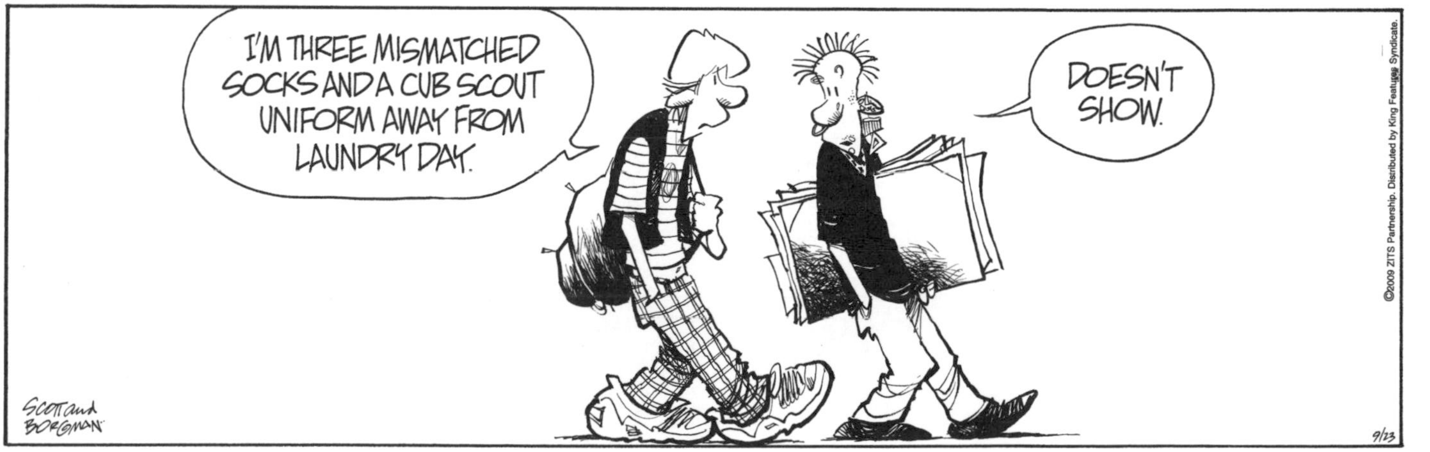
I'M THREE MISMATCHED SOCKS AND A CUB SCOUT UNIFORM AWAY FROM LAUNDRY DAY.
DOESN'T SHOW.
SCOTT and BORGMAN
9/23
©2009 ZITS Partnership. Distributed by King Features Syndicate.

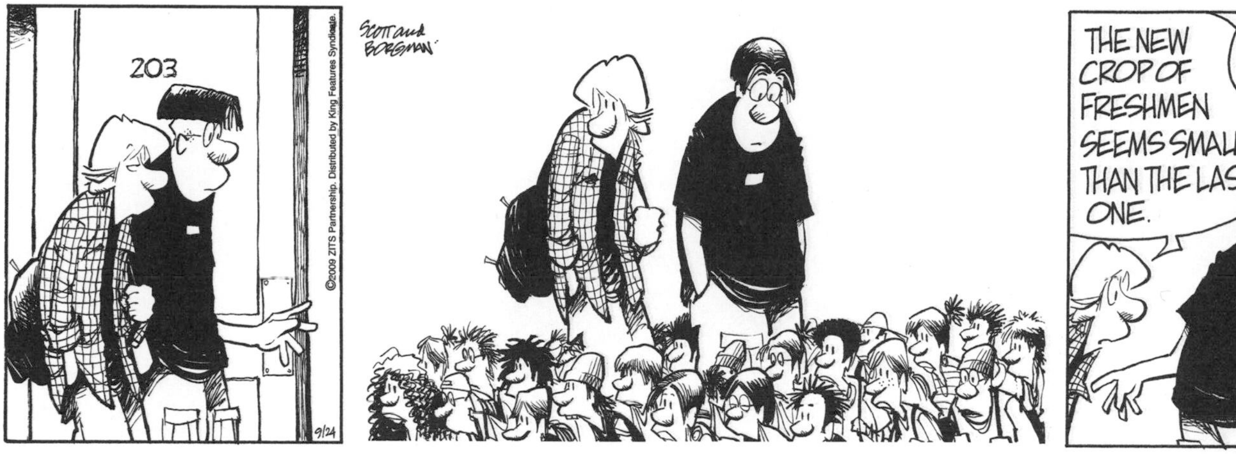
203
©2009 ZITS Partnership. Distributed by King Features Syndicate.
9/24
SCOTT and BORGMAN
THE NEW CROP OF FRESHMEN SEEMS SMALLER THAN THE LAST ONE.
AND GOOIER.

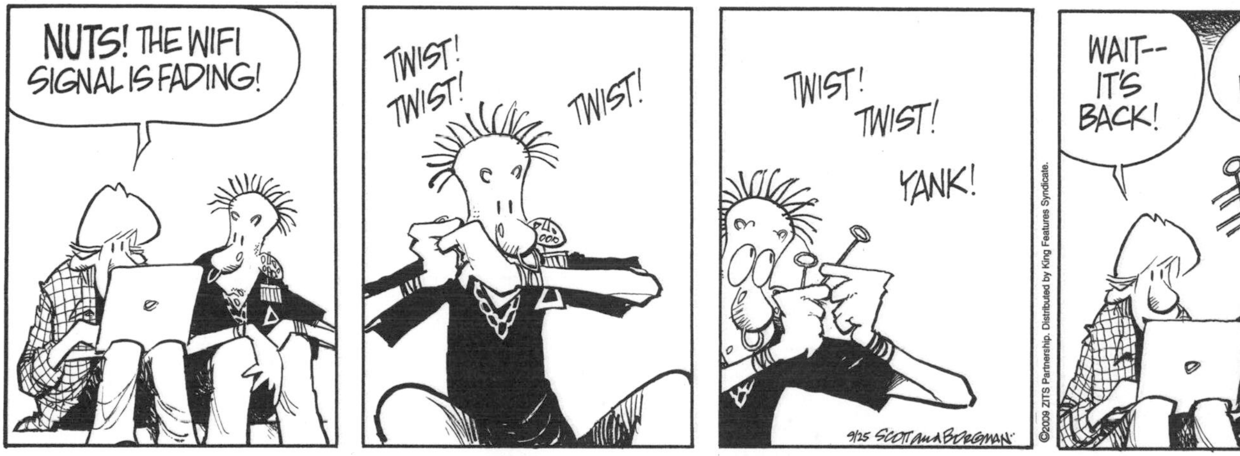
NUTS! THE WIFI SIGNAL IS FADING!
TWIST! TWIST!
TWIST!
TWIST!
TWIST!
YANK!
9/25 SCOTT and BORGMAN
©2009 ZITS Partnership. Distributed by King Features Syndicate.
WAIT-- IT'S BACK!
YOU'RE WELCOME.

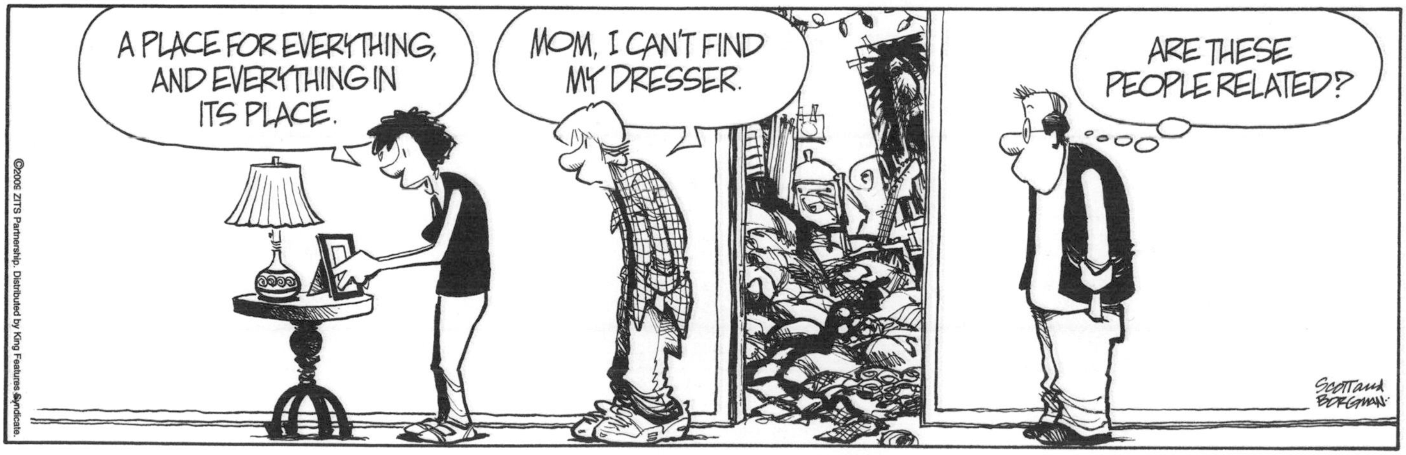
©2006 ZITS Partnership. Distributed by King Features Syndicate.
A PLACE FOR EVERYTHING, AND EVERYTHING IN ITS PLACE.
MOM, I CAN'T FIND MY DRESSER.
ARE THESE PEOPLE RELATED?
SCOTT and BORGMAN

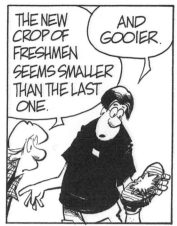

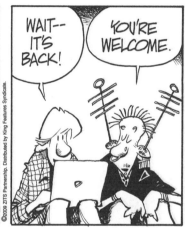

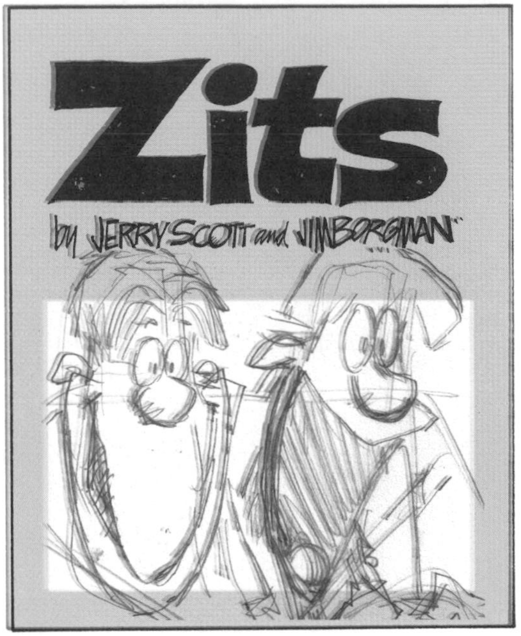
Zits
by JERRY SCOTT and JIM BORGMAN

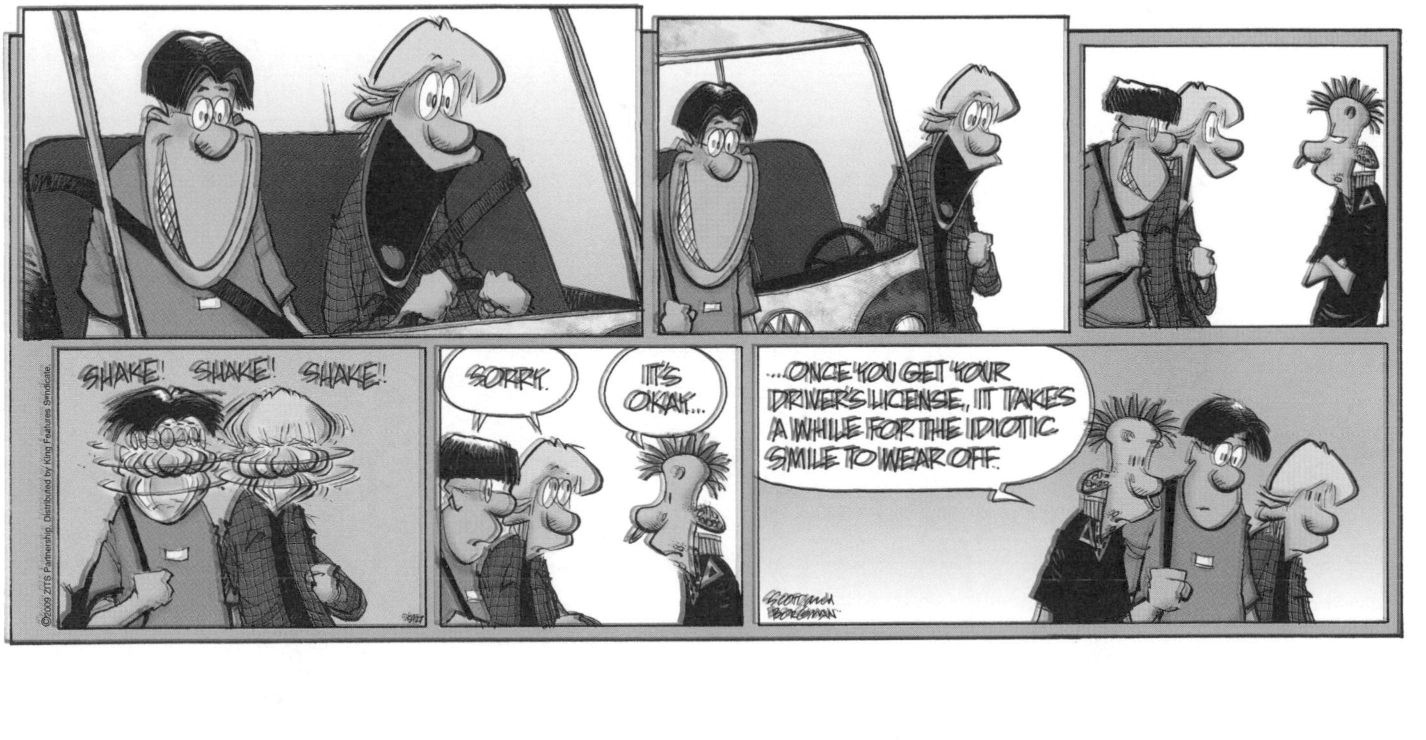
SHAKE! SHAKE! SHAKE!
SORRY.
IT'S OKAY...
...ONCE YOU GET YOUR DRIVER'S LICENSE, IT TAKES A WHILE FOR THE IDIOTIC SMILE TO WEAR OFF.
SCOTT and BORGMAN
©2009 ZITS Partnership. Distributed by King Features Syndicate.

CAN YOU TAKE ME TO THE PARK?
SCOTT and BORGMAN
CAN YOU DRIVE ME TO HECTOR'S?
9/28
CAN YOU GIVE ME A RIDE TO SCHOOL?
©2009 ZITS Partnership, Distributed by King Features Syndicate
WOULD YOU RUN TO THE STORE FOR ME?
WHAT AM I, YOUR SLAVE?

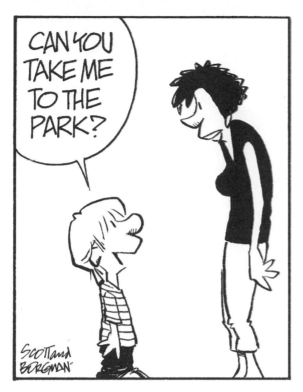

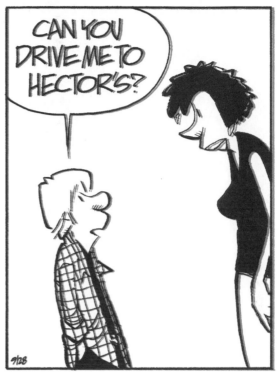

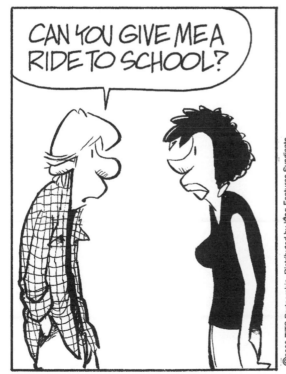

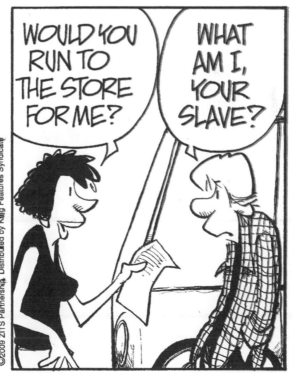

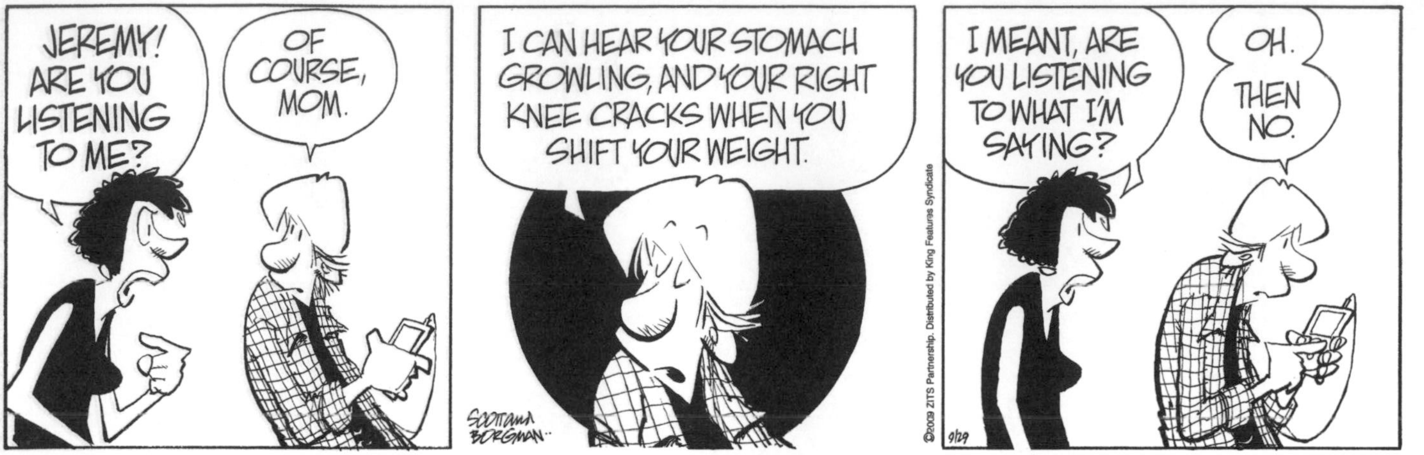

JEREMY! ARE YOU LISTENING TO ME?
OF COURSE, MOM.
I CAN HEAR YOUR STOMACH GROWLING, AND YOUR RIGHT KNEE CRACKS WHEN YOU SHIFT YOUR WEIGHT.
SCOTT and BORGMAN
©2009 ZITS Partnership. Distributed by King Features Syndicate
9/29
I MEANT, ARE YOU LISTENING TO WHAT I'M SAYING?
OH.
THEN NO.

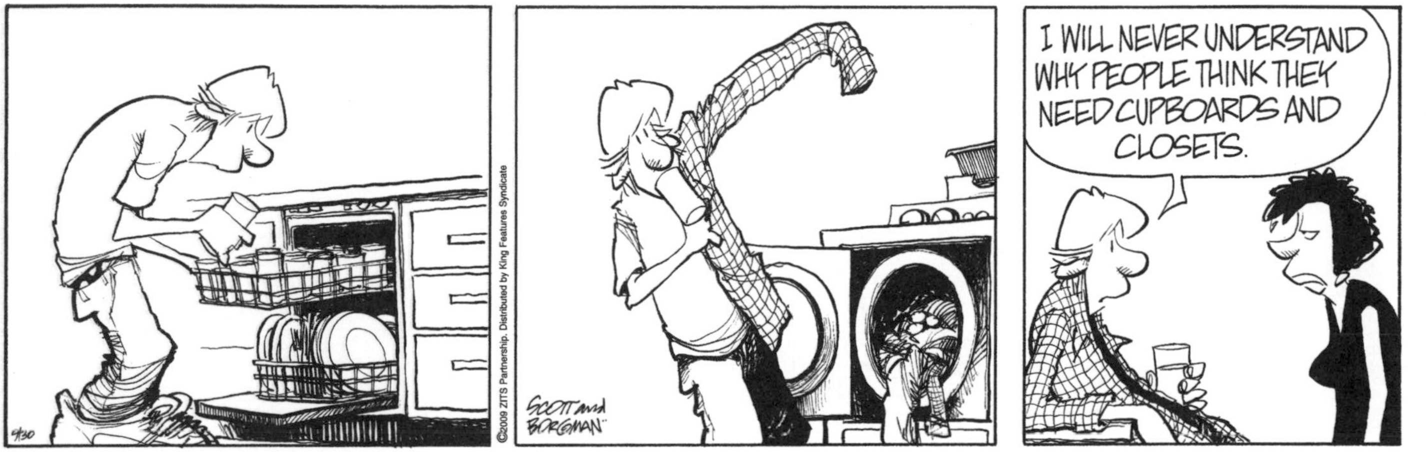

9/30
©2009 ZITS Partnership. Distributed by King Features Syndicate
SCOTT and BORGMAN
I WILL NEVER UNDERSTAND WHY PEOPLE THINK THEY NEED CUPBOARDS AND CLOSETS.

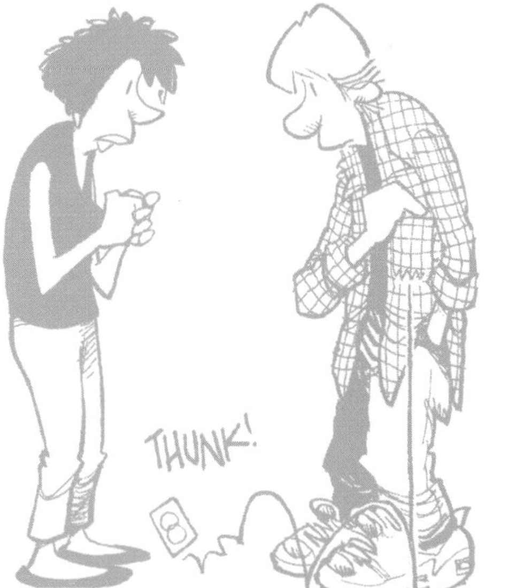

THUNK!

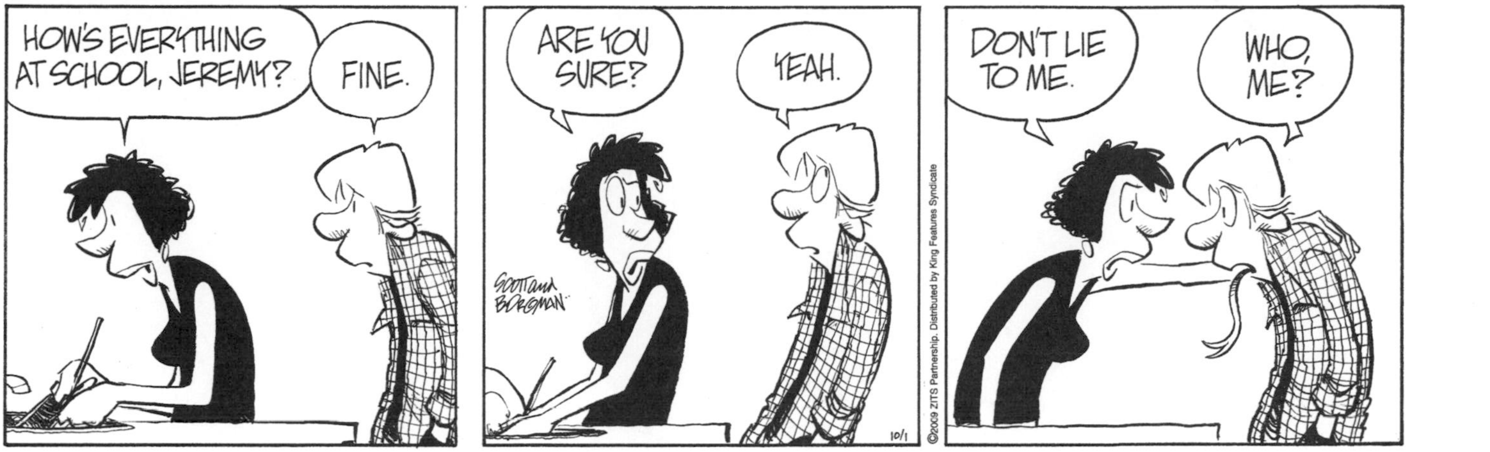
HOW'S EVERYTHING AT SCHOOL, JEREMY?
FINE.
ARE YOU SURE?
YEAH.
SCOTT and BORGMAN
10/1
DON'T LIE TO ME.
WHO, ME?
©2009 ZITS Partnership. Distributed by King Features Syndicate

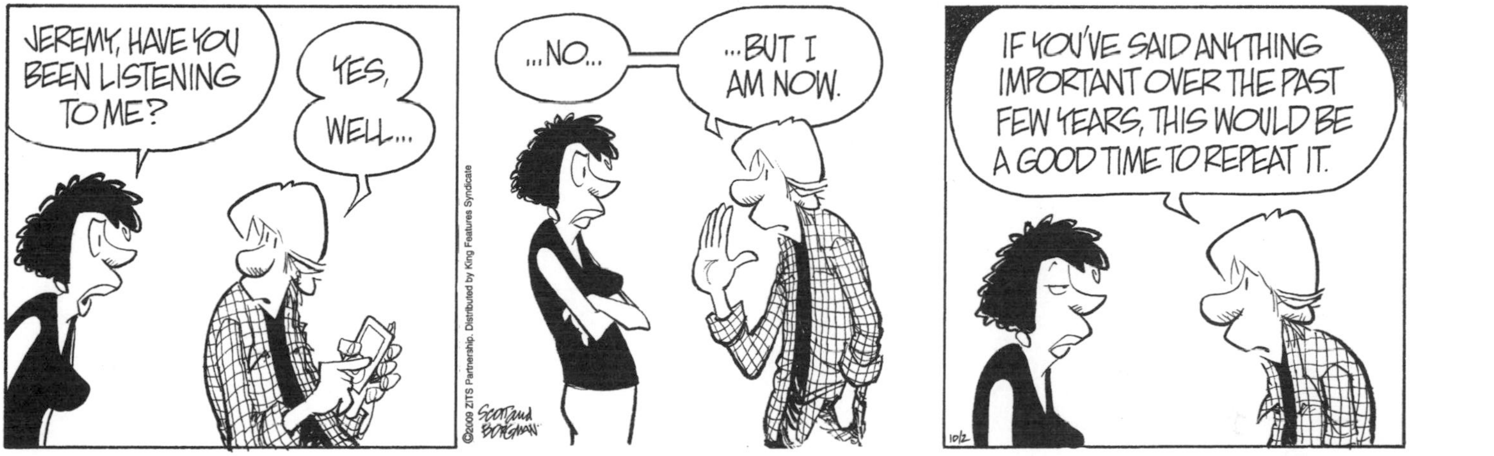
JEREMY, HAVE YOU BEEN LISTENING TO ME?
YES,
WELL...
©2009 ZITS Partnership. Distributed by King Features Syndicate
SCOTT and BORGMAN
...NO...
...BUT I AM NOW.
IF YOU'VE SAID ANYTHING IMPORTANT OVER THE PAST FEW YEARS, THIS WOULD BE A GOOD TIME TO REPEAT IT.
10/2

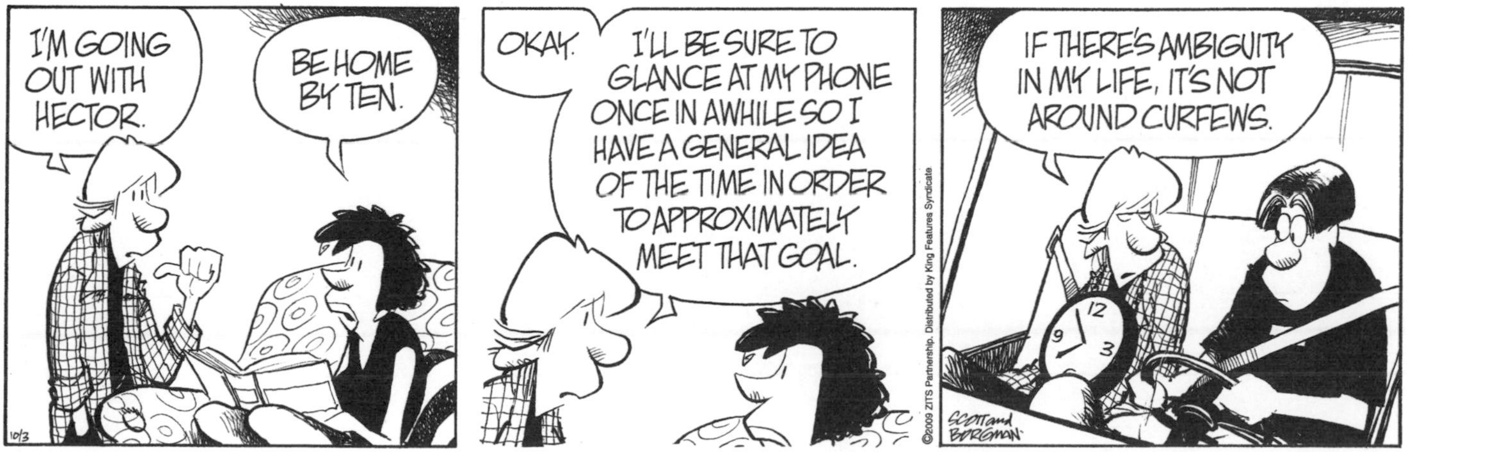
I'M GOING OUT WITH HECTOR.
BE HOME BY TEN.
10/3
OKAY.
I'LL BE SURE TO GLANCE AT MY PHONE ONCE IN AWHILE SO I HAVE A GENERAL IDEA OF THE TIME IN ORDER TO APPROXIMATELY MEET THAT GOAL.
©2009 ZITS Partnership. Distributed by King Features Syndicate
IF THERE'S AMBIGUITY IN MY LIFE, IT'S NOT AROUND CURFEWS.
12
9
3
SCOTT and BORGMAN

Zits
by JERRY SCOTT and JIM BORGMAN

MOM, I'VE BEEN THINKING THAT WITH THE HELP OF A COUPLE OF FRIENDS, SAY, NO MORE THAN FIFTEEN OR TWENTY AT THE MOST, I COULD DO A MUCH BETTER JOB OF HOUSE SITTING WHILE YOU AND DAD ARE AT THE NATIONAL ORTHODONTICS CONVENTION IN ALBUQUER-
NO
10/4 SCOTT and BORGMAN
©2009 ZITS Partnership. Distributed by King Features Syndicate

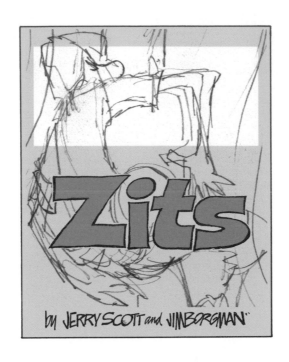

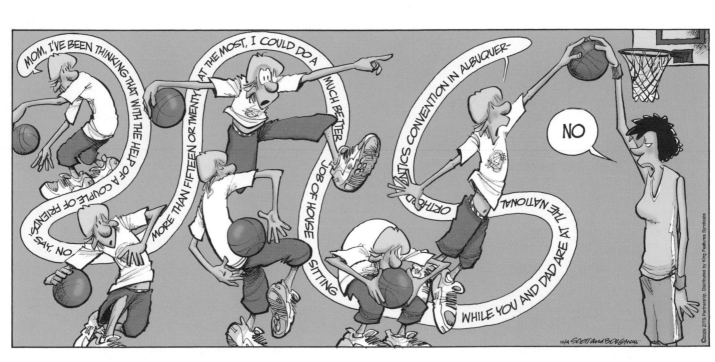

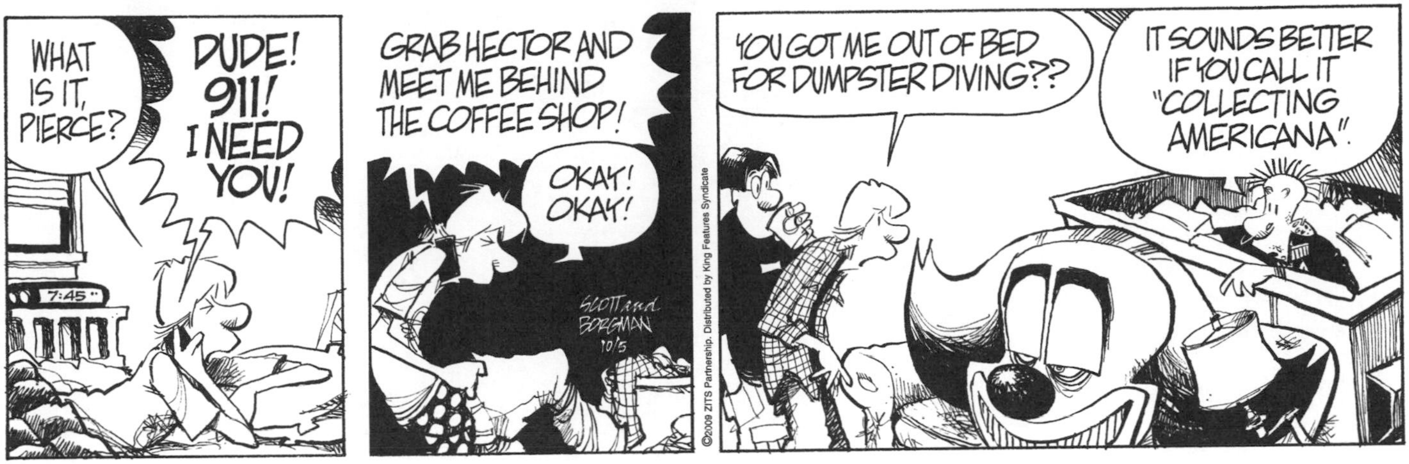
WHAT IS IT, PIERCE?
DUDE! 911! I NEED YOU!
7:45
GRAB HECTOR AND MEET ME BEHIND THE COFFEE SHOP!
OKAY! OKAY!
SCOTT and BORGMAN 10/5
©2009 ZITS Partnership. Distributed by King Features Syndicate
YOU GOT ME OUT OF BED FOR DUMPSTER DIVING??
IT SOUNDS BETTER IF YOU CALL IT "COLLECTING AMERICANA".

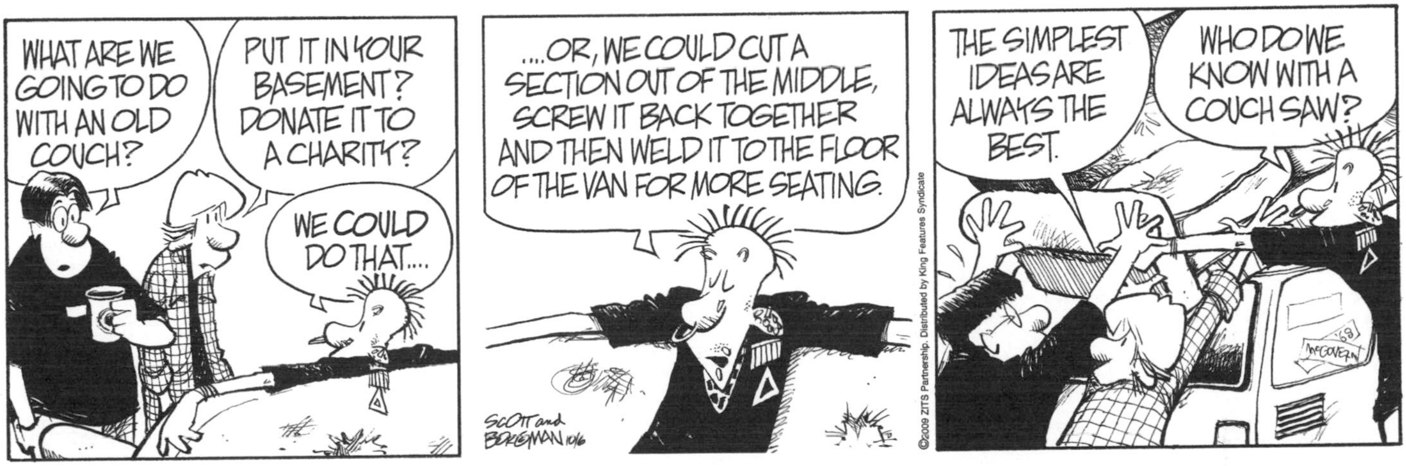
WHAT ARE WE GOING TO DO WITH AN OLD COUCH?
PUT IT IN YOUR BASEMENT? DONATE IT TO A CHARITY?
WE COULD DO THAT....
....OR, WE COULD CUT A SECTION OUT OF THE MIDDLE, SCREW IT BACK TOGETHER AND THEN WELD IT TO THE FLOOR OF THE VAN FOR MORE SEATING.
SCOTT and BORGMAN 10/6
©2009 ZITS Partnership. Distributed by King Features Syndicate
THE SIMPLEST IDEAS ARE ALWAYS THE BEST.
WHO DO WE KNOW WITH A COUCH SAW?
'68
McGOVERN

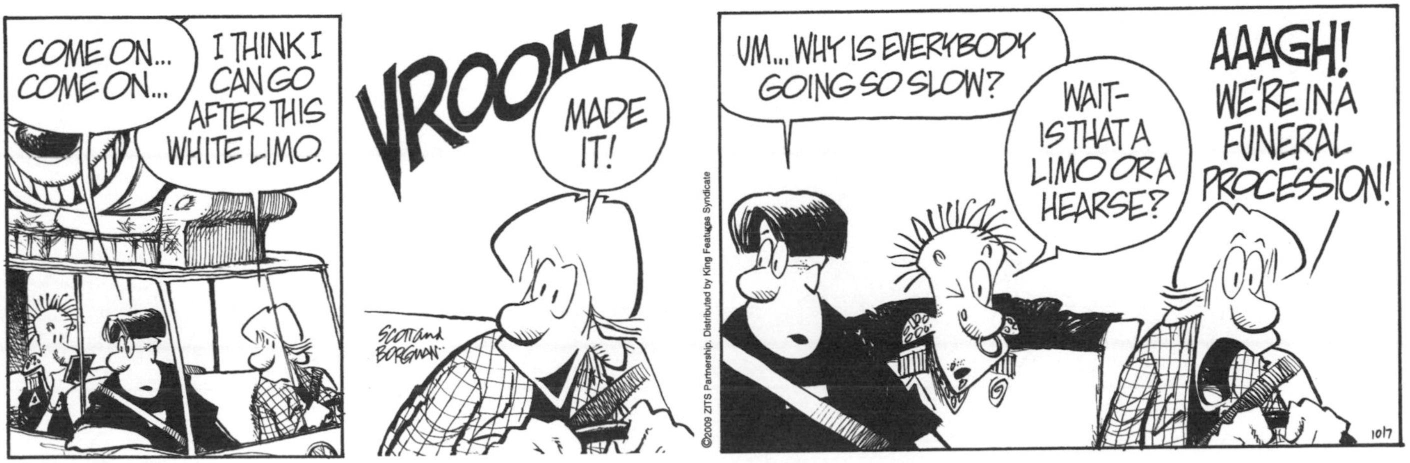
COME ON... COME ON...
I THINK I CAN GO AFTER THIS WHITE LIMO.
VROOM!
MADE IT!
SCOTT and BORGMAN
©2009 ZITS Partnership. Distributed by King Features Syndicate
UM... WHY IS EVERYBODY GOING SO SLOW?
WAIT- IS THAT A LIMO OR A HEARSE?
AAAGH! WE'RE IN A FUNERAL PROCESSION!
10/7

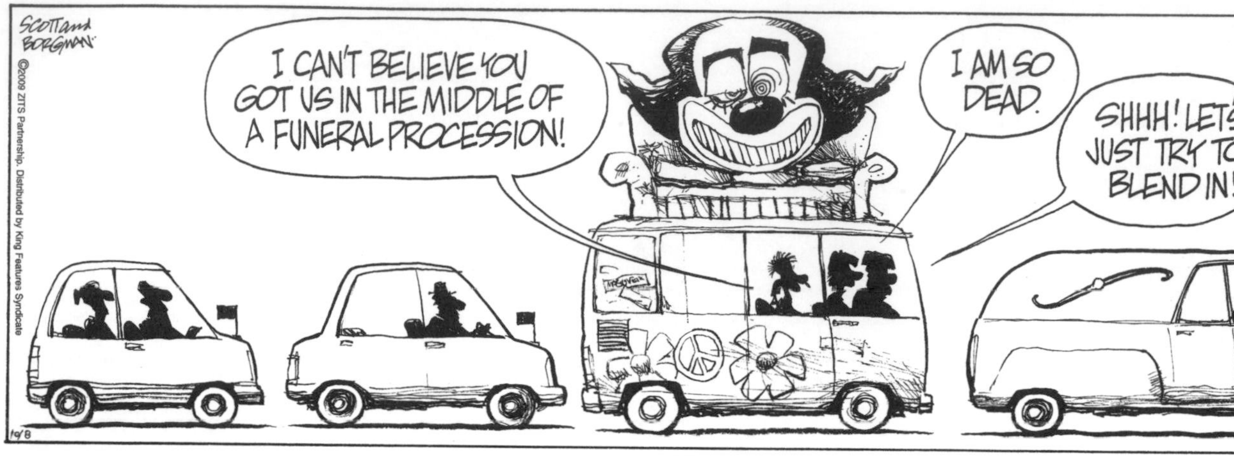
SCOTT and BORGMAN
©2009 ZITS Partnership. Distributed by King Features Syndicate
I CAN'T BELIEVE YOU GOT US IN THE MIDDLE OF A FUNERAL PROCESSION!
I AM SO DEAD.
SHHH! LET'S JUST TRY TO BLEND IN!
10/8

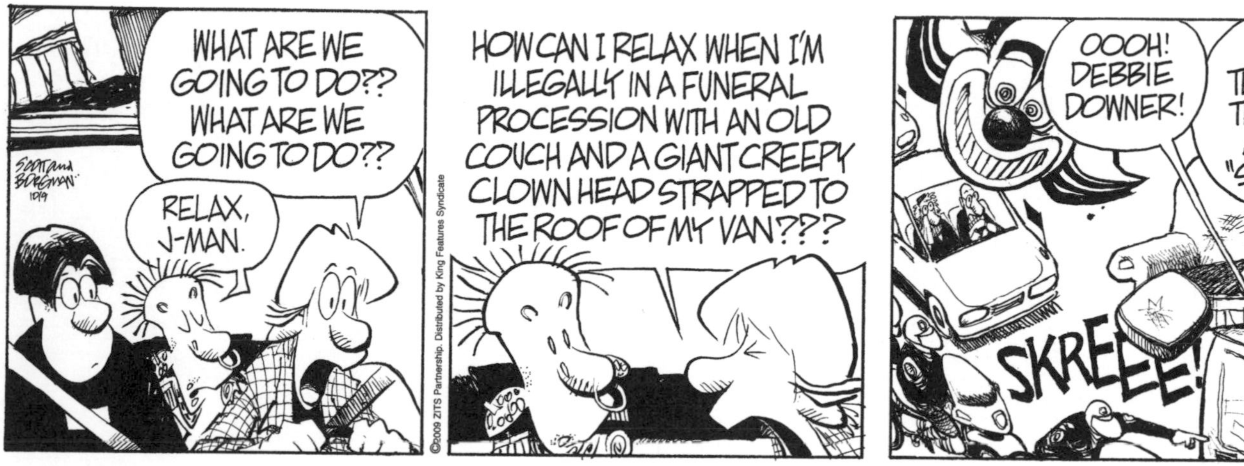
SCOTT and BORGMAN
10/9
WHAT ARE WE GOING TO DO?? WHAT ARE WE GOING TO DO??
RELAX, J-MAN.
©2009 ZITS Partnership. Distributed by King Features Syndicate
HOW CAN I RELAX WHEN I'M ILLEGALLY IN A FUNERAL PROCESSION WITH AN OLD COUCH AND A GIANT CREEPY CLOWN HEAD STRAPPED TO THE ROOF OF MY VAN???
OOOH! DEBBIE DOWNER!
AND TECHNICALLY, THEY'RE NOT ACTUALLY "STRAPPED."
SKREEEE!

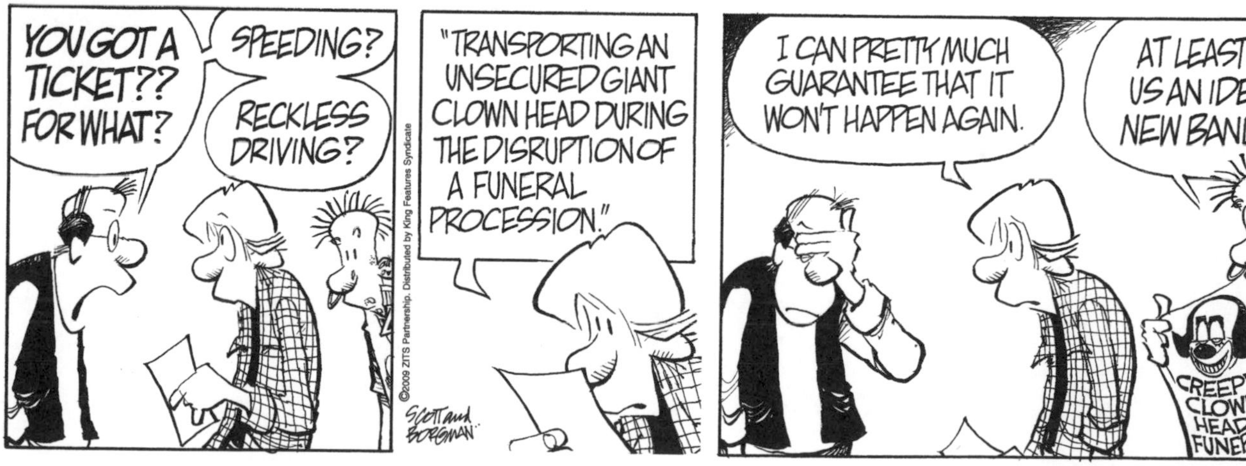
YOU GOT A TICKET?? FOR WHAT?
SPEEDING?
RECKLESS DRIVING?
©2009 ZITS Partnership. Distributed by King Features Syndicate
"TRANSPORTING AN UNSECURED GIANT CLOWN HEAD DURING THE DISRUPTION OF A FUNERAL PROCESSION."
SCOTT and BORGMAN
I CAN PRETTY MUCH GUARANTEE THAT IT WON'T HAPPEN AGAIN.
AT LEAST IT GAVE US AN IDEA FOR A NEW BAND NAME!
CREEPY CLOWN HEAD FUNERAL
10/10

Zits
by
JERRY SCOTT and
JIM BORGMAN

NICE BINGO WINGS, MOM.
WHAT ARE BINGO WINGS?
OKAY, PRETEND YOU'RE PLAYING BINGO.
OKAY...
©2009 ZITS Partnership. Distributed by King Features Syndicate
NOW PRETEND THAT THEY JUST CALLED O-17, WHICH IS THE EXACT SQUARE YOU NEED TO WIN A BRAND NEW CAR- WHAT DO YOU DO?
BINGO!
FLAP FLAP FLAP
FLAP
JIGGLE JIGGLE
SCOTT and BORGMAN
BINGO WINGS.
WE'RE RENEWING OUR GYM MEMBERSHIP.

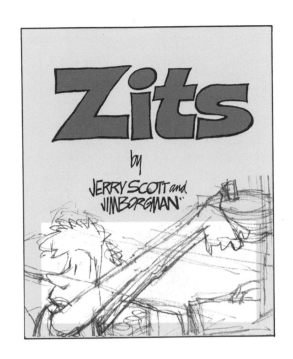

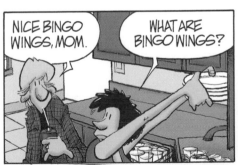

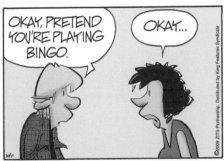

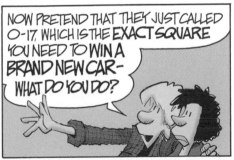

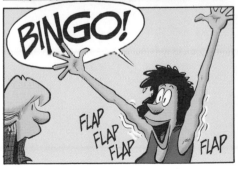

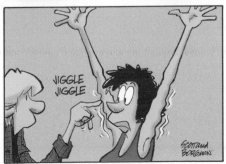

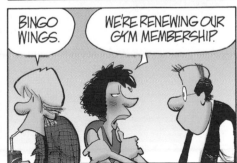

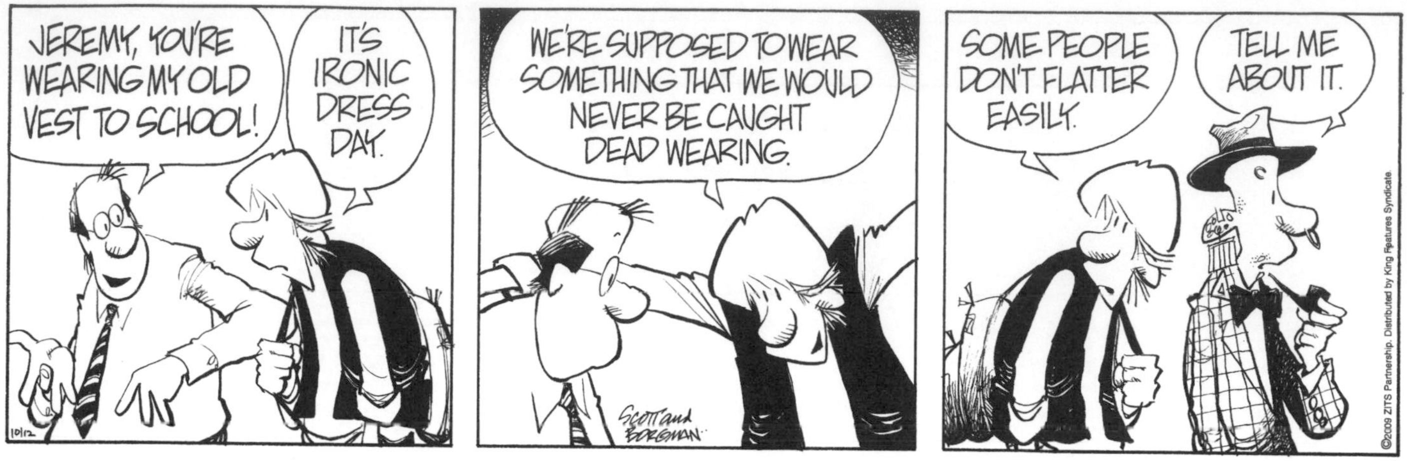
JEREMY, YOU'RE WEARING MY OLD VEST TO SCHOOL!
IT'S IRONIC DRESS DAY.
WE'RE SUPPOSED TO WEAR SOMETHING THAT WE WOULD NEVER BE CAUGHT DEAD WEARING.
SOME PEOPLE DON'T FLATTER EASILY.
TELL ME ABOUT IT.
SCOTT and BORGMAN
10/12
©2009 ZITS Partnership. Distributed by King Features Syndicate.

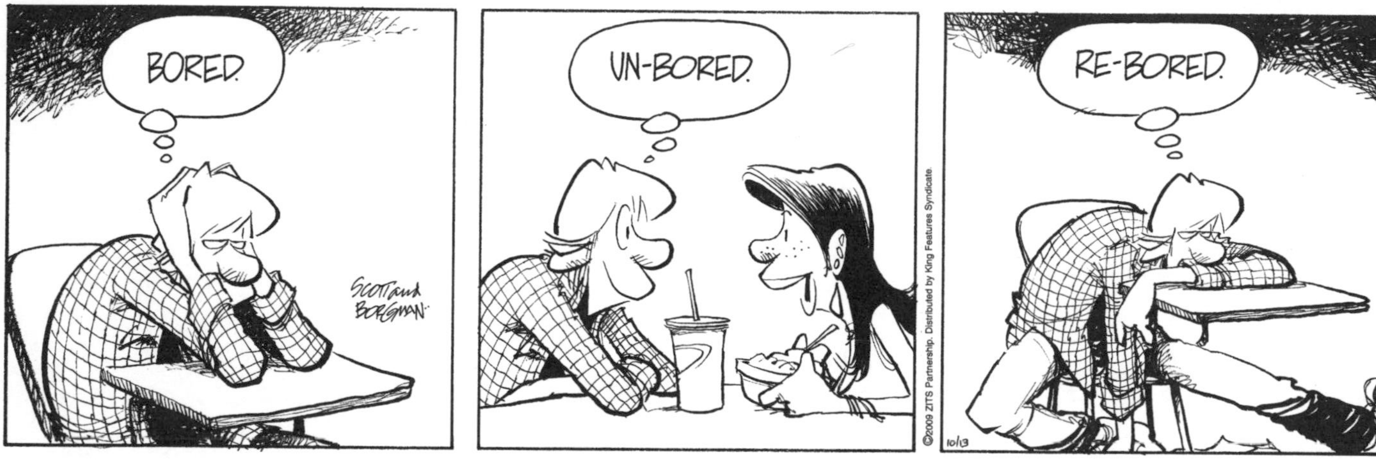
BORED.
UN-BORED.
RE-BORED.
SCOTT and BORGMAN
10/13
©2009 ZITS Partnership. Distributed by King Features Syndicate.

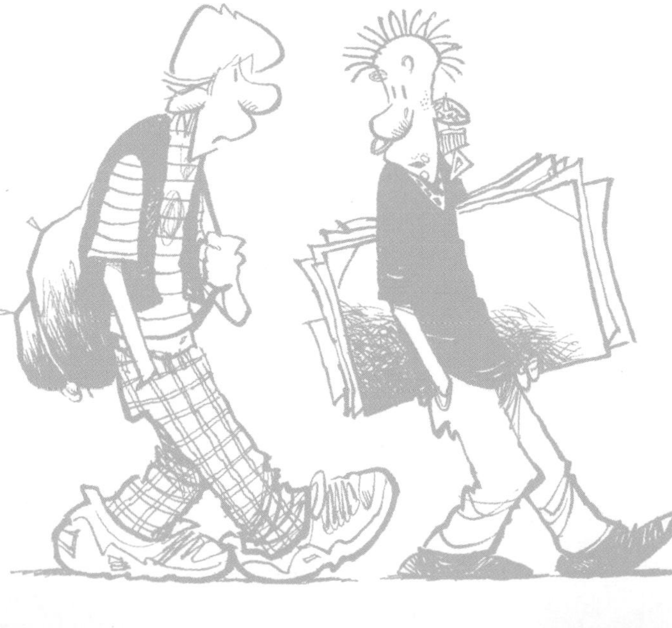

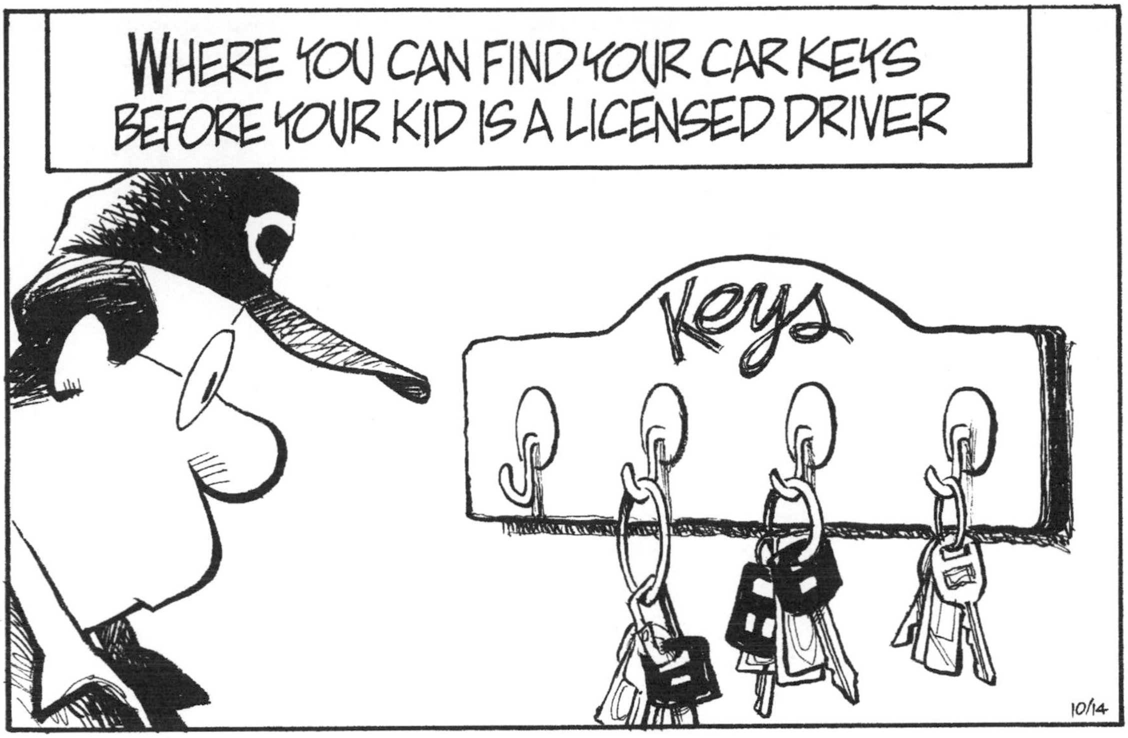
WHERE YOU CAN FIND YOUR CAR KEYS BEFORE YOUR KID IS A LICENSED DRIVER
Keys
10/14

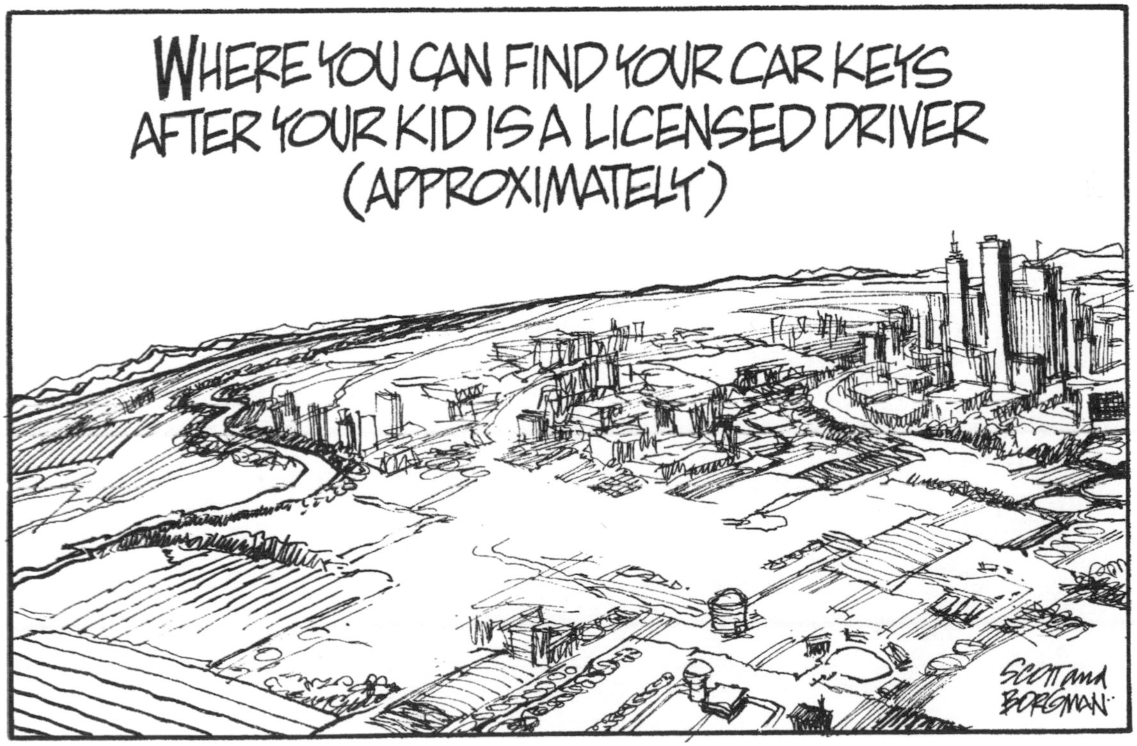
WHERE YOU CAN FIND YOUR CAR KEYS AFTER YOUR KID IS A LICENSED DRIVER (APPROXIMATELY)
SCOTT AND BORGMAN

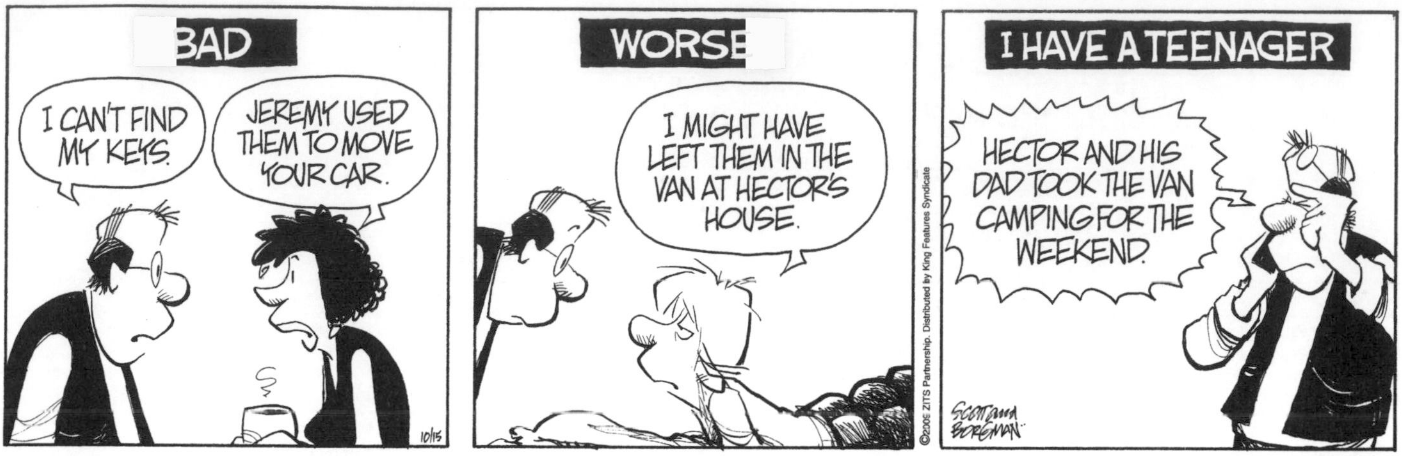
BAD
I CAN'T FIND MY KEYS.
JEREMY USED THEM TO MOVE YOUR CAR.
WORSE
I MIGHT HAVE LEFT THEM IN THE VAN AT HECTOR'S HOUSE.
I HAVE A TEENAGER
HECTOR AND HIS DAD TOOK THE VAN CAMPING FOR THE WEEKEND.
©2005 ZITS Partnership. Distributed by King Features Syndicate

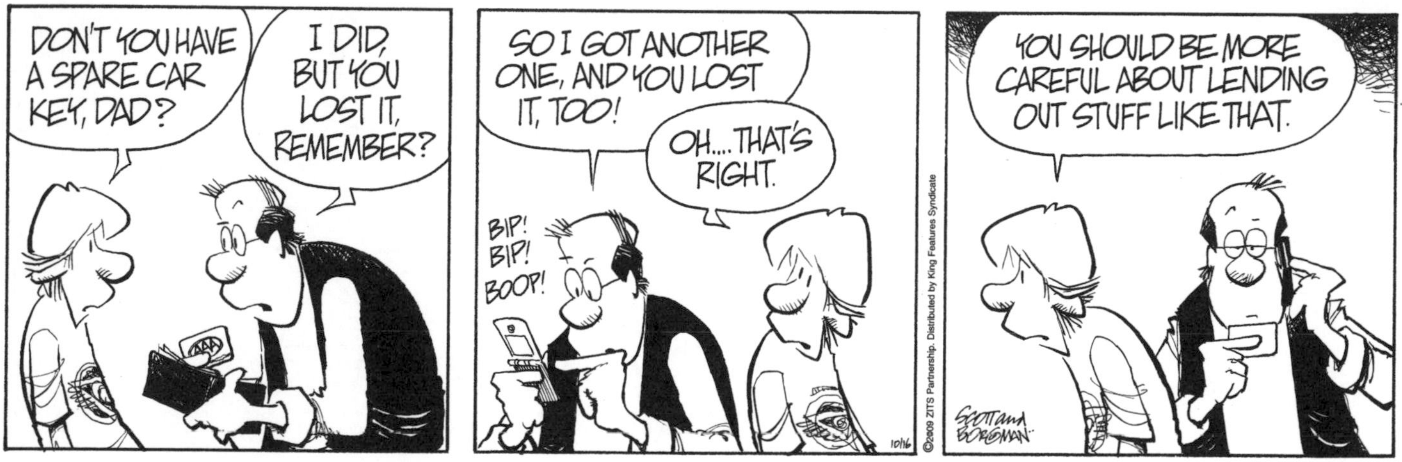
DON'T YOU HAVE A SPARE CAR KEY, DAD?
I DID, BUT YOU LOST IT, REMEMBER?
SO I GOT ANOTHER ONE, AND YOU LOST IT, TOO!
OH.... THAT'S RIGHT.
BIP! BIP! BOOP!
YOU SHOULD BE MORE CAREFUL ABOUT LENDING OUT STUFF LIKE THAT.
©2009 ZITS Partnership. Distributed by King Features Syndicate

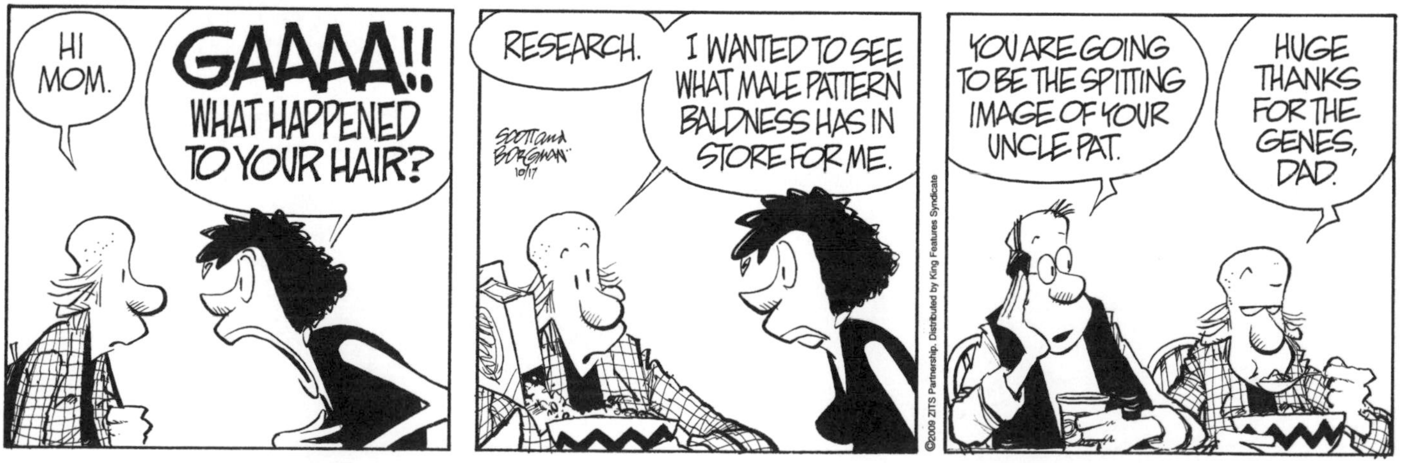
HI MOM.
GAAAA!! WHAT HAPPENED TO YOUR HAIR?
RESEARCH.
I WANTED TO SEE WHAT MALE PATTERN BALDNESS HAS IN STORE FOR ME.
YOU ARE GOING TO BE THE SPITTING IMAGE OF YOUR UNCLE PAT.
HUGE THANKS FOR THE GENES, DAD.
©2009 ZITS Partnership. Distributed by King Features Syndicate

Zits
by JERRY SCOTT and JIM BORGMAN

JE--
I JUST PUT THEM AWAY.
HOW--
--DID I KNOW WHAT YOU WERE GOING TO SAY?
I ALWAYS KNOW WHAT YOU'RE GOING TO SAY.
YOU'RE REALLY PREDICTABLE.
YES, YOU ARE. YES, YOU ARE. YES, YOU ARE.
©2009 ZITS Partnership. Distributed by King Features Syndicate
AND I ALREADY DID.
GO TAKE OUT THE TRASH!
10/18
SCOTT and BORGMAN

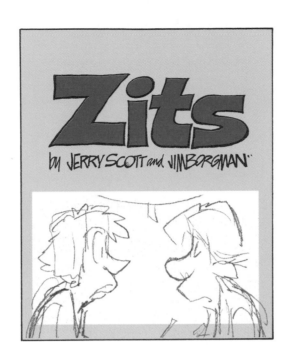

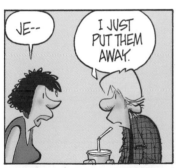

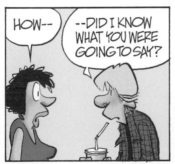

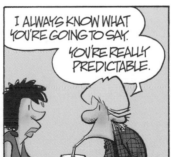

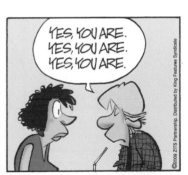

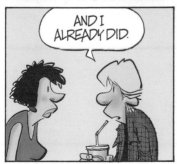

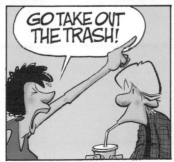

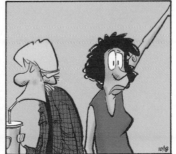

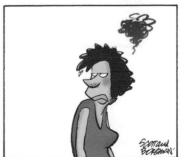

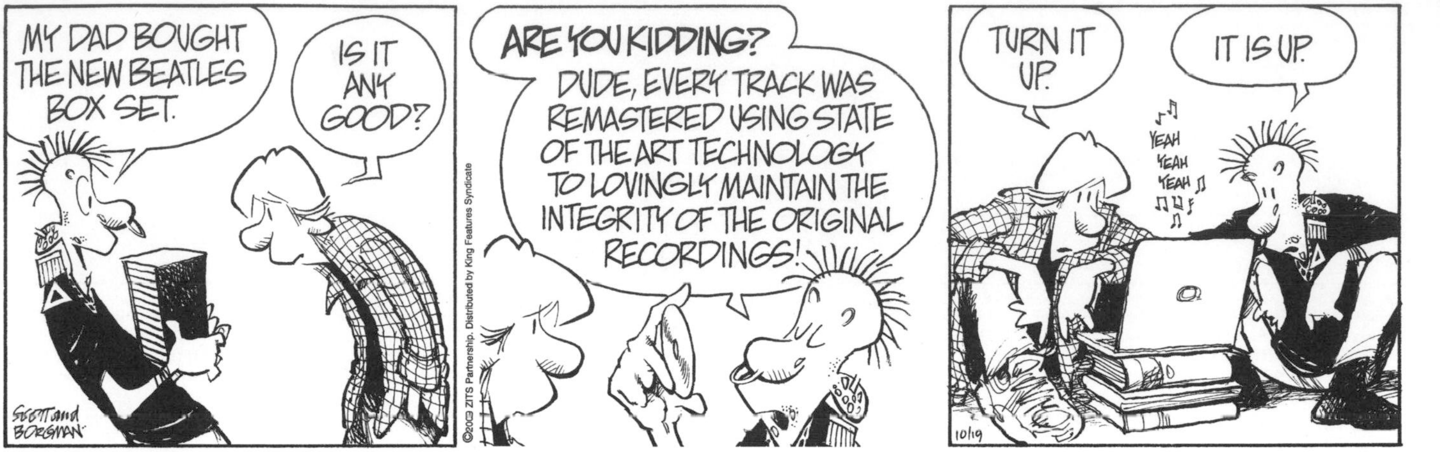
MY DAD BOUGHT THE NEW BEATLES BOX SET.
IS IT ANY GOOD?
SCOTT and BORGMAN
©2009 ZITS Partnership. Distributed by King Features Syndicate
ARE YOU KIDDING?
DUDE, EVERY TRACK WAS REMASTERED USING STATE OF THE ART TECHNOLOGY TO LOVINGLY MAINTAIN THE INTEGRITY OF THE ORIGINAL RECORDINGS!
TURN IT UP.
IT IS UP.
YEAH YEAH YEAH
10/19

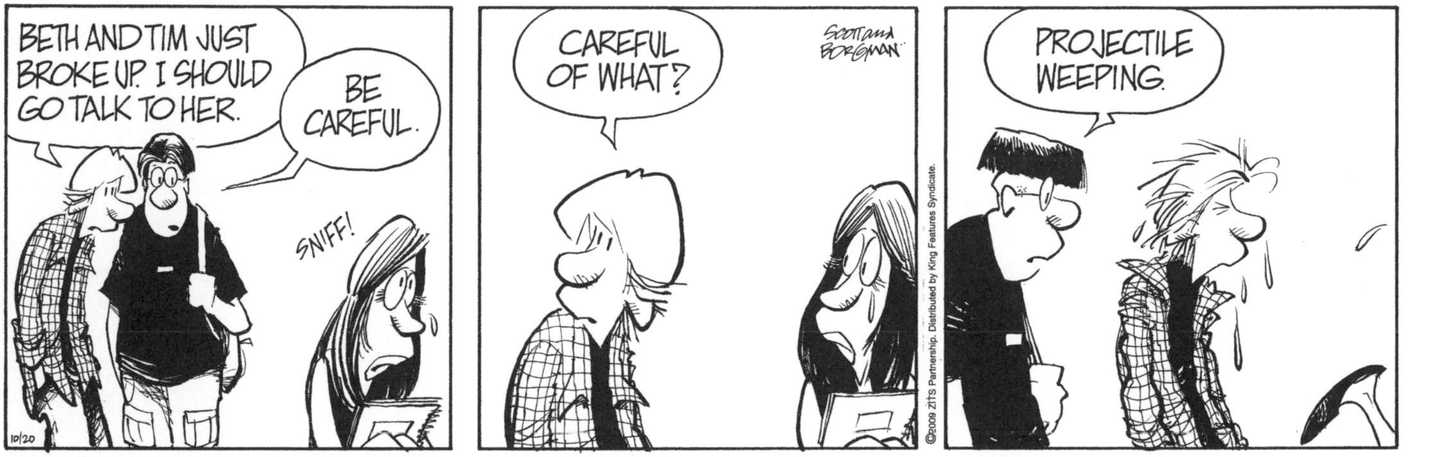
BETH AND TIM JUST BROKE UP. I SHOULD GO TALK TO HER.
BE CAREFUL.
SNIFF!
10/20
CAREFUL OF WHAT?
SCOTT and BORGMAN
©2009 ZITS Partnership. Distributed by King Features Syndicate.
PROJECTILE WEEPING.

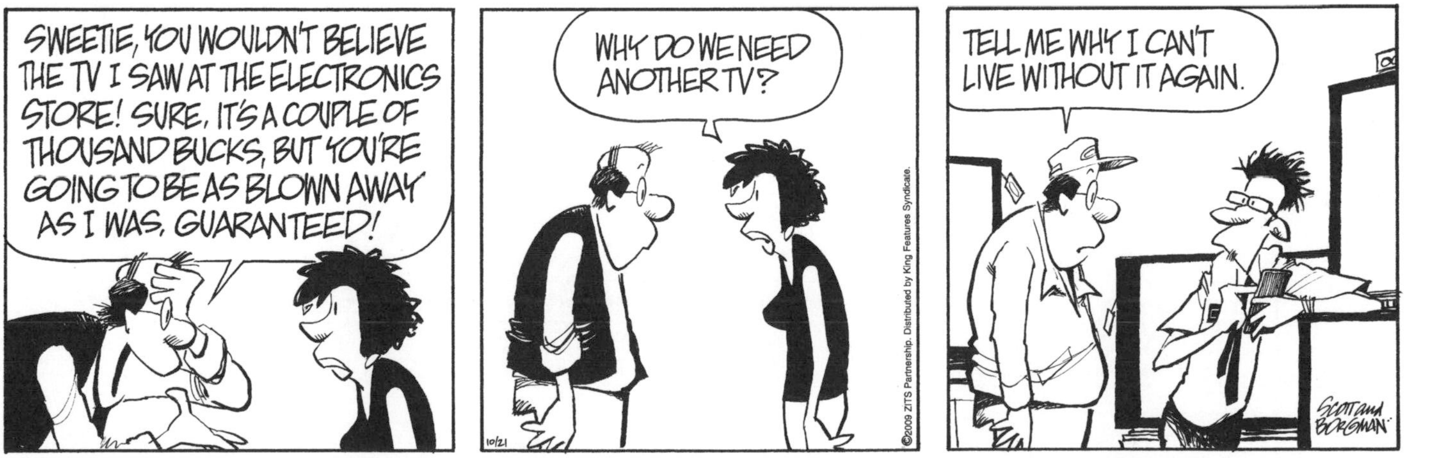
SWEETIE, YOU WOULDN'T BELIEVE THE TV I SAW AT THE ELECTRONICS STORE! SURE, IT'S A COUPLE OF THOUSAND BUCKS, BUT YOU'RE GOING TO BE AS BLOWN AWAY AS I WAS, GUARANTEED!
WHY DO WE NEED ANOTHER TV?
10/21
©2009 ZITS Partnership. Distributed by King Features Syndicate.
TELL ME WHY I CAN'T LIVE WITHOUT IT AGAIN.
SCOTT and BORGMAN

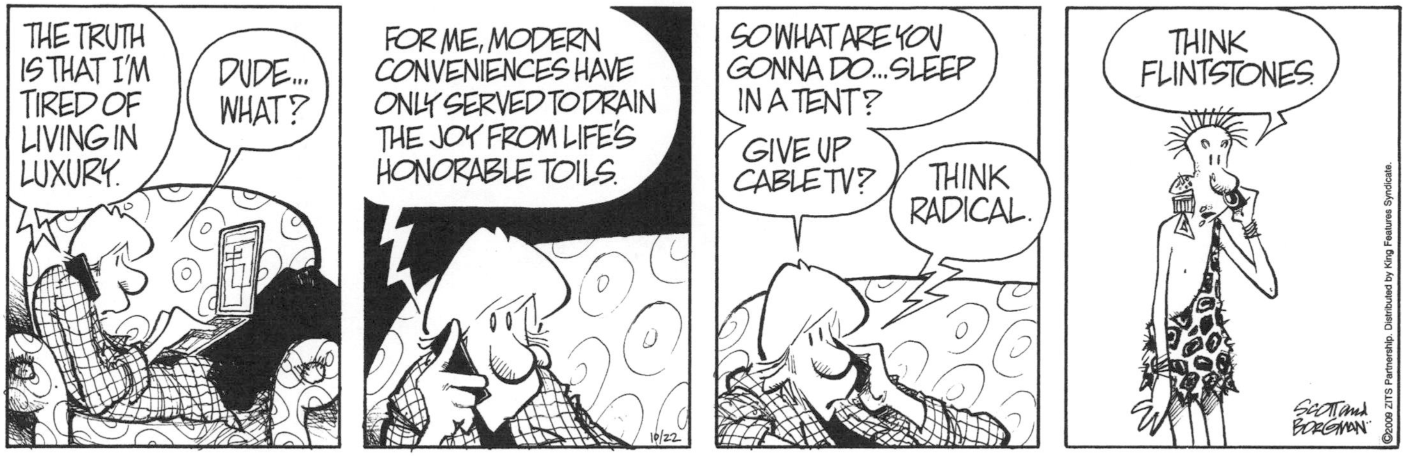
THE TRUTH IS THAT I'M TIRED OF LIVING IN LUXURY.
DUDE... WHAT?
FOR ME, MODERN CONVENIENCES HAVE ONLY SERVED TO DRAIN THE JOY FROM LIFE'S HONORABLE TOILS.
10/22
SO WHAT ARE YOU GONNA DO... SLEEP IN A TENT?
GIVE UP CABLE TV?
THINK RADICAL.
THINK FLINTSTONES.
SCOTT and BORGMAN
©2009 ZITS Partnership. Distributed by King Features Syndicate.

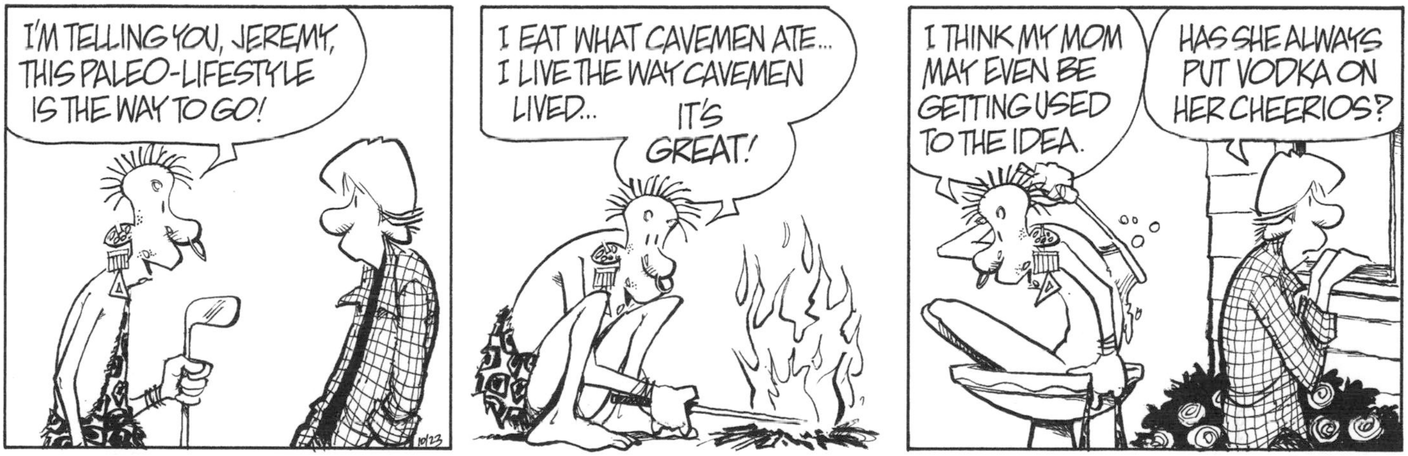
I'M TELLING YOU, JEREMY, THIS PALEO-LIFESTYLE IS THE WAY TO GO!
10/23
I EAT WHAT CAVEMEN ATE... I LIVE THE WAY CAVEMEN LIVED...
IT'S GREAT!
I THINK MY MOM MAY EVEN BE GETTING USED TO THE IDEA.
HAS SHE ALWAYS PUT VODKA ON HER CHEERIOS?

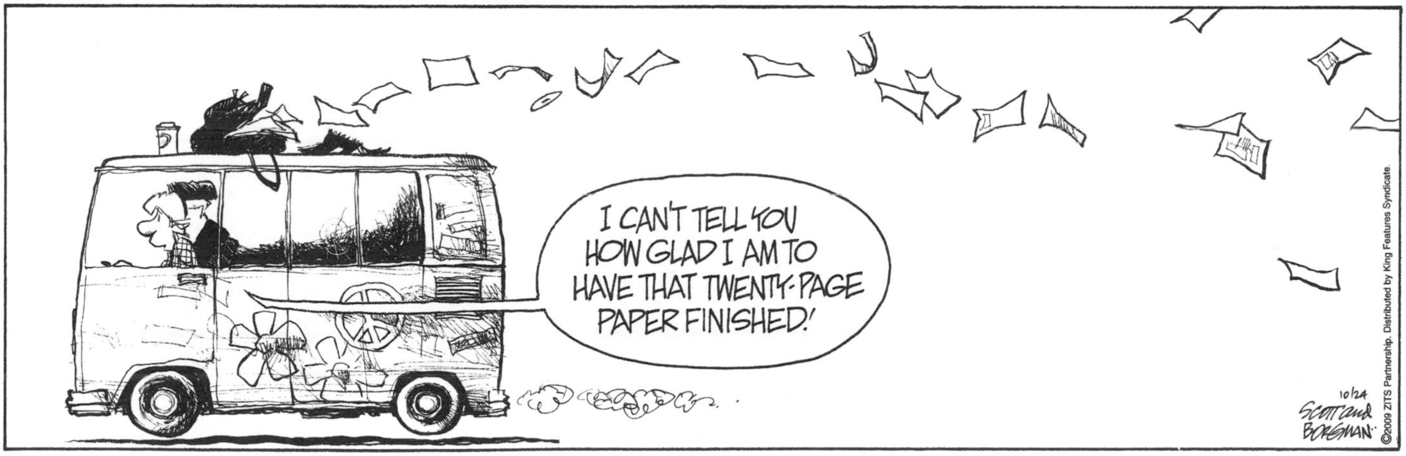
I CAN'T TELL YOU HOW GLAD I AM TO HAVE THAT TWENTY-PAGE PAPER FINISHED!
10/24
SCOTT and BORGMAN
©2009 ZITS Partnership. Distributed by King Features Syndicate.

Zits
by JERRY SCOTT and
JIM BORGMAN

GOT ANY HOMEWORK TONIGHT?
A LITTLE.
SCOTT and BORGMAN
10/25
©2009 ZITS Partnership. Distributed by King Features Syndicate

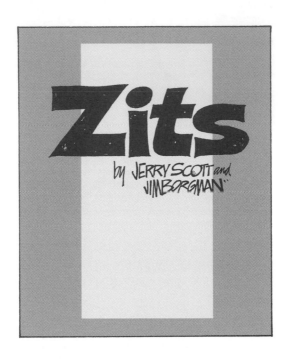

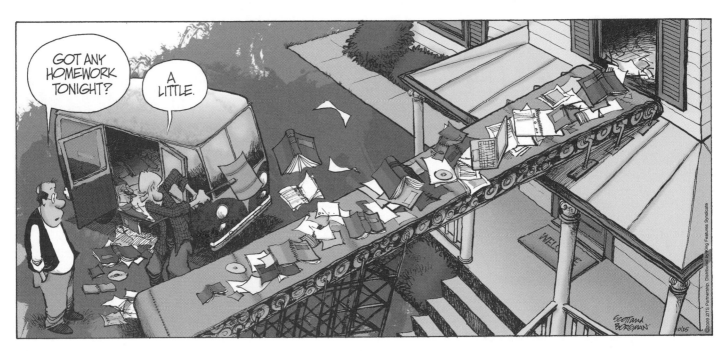

Zits
by
JERRY SCOTT and
JIM BORGMAN

SHAMPOO. MILK. DRYCLEANERS.
GOT IT.
SHOULD I MAKE YOU A LIST?
NO. I GOT IT.
SHAMPOO. MILK. CLEANERS.
I GOT IT.
SHAMP--
I GOT IT!!
HI JEREMY!
LIKE MY NEW JEANS?
SCOTT and BORGMAN
©2009 ZITS Partnership. Distributed by King Features Syndicate
THUD.
COULD WE GO OVER THAT LIST AGAIN?

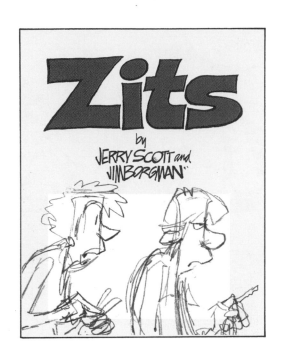

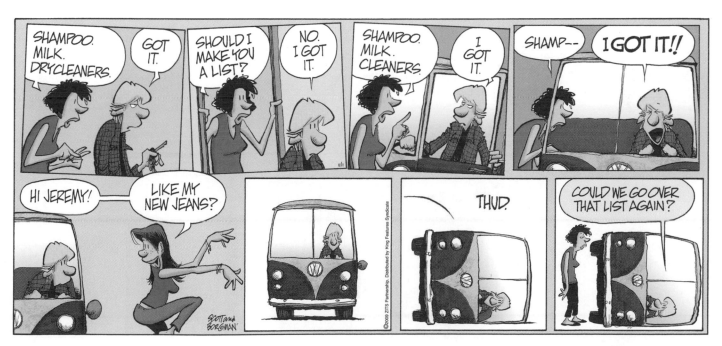

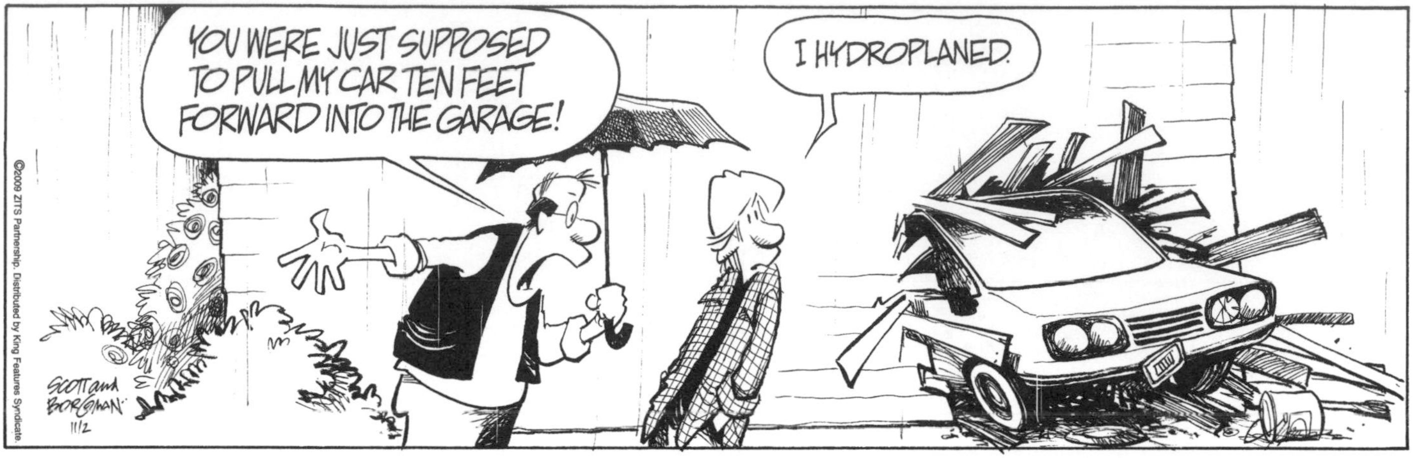
YOU WERE JUST SUPPOSED TO PULL MY CAR TEN FEET FORWARD INTO THE GARAGE!
I HYDROPLANED.
©2009 ZITS Partnership. Distributed by King Features Syndicate.
SCOTT and BORGMAN
11/2

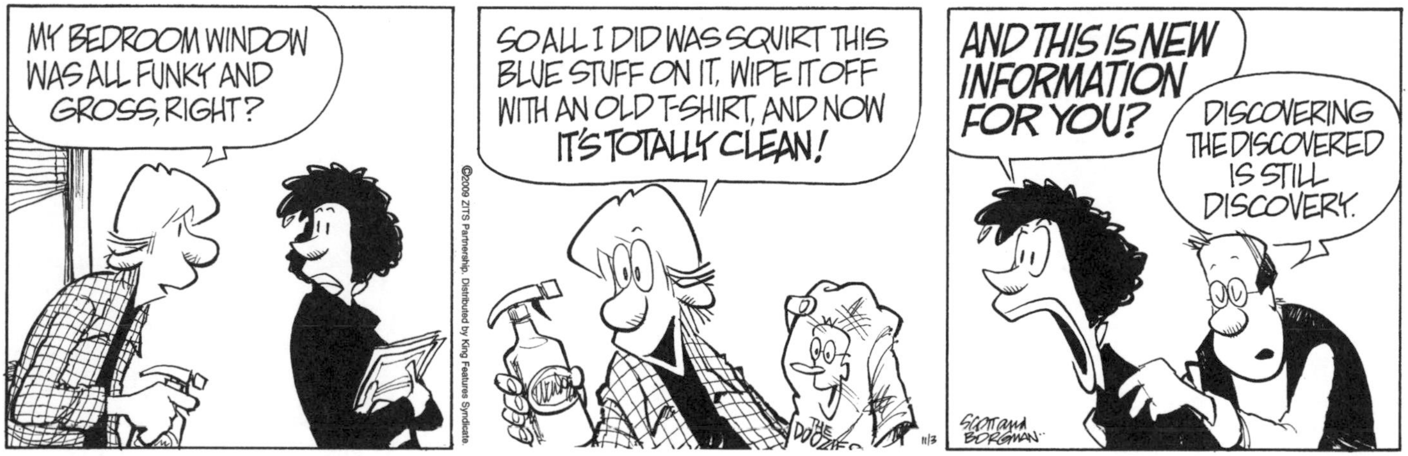
MY BEDROOM WINDOW WAS ALL FUNKY AND GROSS, RIGHT?
SO ALL I DID WAS SQUIRT THIS BLUE STUFF ON IT, WIPE IT OFF WITH AN OLD T-SHIRT, AND NOW IT'S TOTALLY CLEAN!
AND THIS IS NEW INFORMATION FOR YOU?
DISCOVERING THE DISCOVERED IS STILL DISCOVERY.
©2009 ZITS Partnership. Distributed by King Features Syndicate.
11/3
SCOTT and BORGMAN

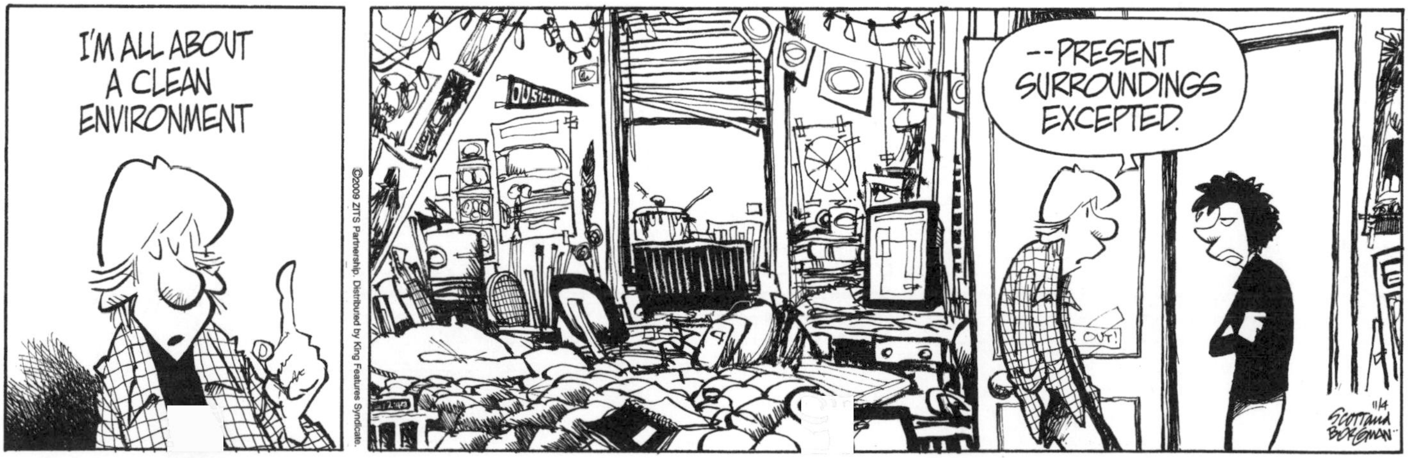
I'M ALL ABOUT A CLEAN ENVIRONMENT
--PRESENT SURROUNDINGS EXCEPTED.
©2009 ZITS Partnership. Distributed by King Features Syndicate.
11/4
SCOTT and BORGMAN

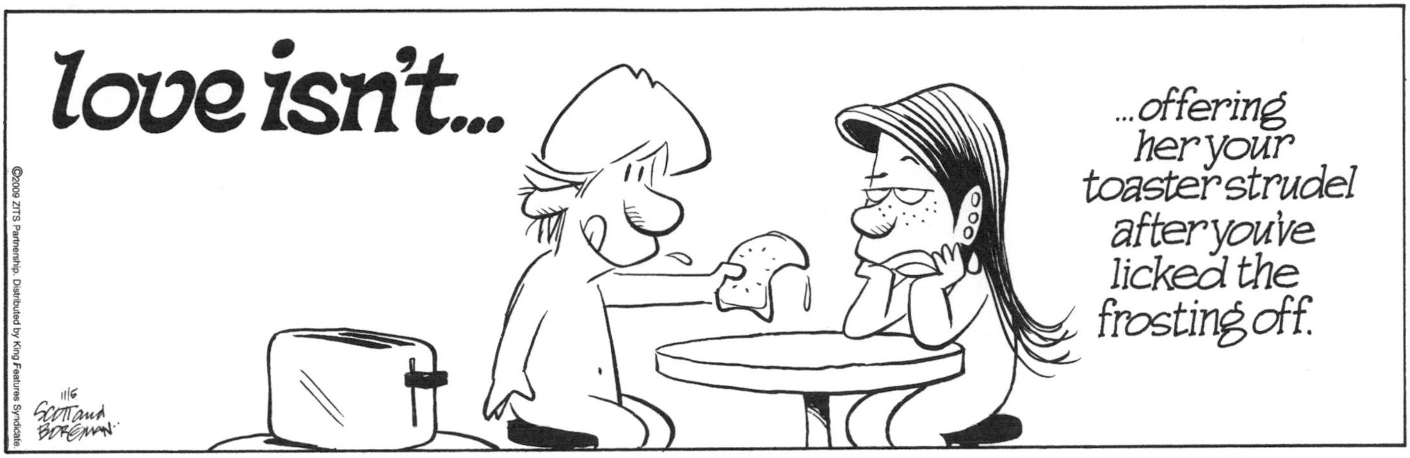
love isn't...
...offering her your toaster strudel after you've licked the frosting off.
©2009 ZITS Partnership. Distributed by King Features Syndicate.
11/6
SCOTT and BORGMAN

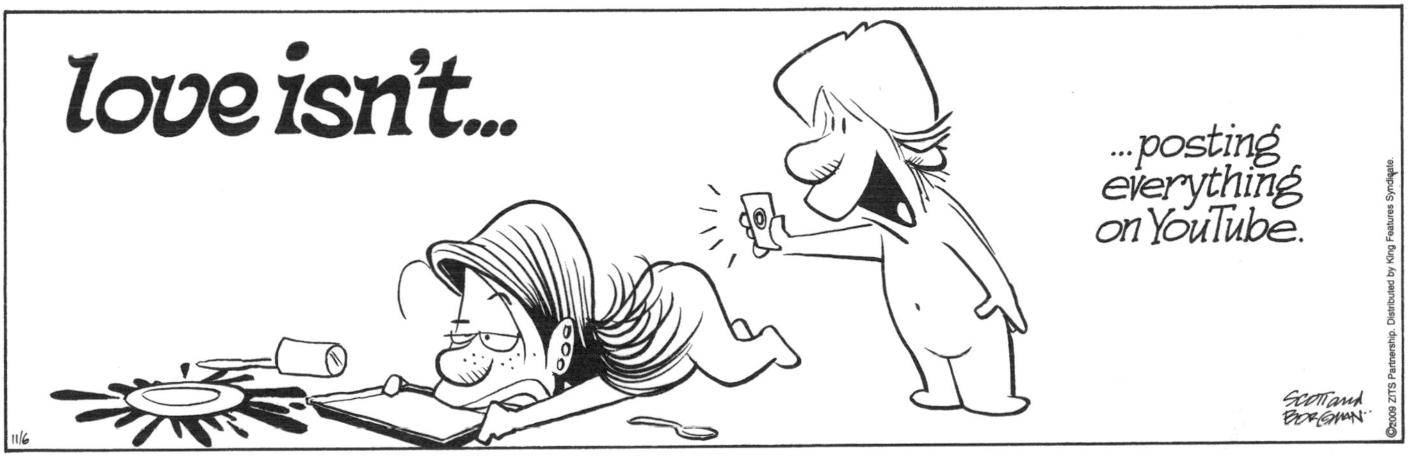
love isn't...
...posting everything on YouTube.
©2009 ZITS Partnership. Distributed by King Features Syndicate.
11/6
SCOTT and BORGMAN

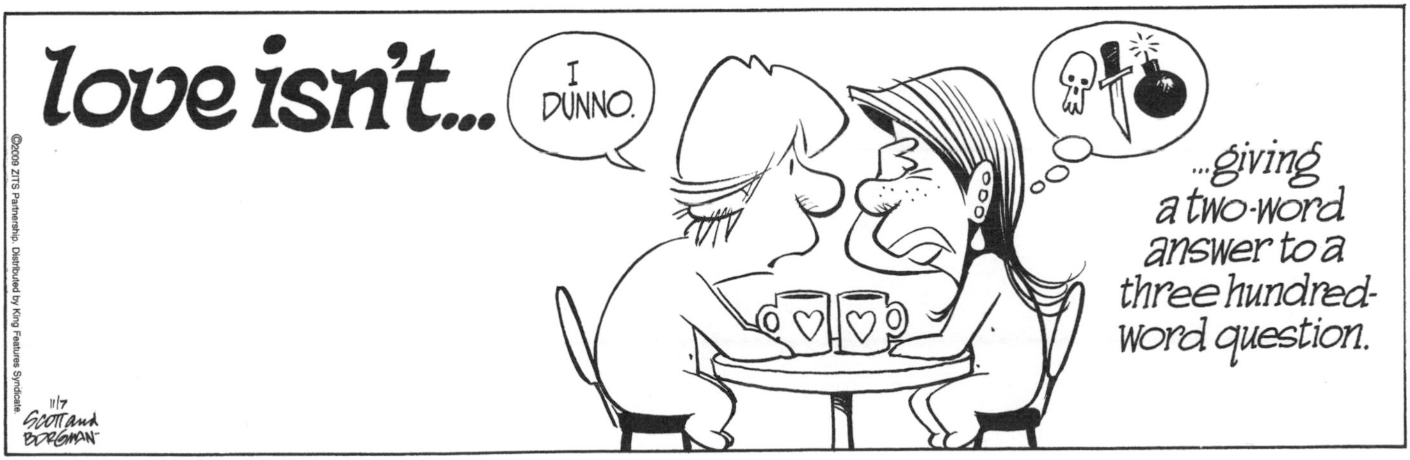
love isn't...
I DUNNO.
...giving a two-word answer to a three hundred-word question.
©2009 ZITS Partnership. Distributed by King Features Syndicate.
11/7
SCOTT and BORGMAN

Zits
by JERRY SCOTT and JIM BORGMAN

BRAKE! BRAKE! BRAKE!
I'D BE A BETTER FULL-TIME MOTHER IF I HAD A PART-TIME TEENAGER.
Z
SCOTT and BORGMAN

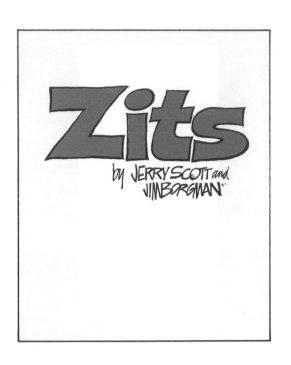

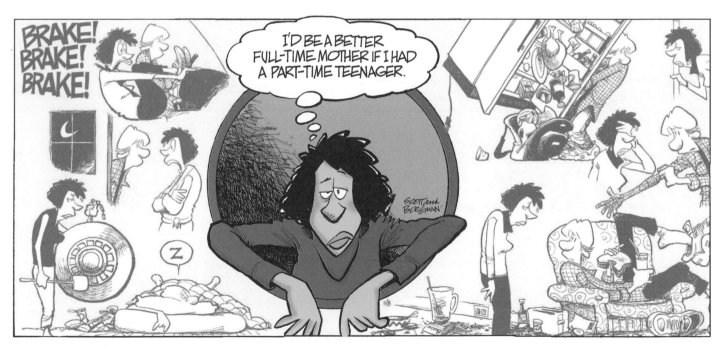

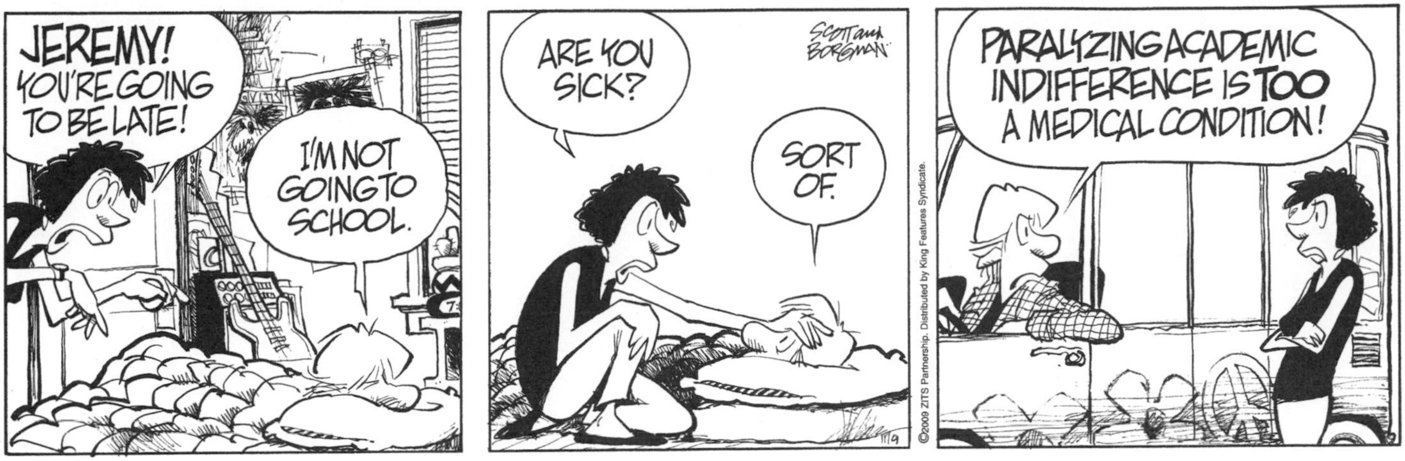
JEREMY! YOU'RE GOING TO BE LATE!
I'M NOT GOING TO SCHOOL.
SCOTT and BORGMAN
ARE YOU SICK?
SORT OF.
11/9
©2009 ZITS Partnership. Distributed by King Features Syndicate.
PARALYZING ACADEMIC INDIFFERENCE IS TOO A MEDICAL CONDITION!

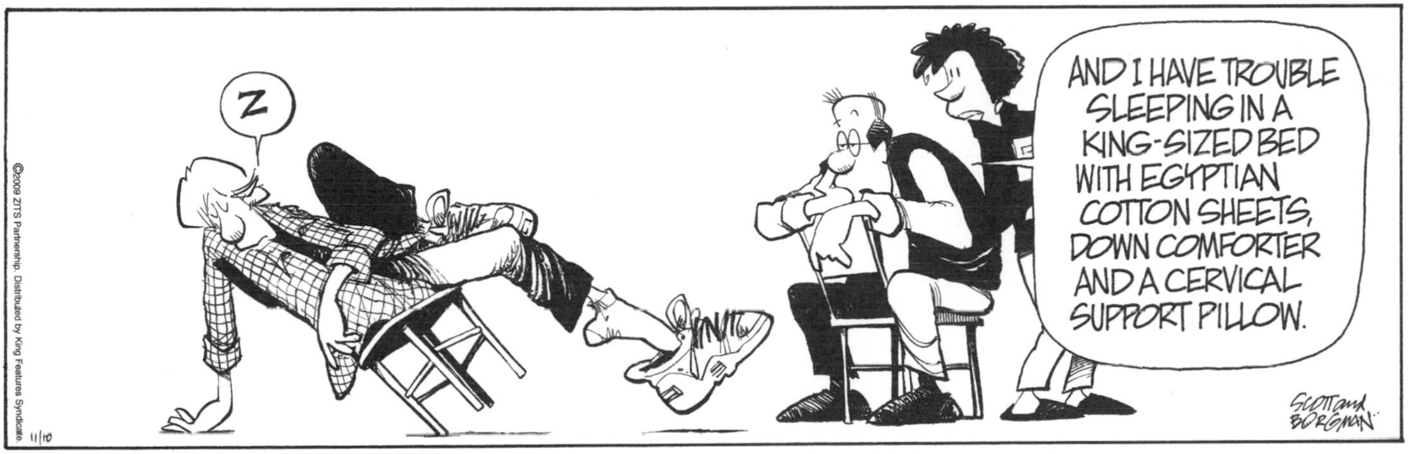
©2009 ZITS Partnership. Distributed by King Features Syndicate.
11/10
Z
AND I HAVE TROUBLE SLEEPING IN A KING-SIZED BED WITH EGYPTIAN COTTON SHEETS, DOWN COMFORTER AND A CERVICAL SUPPORT PILLOW.
SCOTT and BORGMAN

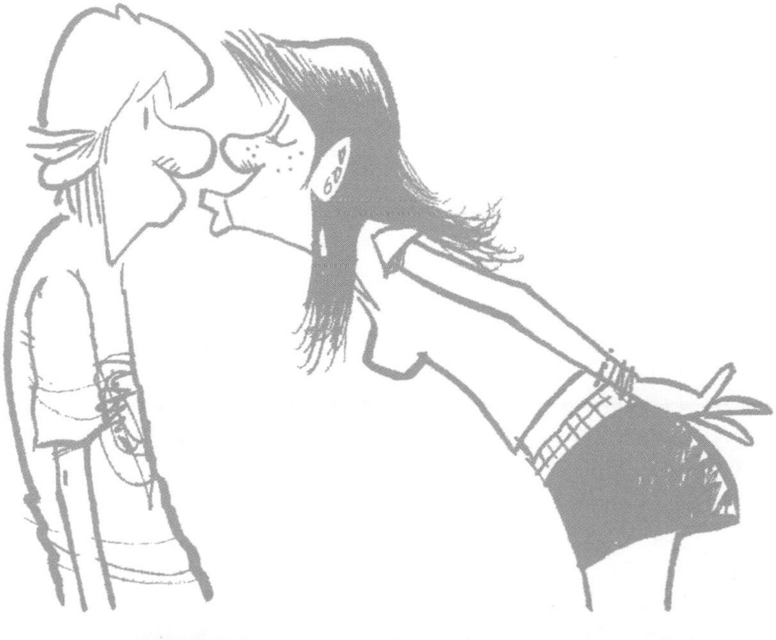

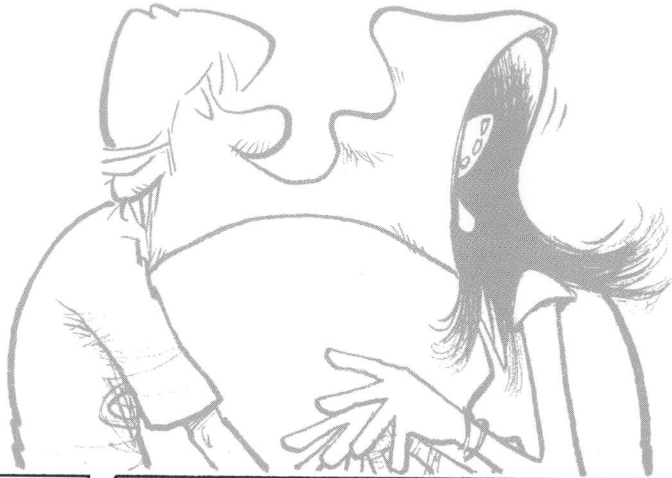

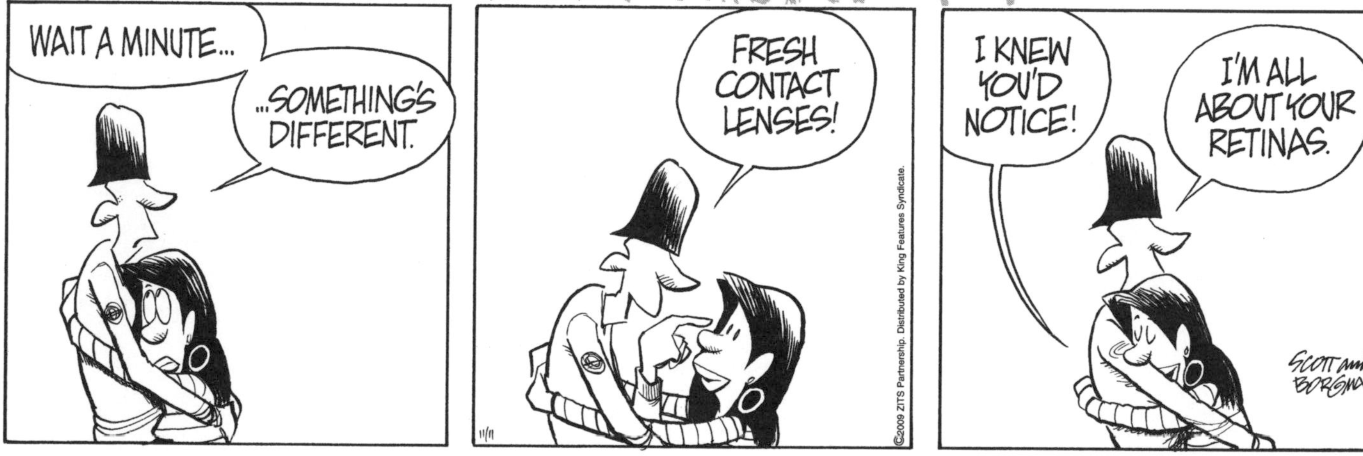

WAIT A MINUTE...
...SOMETHING'S DIFFERENT.
FRESH CONTACT LENSES!
I KNEW YOU'D NOTICE!
I'M ALL ABOUT YOUR RETINAS.
©2009 ZITS Partnership. Distributed by King Features Syndicate.
SCOTT and BORGMAN

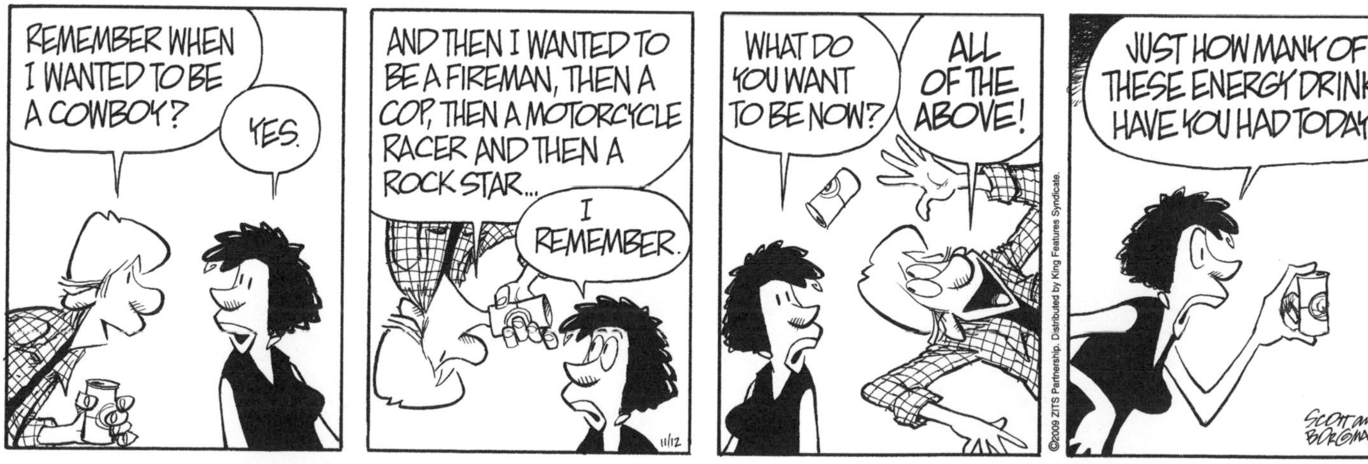

REMEMBER WHEN I WANTED TO BE A COWBOY?
YES.
AND THEN I WANTED TO BE A FIREMAN, THEN A COP, THEN A MOTORCYCLE RACER AND THEN A ROCK STAR...
I REMEMBER.
WHAT DO YOU WANT TO BE NOW?
ALL OF THE ABOVE!
JUST HOW MANY OF THESE ENERGY DRINKS HAVE YOU HAD TODAY?
©2009 ZITS Partnership. Distributed by King Features Syndicate.
SCOTT and BORGMAN

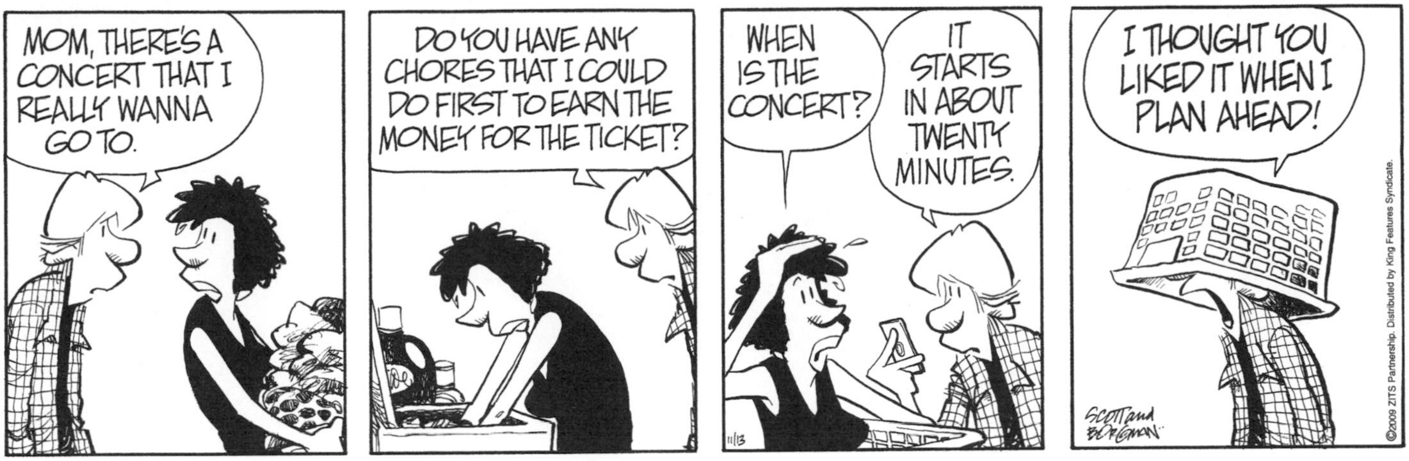

MOM, THERE'S A CONCERT THAT I REALLY WANNA GO TO.
DO YOU HAVE ANY CHORES THAT I COULD DO FIRST TO EARN THE MONEY FOR THE TICKET?
WHEN IS THE CONCERT?
IT STARTS IN ABOUT TWENTY MINUTES.
I THOUGHT YOU LIKED IT WHEN I PLAN AHEAD!
SCOTT and BORGMAN
©2009 ZITS Partnership. Distributed by King Features Syndicate.

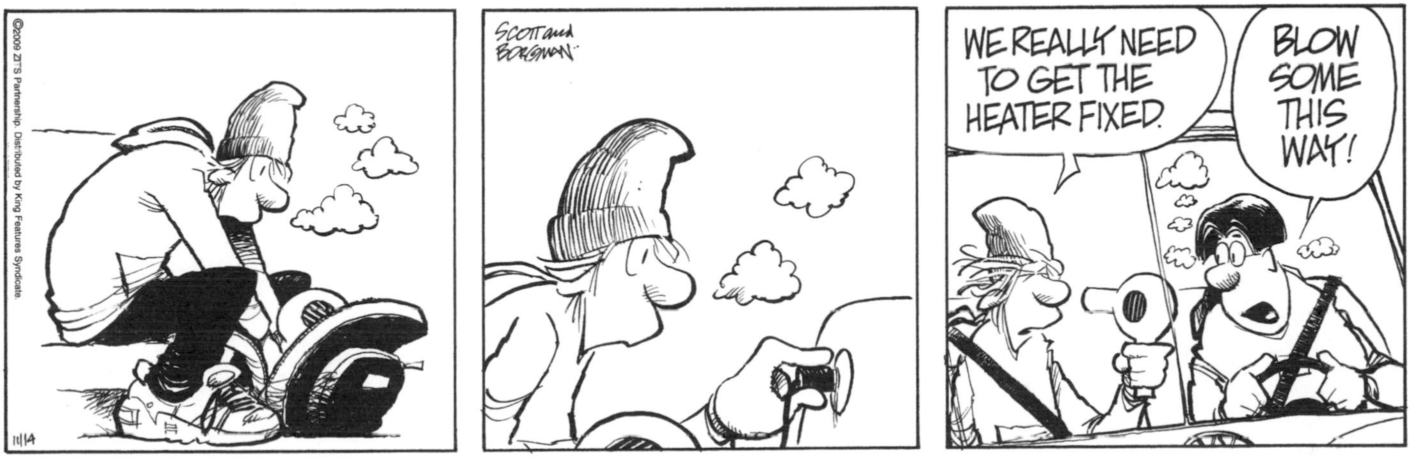

©2009 ZITS Partnership. Distributed by King Features Syndicate.
SCOTT and BORGMAN
WE REALLY NEED TO GET THE HEATER FIXED.
BLOW SOME THIS WAY!

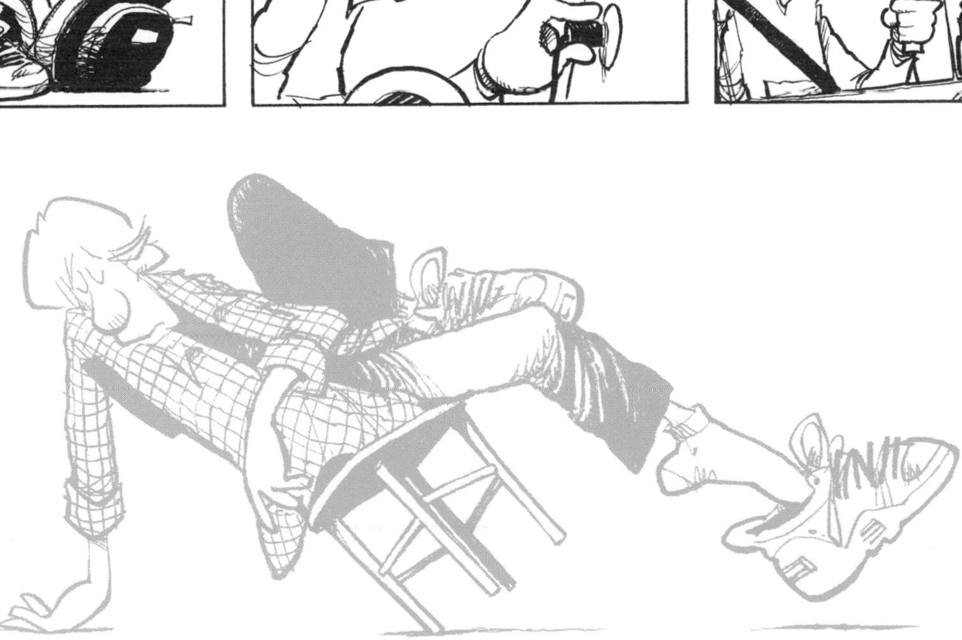

Zits
by
JERRY SCOTT and
JIM BORGMAN

5 QUESTIONS TO Always ANSWER WITH A 'YES'
A ZITS GUIDE TO A MORE PEACEFUL TEENAGE EXPERIENCE
ARE YOU LISTENING TO ME?
IS THERE GOING TO BE ADULT SUPERVISION?
ARE YOU GOING TO CLEAN THAT UP?
HAVE I MADE MYSELF CLEAR?
WILL YOU CALL ME WHEN YOU GET THERE?
©2009 ZITS Partnership. Distributed by King Features Syndicate.
11/15
SCOTT and BORGMAN

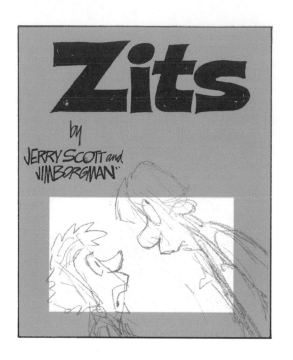

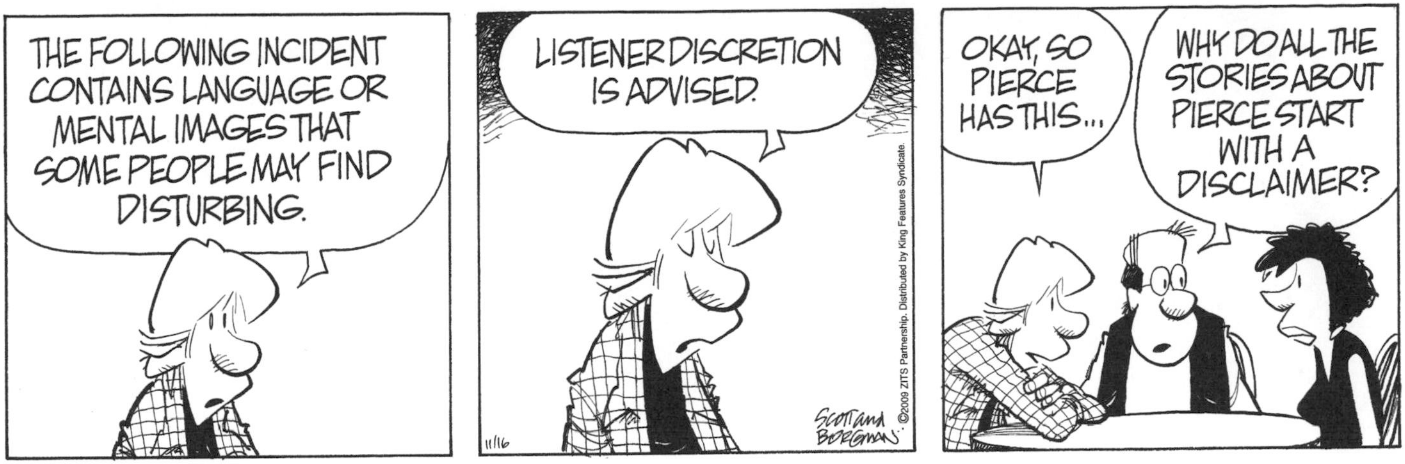
THE FOLLOWING INCIDENT CONTAINS LANGUAGE OR MENTAL IMAGES THAT SOME PEOPLE MAY FIND DISTURBING.
LISTENER DISCRETION IS ADVISED.
©2009 ZITS Partnership. Distributed by King Features Syndicate.
SCOTT and BORGMAN
11/16
OKAY, SO PIERCE HAS THIS...
WHY DO ALL THE STORIES ABOUT PIERCE START WITH A DISCLAIMER?

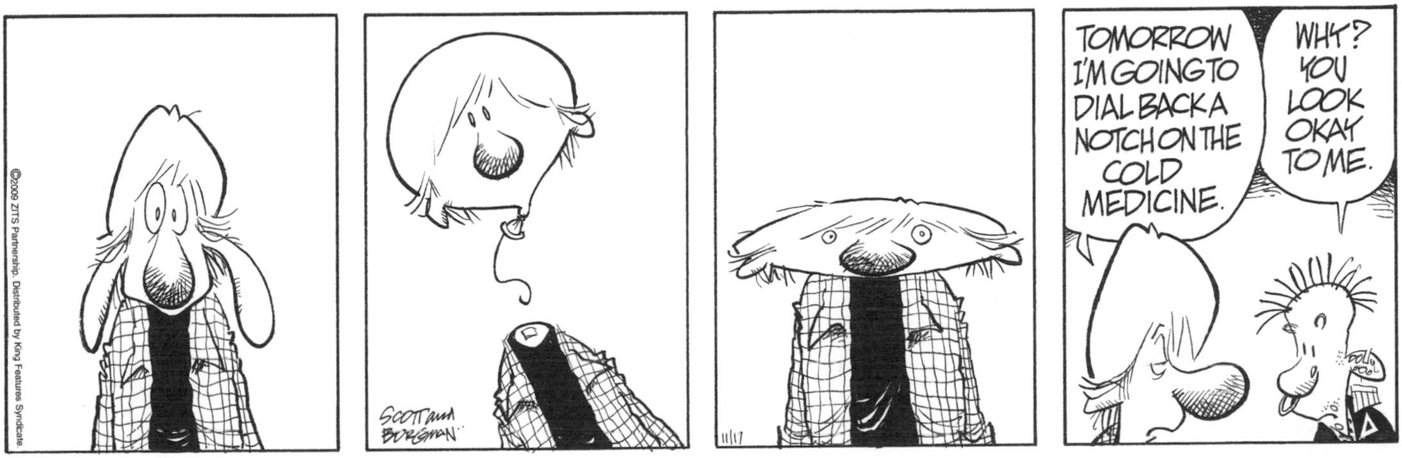
©2009 ZITS Partnership. Distributed by King Features Syndicate.
SCOTT and BORGMAN
11/17
TOMORROW I'M GOING TO DIAL BACK A NOTCH ON THE COLD MEDICINE.
WHY? YOU LOOK OKAY TO ME.

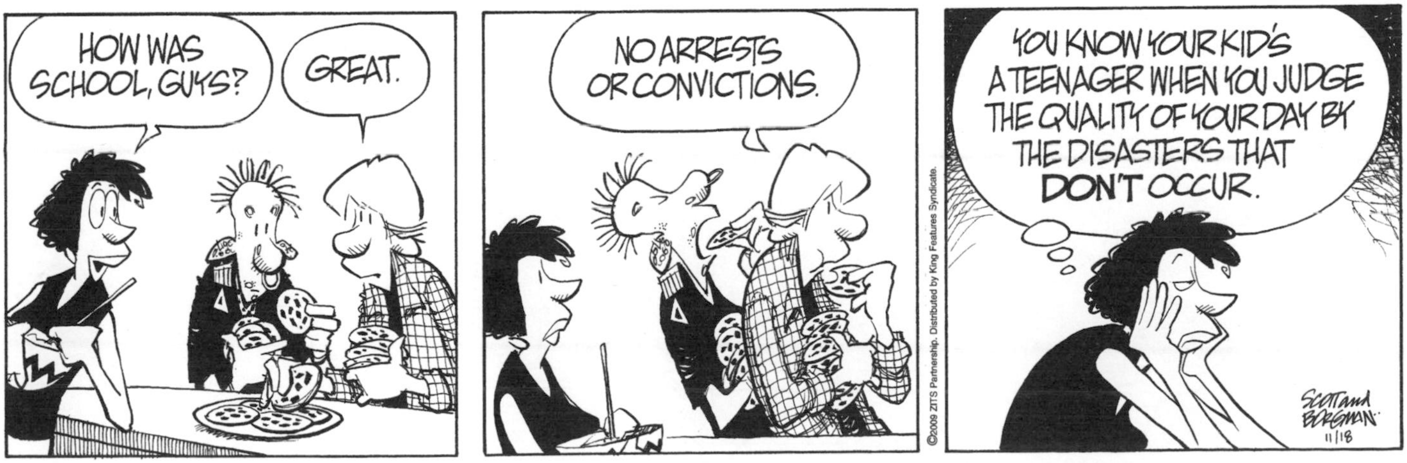
HOW WAS SCHOOL, GUYS?
GREAT.
NO ARRESTS OR CONVICTIONS.
©2009 ZITS Partnership. Distributed by King Features Syndicate.
YOU KNOW YOUR KID'S A TEENAGER WHEN YOU JUDGE THE QUALITY OF YOUR DAY BY THE DISASTERS THAT DON'T OCCUR.
SCOTT and BORGMAN
11/18

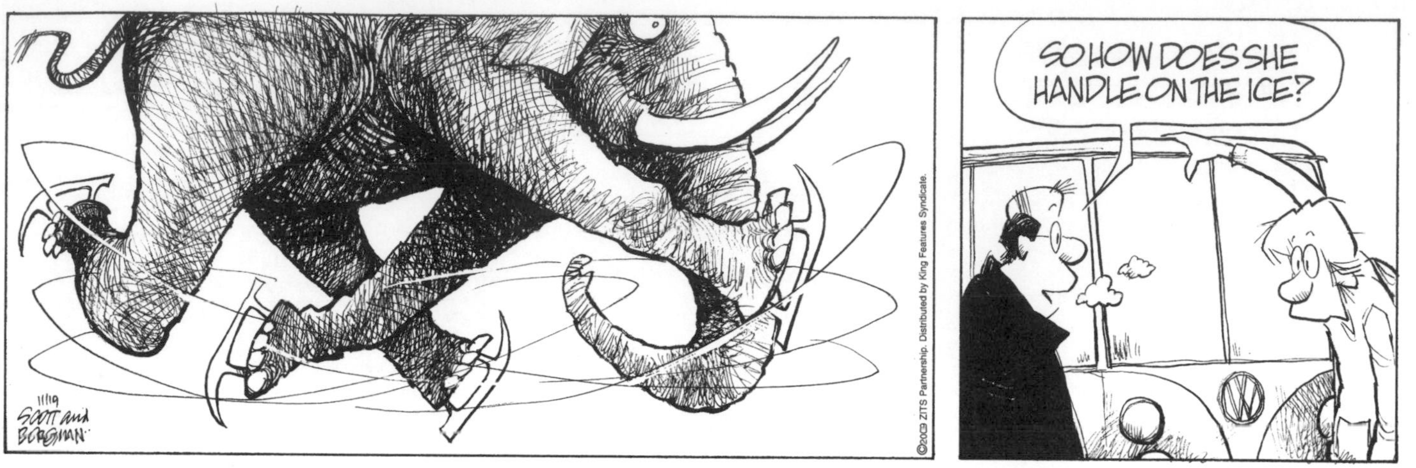
11/19
SCOTT and BORGMAN
SO HOW DOES SHE HANDLE ON THE ICE?
©2009 ZITS Partnership. Distributed by King Features Syndicate.

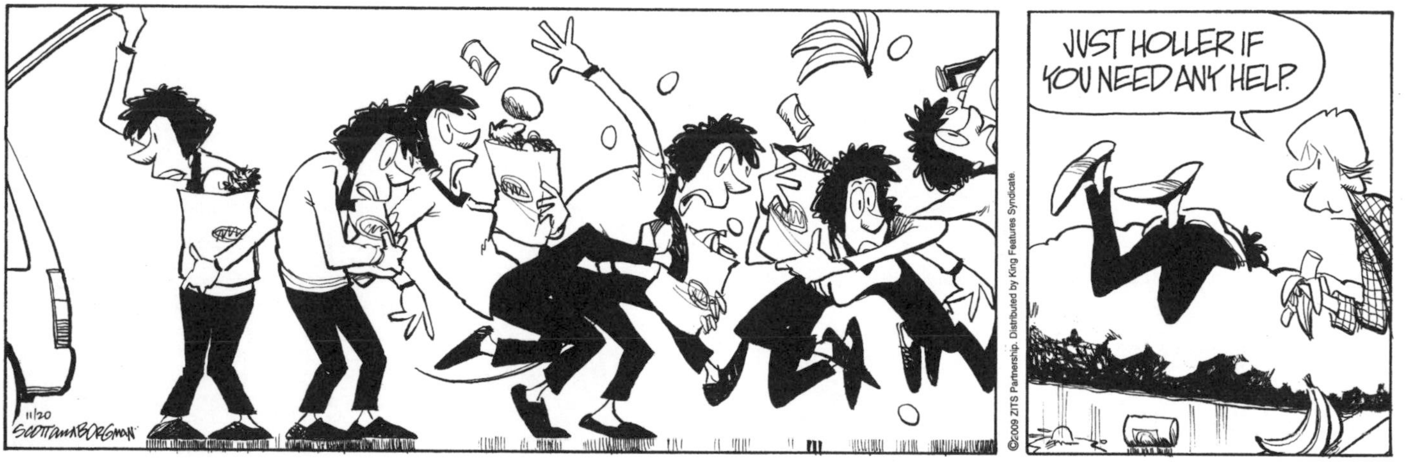
11/20
SCOTT and BORGMAN
JUST HOLLER IF YOU NEED ANY HELP.
©2009 ZITS Partnership. Distributed by King Features Syndicate.

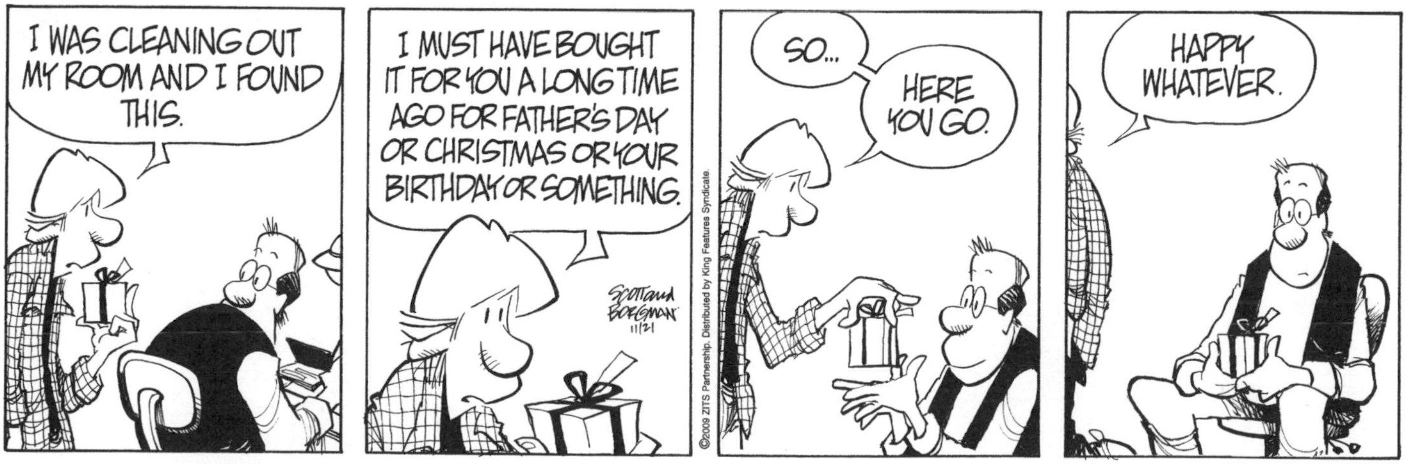
I WAS CLEANING OUT MY ROOM AND I FOUND THIS.
I MUST HAVE BOUGHT IT FOR YOU A LONG TIME AGO FOR FATHER'S DAY OR CHRISTMAS OR YOUR BIRTHDAY OR SOMETHING.
SCOTT and BORGMAN 11/21
©2009 ZITS Partnership. Distributed by King Features Syndicate.
SO...
HERE YOU GO.
HAPPY WHATEVER.

Zits
by JERRY SCOTT and JIM BORGMAN

PSSHHHHHHH
HHHHHHHHHHHHHHHHHH
HHHHHHHHHHHHHHHHHH
HHHHH
JEREMY, ARE YOU THINKING THAT MY PARTY IS TONIGHT? BECAUSE IT'S NOT... IT'S TOMORROW.
OH.
ARE YOU PSYCHIC OR SOMETHING?
NO, YOUR BODY SPRAY GOT PICKED UP BY THE JET STREAM.
SLAM!
©2009 ZITS Partnership. Distributed by King Features Syndicate.

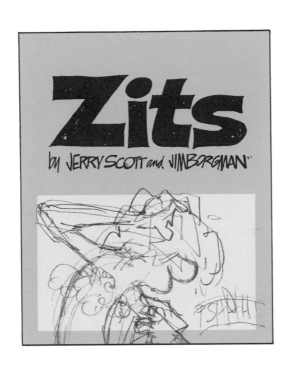

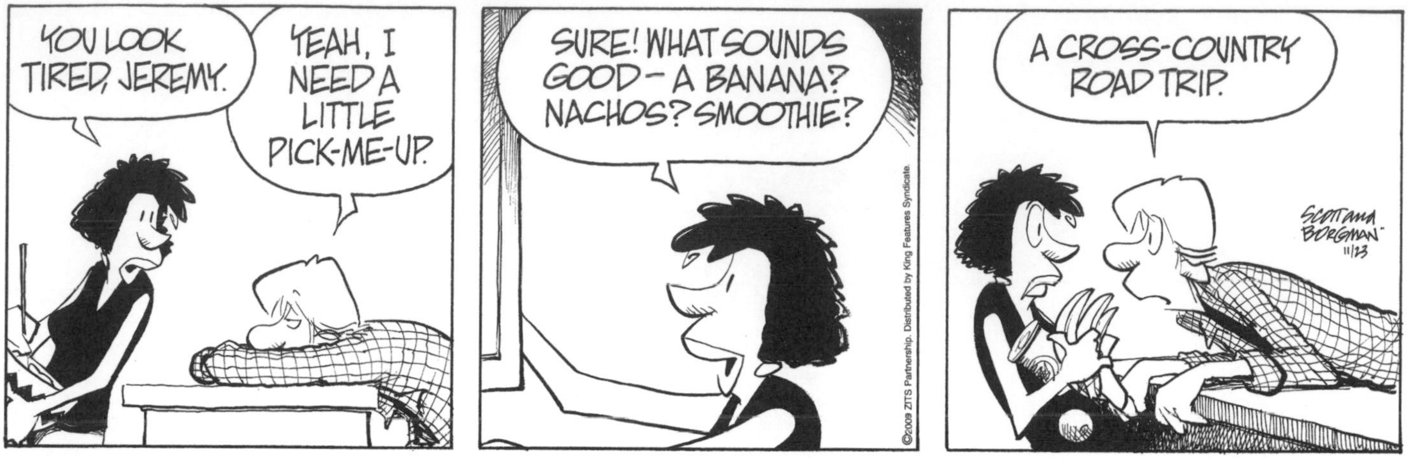
YOU LOOK TIRED, JEREMY.
YEAH, I NEED A LITTLE PICK-ME-UP.
SURE! WHAT SOUNDS GOOD – A BANANA? NACHOS? SMOOTHIE?
A CROSS-COUNTRY ROAD TRIP.
SCOTT and BORGMAN 11/23
©2009 ZITS Partnership. Distributed by King Features Syndicate.

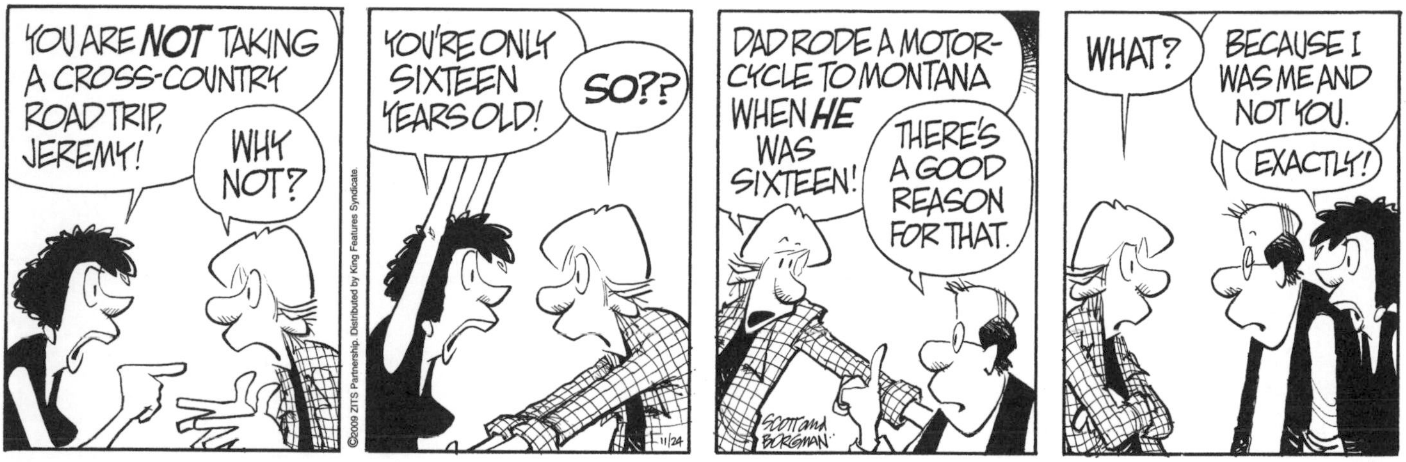
YOU ARE **NOT** TAKING A CROSS-COUNTRY ROAD TRIP, JEREMY!
WHY NOT?
©2009 ZITS Partnership. Distributed by King Features Syndicate.
YOU'RE ONLY SIXTEEN YEARS OLD!
SO??
DAD RODE A MOTORCYCLE TO MONTANA WHEN **HE** WAS SIXTEEN!
THERE'S A GOOD REASON FOR THAT.
SCOTT and BORGMAN 11/24
WHAT?
BECAUSE I WAS ME AND NOT YOU.
EXACTLY!

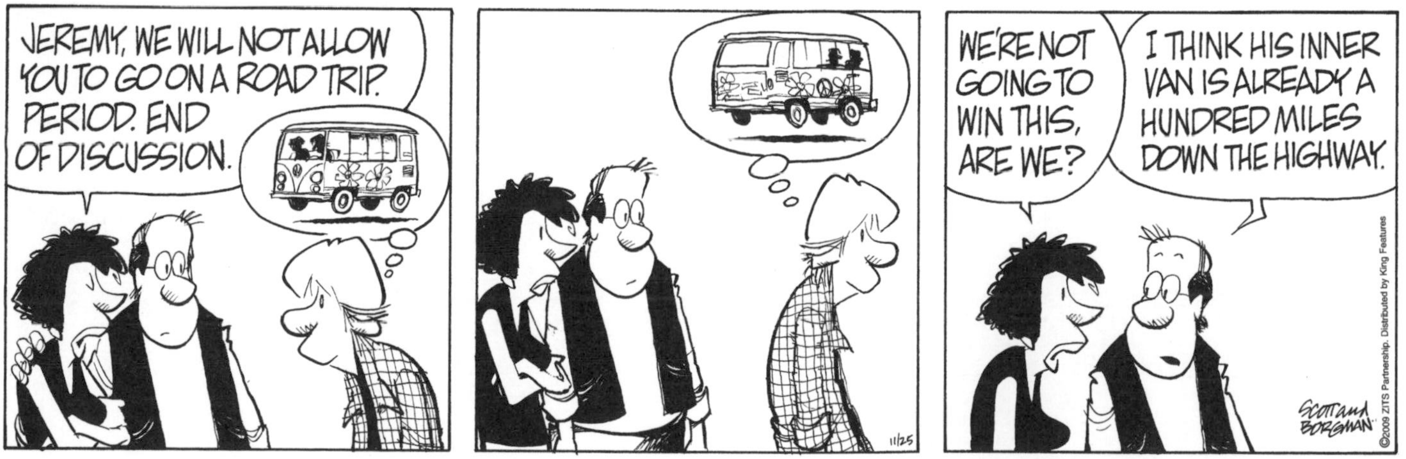
JEREMY, WE WILL NOT ALLOW YOU TO GO ON A ROAD TRIP. PERIOD. END OF DISCUSSION.
11/25
WE'RE NOT GOING TO WIN THIS, ARE WE?
I THINK HIS INNER VAN IS ALREADY A HUNDRED MILES DOWN THE HIGHWAY.
SCOTT and BORGMAN
©2009 ZITS Partnership. Distributed by King Features

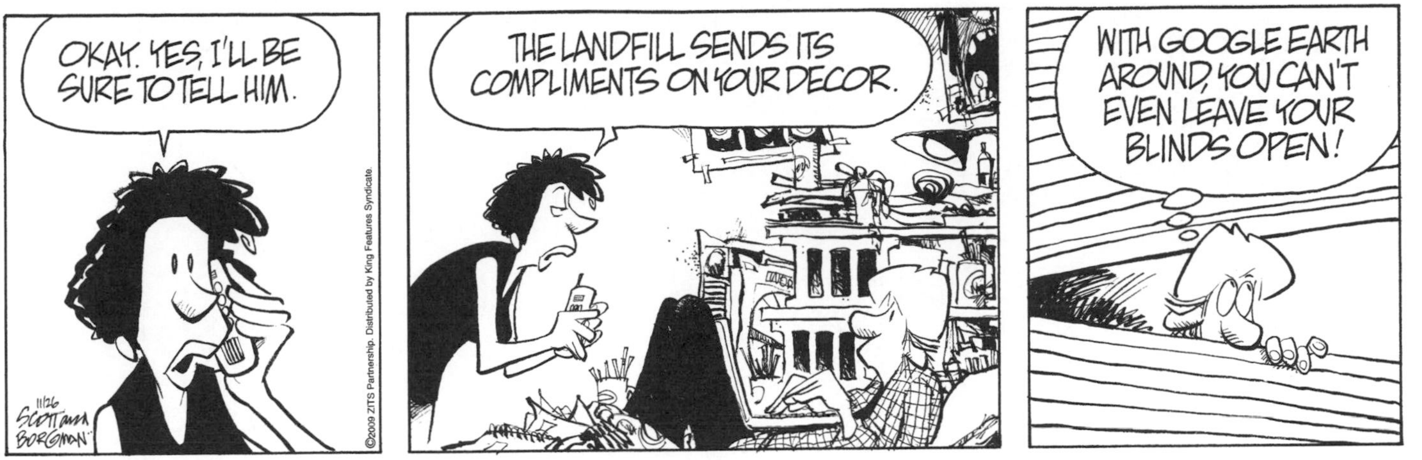
OKAY. YES, I'LL BE SURE TO TELL HIM.
11/26 SCOTT and BORGMAN
©2009 ZITS Partnership. Distributed by King Features Syndicate.
THE LANDFILL SENDS ITS COMPLIMENTS ON YOUR DECOR.
WITH GOOGLE EARTH AROUND, YOU CAN'T EVEN LEAVE YOUR BLINDS OPEN!

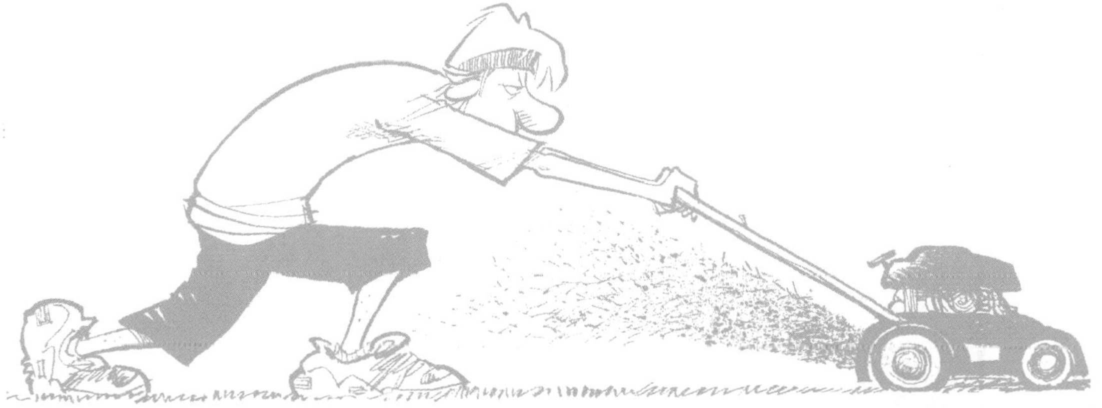

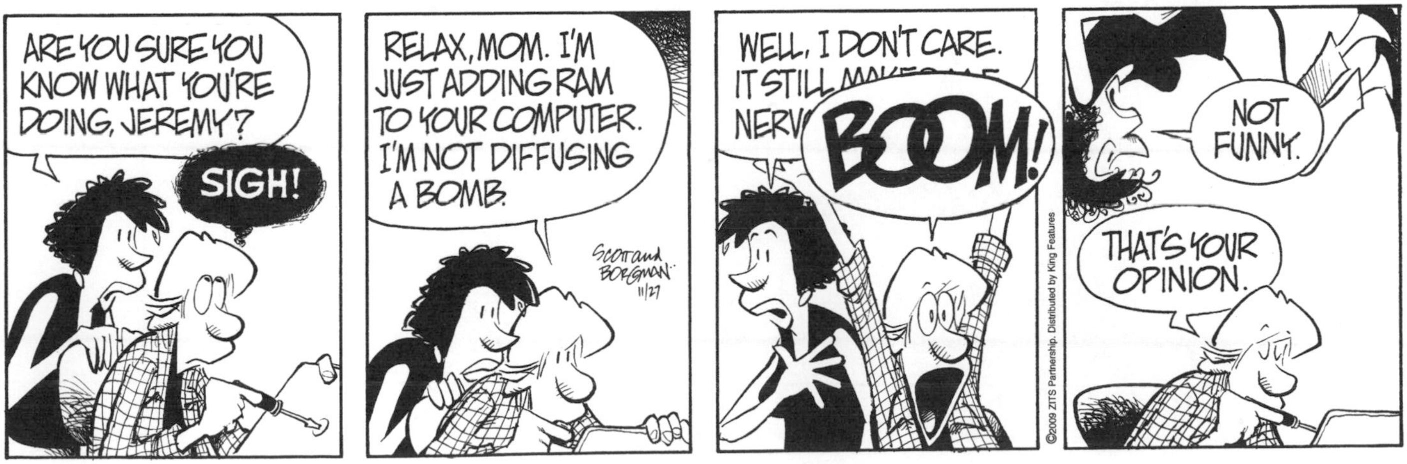
ARE YOU SURE YOU KNOW WHAT YOU'RE DOING, JEREMY?
SIGH!
RELAX, MOM. I'M JUST ADDING RAM TO YOUR COMPUTER. I'M NOT DIFFUSING A BOMB.
SCOTT and BORGMAN 11/27
WELL, I DON'T CARE.
IT STILL
BOOM!
©2009 ZITS Partnership. Distributed by King Features
NOT FUNNY.
THAT'S YOUR OPINION.

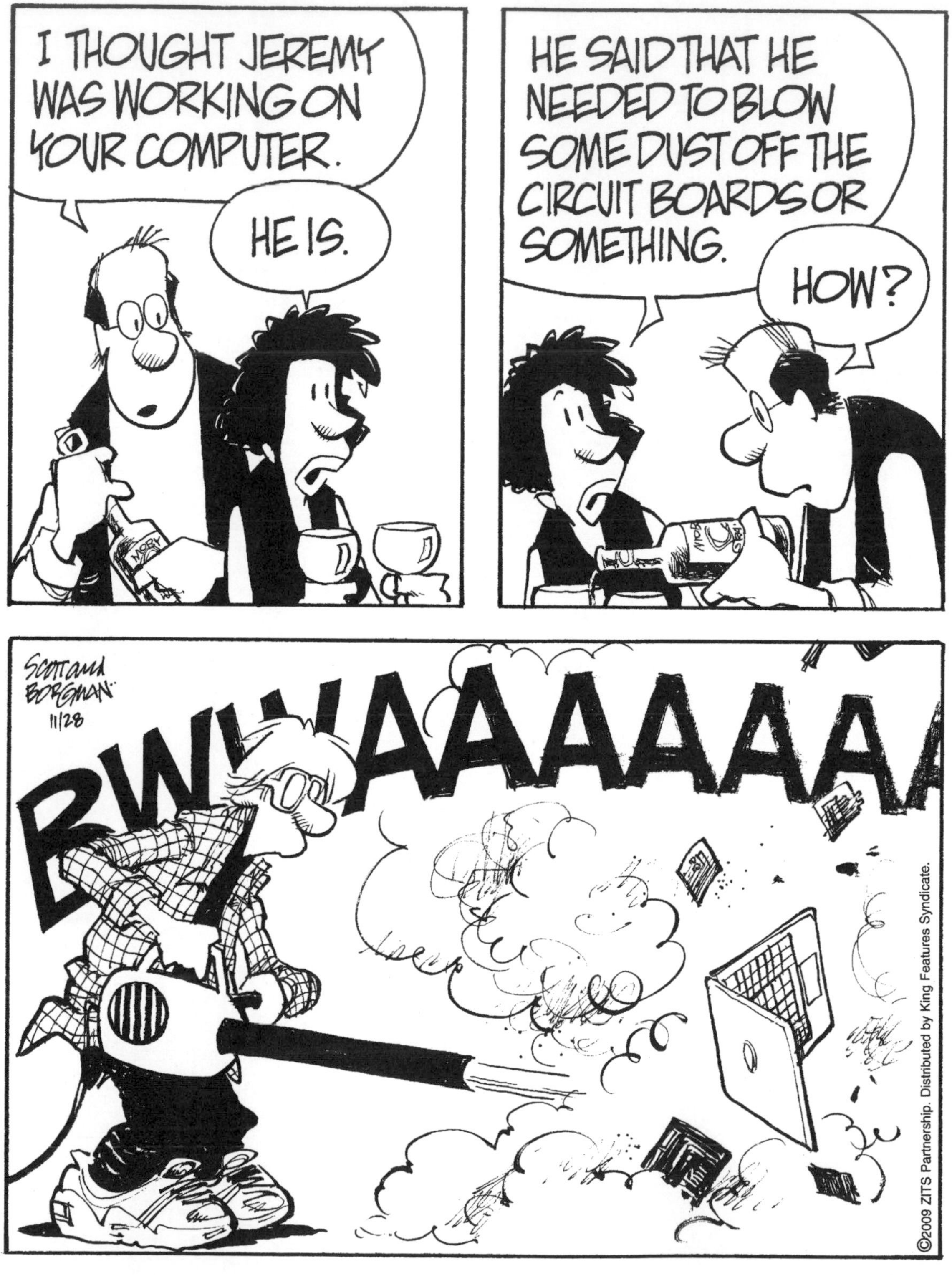
I THOUGHT JEREMY WAS WORKING ON YOUR COMPUTER.
HE IS.
HE SAID THAT HE NEEDED TO BLOW SOME DUST OFF THE CIRCUIT BOARDS OR SOMETHING.
HOW?
SCOTT AND BORGMAN 11/28
BW
AAAAAAA

Zits
by JERRY SCOTT and
JIM BORGMAN

PIZZ
SORRY. I TALK WHEN I'M NERVOUS.
'S OKAY.
SCOTT and BORGMAN

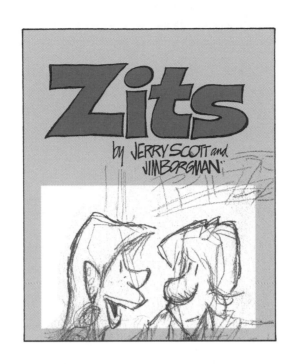

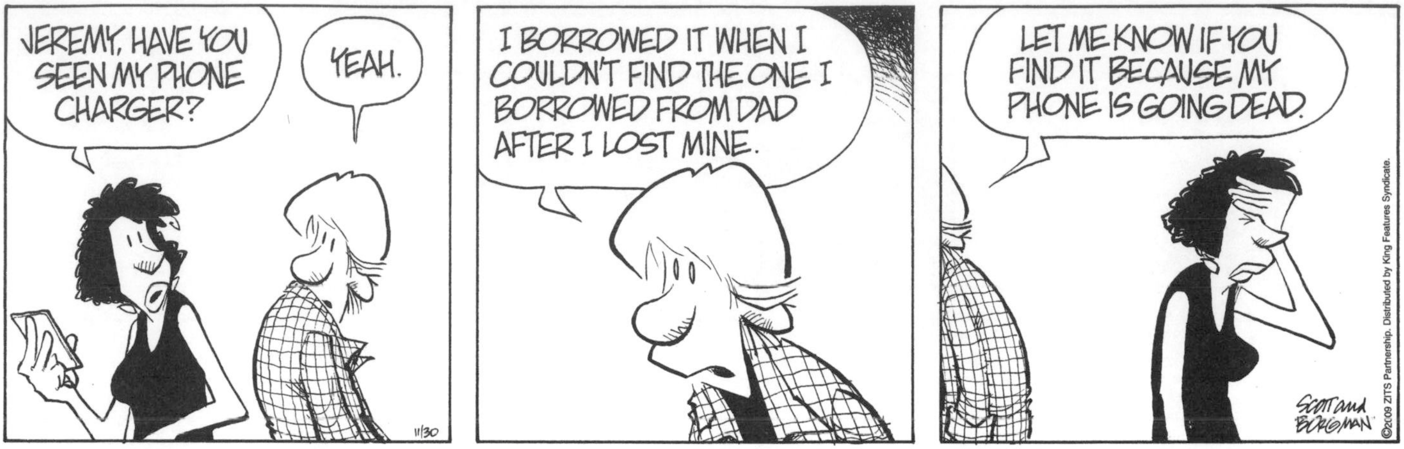
JEREMY, HAVE YOU SEEN MY PHONE CHARGER?
YEAH.
I BORROWED IT WHEN I COULDN'T FIND THE ONE I BORROWED FROM DAD AFTER I LOST MINE.
LET ME KNOW IF YOU FIND IT BECAUSE MY PHONE IS GOING DEAD.
11/30
SCOTT and BORGMAN
©2009 ZITS Partnership. Distributed by King Features Syndicate.

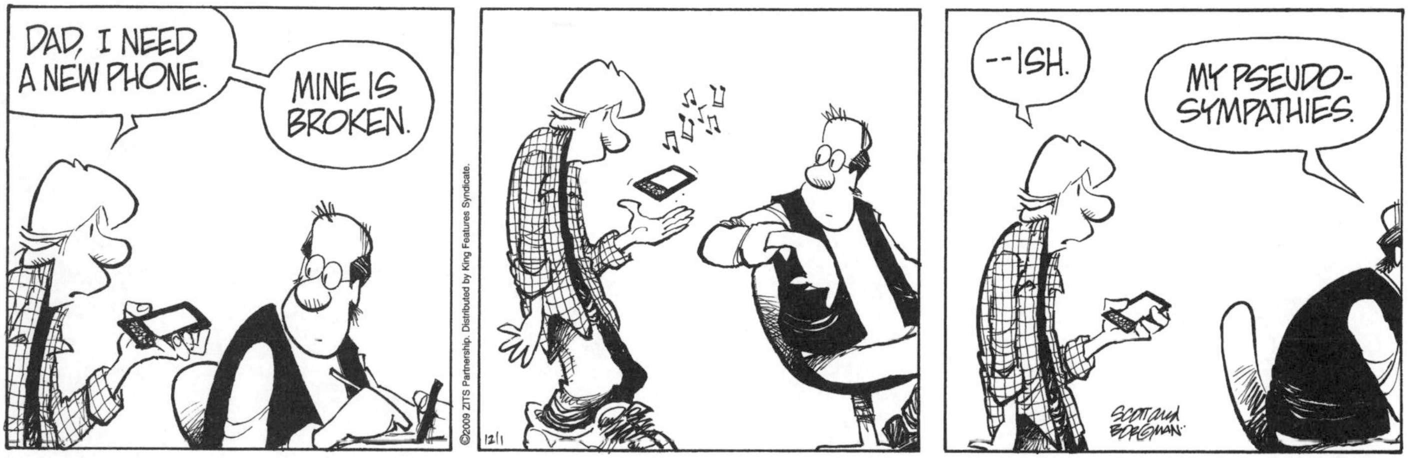
DAD, I NEED A NEW PHONE.
MINE IS BROKEN.
--ISH.
MY PSEUDO-SYMPATHIES.
12/1
SCOTT and BORGMAN
©2009 ZITS Partnership. Distributed by King Features Syndicate.

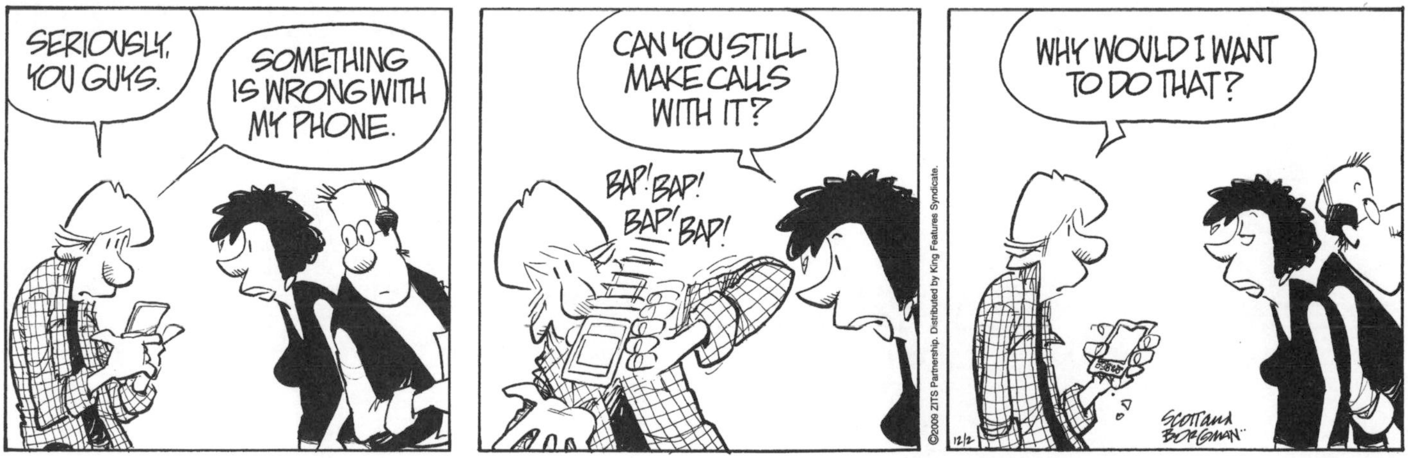
SERIOUSLY, YOU GUYS.
SOMETHING IS WRONG WITH MY PHONE.
CAN YOU STILL MAKE CALLS WITH IT?
BAP! BAP! BAP! BAP!
WHY WOULD I WANT TO DO THAT?
12/2
SCOTT and BORGMAN
©2009 ZITS Partnership. Distributed by King Features Syndicate.

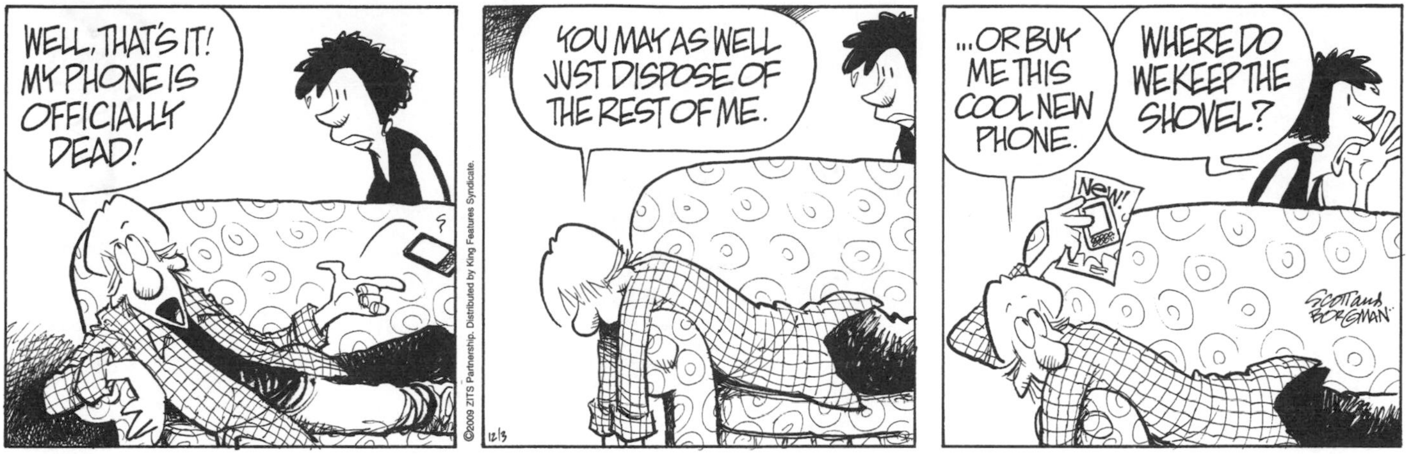
WELL, THAT'S IT! MY PHONE IS OFFICIALLY DEAD!
©2009 ZITS Partnership. Distributed by King Features Syndicate.
12/3
YOU MAY AS WELL JUST DISPOSE OF THE REST OF ME.
...OR BUY ME THIS COOL NEW PHONE.
NEW!
WHERE DO WE KEEP THE SHOVEL?
SCOTT and BORGMAN

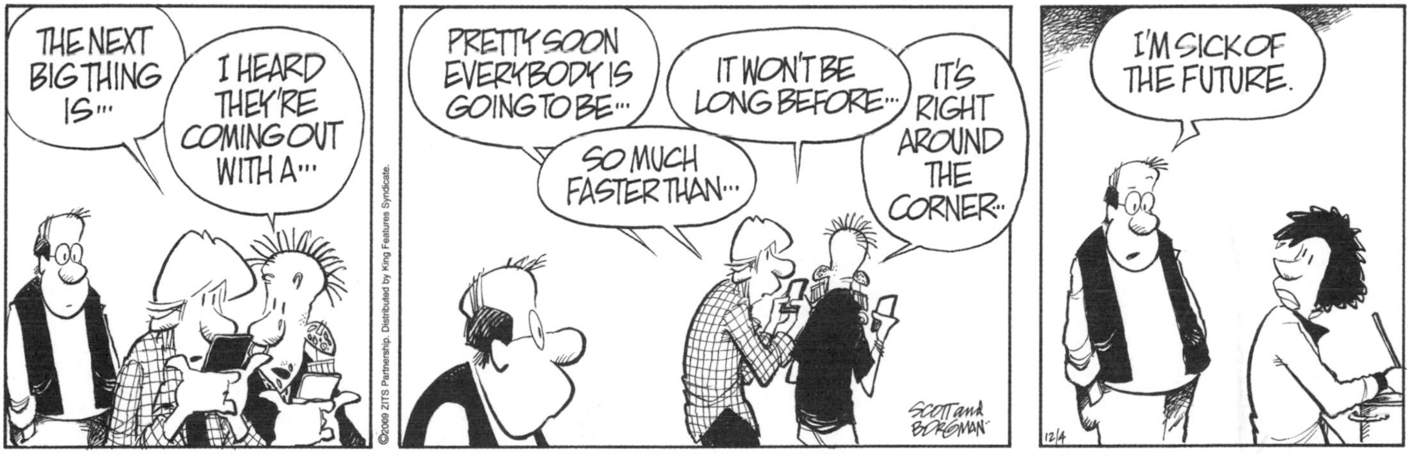
THE NEXT BIG THING IS...
I HEARD THEY'RE COMING OUT WITH A...
©2009 ZITS Partnership. Distributed by King Features Syndicate.
PRETTY SOON EVERYBODY IS GOING TO BE...
SO MUCH FASTER THAN...
IT WON'T BE LONG BEFORE...
IT'S RIGHT AROUND THE CORNER...
SCOTT and BORGMAN
I'M SICK OF THE FUTURE.
12/4

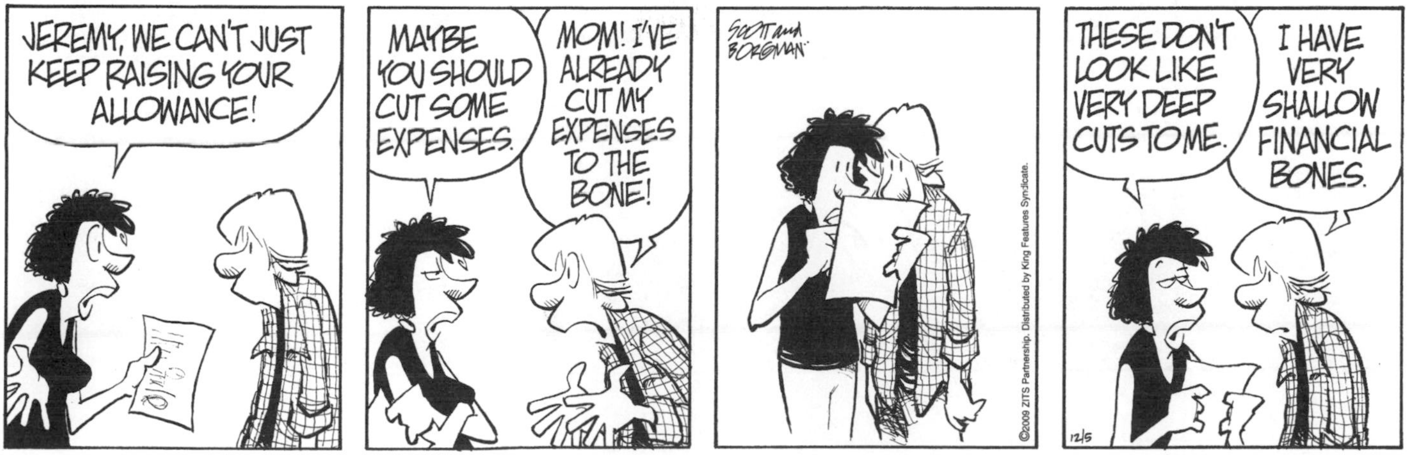
JEREMY, WE CAN'T JUST KEEP RAISING YOUR ALLOWANCE!
MAYBE YOU SHOULD CUT SOME EXPENSES.
MOM! I'VE ALREADY CUT MY EXPENSES TO THE BONE!
SCOTT and BORGMAN
©2009 ZITS Partnership. Distributed by King Features Syndicate.
THESE DON'T LOOK LIKE VERY DEEP CUTS TO ME.
I HAVE VERY SHALLOW FINANCIAL BONES.
12/5

Zits
by JERRY SCOTT and JIM BORGMAN

7:00AM
WALT...?
GO BACK TO SLEEP.
I'M GOING TO MAKE A BIG BREAKFAST FOR JEREMY AND THE GUYS AFTER THEIR POKER PARTY LAST NIGHT.
YAWN!
7:15AM
©2009 ZITS Partnership. Distributed by King Features Syndicate.
7:45AM
Waffle Mix
8:30AM
10:00AM
SCOTT and BORGMAN
SPANG!
12:30PM
(SNIFF!) WHAT SMELLS LIKE STALE BACON?
WHY ARE WE UP SO EARLY?

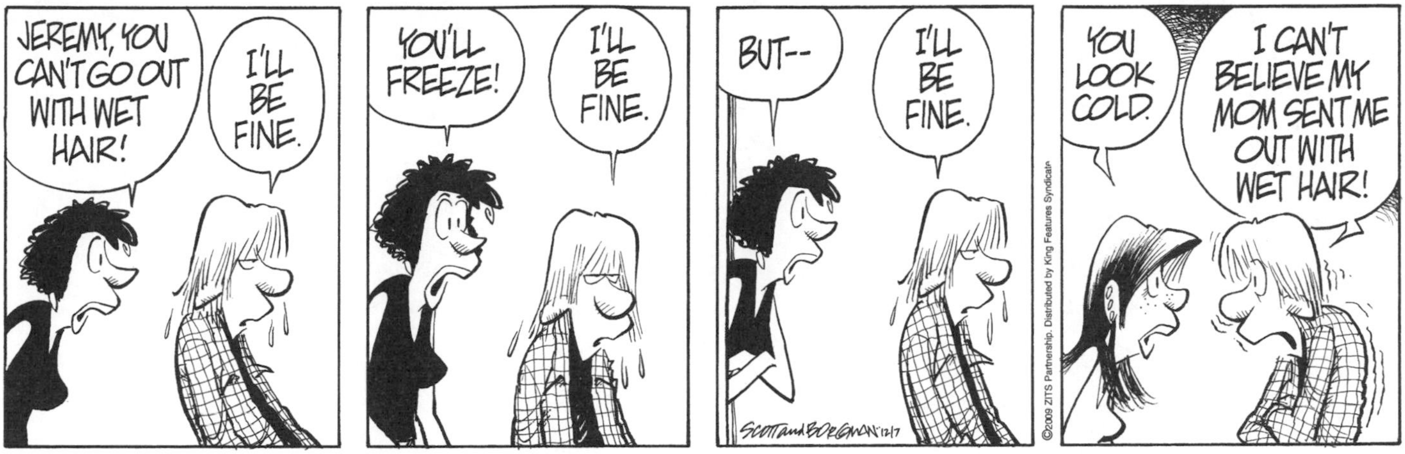
JEREMY, YOU CAN'T GO OUT WITH WET HAIR!
I'LL BE FINE.
YOU'LL FREEZE!
I'LL BE FINE.
BUT--
I'LL BE FINE.
YOU LOOK COLD.
I CAN'T BELIEVE MY MOM SENT ME OUT WITH WET HAIR!
SCOTT and BORGMAN 12/7
©2009 ZITS Partnership. Distributed by King Features Syndicate.

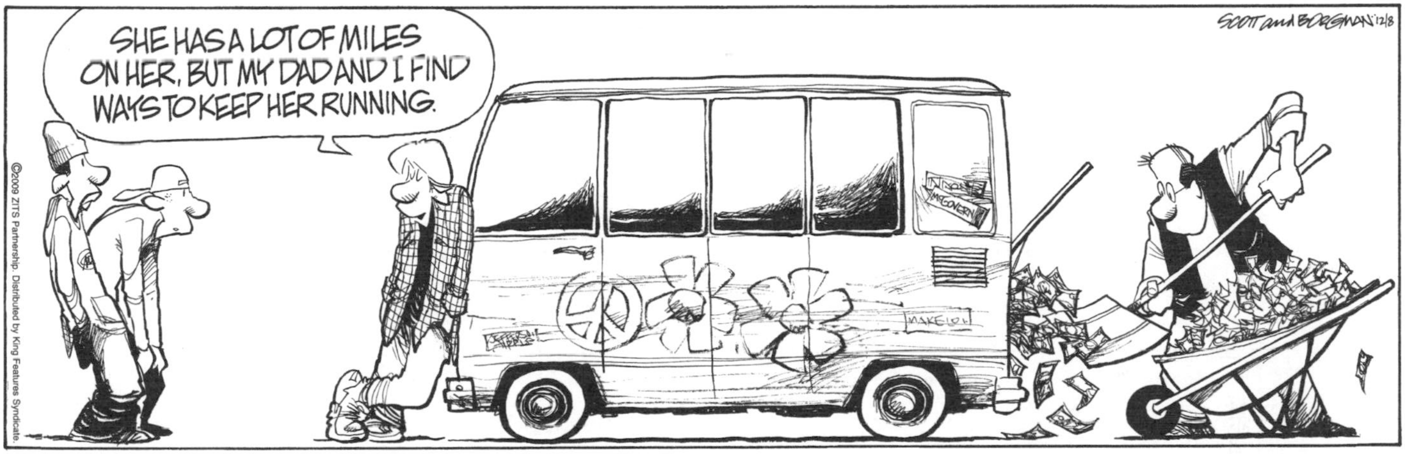
SHE HAS A LOT OF MILES ON HER, BUT MY DAD AND I FIND WAYS TO KEEP HER RUNNING.
SCOTT and BORGMAN 12/8
©2009 ZITS Partnership. Distributed by King Features Syndicate.

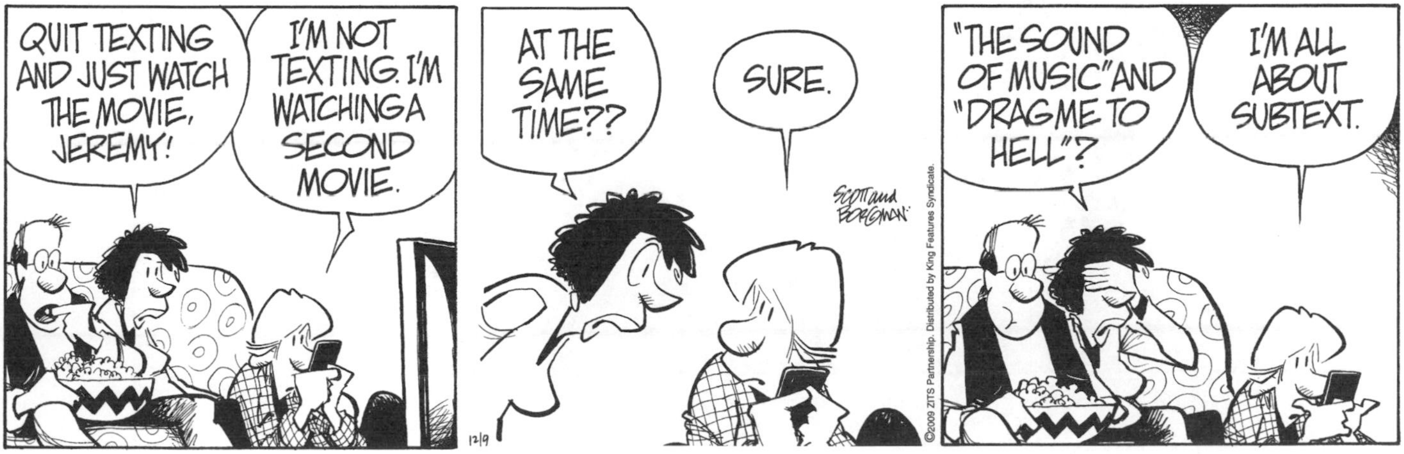
QUIT TEXTING AND JUST WATCH THE MOVIE, JEREMY!
I'M NOT TEXTING. I'M WATCHING A SECOND MOVIE.
AT THE SAME TIME??
SURE.
SCOTT and BORGMAN
12/9
"THE SOUND OF MUSIC" AND "DRAG ME TO HELL"?
I'M ALL ABOUT SUBTEXT.
©2009 ZITS Partnership. Distributed by King Features Syndicate.

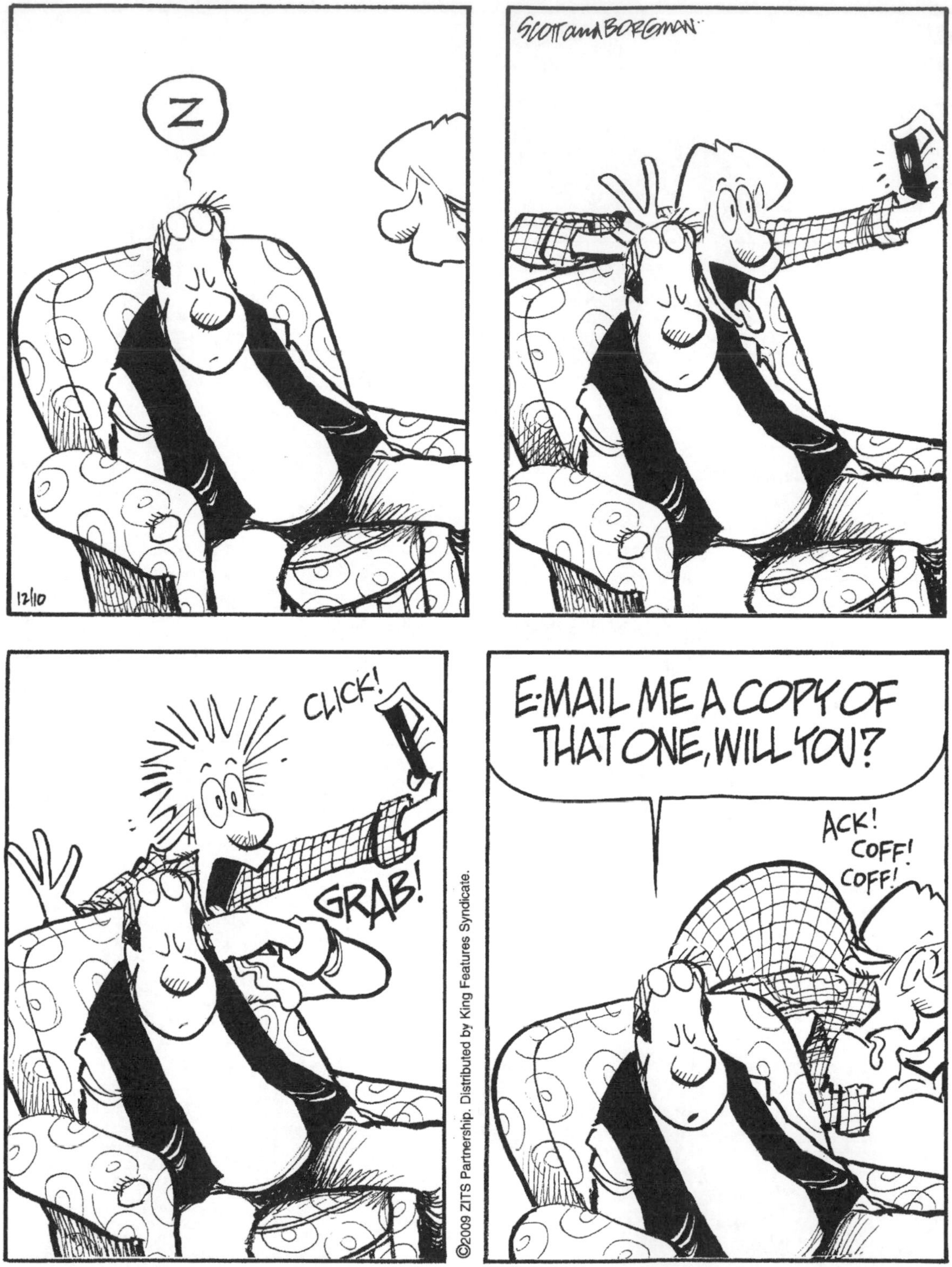
Z
SCOTT and BORGMAN
12/10
CLICK!
GRAB!
E-MAIL ME A COPY OF THAT ONE, WILL YOU?
ACK! COFF! COFF!

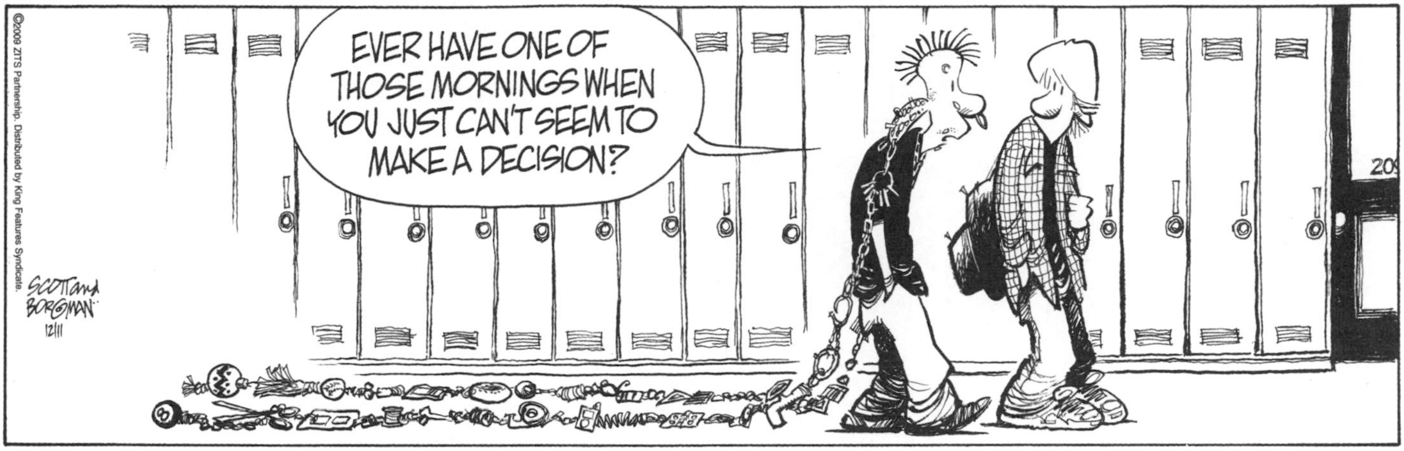
©2009 ZITS Partnership. Distributed by King Features Syndicate.
SCOTT and BORGMAN 12/11
EVER HAVE ONE OF THOSE MORNINGS WHEN YOU JUST CAN'T SEEM TO MAKE A DECISION?

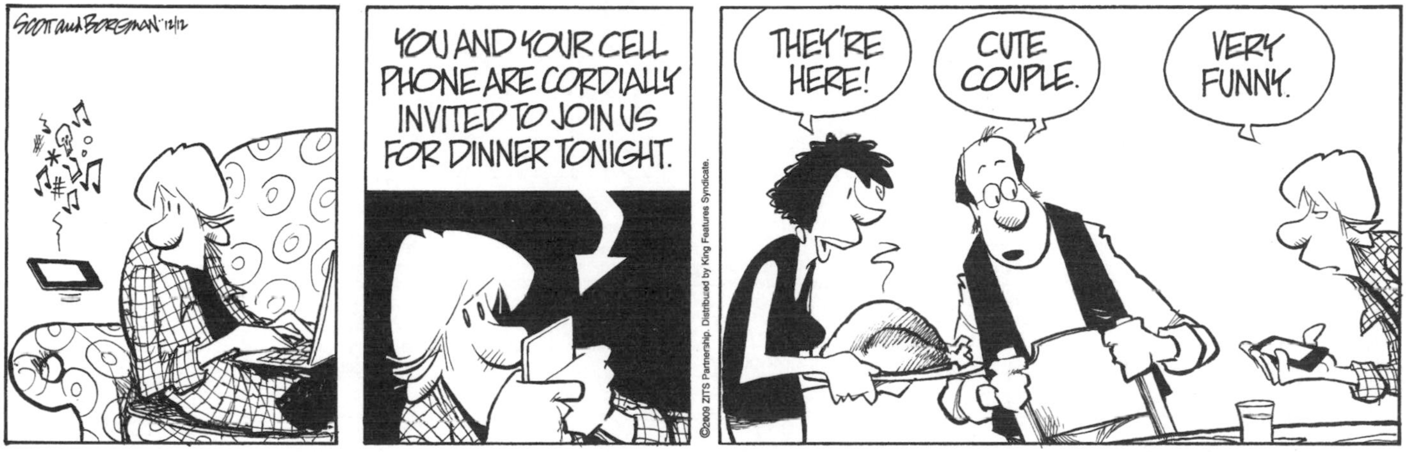
SCOTT and BORGMAN 12/12
YOU AND YOUR CELL PHONE ARE CORDIALLY INVITED TO JOIN US FOR DINNER TONIGHT.
©2009 ZITS Partnership. Distributed by King Features Syndicate.
THEY'RE HERE!
CUTE COUPLE.
VERY FUNNY.

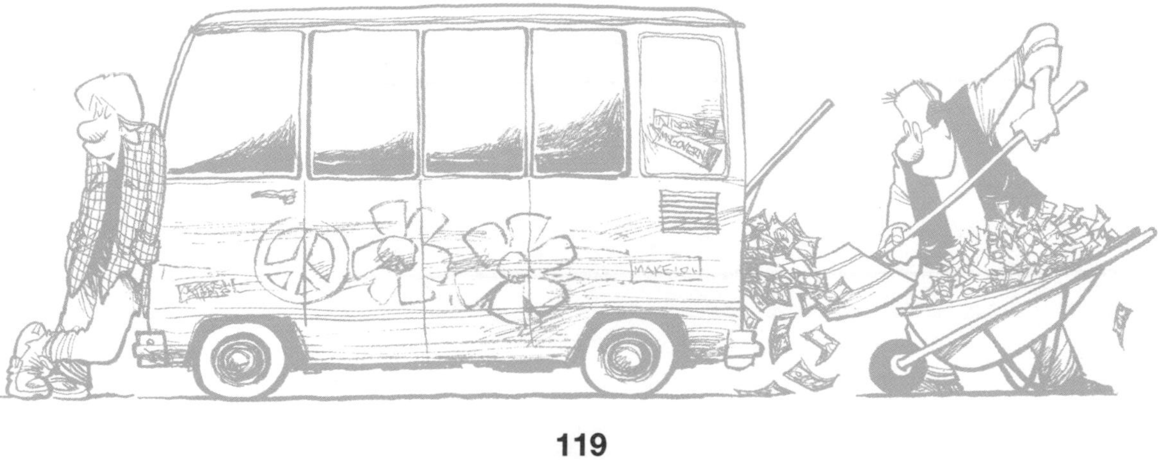

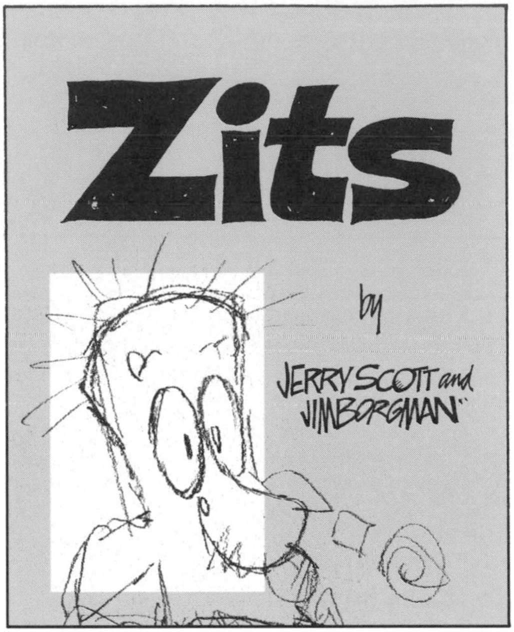
Zits
by
JERRY SCOTT and JIM BORGMAN

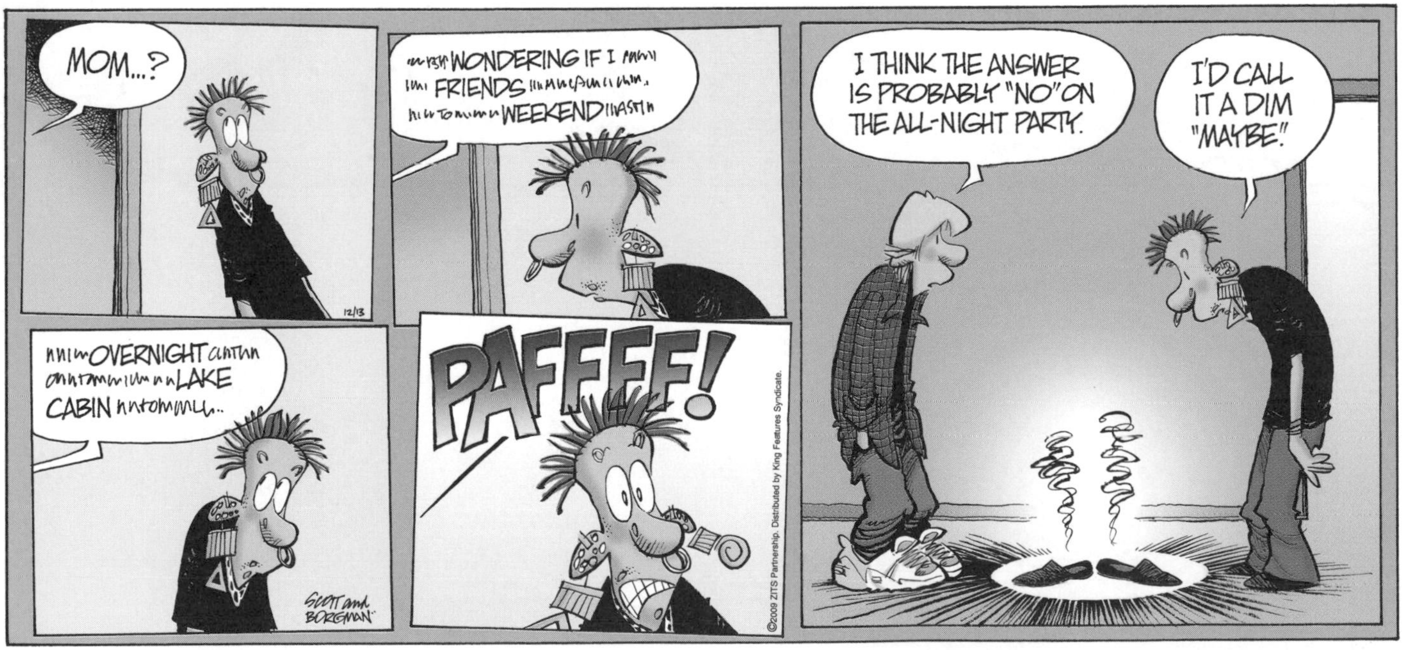
MOM...?
12/13
WONDERING IF I
FRIENDS
WEEKEND
OVERNIGHT
LAKE
CABIN
SCOTT and BORGMAN
PAFFFF!
©2009 ZITS Partnership. Distributed by King Features Syndicate.
I THINK THE ANSWER IS PROBABLY "NO" ON THE ALL-NIGHT PARTY.
I'D CALL IT A DIM "MAYBE."

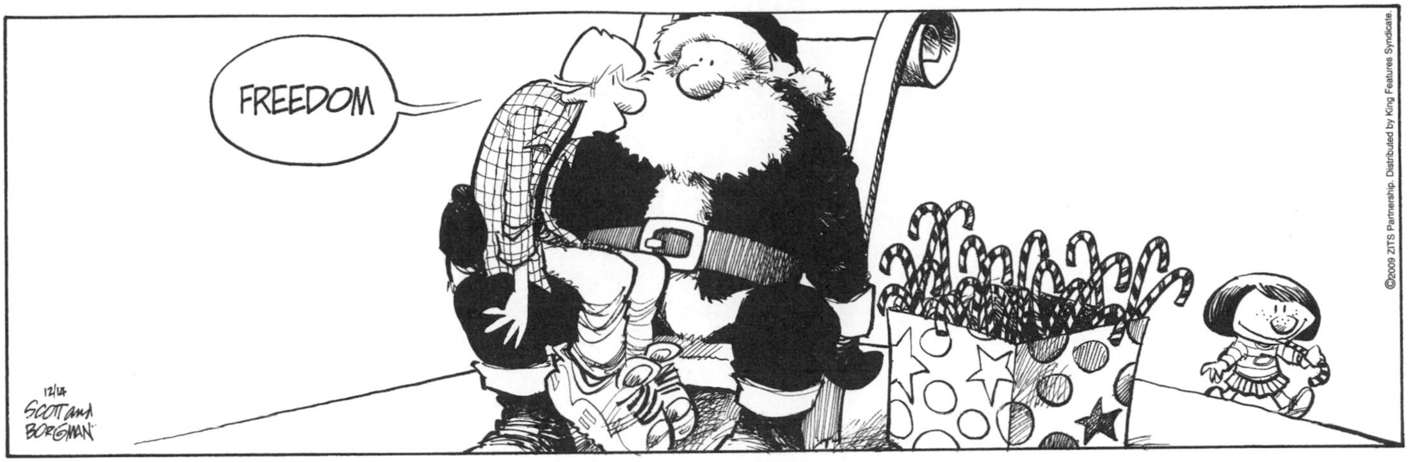
FREEDOM
12/14
SCOTT and BORGMAN
©2009 ZITS Partnership. Distributed by King Features Syndicate.

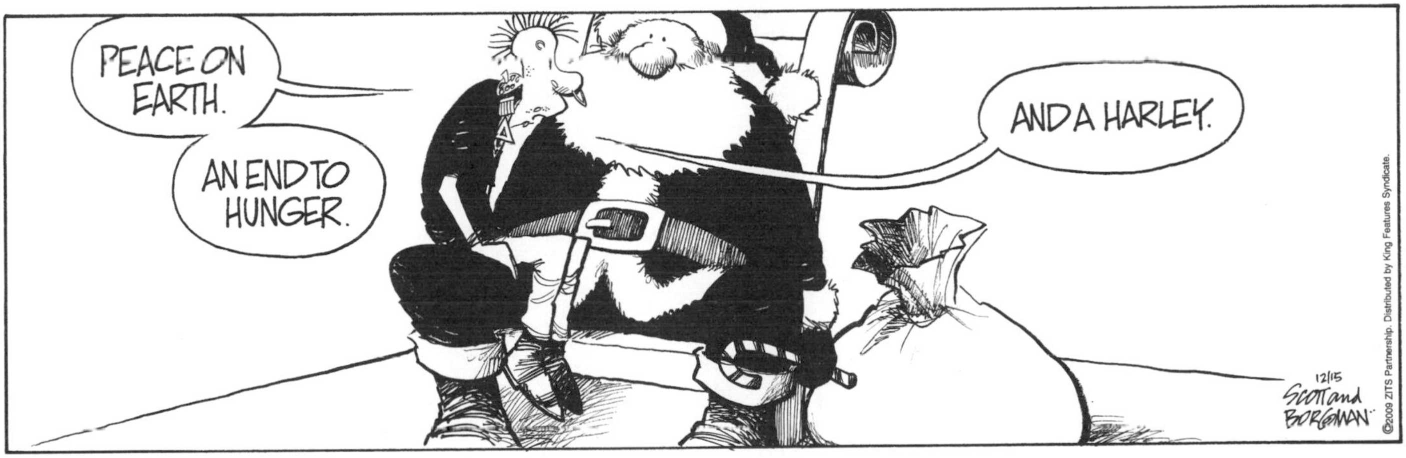
PEACE ON EARTH.
AN END TO HUNGER.
AND A HARLEY.
12/15
SCOTT and BORGMAN
©2009 ZITS Partnership. Distributed by King Features Syndicate.

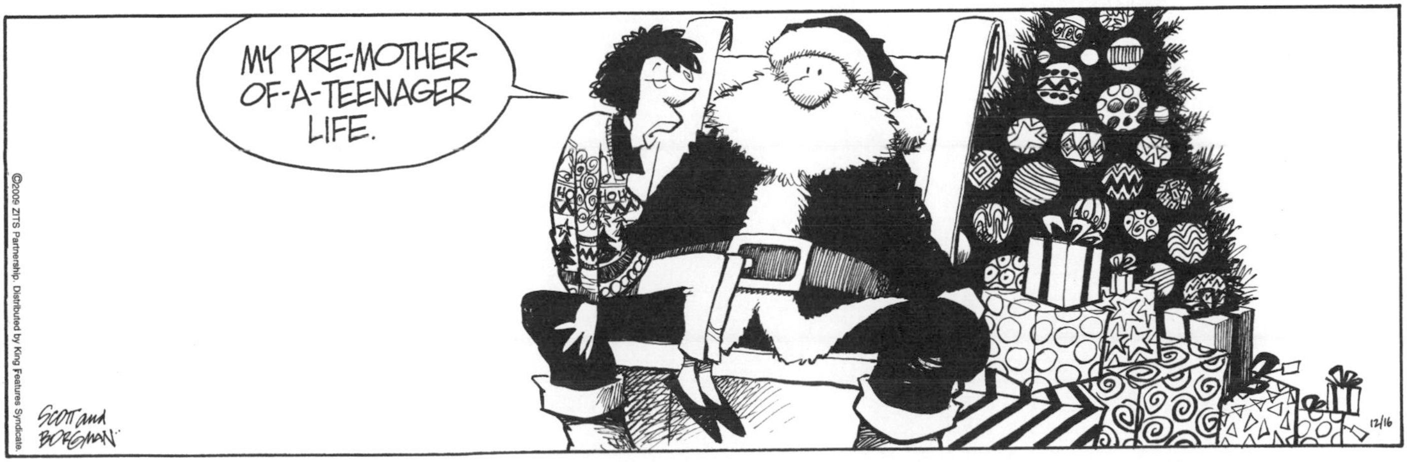
MY PRE-MOTHER-OF-A-TEENAGER LIFE.
SCOTT and BORGMAN
12/16
©2009 ZITS Partnership. Distributed by King Features Syndicate.

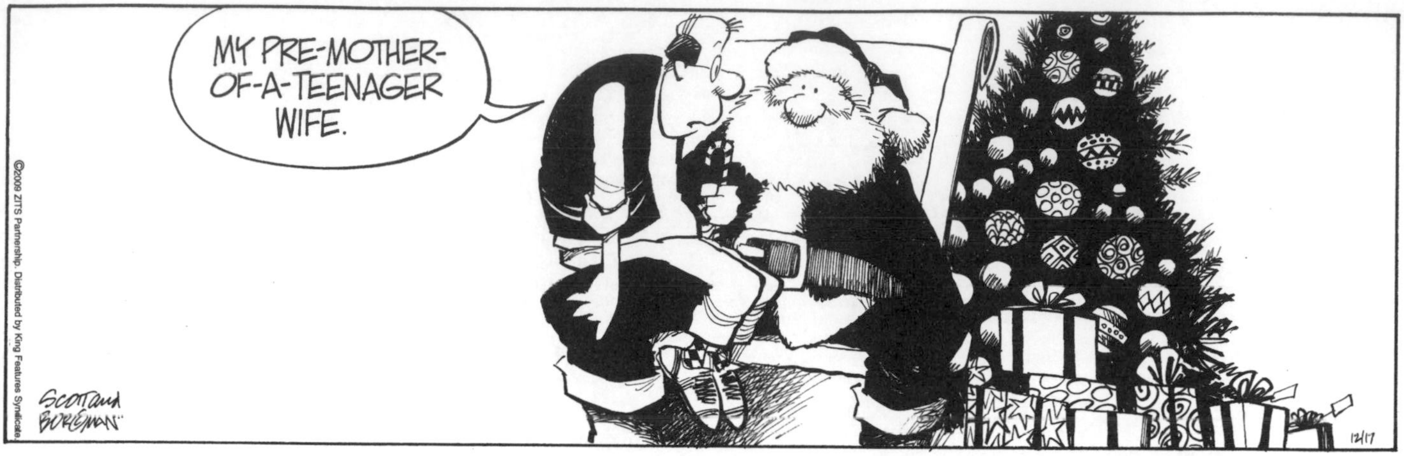
MY PRE-MOTHER-OF-A-TEENAGER WIFE.
©2009 ZITS Partnership. Distributed by King Features Syndicate.
SCOTT and BORGMAN
12/17

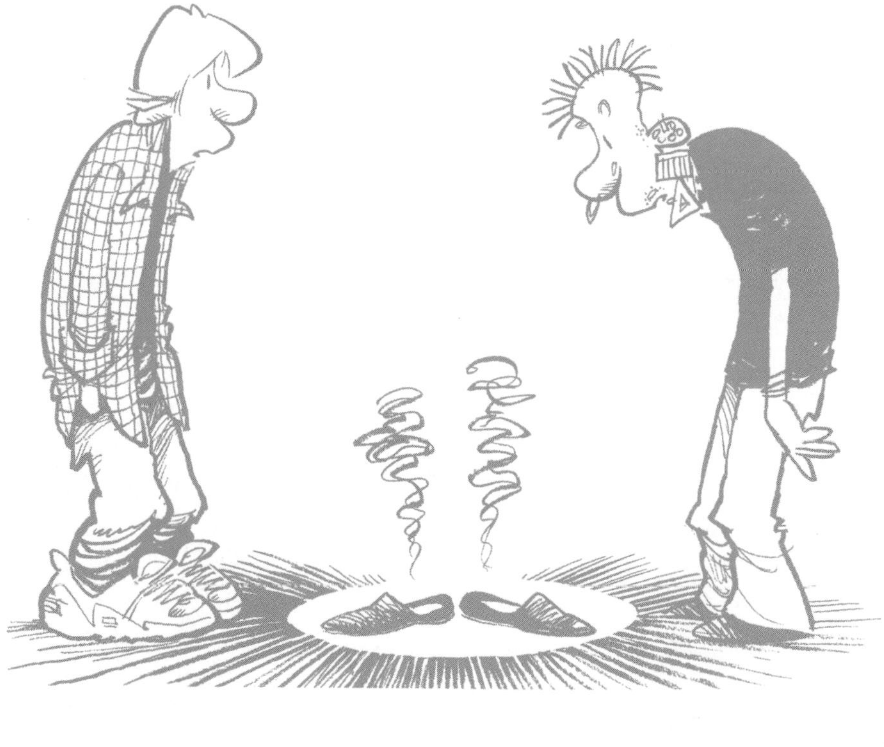

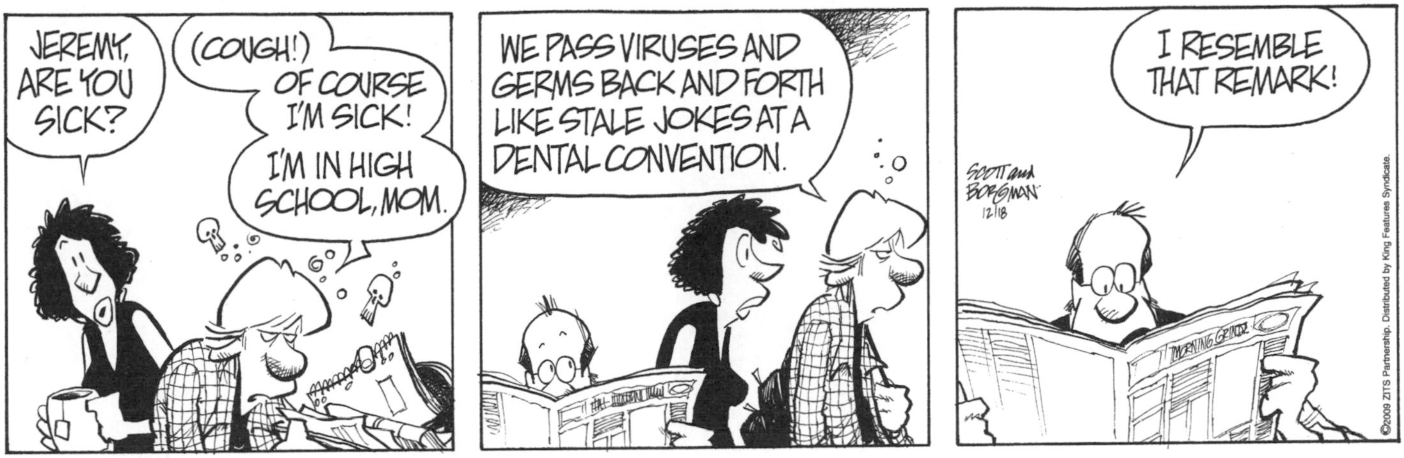
JEREMY, ARE YOU SICK?
(COUGH!) OF COURSE I'M SICK!
I'M IN HIGH SCHOOL, MOM.
WE PASS VIRUSES AND GERMS BACK AND FORTH LIKE STALE JOKES AT A DENTAL CONVENTION.
I RESEMBLE THAT REMARK!
SCOTT and BORGMAN 12/18
©2009 ZITS Partnership. Distributed by King Features Syndicate.

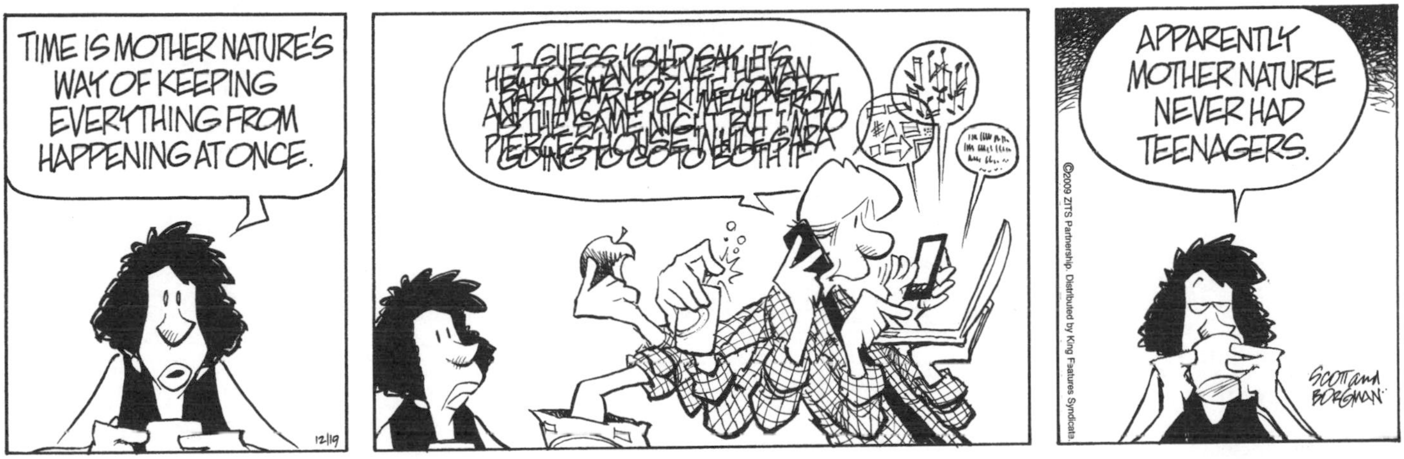
TIME IS MOTHER NATURE'S WAY OF KEEPING EVERYTHING FROM HAPPENING AT ONCE.
12/19
APPARENTLY MOTHER NATURE NEVER HAD TEENAGERS.
©2009 ZITS Partnership. Distributed by King Features Syndicate.
SCOTT and BORGMAN

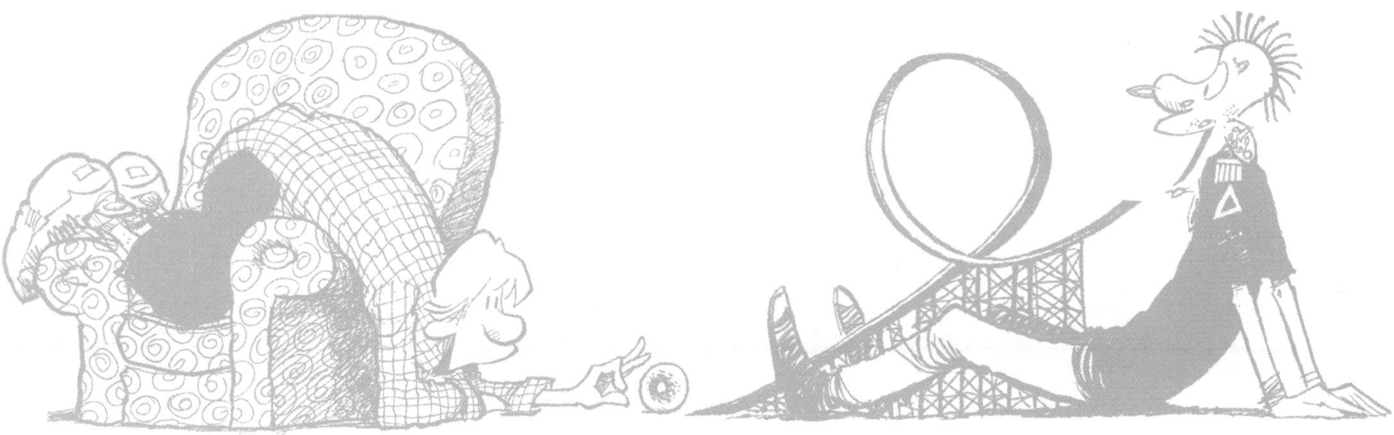

Zits
by JERRY SCOTT and JIM BORGMAN

It's All in the Way You Ask
JEREMY, DO YOU WANT TO HELP US DECORATE THE CHRISTMAS TR
NO.
JEREMY, WILL YOU PLEASE PARTICIP
NO.
IT WILL MEAN A LOT TO ME PERSONALLY IF YOU'LL JUST GIVE US A HAN
NO.
WOULD YOU PREFER TO TEACH ME HOW TO USE FACEBOOK OR HELP US DECORATE THE TR
TREE!
SCOTT and BORGMAN 12/20
©2009 ZITS Partnership. Distributed by King Features Syndicate.

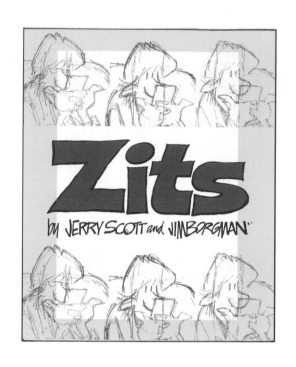

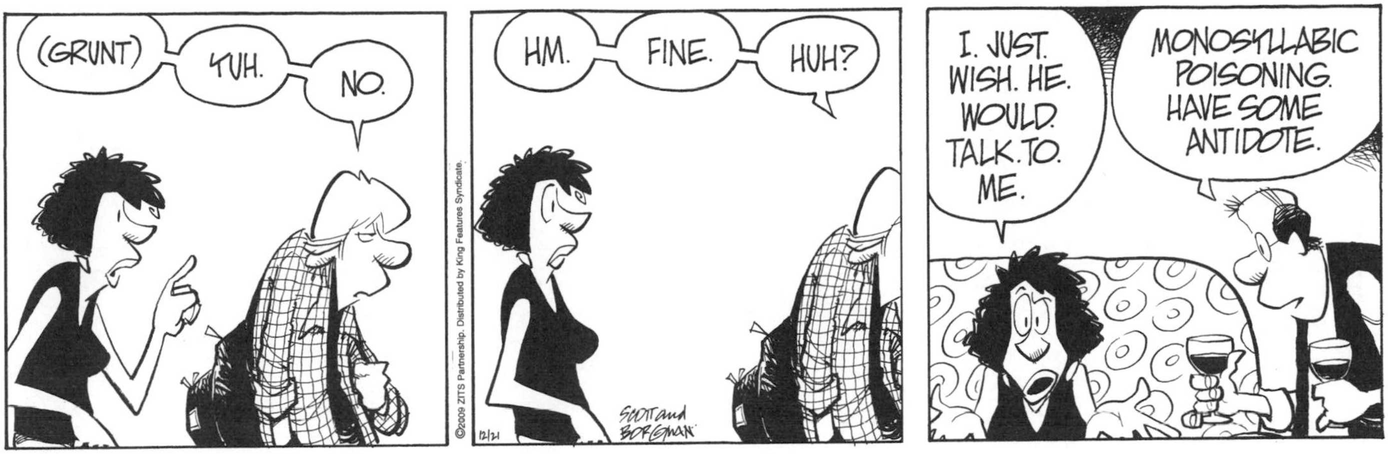
(GRUNT)
YUH.
NO.
HM.
FINE.
HUH?
SCOTT and BORGMAN
12/21
©2009 ZITS Partnership. Distributed by King Features Syndicate.
I. JUST. WISH. HE. WOULD. TALK. TO. ME.
MONOSYLLABIC POISONING. HAVE SOME ANTIDOTE.

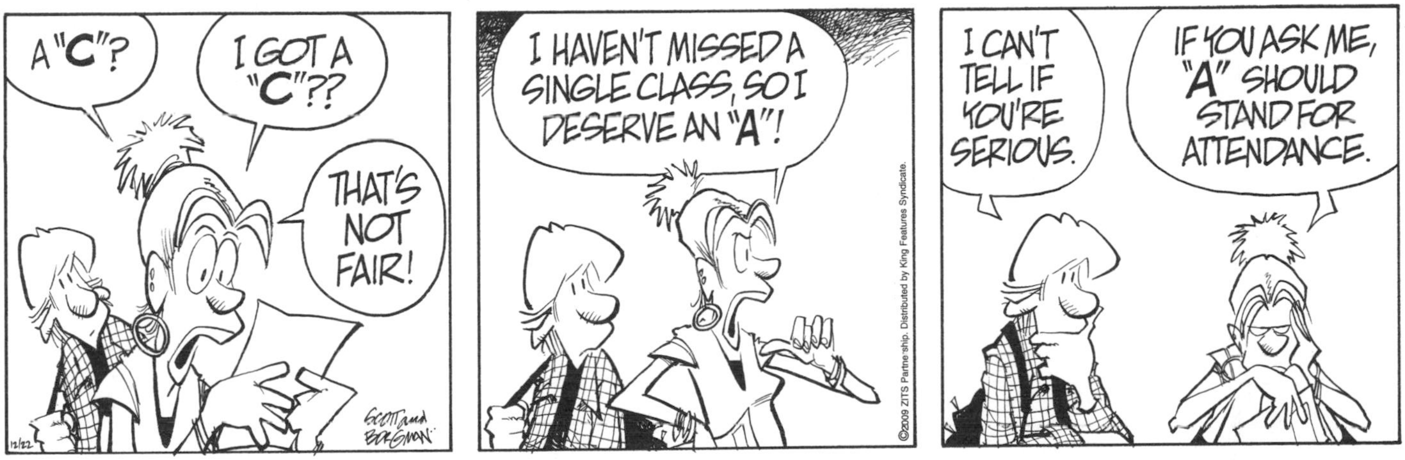
A "C"?
I GOT A "C"??
THAT'S NOT FAIR!
SCOTT and BORGMAN
12/22
I HAVEN'T MISSED A SINGLE CLASS, SO I DESERVE AN "A"!
©2009 ZITS Partnership. Distributed by King Features Syndicate.
I CAN'T TELL IF YOU'RE SERIOUS.
IF YOU ASK ME, "A" SHOULD STAND FOR ATTENDANCE.

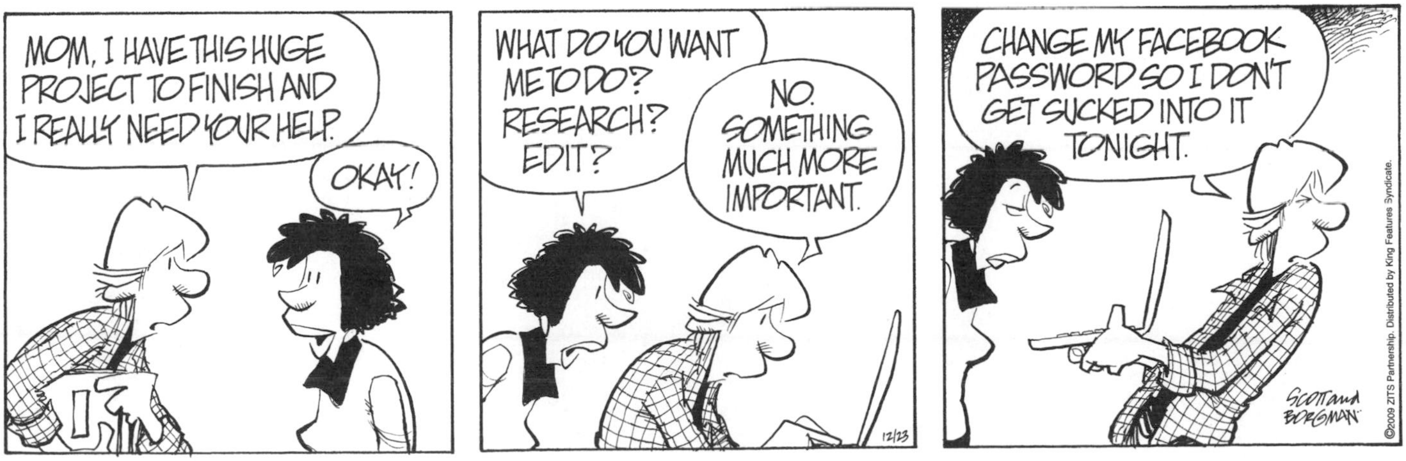
MOM, I HAVE THIS HUGE PROJECT TO FINISH AND I REALLY NEED YOUR HELP.
OKAY!
WHAT DO YOU WANT ME TO DO? RESEARCH? EDIT?
NO. SOMETHING MUCH MORE IMPORTANT.
12/23
CHANGE MY FACEBOOK PASSWORD SO I DON'T GET SUCKED INTO IT TONIGHT.
SCOTT and BORGMAN
©2009 ZITS Partnership. Distributed by King Features Syndicate.

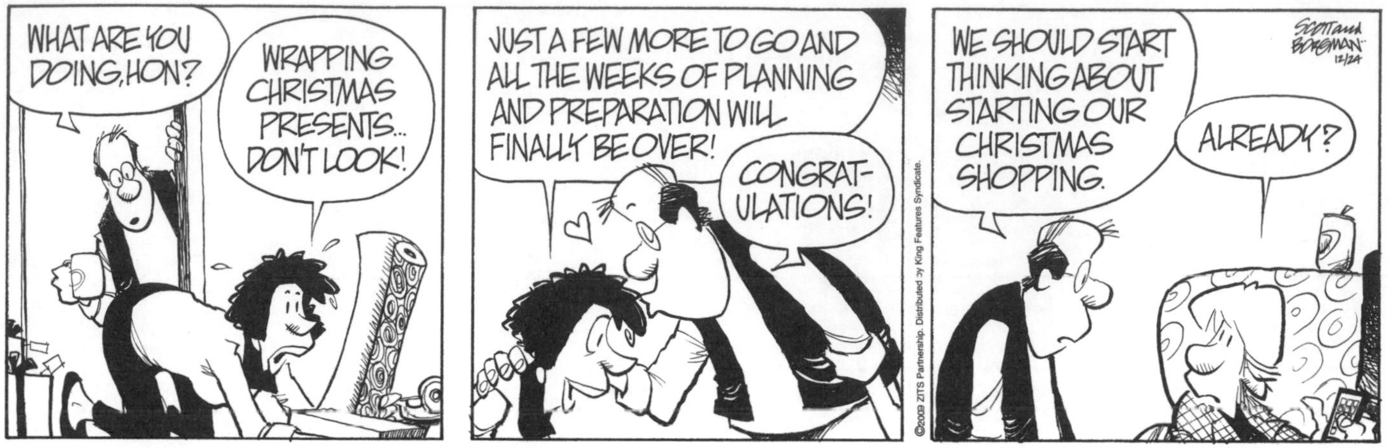
WHAT ARE YOU DOING, HON?
WRAPPING CHRISTMAS PRESENTS... DON'T LOOK!
JUST A FEW MORE TO GO AND ALL THE WEEKS OF PLANNING AND PREPARATION WILL FINALLY BE OVER!
CONGRAT-ULATIONS!
©2009 ZITS Partnership. Distributed by King Features Syndicate.
WE SHOULD START THINKING ABOUT STARTING OUR CHRISTMAS SHOPPING.
ALREADY?
12/24

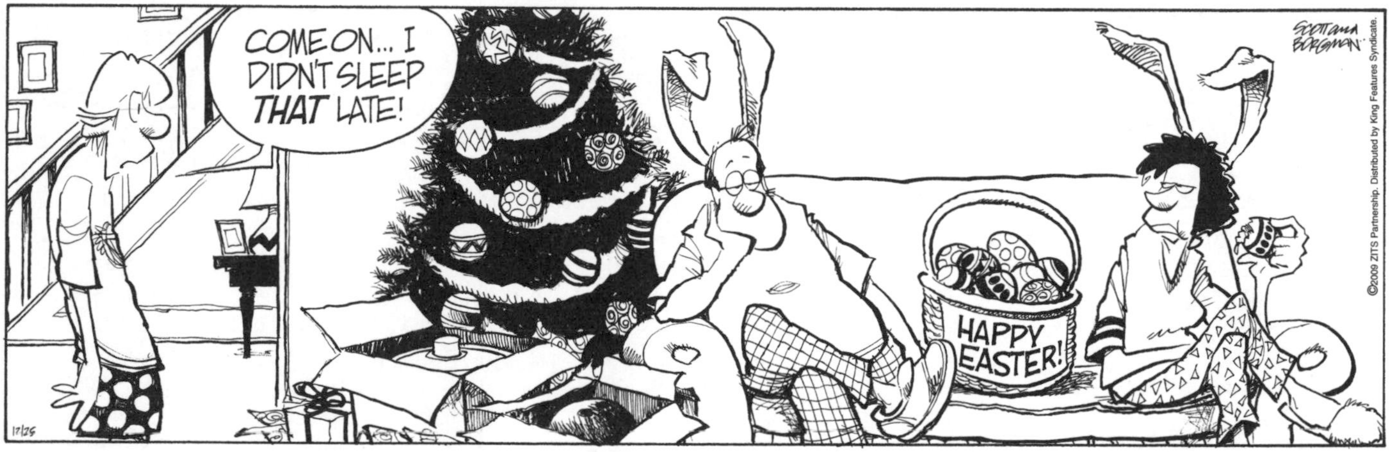
COME ON... I DIDN'T SLEEP ***THAT*** LATE!
HAPPY EASTER!
©2009 ZITS Partnership. Distributed by King Features Syndicate.
12/25

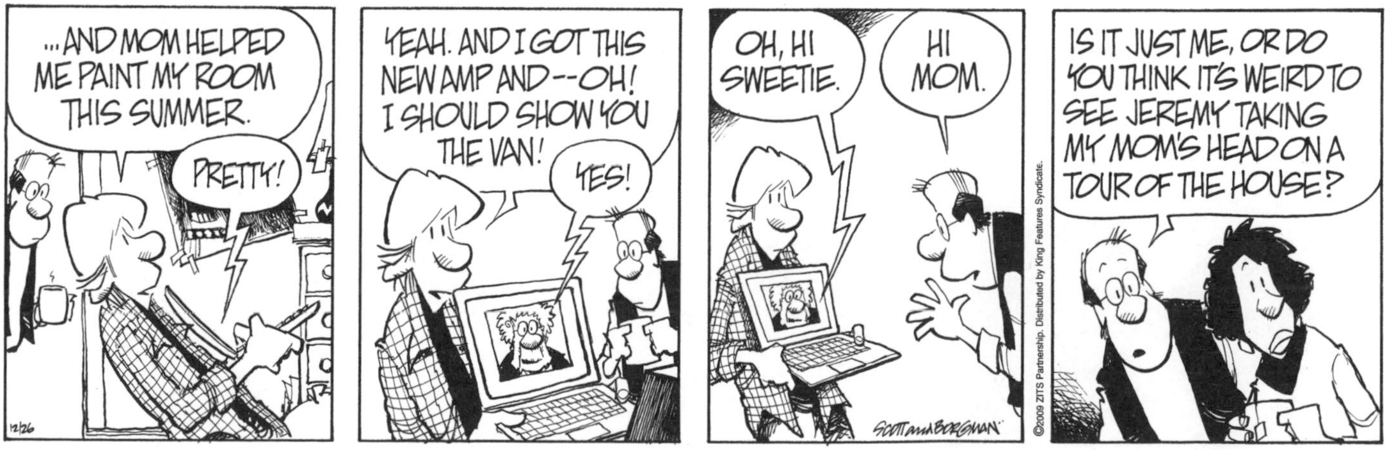
...AND MOM HELPED ME PAINT MY ROOM THIS SUMMER.
PRETTY!
YEAH. AND I GOT THIS NEW AMP AND--OH! I SHOULD SHOW YOU THE VAN!
YES!
OH, HI SWEETIE.
HI MOM.
©2009 ZITS Partnership. Distributed by King Features Syndicate.
IS IT JUST ME, OR DO YOU THINK IT'S WEIRD TO SEE JEREMY TAKING MY MOM'S HEAD ON A TOUR OF THE HOUSE?
12/26

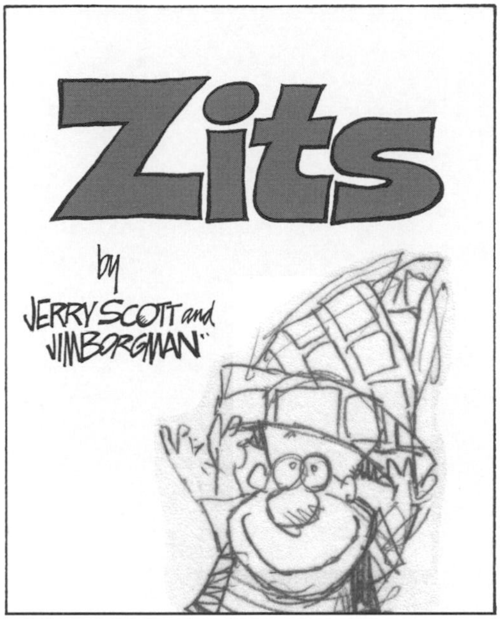
Zits
by
JERRY SCOTT and
JIM BORGMAN

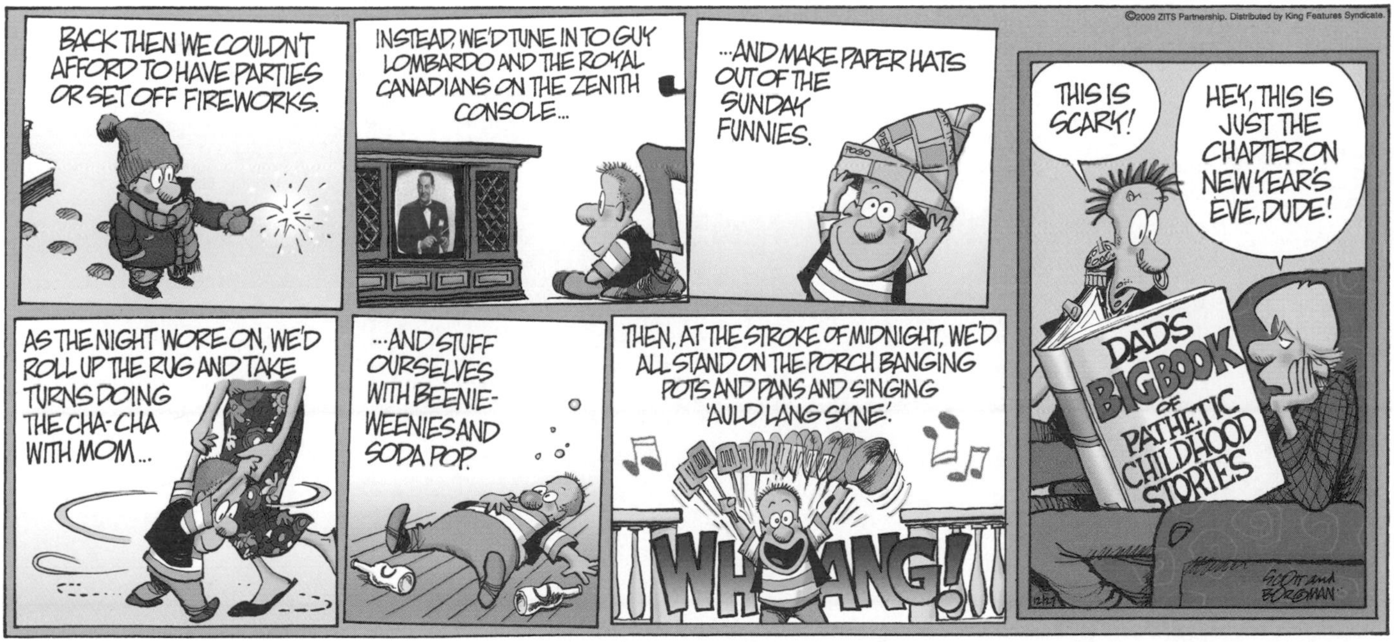
©2009 ZITS Partnership. Distributed by King Features Syndicate.
BACK THEN WE COULDN'T AFFORD TO HAVE PARTIES OR SET OFF FIREWORKS.
INSTEAD, WE'D TUNE IN TO GUY LOMBARDO AND THE ROYAL CANADIANS ON THE ZENITH CONSOLE...
...AND MAKE PAPER HATS OUT OF THE SUNDAY FUNNIES.
POGO
AS THE NIGHT WORE ON, WE'D ROLL UP THE RUG AND TAKE TURNS DOING THE CHA-CHA WITH MOM...
...AND STUFF OURSELVES WITH BEENIE-WEENIES AND SODA POP.
THEN, AT THE STROKE OF MIDNIGHT, WE'D ALL STAND ON THE PORCH BANGING POTS AND PANS AND SINGING 'AULD LANG SYNE'.
WH ANG!
THIS IS SCARY!
HEY, THIS IS JUST THE CHAPTER ON NEW YEAR'S EVE, DUDE!
DAD'S BIG BOOK OF PATHETIC CHILDHOOD STORIES
SCOTT and BORGMAN